More
ONE-STORY HOMES

hanley▲wood
HomePlanners

Published by Home Planners, LLC
3275 W. Ina Road, Suite 220
Tucson, Arizona 85741

DISTRIBUTION CENTER
29333 Lorie Lane
Wixom, Michigan 48393

President, Jayne Fenton
Chief Financial Officer, Joe Carroll
Vice President, Publishing, Jennifer Pearce
Vice President, General Manager, Marc Wheeler
Executive Editor, Linda Bellamy
National Sales Manager, Book Division, Julie Marshall
Marketing Manager, Julie Turetzky
Director, Online Business, David Gallello
Managing Editor, Jason D. Vaughan
Special Projects Editor, Kristin Schneidler
Editor, Nate Ewell
Associate Editor, Kathryn R. Sears
Director, Plan Products, Matt Higgins
Lead Plans Associate, Morenci C. Clark
Plans Associates, Elizabeth Landry, Nick Nieskes
Proofreader/Copywriter, Douglas Jenness
Technical Specialist, Jay C. Walsh
Lead Data Coordinator, Fran Altemose
Data Coordinators, Misty Boler, Melissa Siewert
Production Director, Sara Lisa
Production Manager, Brenda McClary

BIG DESIGNS, INC.
President, Creative Director, Anthony D'Elia
Vice President, Business Manager, Megan D'Elia
Vice President, Design Director, Chris Bonavita
Editorial Director, John Roach
Assistant Editor, Tricia Starkey
Director of Design and Production, Stephen Reinfurt
Group Art Director, Kevin Limongelli
Photo Editor, Christine DiVuolo
Art Director, Jessica Hagenbuch
Graphic Designer, Mary Ellen Mulshine
Graphic Designer, Lindsey O'Neill-Myers
Graphic Designer, Jacque Young
Assistant Photo Editor, Brian Wilson
Project Director, David Barbella
Assistant Production Manager, Rich Fuentes

PHOTO CREDITS
Front Cover: Design 9734 by Donald A. Gardner Architects, Inc. *©1994 Donald A. Gardner Architects, Inc.*
Photography courtesy of Donald A. Gardner Architects, Inc.
Back Cover: Design U112 by by Ahmann Design
Photo provided by Ahmann Design.

10 9 8 7 6 5 4

Printed in the United States of America

Library of Congress Control Number: 2003113856

ISBN: 1-881955-81-8

©1994 Donald A. Gardner Architects, Inc.,
Photography courtesy of Donald A. Gardner Architects, Inc.

Design 9734, pg. 268

Table of Contents

Editor's Note

A long-standing favorite, the one-story home remains a popular choice because of its low-slung, ground-hugging profile, and its easy adaptability and livability. For empty-nesters, the elderly or those who have physical limitations that make it impossible to climb stairs, the one-story is the clear choice. Accessibility to all areas of the house and the freely adaptable floor plan mean that few if any special accommodations need to be made for living comfortably.

For a great investment and a provident addition to the simple one-story house, there is the basement. Full or partial basements are ideal for developing recreational space, hobby areas, laundries and storage facilities. Such inexpensive space can make a one-story house significantly more livable, incorporating economy and effective use of area.

The one-story home also enjoys an advantage over multi-storied houses in providing for today's indoor/outdoor lifestyle. The one-story allows all zones—from living and sleeping areas to work spaces—direct access to patios, terraces and gardens without the expense of second-floor decks and balconies.

In *More One-Story Homes*, you'll find loads of ideas and be impressed with the wide variety and range of sizes offered. From contemporary to traditional, sun country to old country European and more—you're sure to find a favorite in this magnificent new collection!

This home, as shown in the photograph, may differ from the actual blueprints.
For more detailed information, please check the floor plans carefully.

Photo by Oscar Thompson

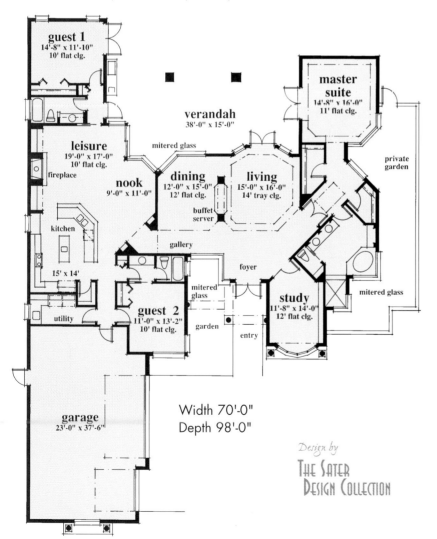

guest 1
14'-8" x 11'-10"
10' flat clg.

master
suite
14'-8" x 16'-0"
11' flat clg.

verandah
38'-0" x 15'-0"

leisure
19'-0" x 17'-0"
10' flat clg.

mitered glass

private
garden

fireplace

dining
12'-0" x 15'-0"
12' flat clg.

living
15'-0" x 16'-0"
14' tray clg.

nook
9'-0" x 11'-0"

kitchen

buffet
server

15' x 14'

gallery

foyer

utility

mitered
glass

guest 2
11'-0" x 13'-2"
10' flat clg.

garden

study
11'-8" x 14'-0"
12' flat clg.

mitered glass

entry

garage
23'-0" x 37'-6"

Width 70'-0"
Depth 98'-0"

Design by
The Sater
Design Collection

Design 6602

Square Footage: 2,794

L

Classic columns, circle-head windows and a bay-windowed study give this stucco home a wonderful street presence. The foyer leads into the formal living and dining areas. An arched buffet server separates these rooms and contributes an open feeling. The kitchen, nook and leisure room are grouped for informal living. A desk/message center in the island kitchen, art niches in the nook and a fireplace with an entertainment center and shelves add custom touches. Two additional suites have private baths and offer full privacy from the master wing—the most gracious guest accommodations. The master suite hosts a private garden area, while the master bath features a walk-in shower that overlooks the garden, and a water closet room with space for books or a television. Large His and Hers walk-in closets complete these private quarters.

This home, as shown in the photograph, may differ from the actual blueprints.
For more detailed information, please check the floor plans carefully.

Photo courtesy The Sater Design Collection

Design by
©The Sater Design Collection

Design HPTM03001

Square Footage: 3,883

■ The Spanish-tile roof and striking stucco exterior of this rambling single-story home introduce an interior that revisits the past. Double doors with sidelights brighten the foyer, which leads directly into the formal living room. To the left of the foyer, the formal dining room features an octagonal tray ceiling and an arched alcove. The well-planned kitchen is easily accessed by the nook and leisure room. To the right of the foyer, the master suite is secluded for privacy and boasts two walk-in closets, a dual-sink vanity, a garden tub and a shower with a seat. Each of the guest suites includes a walk-in closet and a full bath.

Width 101'-4"
Depth 106'-0"

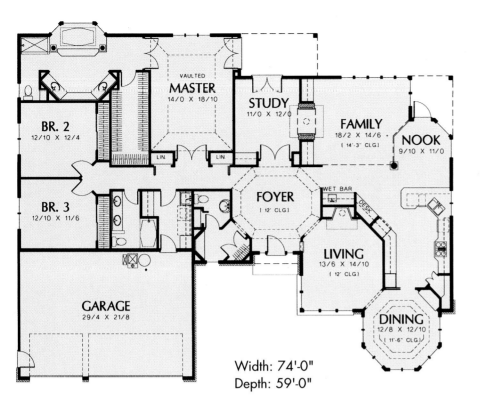

Design 9454

Square Footage: 2,775

L

BR. 2
12/10 X 12/4

BR. 3
12/10 X 11/6

GARAGE
29/4 X 21/8

VAULTED
MASTER
14/0 X 18/10

STUDY
11/0 X 12/0

FAMILY
18/2 X 14/6 +
(14'-3" CLG)

NOOK
9/10 X 11/0

FOYER
(12' CLG)

WET BAR

DESK

LIVING
13/6 X 14/10
(12' CLG)

LIN

LIN

DINING
12/8 X 12/10
(11'-6" CLG)

Width: 74'-0"
Depth: 59'-0"

Design by
© Alan Mascord Design Associates, Inc.

A quaint dining gazebo adds a delightful touch to the facade of this lovely home. It complements the formal living room, with a fireplace, found just to the right of the entry foyer (be sure to notice the elegant guest bath to the left). Family living takes place at the rear of the plan in a large family room with a through-fireplace to the study. A breakfast nook enhances the well-appointed kitchen. The master suite has a vaulted ceiling and boasts a huge walk-in closet and a pampering bath. Two family bedrooms share a full bath.

Photo by Bob Greenspan

This home, as shown in the photograph, may differ from the actual blueprints.
For more detailed information, please check the floor plans carefully.

Photo by Oscar Thompson

Design 6639
Square Footage: 3,944

■ Innovative design and attention to detail create true luxury living. This clean contemporary style features a raised, columned entry with an interesting stucco relief archway. The foyer opens into the formal living room which overlooks the lanai and waterfall through walls of glass. The formal dining room has a curved wall of windows and a built-in buffet table. Two guest suites each have a walk-in closet and private bath. The owners' wing features a foyer with views of a fountain and a sunny sitting area which opens to the lanai. The bath has a soaking tub, a round shower and a large wardrobe area.

Design by
THE SATER
DESIGN COLLECTION

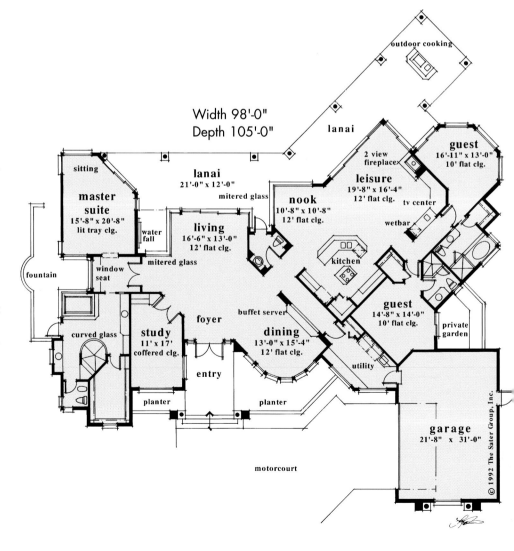

Width 98'-0"
Depth 105'-0"

outdoor cooking

lanai

sitting

master suite
15'-8" x 20'-8"
lit tray clg.

lanai
21'-0" x 12'-0"
mitered glass

nook
10'-8" x 10'-8"
12' flat clg.

leisure
19'-8" x 16'-4"
12' flat clg.

guest
16'-11" x 13'-0"
10' flat clg.

2 view fireplace

tv center

wetbar

water fall

living
16'-6" x 13'-0"
12' flat clg.

fountain

window seat

mitered glass

kitchen

curved glass

study
11' x 17'
coffered clg.

foyer

buffet server

dining
13'-0" x 15'-4"
12' flat clg.

guest
14'-8" x 14'-0"
10' flat clg.

private garden

entry

utility

planter

planter

garage
21'-8" x 31'-0"

motorcourt

© 1992 The Sater Group, Inc.

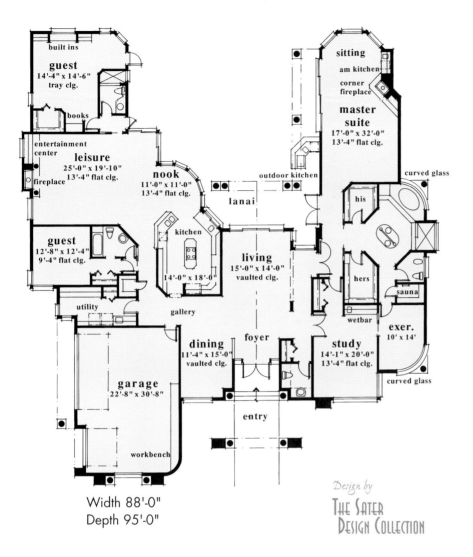

built ins

guest
14'-4" x 14'-6"
tray clg.

books

entertainment center

leisure
25'-0" x 19'-10"
13'-4" flat clg.

fireplace

nook
11'-0" x 11'-0"
13'-4" flat clg.

lanai

guest
12'-8" x 12'-4"
9'-4" flat clg.

kitchen

living
15'-0" x 14'-0"
vaulted clg.
14'-0" x 18'-0"

utility

gallery

dining
11'-4" x 15'-0"
vaulted clg.

foyer

garage
22'-8" x 30'-8"

workbench

entry

sitting

am kitchen

corner fireplace

master suite
17'-0" x 32'-0"
13'-4" flat clg.

outdoor kitchen

curved glass

his

hers

sauna

wetbar

exer.
10' x 14'

study
14'-1" x 20'-0"
13'-4" flat clg.

curved glass

Width 88'-0"
Depth 95'-0"

Design by
The Sater
Design Collection

Design 6636

Square Footage: 4,565

L

■ A free-standing entryway is the focal point of this luxurious residence. It has an arch motif that is carried through to the rear using a gable roof and a vaulted ceiling from the foyer out to the lanai. High ceilings are found throughout the home, creating a spacious atmosphere. The kitchen that features a cooktop island and plenty of counter space, opens to the leisure area with a handy snack bar. Two guest suites with private baths are just off this casual living area. The master wing is truly pampering, stretching the entire length of the home. The suite has a large sitting area, a corner fireplace and a morning kitchen. The bath features an island vanity, a raised tub with a curved glass wall overlooking a private garden, a sauna and separate closets. An exercise room has a curved glass wall and a pocket door to the study, where a wet bar is ready to serve up refreshment. Outdoor living will be welcome, thanks to a lovely rear lanai and an outdoor kitchen.

This home, as shown in the photograph, may differ from the actual blueprints. For more detailed information, please check the floor plans carefully.

Breland & Farmer Desingers, Inc.

Design HPTM03002

Square Footage: 2,396

■ Long and low, but sporting a high roofline, this one-story plan offers the best in family livability. The recessed front porch opens to an entry hall that leads to a huge living area with a fireplace. An angled eating area is close by and connects to the galley-style kitchen. The formal dining area also connects to the kitchen, but retains access to the entry hall for convenience. Family bedrooms on the left side of the plan share a full bath. The master suite sits behind the two-car garage and is graced by patio access and a fine bath. Please specify basement, crawlspace or slab foundation when ordering.

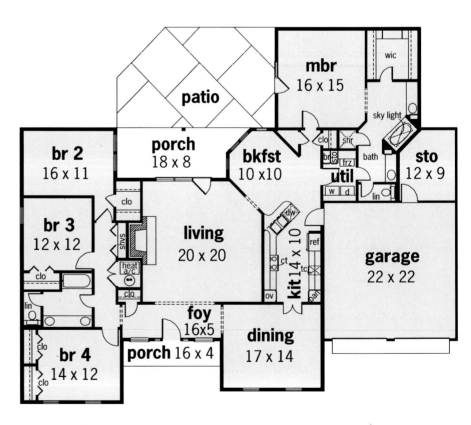

Width 72'-0"
Depth 62'-0"

Design by
©BRELAND & FARMER DESIGNERS, INC.

10

This home, as shown in the photograph, may differ from the actual blueprints. For more detailed information, please check the floor plans carefully.

Mark England

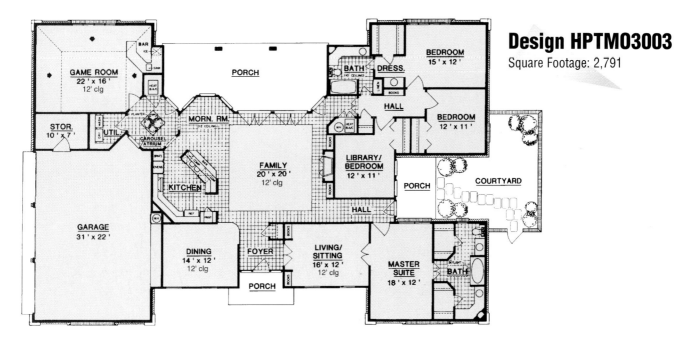

Design HPTM03003
Square Footage: 2,791

GAME ROOM
22' x 16'
12' clg

STOR.
10' x 7'

UTIL.

PORCH

MORN. RM.

KITCHEN

FAMILY
20' x 20'
12' clg

CAROUSEL ATRIUM

GARAGE
31' x 22'

DINING
14' x 12'
12' clg

FOYER

LIVING/ SITTING
16' x 12'
12' clg

PORCH

BATH

DRESS.

BEDROOM
15' x 12'

HALL

BEDROOM
12' x 11'

LIBRARY/ BEDROOM
12' x 11'

PORCH

COURTYARD

HALL

MASTER SUITE
18' x 12'

BATH

Design by
©BRELAND & FARMER DESIGNERS, INC.

Width 84'-0"
Depth 54'-0"

■ This stately country home is a quaint mix of Colonial style and romantic French flavor. Inside, formal living and dining rooms flank the entry foyer. Two sets of double doors open from the family room to the rear patio. A romantic courtyard is placed to the far right of the plan, just beyond the family bedrooms. A three-car garage with an extra storage room offers plenty of space. The family game room is reserved for recreational fun. Please specify crawlspace or slab foundation when ordering.

This home, as shown in the photograph, may differ from the actual blueprints. For more detailed information, please check the floor plans carefully.

Photo provided by Ahmann Design

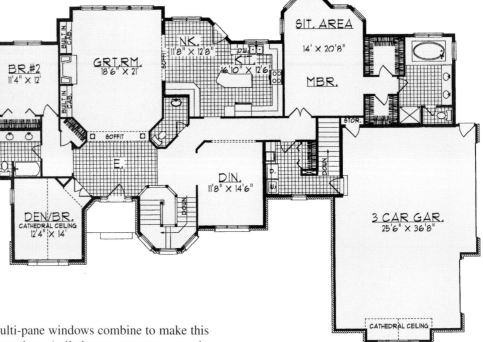

Design U112

Square Footage: 2,600

Design by
©Ahmann Design, Inc.

■ Varied rooflines, shutters and multi-pane windows combine to make this one-story home a neighborhood showpiece. A tiled entry presents a grand view of the spacious great room, which is complete with a warming fireplace and built-in cabinets. A den opens off the foyer through double doors and can be used as a guest bedroom when needed. The island in the kitchen provides extra workspace to an already well-equipped area. With direct access to both the formal dining room and breakfast nook, the kitchen is a warm and bright place to share morning coffee and after-school snacks. A sumptuous master suite features a sitting bay, two walk-in closets and a lavish bath. The three-car garage is reached through the laundry room.

Width 87'-0"
Depth 60'-0"

Photo courtesy of Living Concepts Home Planning

This home, as shown in the photograph, may differ from the actual blueprints. For more detailed information, please check the floor plans carefully.

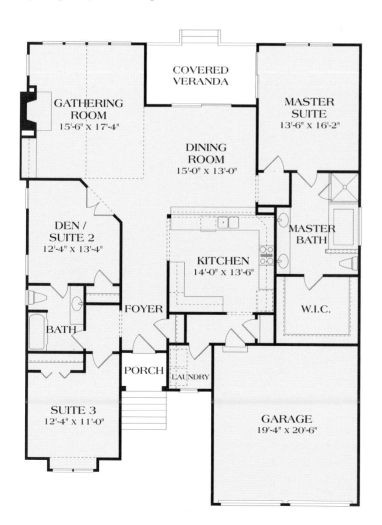

Design A247

Square Footage: 1,915

A sunny bay window and a shady recessed entry create an elegant impression in this lovely design. The sleeping quarters are arranged for privacy along the perimeter of the spacious living areas. The kitchen provides a generous work space, and the dining room is open to the gathering room with its fireplace. To the rear, a covered veranda is accessible from the dining room and the master suite. Note the lavish bath with its oversized tub, separate shower, and twin vanity sinks and the huge walk-in closet in the master suite.

Design by
©Living Concepts Home Planning

Width 46'-0"
Depth 60'-2"

13

This home, as shown in the photograph, may differ from the actual blueprints.
For more detailed information, please check the floor plans carefully.

Photo courtesy of Stephen Fuller, Inc.

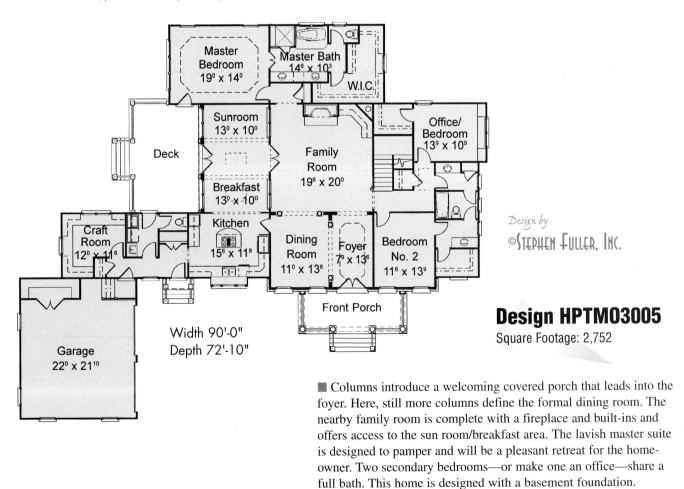

Design by
©Stephen Fuller, Inc.

Width 90'-0"
Depth 72'-10"

Design HPTM03005
Square Footage: 2,752

■ Columns introduce a welcoming covered porch that leads into the foyer. Here, still more columns define the formal dining room. The nearby family room is complete with a fireplace and built-ins and offers access to the sun room/breakfast area. The lavish master suite is designed to pamper and will be a pleasant retreat for the homeowner. Two secondary bedrooms—or make one an office—share a full bath. This home is designed with a basement foundation.

14

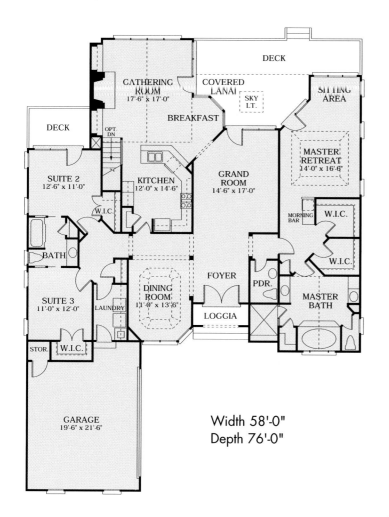

CATHERING ROOM
17'-6" x 17'-0"

DECK

COVERED LANAI

SKY LT.

SITTING AREA

BREAKFAST

DECK

OPT. DN

SUITE 2
12'-6" x 11'-0"

KITCHEN
12'-0" x 14'-6"

GRAND ROOM
14'-6" x 17'-0"

MASTER RETREAT
14'-0" x 16'-6"

W.I.C.

MORNING BAR

W.I.C.

BATH

W.I.C.

SUITE 3
11'-0" x 12'-0"

LAUNDRY

DINING ROOM
11'-0" x 13'-6"

FOYER

PDR.

MASTER BATH

LOGGIA

STOR.

W.I.C.

GARAGE
19'-6" x 21'-6"

Width 58'-0"
Depth 76'-0"

Design HPTMO0001
Square Footage: 2,398

■ Enjoy an exciting floor plan that flows exceptionally well for lots of entertainment possibilities. High-volume ceilings throughout accentuate this open plan. A large gathering room off the full kitchen includes a magnificent Palladian window. An octagonal tray ceiling reflects the bay-window shape in the dining room. The master suite, located away from other bedrooms for enhanced privacy, features its own private sitting area and morning bar, along with huge, dual walk-in closets. The master retreat and gathering room are connected by a covered lanai complete with skylight. A private deck is located off Suite 2. Please specify basement or crawlspace foundation when ordering.

Design by
© LIVING CONCEPTS HOME PLANNING

This home, as shown in the photograph, may differ from the actual blueprints. For more detailed information, please check the floor plans carefully.

Photo courtesy of Living Concepts Home Planning

This home, as shown in the photograph, may differ from the actual blueprints. For more detailed information, please check the floor plans carefully.

Photo by Andrew D. Lautman

■ Split-log siding and a rustic balustrade create country charm with this farmhouse-style retreat. An open living area features a natural stone fireplace and a cathedral ceiling with exposed rough-sawn beam and brackets. A generous kitchen and dining area complement the living room and share the warmth of its fireplace. A master bedroom with complete bath, and a nearby family bedroom with hall bath complete the main floor. Upstairs, a spacious loft affords extra sleeping space—or provides a hobby/recreation area—and offers a full bath.

Design by
HOME PLANNERS

Width 50'-7"
Depth 38'-0"

DINING

DW
KITCHEN   S   RANGE

REFG

LT   W   D
LAUNDRY

LINEN

BATH   LINEN

VANITY   SHWR

MASTER
BATH

LIVING
RM
20^2 x 18^2
VOL. CLG

RAILING

BEDRM
10^{10} x 11^8

UP

MASTER
BEDRM
12^0 x 18^4

COVERED
PORCH

RAILING

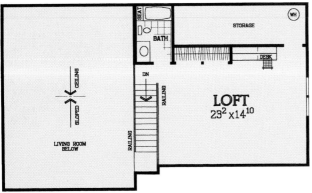

SEAT

WH

BATH

STORAGE

DESK

DN

RAILING

RAILING

LOFT
23^2 x 14^{10}

SLOPED CEILING

LIVING ROOM
BELOW

QUOTE ONE®

Cost to build? See page 434
to order complete cost estimate
to build this house in your area!

Design 3699

Square Footage: 1,356
Loft: 490 square feet

L D

16

Petite and Sweet:

One-story homes of 1,700 square feet and under

Design HPTMO2001
Square Footage: 1,092

MBr
15-4x12-0

Patio

Kit
11-8x11-9

R

L

P

D W

Br 2
8-7x
10-0

Living
11-8x16-7

Garage
11-4x20-4

Dn

Br 3
12-0x10-0

vaulted

Covered Porch
depth 4-0

Width 39'-8"
Depth 41'-0"

Design by
©HOME DESIGN ALTERNATIVES, INC.

■ Cottage accents dazzle the country exterior of this small ranch home, featuring rustic dormers. A front covered porch welcomes you inside to a formal living room. Straight ahead, the casual kitchen area with a pantry accesses a rear patio—perfect for outdoor grilling. A laundry room accesses a single-car garage. The master bedroom provides a walk-in closet and shares a full hall bath with two family bedrooms. A linen closet is placed outside the hall bath nearby. Bedroom 3 features a vaulted area that overlooks the front yard.

QUOTE ONE®

Cost to build? See page 434 to order complete cost estimate to build this house in your area!

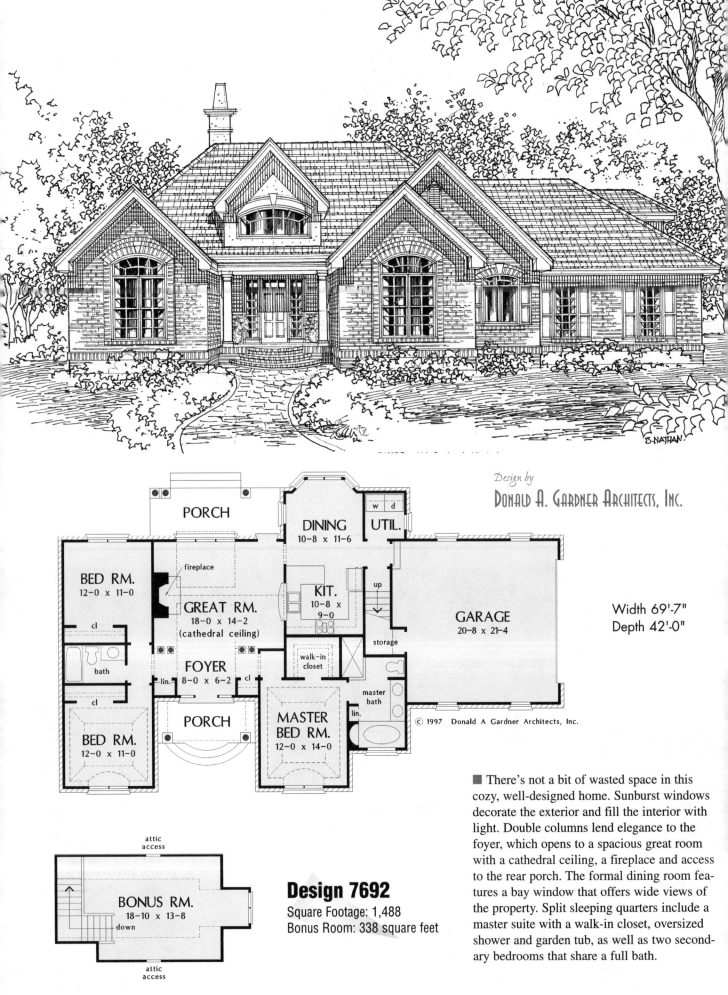

PORCH

DINING
10-8 x 11-6

UTIL.

w d

Design by
Donald A. Gardner Architects, Inc.

BED RM.
12-0 x 11-0

fireplace

cl

bath

cl

BED RM.
12-0 x 11-0

GREAT RM.
18-0 x 14-2
(cathedral ceiling)

KIT.
10-8 x
9-0

up

GARAGE
20-8 x 21-4

Width 69'-7"
Depth 42'-0"

storage

FOYER
8-0 x 6-2

lin.

cl

walk-in
closet

master
bath

PORCH

MASTER
BED RM.
12-0 x 14-0

lin.

© 1997   Donald A Gardner Architects, Inc.

attic
access

BONUS RM.
18-10 x 13-8

down

attic
access

Design 7692
Square Footage: 1,488
Bonus Room: 338 square feet

■ There's not a bit of wasted space in this cozy, well-designed home. Sunburst windows decorate the exterior and fill the interior with light. Double columns lend elegance to the foyer, which opens to a spacious great room with a cathedral ceiling, a fireplace and access to the rear porch. The formal dining room features a bay window that offers wide views of the property. Split sleeping quarters include a master suite with a walk-in closet, oversized shower and garden tub, as well as two secondary bedrooms that share a full bath.

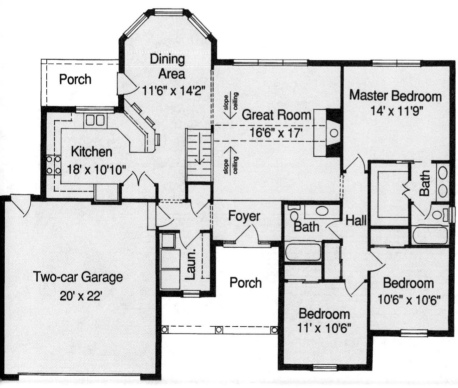

Porch

Dining
Area
11'6" x 14'2"

Kitchen
18' x 10'10"

Great Room
16'6" x 17'
slope ceiling
slope ceiling

Master Bedroom
14' x 11'9"

Bath

Two-car Garage
20' x 22'

Laun.

Foyer

Bath

Hall

Porch

Bedroom
11' x 10'6"

Bedroom
10'6" x 10'6"

Width 60'-0"
Depth 47'-0"

Design by
©Studer Residential Designs, Inc.

Design B518
Square Footage: 1,508

■ Multiple gables and a cozy front porch welcome you to this enchanting one-level home. Whether you are a first-time buyer or an empty-nester, you will appreciate the step-saving convenience of the interior. The grand openings between rooms create a spacious effect and the functional kitchen provides an abundance of counter space. Additional room for quick meals or serving an oversized crowd is provided at the breakfast bar. Double-hung windows and angles add light and dimension to the dining area. The great room features a sloped ceiling. The bright and open floor plan of this three-bedroom ranch makes this home look and feel much larger than its actual size.

Design 7709

Square Footage: 1,629
Bonus Room: 316 square feet

■ A columned, arched entrance and windows provide classic style to the exterior of this plan. The foyer leads to the great room, warmed by an extended-hearth fireplace and lighted by a ribbon of windows. A bay-windowed dining room has views to the rear property and rear deck. One of two family bedrooms is highlighted by a vaulted ceiling; the master bedroom boasts cathedral dimensions and a roomy walk-in closet. An upstairs bonus room offers space for future expansion.

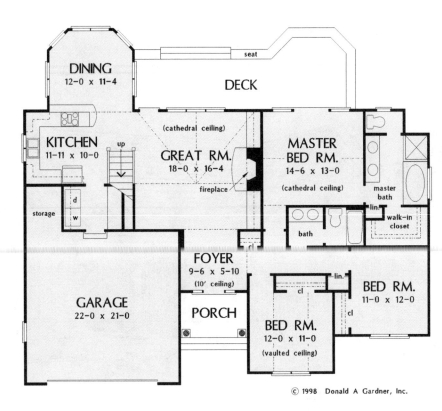

DINING
12-0 x 11-4

DECK

seat

KITCHEN
11-11 x 10-0

up

(cathedral ceiling)

GREAT RM.
18-0 x 16-4

fireplace

MASTER
BED RM.
14-6 x 13-0

(cathedral ceiling)

master bath

d
w

storage

lin.

walk-in closet

bath

FOYER
9-6 x 5-10
(10' ceiling)

lin.

BED RM.
11-0 x 12-0

GARAGE
22-0 x 21-0

PORCH

BED RM.
12-0 x 11-0
(vaulted ceiling)

cl

© 1998 Donald A Gardner, Inc.

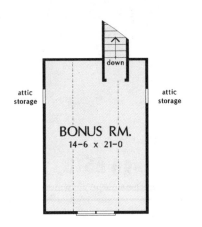

down

attic storage

attic storage

BONUS RM.
14-6 x 21-0

Design by
DONALD A. GARDNER ARCHITECTS, INC.

Width 58'-6"
Depth 49'-8"

B.NATHAN

Design B576

Square Footage: 1,488

■ This one-level home with a front porch showcases an angled fireplace and sloped ceilings. The great room combines with the dining area, creating an open spacious effect. Triple doors lead to a raised deck for a favorable indoor/outdoor relationship. The master suite provides a large walk-in closet and deluxe bath with a unique half-moon tub and a separate shower. A bedroom accessed from the foyer creates an optional den. This house is drawn with a rear walkout basement, enabling the homeowner to increase the square footage.

Design by
©Studer Residential Designs, Inc.

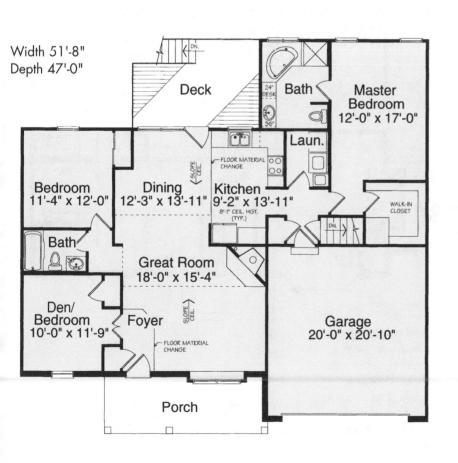

Width 51'-8"
Depth 47'-0"

Deck

Bath

Master Bedroom
12'-0" x 17'-0"

24" DESK

36"

Laun.

WALK-IN CLOSET

FLOOR MATERIAL CHANGE

SLOPE CEIL.

Bedroom
11'-4" x 12'-0"

Dining
12'-3" x 13'-11"

Kitchen
9'-2" x 13'-11"
8'-1" CEIL. HGT. (TYP.)

Bath

Great Room
18'-0" x 15'-4"

DN.

Den/ Bedroom
10'-0" x 11'-9"

Foyer

SLOPE CEIL.

FLOOR MATERIAL CHANGE

Garage
20'-0" x 20'-10"

Porch

DN.

21

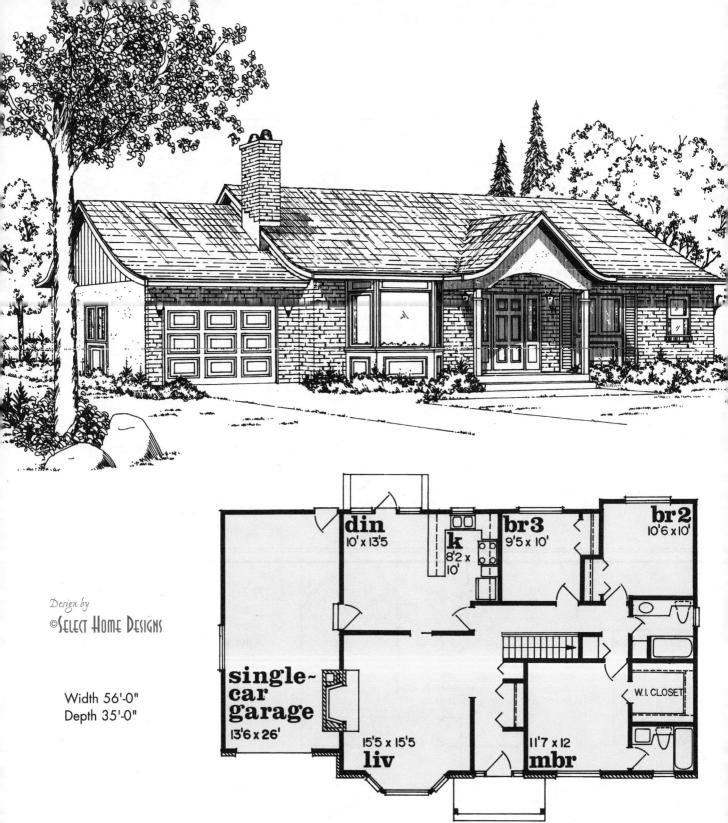

Design by
©Select Home Designs

Width 56'-0"
Depth 35'-0"

din
10' x 13'5

k
8'2 x 10'

br3
9'5 x 10'

br2
10'6 x 10'

single-car garage
13'6 x 26'

W. I. CLOSET

15'5 x 15'5
liv

11'7 x 12
mbr

■ A charming bay window and a distinctive covered porch lend this compact starter or retirement home curb appeal. The foyer—with a coat closet—leads to a comfortable living room featuring a bay window and warming fireplace. For convenience, a pocket door separates the living room from the dining area and kitchen. This country kitchen is sure to please, with ample counter space and a window over the sink. To the right of the kitchen, two family bedrooms share a fully appointed bathroom. Nearby, the master suite enjoys a walk-in closet and private bath with soaking tub.

Design Q544
Square Footage: 1,285

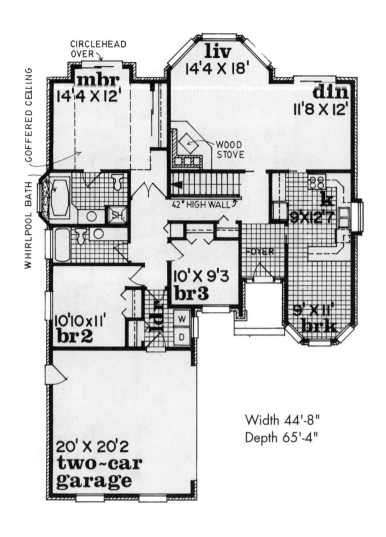

CIRCLEHEAD
OVER

mbr
14'4 X 12'

COFFERED CEILING

WHIRLPOOL BATH

SH

liv
14'4 X 18'

WOOD
STOVE

42" HIGH WALL

din
11'8 X 12'

k
9'X12'7

FOYER

10' X 9'3
br3

ldr

W
D

10'10x11'
br2

9' X 11'
brk

20' X 20'2
**two-car
garage**

Width 44'-8"
Depth 65'-4"

Design Q579

Square Footage: 1,652

■ This entrancing brick home combines multiple rooflines and interesting window details for eye appeal,
while the floor plan is designed to
capture the view to the rear of the
home. The kitchen, with a peninsular
counter, conveniently serves a win-
dowed-bay breakfast room and dining
room. Another, larger, bay window in
the living room offers a cozy sitting
area and full view of the panorama.
The circle-head window, over the sliding glass door, enhances the coffered
ceiling in the master bedroom. The
master suite enjoys a whirlpool spa,
separate shower and plant shelf.

Design by
©Select Home Designs

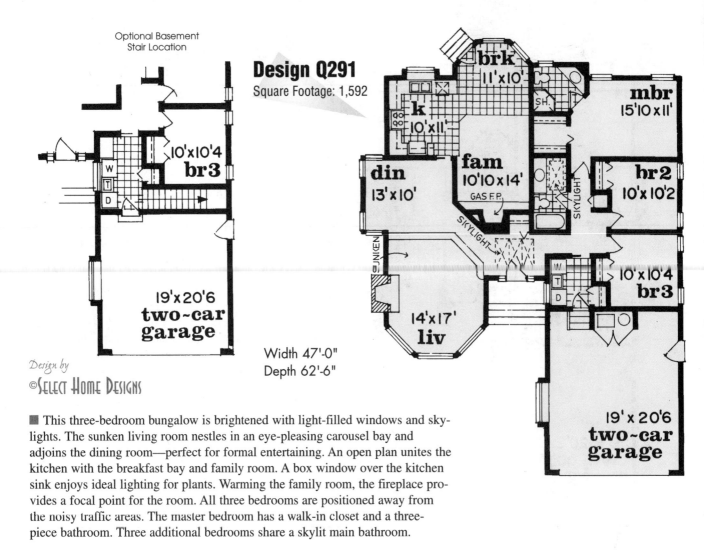

Design Q291
Square Footage: 1,592

10'x10'4
br3

W
T
D

19'x20'6
**two-car
garage**

Width 47'-0"
Depth 62'-6"

Design by
©Select Home Designs

brk
11'x10'

SH.

mbr
15'10 x 11'

k
10'x11'

fam
10'10 x 14'
GAS F.P.

din
13'x10'

br2
10'x10'2

SKYLIGHT

SKYLIGHT

SUNKEN

14'x17'
liv

W
T
D

10'x10'4
br3

19' x 20'6
**two-car
garage**

■ This three-bedroom bungalow is brightened with light-filled windows and sky-lights. The sunken living room nestles in an eye-pleasing carousel bay and adjoins the dining room—perfect for formal entertaining. An open plan unites the kitchen with the breakfast bay and family room. A box window over the kitchen sink enjoys ideal lighting for plants. Warming the family room, the fireplace provides a focal point for the room. All three bedrooms are positioned away from the noisy traffic areas. The master bedroom has a walk-in closet and a three-piece bathroom. Three additional bedrooms share a skylit main bathroom.

Design Z025
Square Footage: 972

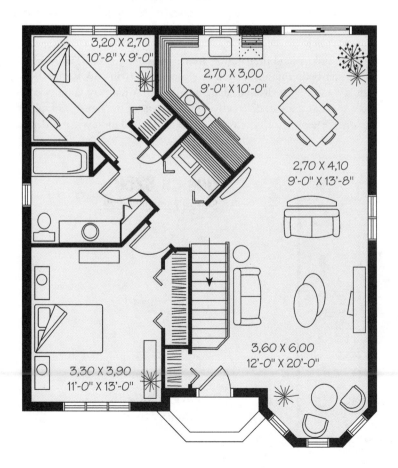

3,20 X 2,70
10'-8" X 9'-0"

2,70 X 3,00
9'-0" X 10'-0"

2,70 X 4,10
9'-0" X 13'-8"

3,60 X 6,00
12'-0" X 20'-0"

3,30 X 3,90
11'-0" X 13'-0"

■ Eye-catching exterior details distin-
guish this small Victorian design.
Inside, natural light flows through the
living area from the turret's windows,
where there's a sitting bay. The living
room and dining room make one open
space, which is helpful for entertaining.
A sliding door in the dining room leads
to the backyard. An angled kitchen provides plenty of work space. The master
bedroom and a second bedroom share a
full bath. This home is designed with a
basement foundation.

Design by
©DRUMMOND DESIGNS, INC.

Width 30'-0"
Depth 35'-0"

■ A fine first impression is offered with the delightful chalet roofline on the entry of this efficient country design. A traditional foyer opens to the large living room. Accents include a sloped ten-foot ceiling, a snack bar from the kitchen and windows that frame the fireplace. The kitchen has a corner sink, island preparation area and a dining nook. The front-facing master bedroom has a walk-in closet and a twin-sink vanity in the bath. Two family bedrooms share a hall bath. A hallway laundry center and a two-car garage, discreetly sit at the rear of the house, complete this plan. Please specify crawlspace or slab foundation when ordering.

Design 8250
Square Footage: 1,322

Design by
©Larry E. Belk Designs

Width 44'-6"
Depth 58'-2"

Design A101

Square Footage: 1,383

■ Starter homebuyers and retirees alike will take pleasure in this modest-yet-handsome one-story, which can be constructed in brick or frame. A vaulted ceiling in the great room and high glass windows on the rear wall combine to create an open, spacious feel. Off the great room is an open dining room. The ample kitchen layout features a built-in pantry. A generous walk-in closet is found in the master suite. Please specify basement, slab or crawlspace foundation when ordering.

Design by
LIVING CONCEPTS HOME PLANNING

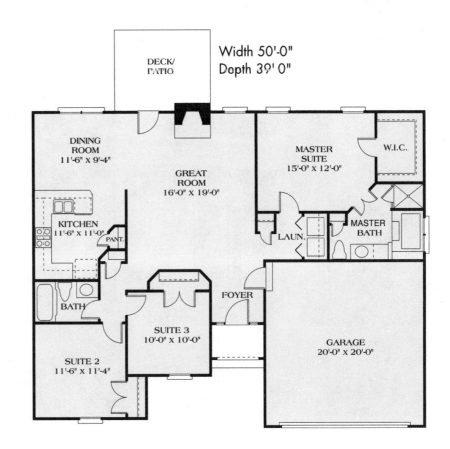

Width 50'-0"
Depth 39'-0"

DECK/PATIO

DINING ROOM
11'-6" x 9'-4"

GREAT ROOM
16'-0" x 19'-0"

MASTER SUITE
15'-0" x 12'-0"

W.I.C.

KITCHEN
11'-6" x 11'-0"

PANT.

LAUN.

MASTER BATH

BATH

FOYER

SUITE 3
10'-0" x 10'-0"

GARAGE
20'-0" x 20'-0"

SUITE 2
11'-6" x 11'-4"

Design HPTM03006

Square Footage: 1,282

■ An endearing exterior with a large living room window, a sunburst and sidelight will gratify homeowners. Inside, the spacious kitchen includes an island with room for gourmet cooking and a snack bar for an afternoon lunch. A nearby dining area is available while the living room is ready to greet friends and family. One of two family bedrooms includes two spacious closets, while both share a full bath located just steps away. This home is designed with a basement foundation.

Design by
©Drummond Designs, Inc.

Width 40'-0"
Depth 46'-0"

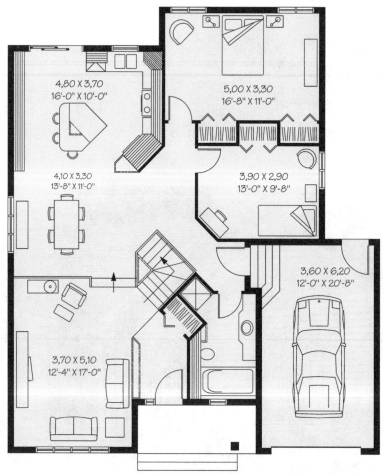

4,80 X 3,70
16'-0" X 10'-0"

5,00 X 3,30
16'-8" X 11'-0"

4,10 X 3,30
13'-8" X 11'-0"

3,90 X 2,90
13'-0" X 9'-8"

3,60 X 6,20
12'-0" X 20'-8"

3,70 X 5,10
12'-4" X 17'-0"

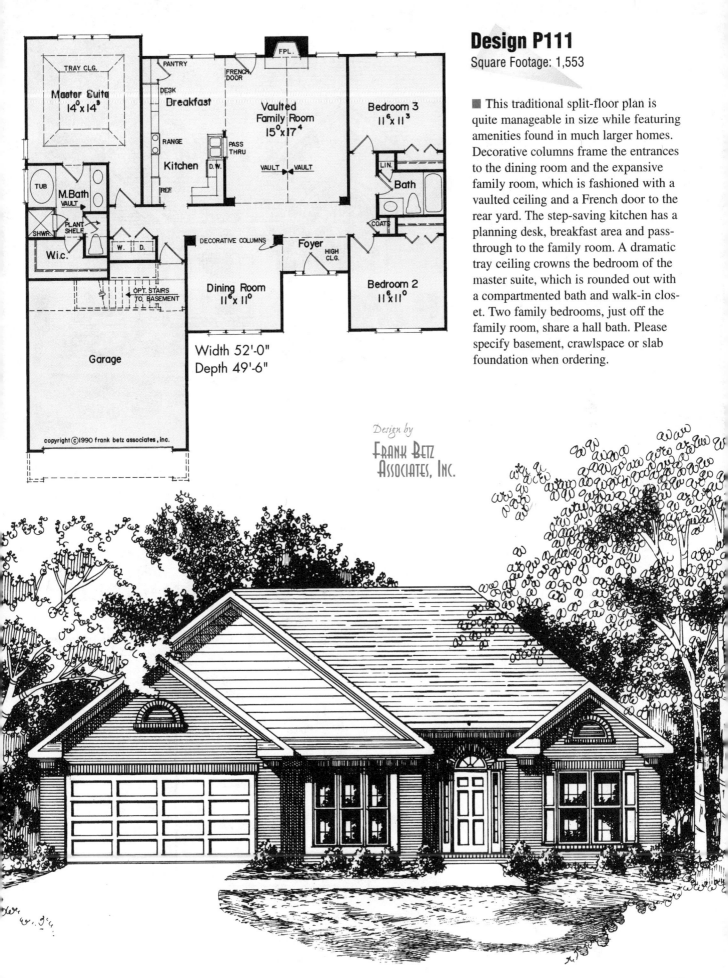

Design P111

Square Footage: 1,553

■ This traditional split-floor plan is quite manageable in size while featuring amenities found in much larger homes. Decorative columns frame the entrances to the dining room and the expansive family room, which is fashioned with a vaulted ceiling and a French door to the rear yard. The step-saving kitchen has a planning desk, breakfast area and pass-through to the family room. A dramatic tray ceiling crowns the bedroom of the master suite, which is rounded out with a compartmented bath and walk-in closet. Two family bedrooms, just off the family room, share a hall bath. Please specify basement, crawlspace or slab foundation when ordering.

TRAY CLG.

Master Suite
14⁰ x 14³

PANTRY

Breakfast

DESK

FPL.

FRENCH DOOR

Vaulted Family Room
15⁰ x 17⁴

Bedroom 3
11⁶ x 11³

RANGE

Kitchen

PASS THRU

VAULT   VAULT

D.W.

REF.

LIN.

Bath

TUB

M. Bath
VAULT

COATS

PLANT SHELF

SHWR.

W.i.c.

W. D.

DECORATIVE COLUMNS

Foyer

HIGH CLG.

OPT. STAIRS TO BASEMENT

Dining Room
11⁶ x 11⁰

Bedroom 2
11⁶ x 11⁰

Garage

copyright ©1990 frank betz associates, inc.

Width 52'-0"
Depth 49'-6"

Design by
FRANK BETZ ASSOCIATES, INC.

29

Design P189

Square Footage: 1,502

■ This ambitious plan masterfully combines stylish architectural elements in a smaller square footage. Elegant ceiling details, decorative columns and fancy window treatment prevail throughout this split-bedroom design. The great room is fashioned with a fireplace and has an open view into the breakfast room and serving bar. The modified galley kitchen has a convenient rear entry to the formal dining room and a service entrance through the two-car garage. Two family bedrooms and a full bath are neatly tucked behind the breakfast nook. The master suite is truly an owner's retreat with a cozy sitting room that's accented with a vaulted ceiling and sunny windows. The compartmented bath has a twin vanity and a walk-in closet. Please specify crawlspace or basement foundation when ordering.

Design by
FRANK BETZ
ASSOCIATES, INC.

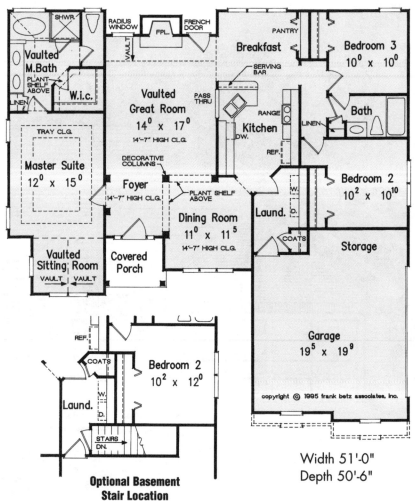

SHWR.

RADIUS WINDOW

FPL.

FRENCH DOOR

PANTRY

Breakfast

Bedroom 3
10⁰ x 10⁰

Vaulted M.Bath

PLANT SHELF ABOVE

W.i.c.

LINEN

VAULT

SERVING BAR

PASS THRU

Vaulted Great Room
14⁰ x 17⁰
14'-7" HIGH CLG.

RANGE

DW.

Kitchen

REF.

LINEN

Bath

TRAY CLG.

DECORATIVE COLUMNS

Master Suite
12⁰ x 15⁰

Foyer
14'-7" HIGH CLG.

PLANT SHELF ABOVE

Bedroom 2
10² x 10¹⁰

Laund.

W. D.

COATS

Dining Room
11⁰ x 11⁵
14'-7" HIGH CLG.

Storage

Vaulted Sitting Room
VAULT | VAULT

Covered Porch

REF.

COATS

W. D.

Bedroom 2
10² x 12⁰

Laund.

STAIRS DN.

Garage
19⁵ x 19⁹

copyright © 1995 frank betz associates, inc.

Optional Basement Stair Location

Width 51'-0"
Depth 50'-6"

Design HPTM00005

Square Footage: 1,434

■ This compact French country cottage has a lovely exterior and an efficient floor plan. The secluded master suite has a grand bath and a roomy walk-in closet. Both of the secondary bedrooms also contain walk-in closets. French doors in the living room open to front and rear porches. The kitchen is conveniently located between the dining room and a snug dinette. The two-car garage is complete with storage space for all the family treasures. Please specify crawlspace or slab foundation when ordering.

Width 70'-0"
Depth 44'-0"

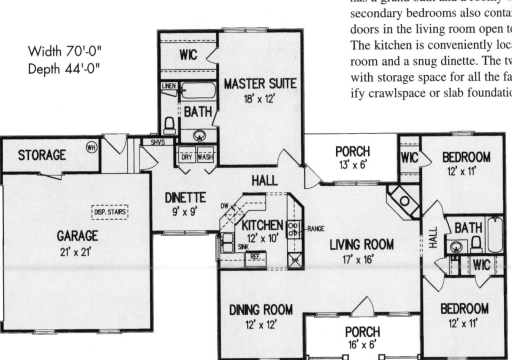

STORAGE
WH

GARAGE
21' x 21'
DISP. STARS

WIC
MASTER SUITE
18' x 12'
LINEN
BATH
SHVS
DRY WASH

DINETTE
9' x 9'
HALL

KITCHEN
12' x 10'
DW
SINK
REF
RANGE

PORCH
13' x 6'
WIC
BEDROOM
12' x 11'

LIVING ROOM
17' x 16'
HALL
BATH
WIC

DINING ROOM
12' x 12'

PORCH
16' x 6'

BEDROOM
12' x 11'

Design 7229

Square Footage: 1,696

■ This convenient split-entry traditional home features a great room with a fireplace flanked by bookcases and a floor-to-ceiling view of the backyard. The efficient kitchen includes a sunny bay window in the breakfast area. Box ceilings grace both the breakfast nook and the formal dining room. The laundry room is strategically located near the sleeping wing. Two secondary bedrooms offer abundant closet space and a shared full bath. The deluxe master bedroom offers a vaulted ceiling, a large walk-in closet and a bath with a whirlpool tub.

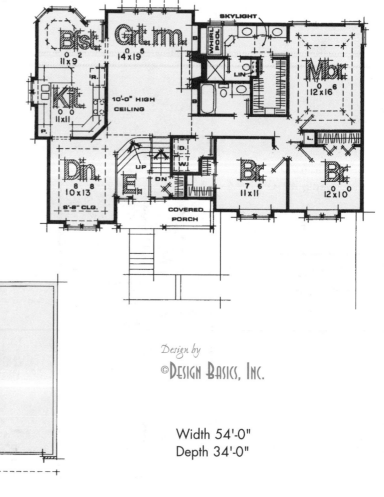

Design by
©Design Basics, Inc.

Width 54'-0"
Depth 34'-0"

3,00 X 3,00
10'-0" X 10'-0"

6,10 X 3,70
20'-4" X 12'-4"

3,90 X 4,80
13'-0" X 16'-0"

3,60 X 3,60
12'-0" X 12'-0"

Design HPTM03007
Square Footage: 1,098

■ A traditional feel exudes from the European Chateau exterior of this compact two-bedroom home. The front entry smartly blocks cold winter breezes with an interior door. A fireplace column adorns the living room, which sits open to the dining room at the rear. A unique angle to the kitchen makes wonderful use of space and provides privacy to one of the two family bedrooms. A full bath includes a separate shower and a tub. This home is designed with a basement foundation.

Design by
©DRUMMOND DESIGNS, INC.

Width 32'-0"
Depth 36'-8"

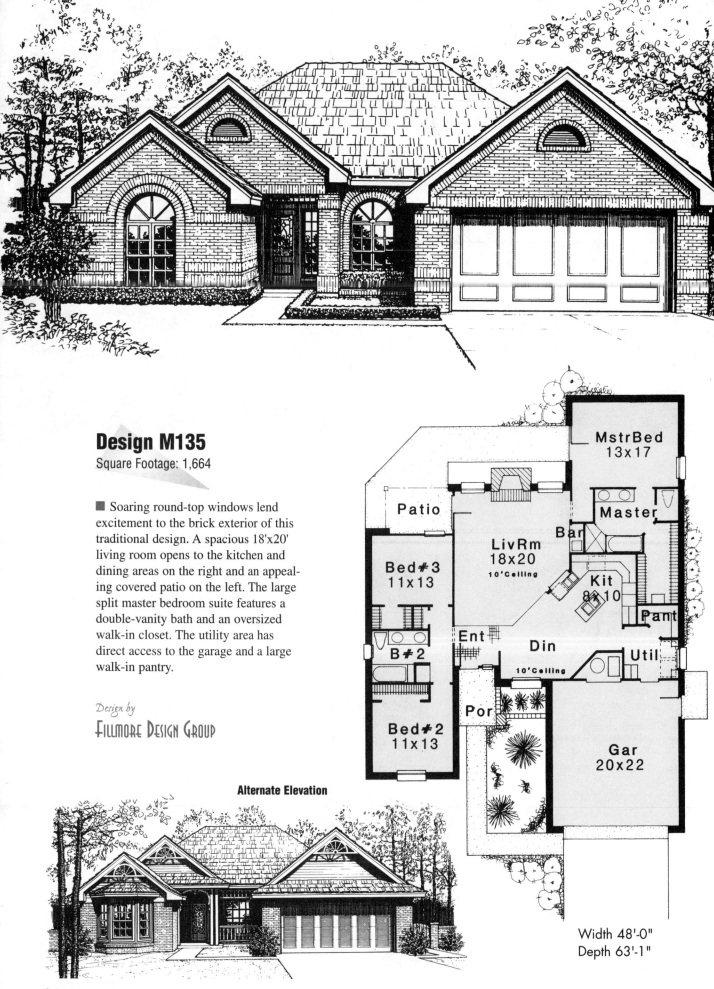

Design M135

Square Footage: 1,664

■ Soaring round-top windows lend excitement to the brick exterior of this traditional design. A spacious 18'x20' living room opens to the kitchen and dining areas on the right and an appealing covered patio on the left. The large split master bedroom suite features a double-vanity bath and an oversized walk-in closet. The utility area has direct access to the garage and a large walk-in pantry.

Design by

FILLMORE DESIGN GROUP

Alternate Elevation

MstrBed
13x17

Master

Patio

Bar

LivRm
18x20
10'Ceiling

Kit
8x10

Pant

Bed#3
11x13

Ent

Din

Util

B#2

10'Ceiling

Por

Bed#2
11x13

Gar
20x22

Width 48'-0"
Depth 63'-1"

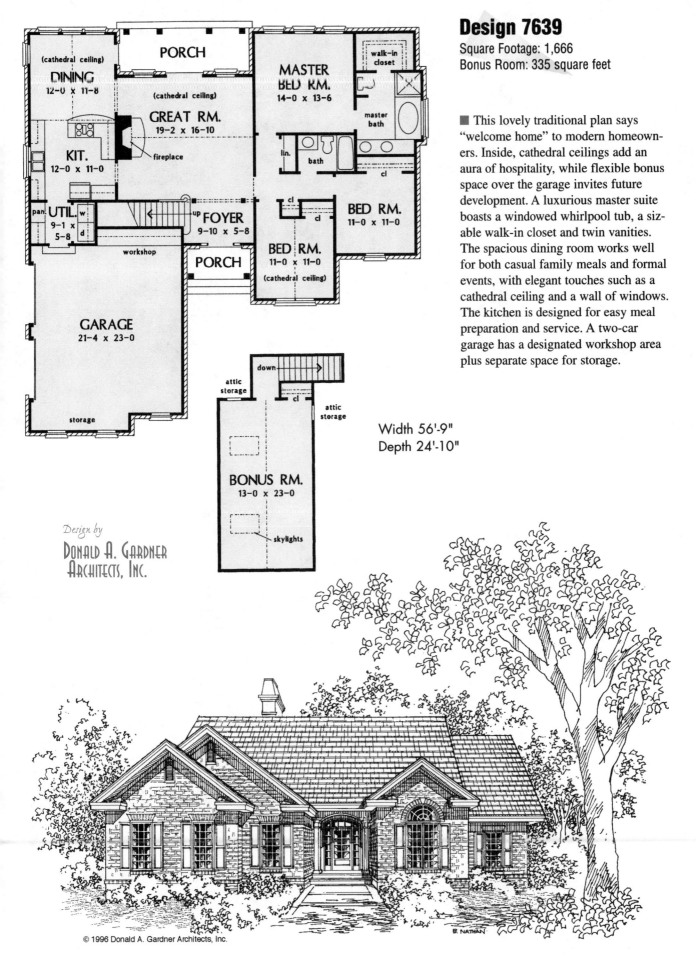

Design 7639

Square Footage: 1,666
Bonus Room: 335 square feet

■ This lovely traditional plan says "welcome home" to modern homeowners. Inside, cathedral ceilings add an aura of hospitality, while flexible bonus space over the garage invites future development. A luxurious master suite boasts a windowed whirlpool tub, a sizable walk-in closet and twin vanities. The spacious dining room works well for both casual family meals and formal events, with elegant touches such as a cathedral ceiling and a wall of windows. The kitchen is designed for easy meal preparation and service. A two-car garage has a designated workshop area plus separate space for storage.

Width 56'-9"
Depth 24'-10"

(cathedral ceiling)
DINING
12-0 x 11-8

PORCH

MASTER
BED RM.
14-0 x 13-6

walk-in closet

master bath

(cathedral ceiling)

GREAT RM.
19-2 x 16-10

lin. | bath

KIT.
12-0 x 11-0

fireplace

cl

BED RM.
11-0 x 11-0

pan. UTIL.
9-1 x 5-8

w d

FOYER
9-10 x 5-8

up

cl
cl

workshop

PORCH

BED RM.
11-0 x 11-0
(cathedral ceiling)

GARAGE
21-4 x 23-0

storage

down

attic storage

cl

attic storage

BONUS RM.
13-0 x 23-0

skylights

Design by

Donald A. Gardner
Architects, Inc.

B. NATHAN

© 1996 Donald A. Gardner Architects, Inc.

Design HPTM03008

Square Footage: 1,207

■ Two bay windows fill the interior of this charming brick home with natural light. The living spaces radiate off the central foyer, eliminating the need for a hallway and creating a very efficient use of space. The master bedroom is on the right with a lavish bath close at hand. A second bedroom finds privacy on the left surrounded by the enclosed entry, the foyer, the basement stairs and the mudroom that leads to the garage. The dining/living room looks out to the rear deck, enhancing the spaciousness of this open plan. The breakfast nook, nestled in the rear bay window, adjoins the well-equipped kitchen—note the rear exit to the deck. This home is designed with a basement foundation.

Width 48'-0"
Depth 48'-0"

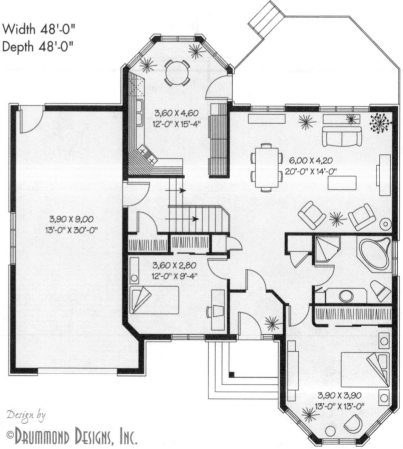

Design by
©Drummond Designs, Inc.

36

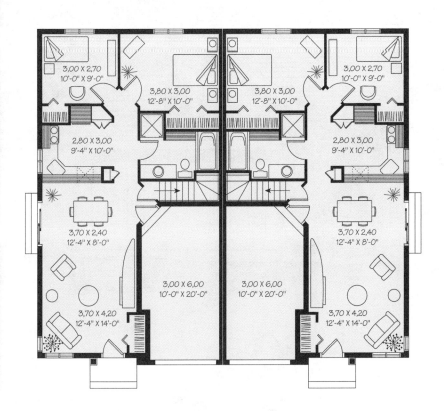

Design Z047

Total: 834 square feet (per unit)

■ Two gables adorn the front of this fine duplex, while inside, matching units offer a place to call home. The foyer opens directly into the living area where there is space for both a living room and a dining area. The open kitchen offers a cheerful pass-through to the dining area. Here, sliding glass doors access the side yard, letting natural light flood the area. Two bedrooms share a full hall bath which features both a shower as well as a tub. The one-car garage offers some storage for yard equipment. This home is designed with a basement foundation.

Width 48'-0"
Depth 44'-0"

Design by
©Drummond Designs, Inc.

Design 7304

Square Footage: 1,341

■ For great livability, this one-story home places its living areas to the back of the plan. The foyer leads directly to the great room and its focal-point fireplace. Extras include a built-in entertainment center and bookcase in the great room and a snack bar separating the sunny breakfast room from the U-shaped kitchen. The master suite includes a large walk-in closet and a pampering bath with a whirlpool tub, separate shower and dual-bowl vanity. Two front-facing family bedrooms share a full hall bath.

Design by
DESIGN BASICS, INC.

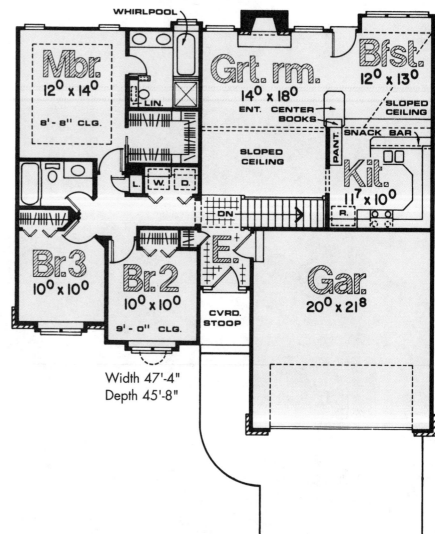

WHIRLPOOL

Mbr.
12⁰ x 14⁰
8'-8" CLG.

LIN.

Grt. rm.
14⁰ x 18⁰
ENT. CENTER
BOOKS
SLOPED CEILING
PANT.

Bfst.
12⁰ x 13⁰
SLOPED CEILING
SNACK BAR

Kit.
11⁷ x 10⁰

L W D

DN

Br. 3
10⁰ x 10⁰

Br. 2
10⁰ x 10⁰
9'-0" CLG.

CVRD. STOOP

Gar.
20⁰ x 21⁸

Width 47'-4"
Depth 45'-8"

38

2,50 X 3,10
8'-4" X 10'-4"

3,50 X 3,10
11'-8" X 10'-4"

4,20 X 3,30
14'-0" X 11'-0"

3,70 X 4,50
12'-4" X 15'-0"

3,30 X 2,70
11'-0" X 9'-0"

Width 39'-0"
Depth 32'-8"

Design HPTM03009

Square Footage: 1,103

■ Plenty of windows decorate the exterior and illuminate the interior of this cozy contemporary design. The living room sits to the left of the entry and opens to the kitchen and dining area, The kitchen includes a pantry and a snack bar, while the dining room provides a bay window and access to the outdoors. Two bedrooms share a full hall bath that includes a corner shower. The rear bedroom, accessed by French doors, features a wall closet that spans the length of the room. This home is designed with a basement foundation.

Design by
©DRUMMOND DESIGNS, INC.

Design R155
Square Footage: 1,440

■ A covered porch welcomes both family and friends to this fine three-bedroom home. The vaulted great room gives this plan a much larger feel than the square footage would indicate, and the openness of the dining bay and kitchen contributes to this airiness. The cathedral ceiling in the great room enhances the spaciousness, and the fireplace adds a touch of warmth to the atmosphere. Three bedrooms, including an indulgent master suite, are located down a short hall. The optional two-car garage will be perfect to shelter the family fleet.

Design by
DONALD A. GARDNER ARCHITECTS, INC.

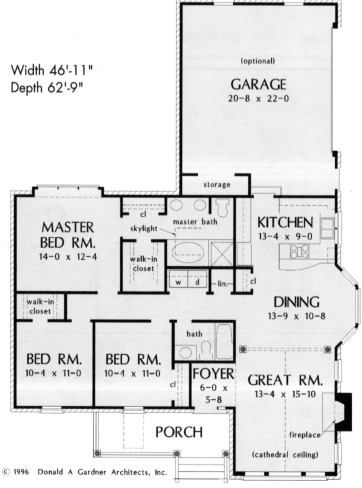

Width 46'-11"
Depth 62'-9"

(optional)
GARAGE
20-8 x 22-0

storage

MASTER BED RM.
14-0 x 12-4

cl

skylight

master bath

KITCHEN
13-4 x 9-0

walk-in closet

w d lin. cl

walk-in closet

DINING
13-9 x 10-8

bath

BED RM.
10-4 x 11-0

BED RM.
10-4 x 11-0

FOYER
6-0 x 5-8

cl

GREAT RM.
13-4 x 15-10

PORCH

fireplace

(cathedral ceiling)

PATIO

DINING
13-0 x 10-6

GREAT RM.
18-8 x 16-8
(cathedral ceiling)

fireplace

MASTER
BED RM.
15-0 x 13-8
(cathedral ceiling)

master
bath

KITCHEN
13-0 x 12-2

FOYER
9-0 x 5-8

cl

bath

walk-in
closet

d
w

cl

cl

storage

up

PORCH

cl

BED RM.
11-0 x 12-0

GARAGE
22-8 x 20-0

BED RM.
11-0 x 12-0
(cathedral ceiling)

© 1998 Donald A Gardner, Inc.

BONUS RM.
14-10 x 20-0

attic
storage

attic
storage

down

Design by
DONALD A. GARDNER ARCHITECTS, INC.

Design 7763

Square Footage: 1,658
Bonus Room: 359 square feet

■ This traditional home appeals with architectural details often found only on much larger homes: keystone arches above garage doors, a dormer window and a recessed entry. The floor plan puts the sleeping zone— with a master suite and family bed-rooms—on the right side of the plan and the living and dining areas on the left. The great room features a cathe-dral ceiling and a fireplace, plus patio access. The U-shaped kitchen serves a sunny dining room. Stairs in the two-car garage lead up to bonus space that can be developed later.

Width 57'-8"
Depth 47'-4"

Design 7704

Square Footage: 1,246

■ Open living spaces allow an easy flow in this gracious country cottage, and vaulted ceilings add volume. The front porch wraps slightly, giving the illusion of a larger home, while a cathedral ceiling maximizes space in the open great room and dining room. The kitchen features a center skylight, breakfast bar and screened-porch access. Two bedrooms share a bath near the entry, while the master suite enjoys a private location at the back of the plan. Luxuriate in the master bath with its separate shower, garden tub and twin-sink vanity.

Design by
DONALD A. GARDNER ARCHITECTS, INC.

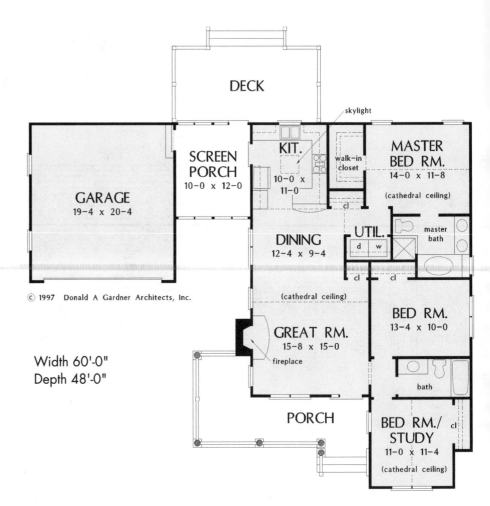

Width 60'-0"
Depth 48'-0"

© 1997   Donald A Gardner Architects, Inc.

© 1995 Donald A. Gardner Architects, Inc.

Design by
DONALD A. GARDNER ARCHITECTS, INC.

Width 60'-0"
Depth 48'-0"

DECK

SCREEN PORCH
10-0 x 11-4

DINING
10-0 x 11-0
(cathedral ceiling)

sto.

master bath

(cathedral ceiling)

MASTER BED. RM.
11-8 x 14-4

GARAGE
19-4 x 20-4

pan.

skylight

KIT.
11-8 x 9-4

UTIL.
d   w

lin.

walk-in closet

cl   cl

plant shelf above

© 1995   Donald A Gardner Architects, Inc.

(cathedral ceiling)

GREAT RM.
15-8 x 15-4

fireplace

BED. RM.
13-4 x 10-0

bath

skylight

Design 7733
Square Footage: 1,253

PORCH

BED. RM./ STUDY
11-0 x 11-4
(cathedral ceiling)

cl

■ Three inset gables and a covered, wraparound porch welcomes both family and friends to this fine three-bedroom home. The vaulted great room gives this plan a much larger feel than the square footage would indicate, and the openness of the dining bay and kitchen contributes to this airiness. The fireplace adds a touch of warmth to the great room for those chilly days. Three bedrooms, including an indulgent master suite, are located to the right of the plan. The two-car garage will be perfect to shelter the family fleet and accesses the screened porch by the dining room.

Design by
Frank Betz
Associates, Inc.

Design P110

Square Footage: 1,429

■ This home's gracious exterior is indicative of the elegant, yet extremely livable, floor plan inside. Volume ceilings that crown the family living areas combine with an open floor plan to give the modest square footage a more spacious feel. The formal dining room is set off from the foyer and vaulted family room with stately columns. The spacious family room has a corner fireplace, rear yard access and serving bar from the open galley kitchen. A bay windowed breakfast nook flanks the kitchen on one end while a laundry center and wet-bar/serving pantry lead to the dining room on the other. The split-bedroom plan allows the amenity-rich master suite maximum privacy. A pocket door off the family room leads to the hall housing the two family bedrooms and a full bath. Please specify basement, crawlspace or slab foundation when ordering.

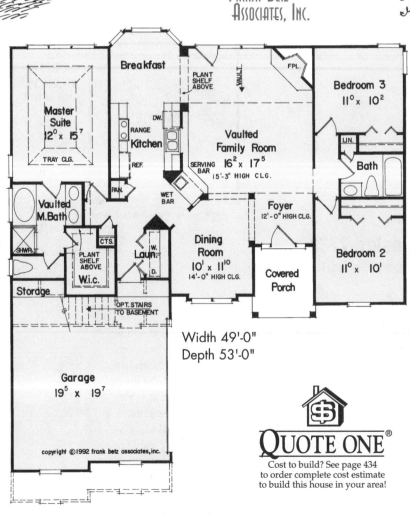

Width 49'-0"
Depth 53'-0"

QUOTE ONE®

Cost to build? See page 434 to order complete cost estimate to build this house in your area!

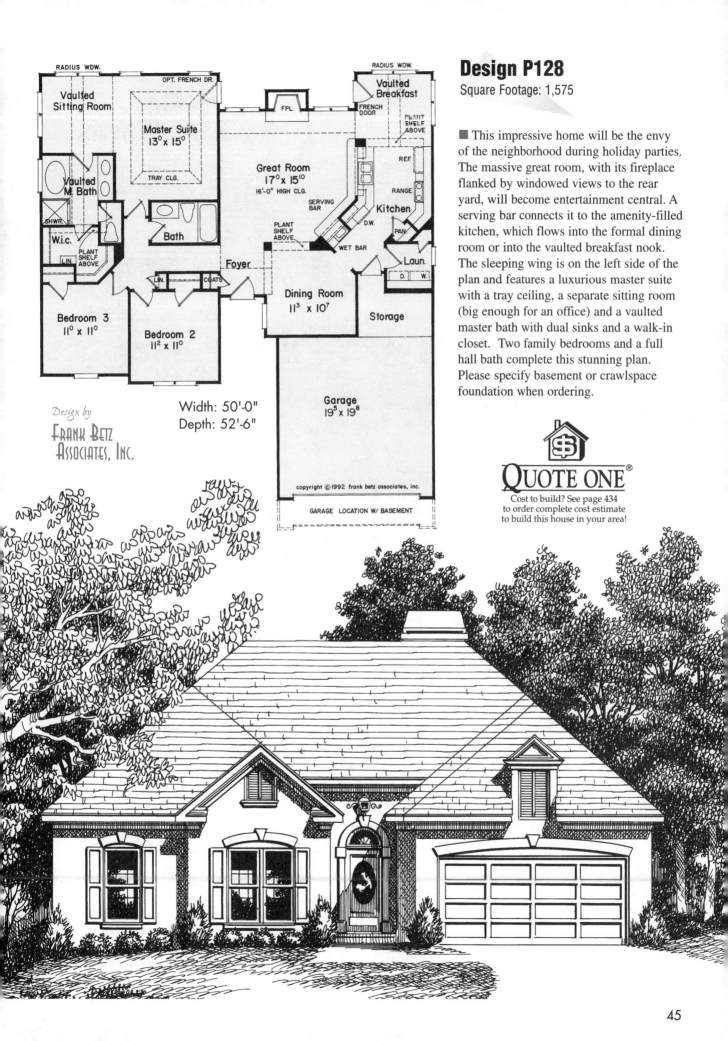

Design P128

Square Footage: 1,575

RADIUS WDW.

Vaulted Sitting Room

Master Suite
13⁰ x 15⁰

OPT. FRENCH DR.

TRAY CLG.

Vaulted M. Bath

SHWR.

W.i.c.

PLANT SHELF ABOVE

LIN.

Bath

Bedroom 3
11⁰ x 11⁰

LIN.

COATS

Bedroom 2
11² x 11⁰

Foyer

RADIUS WDW.

Vaulted Breakfast

FPL.

FRENCH DOOR

PLANT SHELF ABOVE

Great Room
17⁰ x 15¹⁰
16'-0" HIGH CLG.

REF.

RANGE

SERVING BAR

Kitchen

D.W.

PAN.

PLANT SHELF ABOVE

WET BAR

Laun.

D. W.

Dining Room
11³ x 10⁷

Storage

Garage
19⁵ x 19⁸

Width: 50'-0"
Depth: 52'-6"

Design by
Frank Betz Associates, Inc.

copyright © 1992 frank betz associates, inc.

GARAGE LOCATION W/ BASEMENT

■ This impressive home will be the envy of the neighborhood during holiday parties. The massive great room, with its fireplace flanked by windowed views to the rear yard, will become entertainment central. A serving bar connects it to the amenity-filled kitchen, which flows into the formal dining room or into the vaulted breakfast nook. The sleeping wing is on the left side of the plan and features a luxurious master suite with a tray ceiling, a separate sitting room (big enough for an office) and a vaulted master bath with dual sinks and a walk-in closet. Two family bedrooms and a full hall bath complete this stunning plan. Please specify basement or crawlspace foundation when ordering.

QUOTE ONE®

Cost to build? See page 434 to order complete cost estimate to build this house in your area!

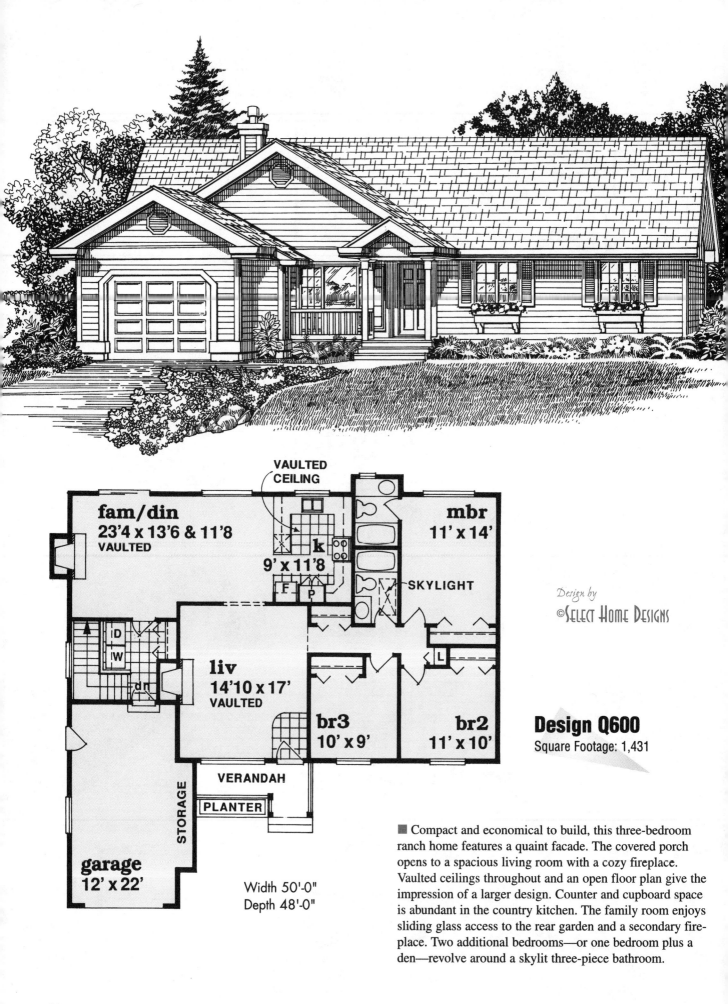

VAULTED CEILING

fam/din
23'4 x 13'6 & 11'8
VAULTED

mbr
11' x 14'

k
9' x 11'8

F   P

SKYLIGHT

Design by
©Select Home Designs

D W

dn

liv
14'10 x 17'
VAULTED

L

br3
10' x 9'

br2
11' x 10'

Design Q600
Square Footage: 1,431

VERANDAH

STORAGE

PLANTER

garage
12' x 22'

Width 50'-0"
Depth 48'-0"

■ Compact and economical to build, this three-bedroom
ranch home features a quaint facade. The covered porch
opens to a spacious living room with a cozy fireplace.
Vaulted ceilings throughout and an open floor plan give the
impression of a larger design. Counter and cupboard space
is abundant in the country kitchen. The family room enjoys
sliding glass access to the rear garden and a secondary fireplace. Two additional bedrooms—or one bedroom plus a
den—revolve around a skylit three-piece bathroom.

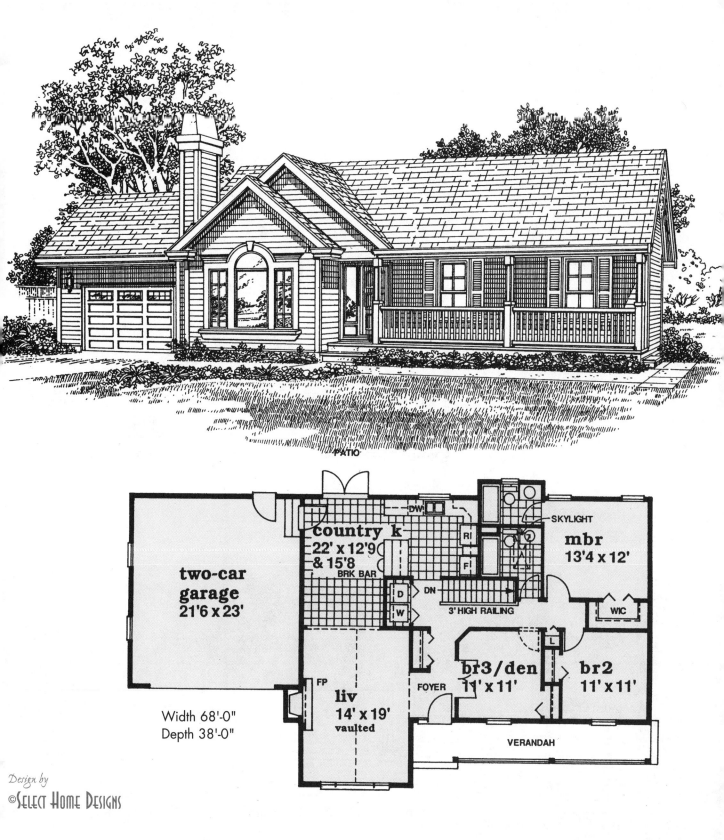

two-car
garage
21'6 x 23'

country k
22' x 12'9
& 15'8
BRK BAR

DW

SKYLIGHT

mbr
13'4 x 12'

WIC

DN

3' HIGH RAILING

FP

liv
14' x 19'
vaulted

FOYER

br3/den
11' x 11'

br2
11' x 11'

VERANDAH

Width 68'-0"
Depth 38'-0"

PATIO

Design by
©Select Home Designs

■ This clever one-story ranch home features a covered veranda at the front to enhance outdoor livability. The entry opens to a foyer that leads into a vaulted living room with fireplace on the left and a den or third bedroom on the right. The country kitchen is found to the back and is highlighted by a breakfast bar and sliding glass door to the rear patio. The hallway contains an open-railed stairway to the basement and a laundry alcove. The large bedrooms include ample closet space. The master bedroom features a walk-in closet and a full, private bath. Family bedrooms share the use of a skylit main bath. A two-car garage handles the family vehicles and faces front for convenience.

Design Q447
Square Footage: 1,428

Design Q632

Square Footage: 839

■ This quaint get-away home presents lovely shutters and multi-pane windows. Inside, a ribbon of windows lends natural lighting to the living room. This room is warmed by a wood stove, set opposite sliding glass doors to the covered deck. Relax on the deck, leaning against the wooden balustrade. When you aren't dining out, eat in the L-shaped kitchen. The plan has two bedrooms—a master suite and a secondary bedroom, sharing a full bath.

Design by
©Select Home Designs

Width 36'-6"
Depth 26'-0"

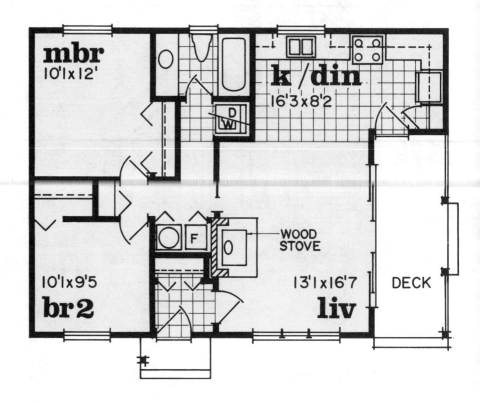

mbr 10'1x12'

k/din 16'3x8'2

D/W

WOOD STOVE

10'1x9'5 **br2**

13'1x16'7 **liv**

DECK

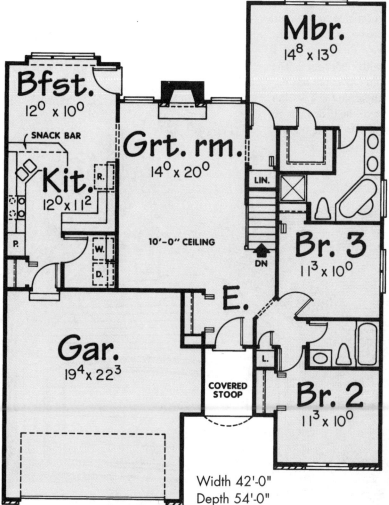

Mbr.
14⁸ x 13⁰

Bfst.
12⁰ x 10⁰

SNACK BAR

Grt. rm.
14⁰ x 20⁰

LIN.

Kit.
12⁰ x 11²

R.

10'-0" CEILING

P.

W.
D.

DN

Br. 3
11³ x 10⁰

E.

Gar.
19⁴ x 22³

COVERED
STOOP

L.

Br. 2
11³ x 10⁰

Width 42'-0"
Depth 54'-0"

© design basics inc.

Design 7349

Square Footage: 1,392

■ With an unusually narrow footprint, this one-story will fit on most slender lots and still provide a great floor plan. The entry is graced with a handy coat closet and leads back to the spacious great room (note the ten-foot ceiling here) and to the right to two family bedrooms and a full bath. Stairs to the basement level are also found, just beyond the entry hall. The breakfast room and kitchen dominate the left side of the plan. Separating them is a snack-bar counter for quick meals-on-the-go. To the rear on the right is the master suite. Pampered amenities include a walk-in closet, windowed corner whirlpool tub, dual sinks and separate shower. A service entrance through the kitchen to the garage leads to a convenient laundry area and broom closet.

Design by
DESIGN BASICS, INC.

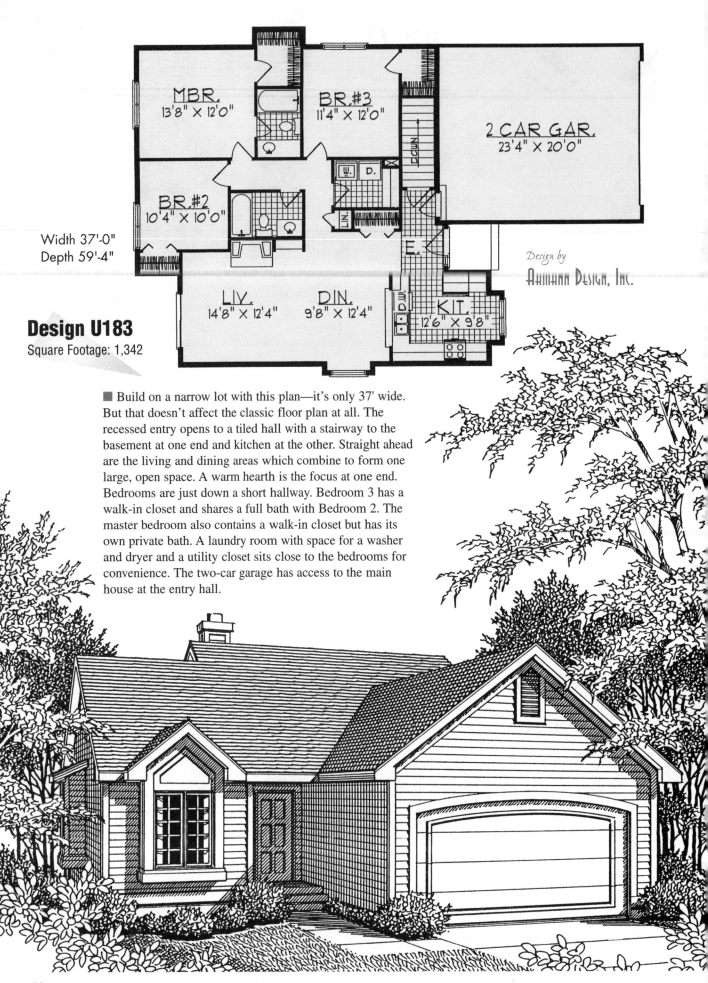

MBR.
13'8" X 12'0"

BR. #3
11'4" X 12'0"

2 CAR GAR.
23'4" X 20'0"

W. D.

LIN.

DOWN

E.

BR. #2
10'4" X 10'0"

Width 37'-0"
Depth 59'-4"

Design by
Ahmann Design, Inc.

LIV.
14'8" X 12'4"

DIN.
9'8" X 12'4"

KIT.
12'6" X 9'8"

Design U183

Square Footage: 1,342

■ Build on a narrow lot with this plan—it's only 37' wide. But that doesn't affect the classic floor plan at all. The recessed entry opens to a tiled hall with a stairway to the basement at one end and kitchen at the other. Straight ahead are the living and dining areas which combine to form one large, open space. A warm hearth is the focus at one end. Bedrooms are just down a short hallway. Bedroom 3 has a walk-in closet and shares a full bath with Bedroom 2. The master bedroom also contains a walk-in closet but has its own private bath. A laundry room with space for a washer and dryer and a utility closet sits close to the bedrooms for convenience. The two-car garage has access to the main house at the entry hall.

Design Q618

Square Footage: 988

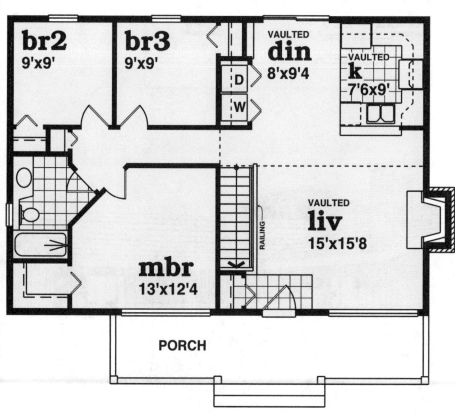

br2
9'x9'

br3
9'x9'

VAULTED
din
8'x9'4

VAULTED
k
7'6x9'

D

W

VAULTED
liv
15'x15'8

RAILING

mbr
13'x12'4

PORCH

■ This economical, compact home is the ultimate in the efficient use of space. Rest a while on the casual country porch which shelters the entry door. Inside, the central living room features a cozy fireplace and a lovely view of the front yard. The U-shaped kitchen and nearby dining room enjoy vaulted ceilings and sliding glass-door access to the rear garden. The uniquely-shaped master bedroom features a walk-in closet and shares a full, tiled bath with the two secondary bedrooms.

Quote One®

Cost to build? See page 434
to order complete cost estimate
to build this house in your area!

Design by
©SELECT HOME DESIGNS

Width 38'-0"
Depth 32'-0"

Design Q530

Square Footage: 1,244

■ With a simple floor plan and a lovely facade—including vertical siding
and brick—this casual ranch design is
the ideal retirement home. It features
an open plan with a living/dining area
to the front and bedrooms to the rear.
The convenient kitchen connects
directly to the dining room and shares
its view of the front deck through sliding glass doors. The master suite holds
His and Hers closets and a private half-
bath. Family bedrooms share a full hall
bath. Make one of them into a den or
guest room to fit your lifestyle. If you
choose, a full basement could be developed later into livable space—or keep
it as a storage area.

Design by
©Select Home Designs

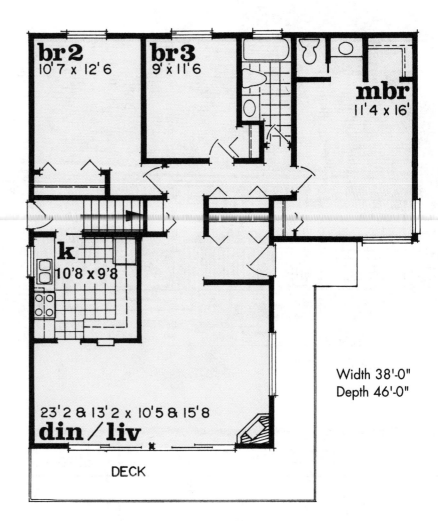

br2 10'7 x 12'6

br3 9' x 11'6

mbr 11'4 x 16'

k 10'8 x 9'8

23'2 & 13'2 x 10'5 & 15'8
din / liv

DECK

Width 38'-0"
Depth 46'-0"

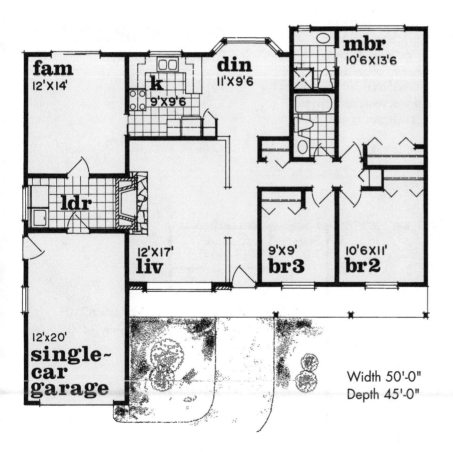

fam
12'X14'

k
9'X9'6

din
11'X9'6

mbr
10'6X13'6

ldr

liv
12'X17'

br3
9'X9'

br2
10'6X11'

single-car garage
12'x20'

Width 50'-0"
Depth 45'-0"

Design Q539

Square Footage: 1,377

■ Brick and siding lend country charm to the exterior of this three-bedroom home. Inside, a raised-hearth fireplace enhances the spacious living room. The U-shaped kitchen features a large window over the sink and enjoys convenient access to the family room and the dining area. Light will spill in through the bay window in the dining room. The family room has rear-yard access. The laundry room—also great as a mudroom—blocks noise from the single-car garage. Three bedrooms reside to the right of the plan. The master bedroom includes a private bath with a shower and the two secondary bedrooms share a full bath.

Design by
© Select Home Designs

53

■ Ranch-style homes continue to be a popular choice all over the continent, because of their casual, rustic appeal. This one is a classic, with a large great room with fireplace, a dining area and a galley-style kitchen. The two-car garage connects to the main home at an entry near the kitchen. It features two storage areas. Bedrooms sit on the far left: a master suite and two family bedrooms. The master bedroom contains a private bath and walk-in closet. Please specify basement, crawlspace or slab foundation when ordering.

Design HPTM00008
Square Footage: 1,441

Design by
©Larry James & Associates, Inc.

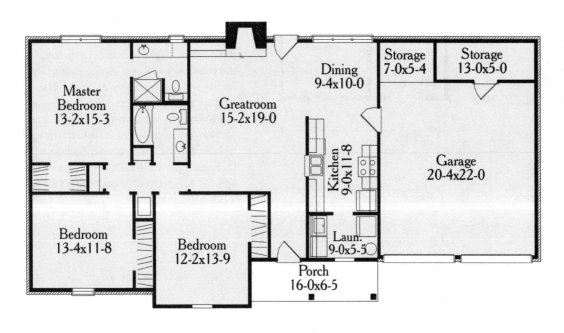

Master Bedroom
13-2x15-3

Dining
9-4x10-0

Storage
7-0x5-4

Storage
13-0x5-0

Greatroom
15-2x19-0

Kitchen
9-0x11-8

Garage
20-4x22-0

Bedroom
13-4x11-8

Bedroom
12-2x13-9

Laun.
9-0x5-5

Porch
16-0x6-5

Width 67'-0"
Depth 34'-0"

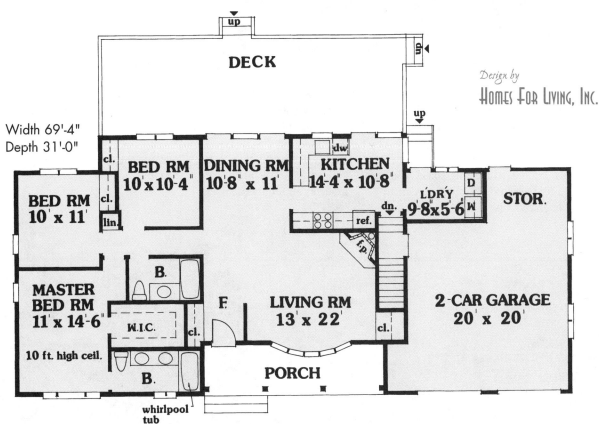

Width 69'-4"
Depth 31'-0"

DECK

up

up

up

Design by
Homes For Living, Inc.

BED RM
10' x 11'

cl.
cl.
lin.

BED RM
10' x 10'-4"

DINING RM
10'-8" x 11'

KITCHEN
14'-4" x 10'-8"

dw

LDRY
9'-8"x5'-6"

D
W

STOR.

ref.

dn.

f.p.

MASTER
BED RM
11' x 14'-6"

W.I.C.

10 ft. high ceil.

B.

cl.

F.

LIVING RM
13' x 22'

cl.

2-CAR GARAGE
20' x 20'

B.

whirlpool
tub

PORCH

Design N107
Square Footage: 1,387

■ Entering from a gracious front porch, the main activity spaces of this
traditional, one-story farmhouse are grouped to the right of the foyer.
The large living room has a corner fireplace and front-facing bow window. The dining room and kitchen have French doors leading to an outside deck. In the sleeping area, the master bedroom has a vaulted ceiling and a spacious walk-in closet. The master bath has a whirlpool tub
and two sinks. Two bedrooms off the hall share a bathroom.

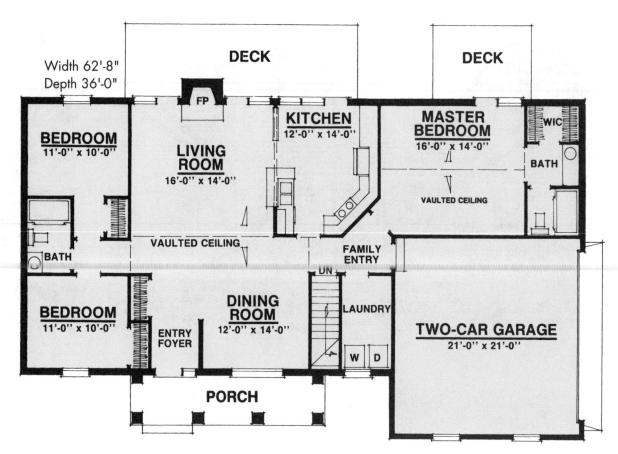

Width 62'-8"
Depth 36'-0"

DECK

DECK

FP

KITCHEN
12'-0'' x 14'-0''

MASTER BEDROOM
16'-0'' x 14'-0''

WIC

BEDROOM
11'-0'' x 10'-0''

LIVING ROOM
16'-0'' x 14'-0''

BATH

VAULTED CEILING

BATH

VAULTED CEILING

FAMILY ENTRY

DN

BEDROOM
11'-0'' x 10'-0''

DINING ROOM
12'-0'' x 14'-0''

LAUNDRY

TWO-CAR GARAGE
21'-0'' x 21'-0''

ENTRY FOYER

W   D

PORCH

■ A handsome porch dressed up with Greek Revival details greets visitors warmly into this one-story Early American home. From the entry, one is struck by the volume of space provided by the vaulted ceiling in the dining room, the living room, and the kitchen with eating space. The secluded master bedroom also sports a vaulted ceiling and is graced with a dressing area, a pri-vate bath and a walk-in closet. Two decks located at the rear of the plan are conveniently accessed by the master bedroom, kitchen and living room. A full bath serves the two family bedrooms and is readily accessible by guests. Adjacent to the two-car garage is a laundry room that handily accom-modates all family members.

Design F117
Square Footage: 1,550

Design by
R.L Pfotenhauer

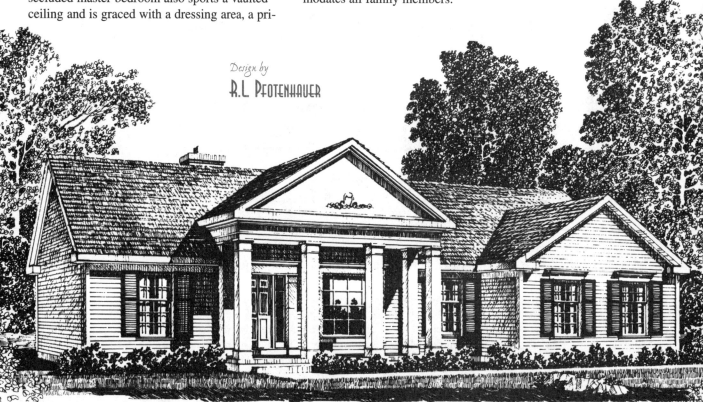

Design by
Homes For Living, Inc.

■ The exterior of this warm farmhouse style reflects this country's rich design heritage and has a plan firmly grounded in today's lifestyles. The sheltering entrance porch opens to a central foyer which leads to the main living space. Filling the large central area is a high-ceilinged living room with natural light flowing in through the skylight and the tall windows on either side of the fireplace. To the right of the foyer is a comfortable dining room with a bow window facing the front porch. Adjacent to the formal dining room is a large kitchen and convenient dinette area. The master bedroom suite contains a five-fixture bath and a large walk-in closet. Two additional bedrooms share a bath. An extra "flex"room near the entrance can be used as a den which opens directly into the living room, or closed, as a private fourth bedroom or home office with optional exterior door.

Design N101
Square Footage: 1,598

H.
cl.
B. R.
10' x 10'
Alternate Plan

H.
cl.
optional door
OFFICE
10' x 10'
Alternate Plan

TERR.

M. B. R.
16'-8" x 12'

B. R.
10 x 13'-2"

L. R.
high ceiling
skylight
13' x 20'-6"

KIT.
18'-6" x 10'
DIN.

ref.

dw

w d

dn.

up

2 - CAR GAR.
20' x 20'

w. i. cl.

lin.

cl.

whirlpool tub

shower

cl.

B. R.
11' x 10'
cath. ceiling

H.

cl.

DEN
10' x 10'
cath. ceiling

F.

D. R.
11'-4" x 10'

cl.

PORCH

up

Width 76'-4"
Depth 35'-10"

Design HPTM03010

Square Footage: 1,175

■ The contemporary style of this home influences the shape of the lovely brick exterior. The entry opens to a living area warmed by a fireplace—flanking windows illuminate the interior. The island snack-bar kitchen combines with a circular bayed breakfast room for casual family meals. The two family bedrooms share a hall bath that includes a corner tub, separate shower and double-bowl vanity—the master bedroom features ample closet space. A garage completes the floor plan. This home is designed with a basement foundation.

Design by
© DRUMMOND DESIGNS, INC.

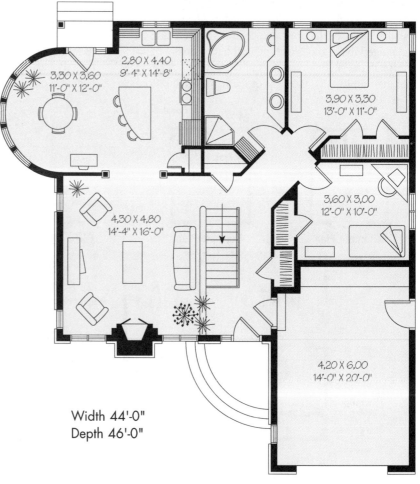

3.30 X 3.60
11'-0" X 12'-0"

2.80 X 4.40
9'-4" X 14'-8"

3.90 X 3.30
13'-0" X 11'-0"

4.30 X 4.80
14'-4" X 16'-0"

3.60 X 3.00
12'-0" X 10'-0"

4.20 X 6.00
14'-0" X 20'-0"

Width 44'-0"
Depth 46'-0"

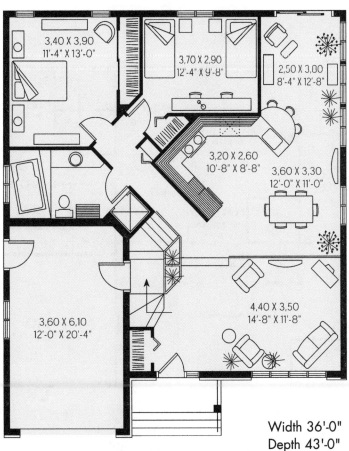

3,40 X 3,90
11'-4" X 13'-0"

3,70 X 2,90
12'-4" X 9'-8"

2,50 X 3,00
8'-4" X 12'-8"

3,20 X 2,60
10'-8" X 8'-8"

3,60 X 3,30
12'-0" X 11'-0"

3,60 X 6,10
12'-0" X 20'-4"

4,40 X 3,50
14'-8" X 11'-8"

Width 36'-0"
Depth 43'-0"

Design HPTM03011

Square Footage: 1,145

■ This brick cottage would fit into any
neighborhood and is a darling addition to
a narrow space. A coat closet is conveniently located near the front entrance.
The living room is creatively set apart
from the dining room by a set of short
stairs. The open kitchen features a breakfast bar and is within steps of the dining
room. A sun room enjoys the natural light
pouring through a wall of windows. Two
bedrooms share a full hall bath. This home
is designed with a basement foundation.

Design by
© DRUMMOND DESIGNS, INC.

©1997 Donald A. Gardner Architects, Inc.

Design 7679

Square Footage: 1,517
Bonus Room: 287 square feet

■ The foyer opens to a spacious great room with a fireplace and a cathedral ceiling in this lovely traditional home. Sliding doors open to a rear deck from the great room, posing a warm welcome to enjoy the outdoors. The L-shaped kitchen features an angled peninsula counter with a cooktop. A private hall leads to the family sleeping quarters, which include two bedrooms and a full bath with a double-bowl lavatory. A sizable bonus space above the garage provides plenty of room to grow.

Design by
DONALD A. GARDNER ARCHITECTS, INC.

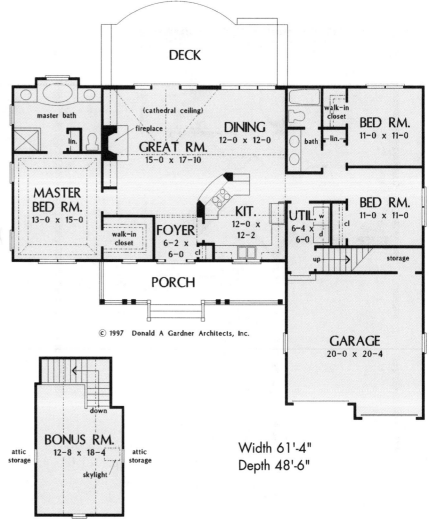

DECK

master bath

(cathedral ceiling)

fireplace

GREAT RM.
15-0 x 17-10

DINING
12-0 x 12-0

walk-in closet

BED RM.
11-0 x 11-0

bath

lin.

MASTER BED RM.
13-0 x 15-0

walk-in closet

FOYER
6-2 x 6-0

KIT.
12-0 x 12-2

UTIL.
6-4 x 6-0

BED RM.
11-0 x 11-0

up

storage

PORCH

© 1997   Donald A Gardner Architects, Inc.

GARAGE
20-0 x 20-4

BONUS RM.
12-8 x 18-4

down

attic storage

attic storage

skylight

Width 61'-4"
Depth 48'-6"

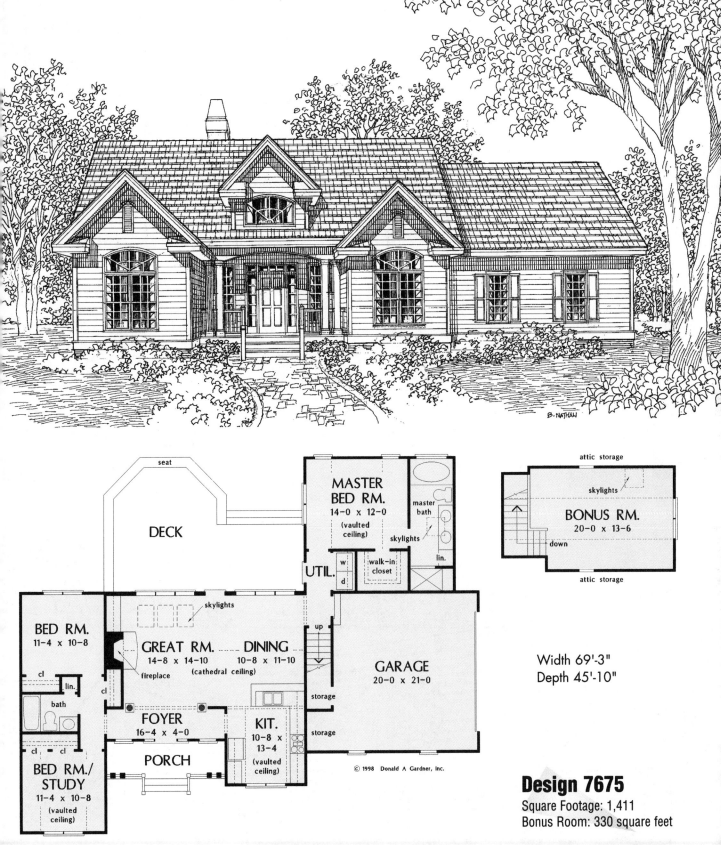

seat

DECK

MASTER BED RM.
14-0 x 12-0
(vaulted ceiling)

master bath

skylights

UTIL.

w d

walk-in closet

lin.

attic storage

skylights

BONUS RM.
20-0 x 13-6

down

attic storage

skylights

BED RM.
11-4 x 10-8

cl

lin.

bath

cl cl

BED RM./ STUDY
11-4 x 10-8
(vaulted ceiling)

GREAT RM.
14-8 x 14-10

fireplace

cl

DINING
10-8 x 11-10
(cathedral ceiling)

up

GARAGE
20-0 x 21-0

storage

storage

FOYER
16-4 x 4-0

KIT.
10-8 x 13-4
(vaulted ceiling)

PORCH

© 1998   Donald A Gardner, Inc.

Width 69'-3"
Depth 45'-10"

Design 7675
Square Footage: 1,411
Bonus Room: 330 square feet

Design by
DONALD A. GARDNER ARCHITECTS, INC.

■ With a smaller square footage, this country-style one-story home provides cozy comfort. The covered front porch opens to a central foyer, divided from the great room by decorative columns. Bookcases flank a fireplace in the great room, while skylights add brightness. The L-shaped kitchen serves a nearby dining room. Family bedrooms occupy the left side of the plan, split from the master suite on the right. A large deck along the back of the plan adds to outdoor fun.

Design 7771

Square Footage: 1,559

■ Both formal and informal rooms are found in this country one-story—even though it contains a smaller square footage. The foyer opens to a formal dining room to the right and a great room with cathedral ceiling straight ahead. The breakfast room and kitchen lie just to the right of the great room. Family bedrooms on the left side of the plan share a full hall bath. The master suite is tucked behind the two-car garage and accesses the rear deck, as does the great room.

Design by
DONALD A. GARDNER ARCHITECTS, INC.

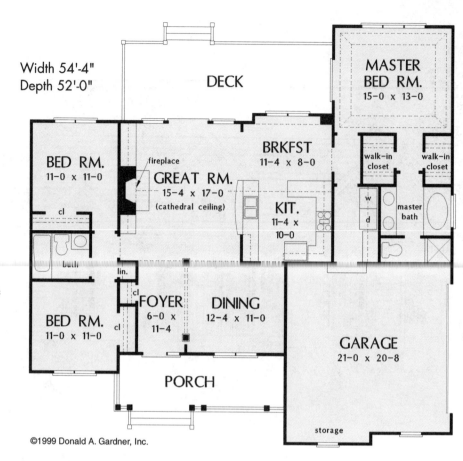

Width 54'-4"
Depth 52'-0"

DECK

MASTER BED RM.
15-0 x 13-0

BED RM.
11-0 x 11-0

fireplace

GREAT RM.
15-4 x 17-0
(cathedral ceiling)

BRKFST
11-4 x 8-0

walk-in closet

walk-in closet

cl

KIT.
11-4 x 10-0

w

d

master bath

bath

BED RM.
11-0 x 11-0

lin.

cl

cl

FOYER
6-0 x 11-4

DINING
12-4 x 11-0

GARAGE
21-0 x 20-8

PORCH

storage

©1999 Donald A. Gardner, Inc.

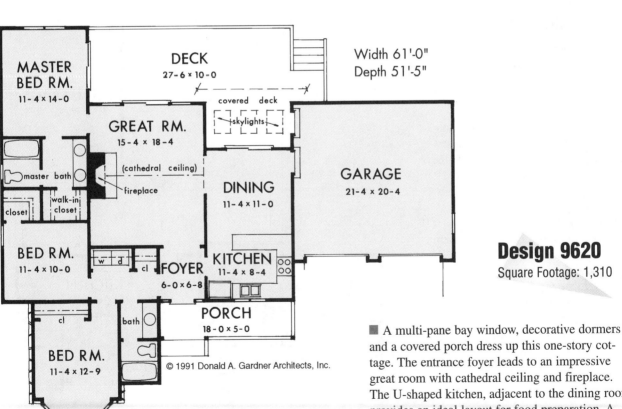

MASTER BED RM.
11-4 x 14-0

DECK
27-6 x 10-0

Width 61'-0"
Depth 51'-5"

covered deck
skylights

GREAT RM.
15-4 x 18-4

(cathedral ceiling)

fireplace

master bath

walk-in closet

closet

DINING
11-4 x 11-0

GARAGE
21-4 x 20-4

BED RM.
11-4 x 10-0

w d cl

FOYER
6-0 x 6-8

KITCHEN
11-4 x 8-4

Design 9620
Square Footage: 1,310

cl

bath

PORCH
18-0 x 5-0

BED RM.
11-4 x 12-9

Design by
DONALD A. GARDNER ARCHITECTS, INC.

■ A multi-pane bay window, decorative dormers and a covered porch dress up this one-story cottage. The entrance foyer leads to an impressive great room with cathedral ceiling and fireplace. The U-shaped kitchen, adjacent to the dining room, provides an ideal layout for food preparation. A large deck offers shelter while admitting cheery sunlight through skylights. A luxurious master bedroom, located to the rear of the house, takes advantage of the deck area and is assured privacy from two other bedrooms at the front of the house. These family bedrooms share a full bath.

Design 9665

Square Footage: 1,345

Width 56'-6"
Depth 62'-2"

■ A dormer above the great room and a round-top window add special features to this cozy traditional plan. Inside, the great room contains a fireplace and a sloped ceiling. Elegant round columns define the dining and kitchen areas while creating an openness with the great room. Ceilings in the dining room, kitchen and great room all slope up to a ridge above the columns. A bedroom adjacent to the foyer can double as a study. The master bedroom enjoys a fine bath, which includes a double-bowl vanity, shower and whirlpool tub. The garage connects to the house with a breezeway for flexibility.

Design by

DONALD A. GARDNER ARCHITECTS, INC.

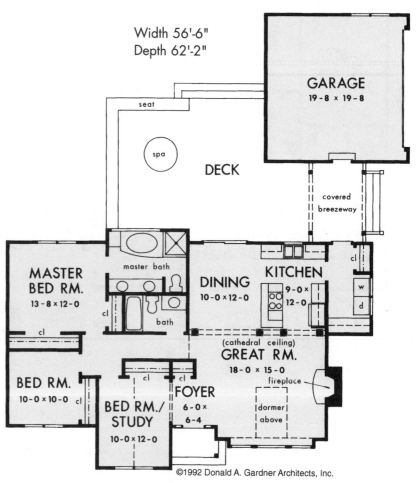

GARAGE
19-8 × 19-8

seat

spa

DECK

covered
breezeway

MASTER
BED RM.
13-8 × 12-0

master bath

cl

bath

DINING
10-0 × 12-0

KITCHEN

9-0 ×
12-0

cl

w
d

(cathedral ceiling)
GREAT RM.
18-0 × 15-0

fireplace

BED RM.
10-0 × 10-0

cl

cl

cl

FOYER
6-0 ×
6-4

dormer
above

BED RM./
STUDY
10-0 × 12-0

©1992 Donald A. Gardner Architects, Inc.

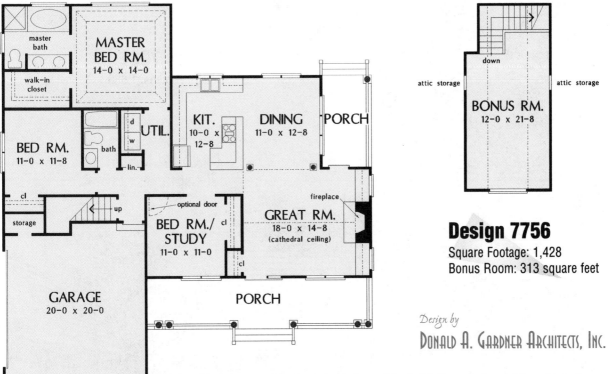

master
bath

walk-in
closet

MASTER
BED RM.
14-0 x 14-0

KIT.
10-0 x
12-8

DINING
11-0 x 12-8

PORCH

BED RM.
11-0 x 11-8

d

w

bath

UTIL.

lin.

cl

fireplace

cl

storage

up

optional door

BED RM./
STUDY
11-0 x 11-0

cl

GREAT RM.
18-0 x 14-8
(cathedral ceiling)

cl

GARAGE
20-0 x 20-0

PORCH

© 1998   Donald A Gardner, Inc.

down

attic storage

attic storage

BONUS RM.
12-0 x 21-8

Design 7756

Square Footage: 1,428
Bonus Room: 313 square feet

Design by
DONALD A. GARDNER ARCHITECTS, INC.

Width 52'-8"
Depth 52'-4"

■ Stunning arched windows framed by bold, front-facing gables add to the tremendous curb appeal of this modest home. Topped by a cathedral ceiling and with porches on either side, the great room is expanded further by its openness to the dining room and kitchen. Built-ins flank the fireplace for added convenience. Flexibility, which is so important in a home this size, is found in the versatile bedroom/study as well as the optional bonus room over the garage. The master suite is positioned for privacy at the rear of the home, with a graceful tray ceiling, walk-in closet and private bath. An additional bedroom and a hall bath complete the plan.

■ This rustic retreat is updated with contemporary angles and packs a lot of living into a small space. Indoor/outdoor relationships are well developed and help to create a comfortable home. Start off with the covered front porch, which leads to a welcoming foyer. The beamed-ceiling great room opens directly ahead and features a fireplace, a wall of windows, access to the screened porch (with its own fireplace!) and is adjacent to the angled dining area. A highly efficient island kitchen is sure to please with a cathedral ceiling, access to the rear deck and tons of counter and cabinet space. Two family bedrooms, sharing a full bath, are located on one end of the plan while the master suite is secluded for complete privacy at the other end. The master suite includes a walk-in closet and a pampering bath.

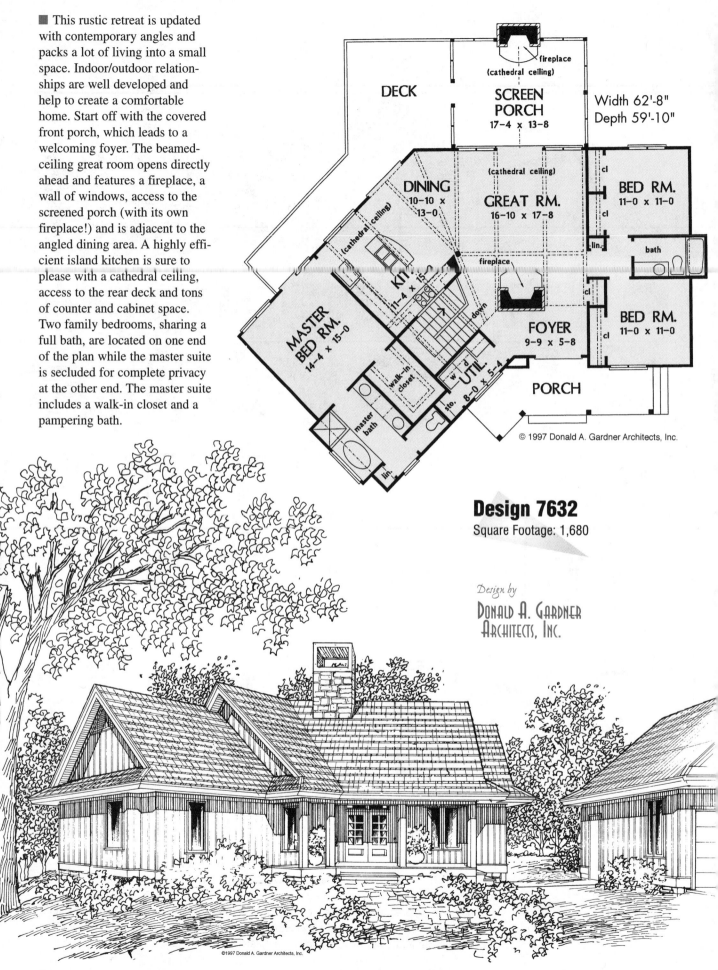

Width 62'-8"
Depth 59'-10"

DECK

SCREEN PORCH
17-4 x 13-8

fireplace
(cathedral ceiling)

(cathedral ceiling)

DINING
10-10 x 13-0

GREAT RM.
16-10 x 17-8

BED RM.
11-0 x 11-0

cl
cl
lin.

bath

(cathedral ceiling)

KIT.
11-4 x 15-2

fireplace

MASTER BED RM.
14-4 x 15-0

down

FOYER
9-9 x 5-8

cl

BED RM.
11-0 x 11-0

walk-in closet

w d
UTIL.
8-0 x 5-4

sto.

master bath

PORCH

lin.

cl

© 1997 Donald A. Gardner Architects, Inc.

Design 7632
Square Footage: 1,680

Design by
DONALD A. GARDNER
ARCHITECTS, INC.

©1997 Donald A. Gardner Architects, Inc.

Design 7673

Square Footage: 1,544
Bonus Room: 320 square feet

■ This home would look good in any neighborhood. From the covered front porch to the trio of gables, this design has a lot of appeal. Inside, the Craftsman styling continues in the manner of built-in shelves and a warming fireplace in the great room and plenty of windows to bring in the outdoors. The U-shaped kitchen offers easy access to the formal dining area. Expansion is possible with an optional bonus room, adding a second level. A tray ceiling adorns the master suite and the owner will enjoy His and Hers walk-in closets and a pampering bath complete with a twin-sink vanity and a separate shower and garden tub.

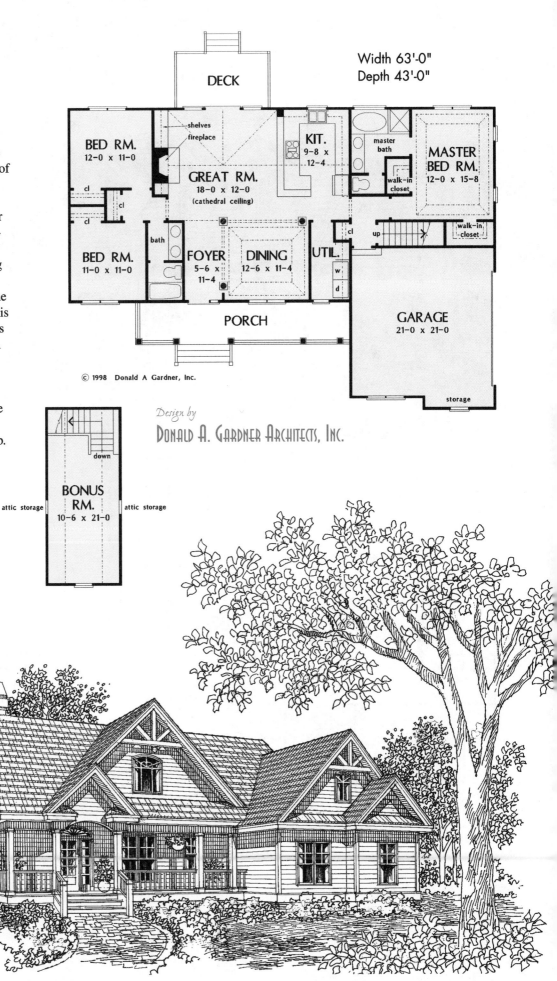

Width 63'-0"
Depth 43'-0"

DECK

BED RM.
12-0 x 11-0

shelves
fireplace

KIT.
9-8 x 12-4

master bath

MASTER BED RM.
12-0 x 15-8

GREAT RM.
18-0 x 12-0
(cathedral ceiling)

walk-in closet

cl

cl

cl

BED RM.
11-0 x 11-0

bath

FOYER
5-6 x 11-4

DINING
12-6 x 11-4

UTIL.

up

walk-in closet

cl

w
d

GARAGE
21-0 x 21-0

PORCH

© 1998 Donald A Gardner, Inc.

storage

Design by
Donald A. Gardner Architects, Inc.

down

BONUS RM.
10-6 x 21-0

attic storage

attic storage

67

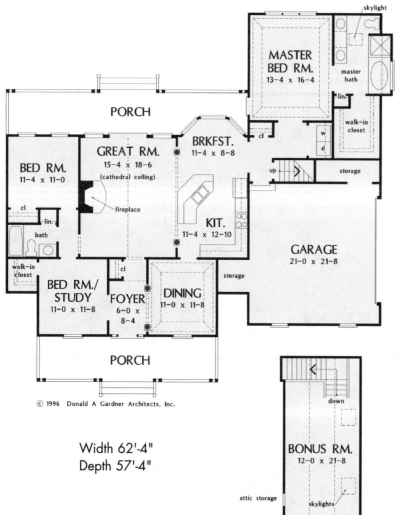

© 1996 Donald A Gardner Architects, Inc.

Width 62'-4"
Depth 57'-4"

Design 7711

Square Footage: 1,685
Bonus Room: 331 square feet

■ This lovely country home features many luxurious amenities beyond its comfortable country facade. The foyer leads to a great room adorned with a cathedral ceiling, a warming fireplace and views of the rear porch and yard. The master suite enjoys a tray ceiling and lavish bath with a garden tub and picture window. An open island kitchen and a great room with a cathedral ceiling split the master bedroom from two additional bedrooms. The formal dining room is dressed up with a tray ceiling, while outside, full front and back porches expand the living area.

Design by
Donald A. Gardner Architects, Inc.

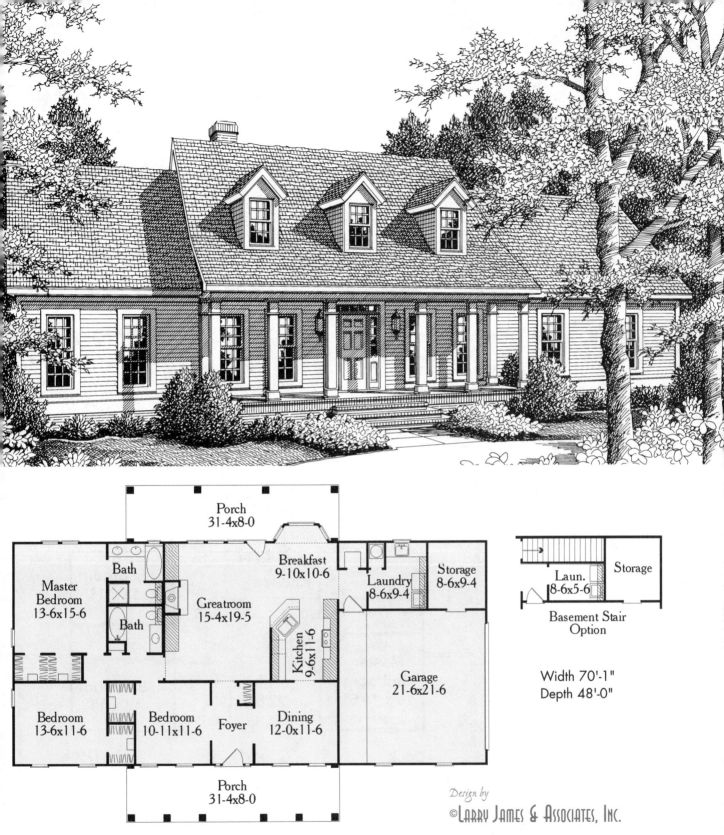

Porch
31-4x8-0

Breakfast
9-10x10-6

Bath

Laundry
8-6x9-4

Storage
8-6x9-4

Master
Bedroom
13-6x15-6

Greatroom
15-4x19-5

Bath

Kitchen
9-6x11-6

Garage
21-6x21-6

Bedroom
13-6x11-6

Bedroom
10-11x11-6

Foyer

Dining
12-0x11-6

Porch
31-4x8-0

Laun.
8-6x5-6

Storage

Basement Stair
Option

Width 70'-1"
Depth 48'-0"

Design by
© Larry James & Associates, Inc.

Design HPTM00009
Square Footage: 1,688

■ Dormers and columns decorate the exterior of this three-bedroom country home. Inside, the foyer has immediate access to one family bedroom and the formal dining area. Ahead is the great room with a warming fireplace and ribbon windows for natural lighting. The galley kitchen adjoins a breakfast area with a lovely bay window. The master suite is set to the back of the plan and features a lavish bath with a garden tub, separate shower and two vanities. Storage is not a problem in this comfortable home, with walk-in closets in each bedroom and an additional storage room off the two-car garage. Please specify basement, crawlspace or slab foundation when ordering.

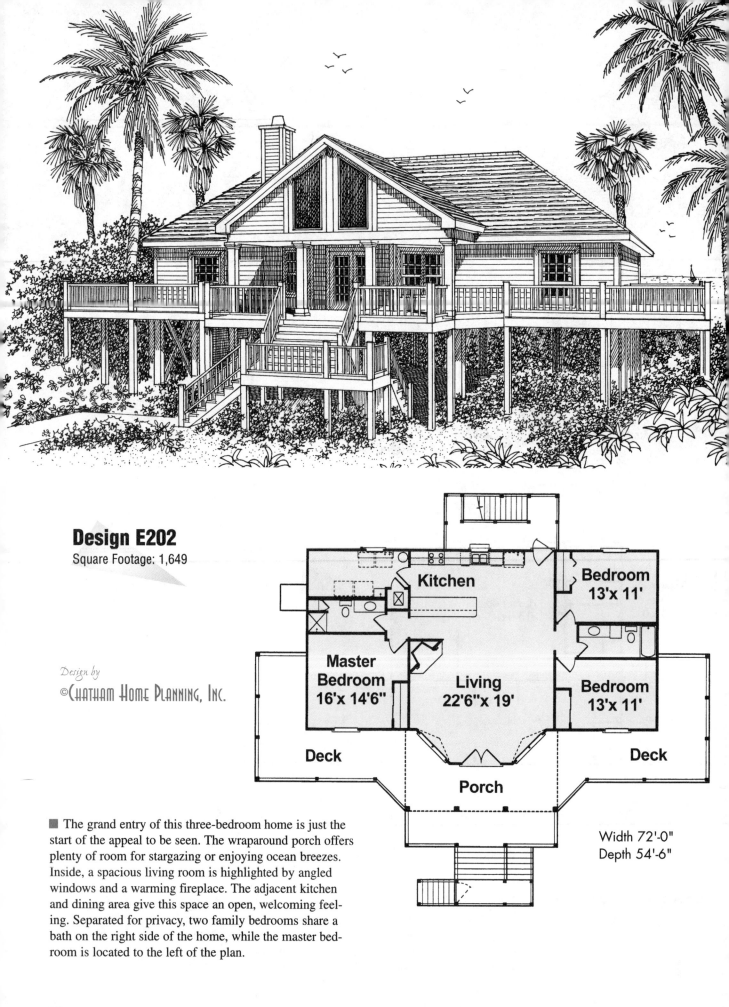

Design E202

Square Footage: 1,649

Design by
©Chatham Home Planning, Inc.

Kitchen

Bedroom
13' x 11'

Master Bedroom
16' x 14'6"

Living
22'6" x 19'

Bedroom
13' x 11'

Deck

Deck

Porch

Width 72'-0"
Depth 54'-6"

■ The grand entry of this three-bedroom home is just the start of the appeal to be seen. The wraparound porch offers plenty of room for stargazing or enjoying ocean breezes. Inside, a spacious living room is highlighted by angled windows and a warming fireplace. The adjacent kitchen and dining area give this space an open, welcoming feeling. Separated for privacy, two family bedrooms share a bath on the right side of the home, while the master bedroom is located to the left of the plan.

Design E154
Square Footage: 1,520

Deck

Bedroom
10'x 11'

Bedroom
10'4"x 9'6"

Bedroom
11'6"x 9'6"

Master
Bedroom
11'x 14'4"

Living
16'x 28'

Kitchen

Deck

■ Size doesn't always predict amenities! This one-story, pier-foundation
home is only 1,520 square feet, but
it's packed with surprises. A skylight
brings sunshine to the foyer, which
leads to the spacious living room.
Here, a huge wall of windows shows
off the beach, while a fireplace offers
warmth on cool winter evenings. The
L-shaped kitchen features an angled
work island and easily accesses the
adjacent dining area. Three secondary
bedrooms share a full bath and provide ample room for family or guests.
The master bedroom is complete with
a walk-in closet and a private bath.

Design by
©Chatham Home Planning, Inc.

Width 40'-0"
Depth 59'-0"

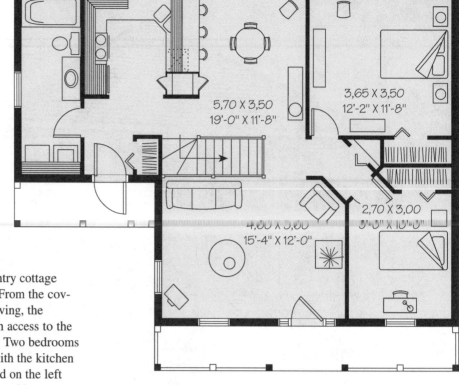

Design Z050

Square Footage: 920

5,70 X 3,50
19'-0" X 11'-8"

3,65 X 3,50
12'-2" X 11'-8"

2,70 X 3,00
8'-8" X 10'-0"

4,00 X 3,60
15'-4" X 12'-0"

Width 38'-0"
Depth 28'-0"

■ Compact yet comfortable, this country cottage possesses many appealing amenities. From the covered front porch that invites relaxed living, the entrance opens to the living room with access to the dining room and snack bar at the rear. Two bedrooms are secluded to the right of the plan with the kitchen and bathroom/laundry facilities located on the left side. A second porch off the kitchen provides room for more casual dining and quiet moments. This home is designed with a basement foundation.

On the Level with Luxury:
One-story homes of 2,800 square feet and up

Design M150

Square Footage: 4,615

■ The hip-roof French country exterior and porte cochere entrance are just the beginning of this unique, and impressive, design. An unusual pullman ceiling graces the foyer as it leads to the formal dining room on the right, to the study with a fireplace on the left and straight ahead to the formal living room with its covered patio access. A gallery directs you to the island kitchen with its abundant counter space and adjacent sun-filled breakfast bay. On the left side of the home, a spectacular master suite will become your favorite haven and the envy of your guests. The master bedroom includes a coffered ceiling, a bayed sitting area and patio access. The master bath features a large doorless shower, a separate exercise room and a huge walk-in closet with built-in chests. All of the family bedrooms offer private baths and walk-in closets.

Width 109'-10"
Depth 89'-4"

MstrBed 18x25
Exercise Area 11'8x11'8
Covered Patio
Brkfst 12x15
3-Car Gar 26x38
Kit
LivRm 16x18½
FamilyRm 18x24
Gallery
Hall
Bed#2 13x15
Study 17x15
Foyer
FmlDin 14x15
Pwdr
Util
Bed#3 15x13½
Bed#4 13x15
Hall
Covered Porch
Porte-Cochere

Design by
FILLMORE DESIGN GROUP

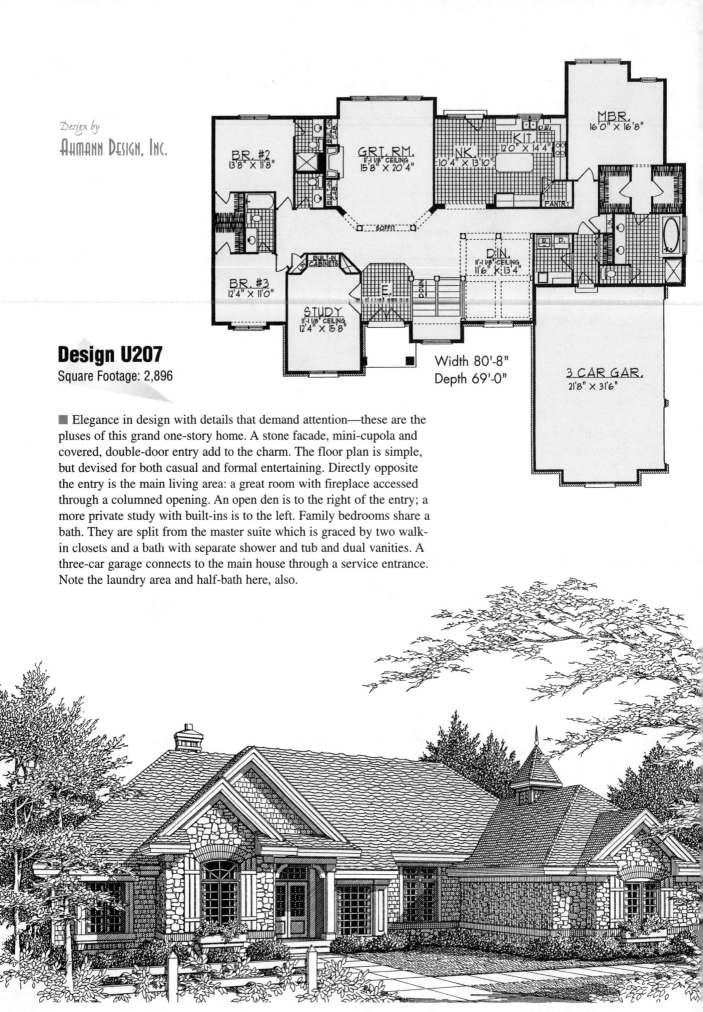

Design by

Ahmann Design, Inc.

BR. #2
13'8" X 11'8"

GRT. RM.
11'-1 1/8" CEILING
15'8" X 20'4"

NK.
10'4" X 13'0"

KIT.
12'0" X 14'4"

MBR.
16'0" X 16'8"

BUILT-IN CAB.

PANTRY

SOFFIT

BR. #3
12'4" X 11'0"

BUILT-IN CABINETS

STUDY
11'-1 1/8" CEILING
12'4" X 15'8"

DIN.
11'-1 1/8" CEILING
11'6" X 13'4"

DOWN

3 CAR GAR.
21'8" X 31'6"

Design U207

Square Footage: 2,896

Width 80'-8"
Depth 69'-0"

■ Elegance in design with details that demand attention—these are the pluses of this grand one-story home. A stone facade, mini-cupola and covered, double-door entry add to the charm. The floor plan is simple, but devised for both casual and formal entertaining. Directly opposite the entry is the main living area: a great room with fireplace accessed through a columned opening. An open den is to the right of the entry; a more private study with built-ins is to the left. Family bedrooms share a bath. They are split from the master suite which is graced by two walk-in closets and a bath with separate shower and tub and dual vanities. A three-car garage connects to the main house through a service entrance. Note the laundry area and half-bath here, also.

Alternate Elevation

Design M103

Square Footage: 2,985

Design by
FILLMORE DESIGN GROUP

Width 80'-0"
Depth 68'-0"

■ Varying rooflines, a stately brick exterior and classic window treatment accentuates the beauty of this traditional one-story home. Inside, formal living areas flank the entry—living room to the left and dining room to the right—presenting a fine introduction. Double French doors provide an elegant entrance to the centrally-located study. To the right you will find the casual living areas: a U-shaped kitchen, a dinette and a large family room with a cathedral ceiling. Three secondary bedrooms and two full baths complete this side of the plan. Tucked behind the living room is the master suite. Amenities enhancing this private getaway include a sitting area with built-in space for a TV, a huge walk in closet, and a master bath with a whirlpool tub and a separate shower.

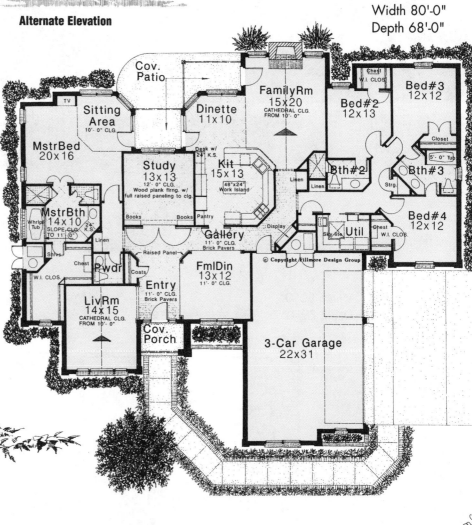

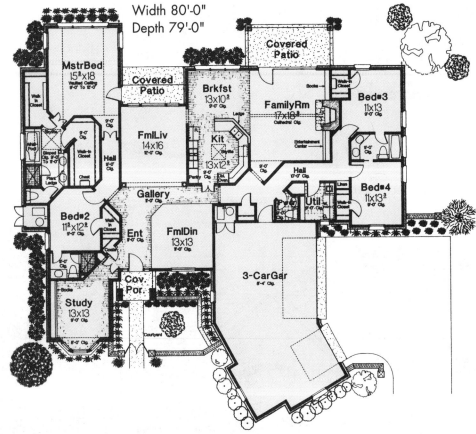

Width 80'-0"
Depth 79'-0"

MstrBed
15³x18
Vaulted Ceiling

Covered
Patio

Brkfst
13x10³

Covered
Patio

FamilyRm
17x18³
Cathedral Clg.

Bed#3
11x13

FmlLiv
14x16

Kit
13x12³

Hall

Bed#4
11x13³

Bed#2
11³x12³

Gallery

Ent

FmlDin
13x13

3-CarGar

Cov.
Por.

Study
13x13

Courtyard

Design by
FILLMORE DESIGN GROUP

Design M156

Square Footage: 3,056

■ Depending on European and French influences for its exterior beauty, this regal one-story belies the theory that a single-story has no character. A volume roofline helps make the difference, both inside and out, allowing for vaulted ceilings in many of the interior spaces. There are more than enough living areas in this plan: formal living and dining rooms, a huge family room with fireplace and a study with bay window. The kitchen has an attached, light-filled breakfast area and is open to the family room. Four bedrooms include three family bedrooms; two on the right side of the plan and one on the left. The master suite has a private covered patio, a vaulted ceiling, two walk-in closets and a bath fit for a king. A three-car garage contains ample space for cars and recreational vehicles.

Design M158

Square Footage: 3,352

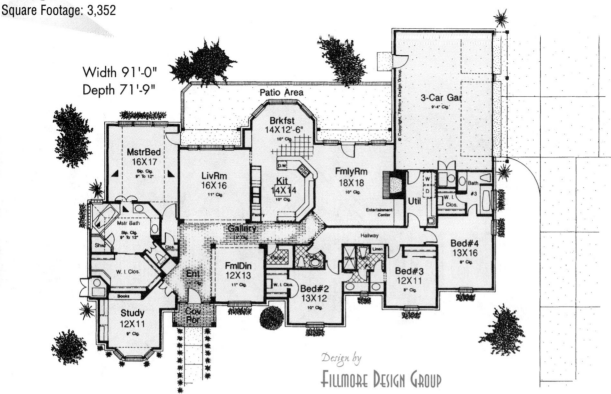

Width 91'-0"
Depth 71'-9"

Patio Area

Brkfst
14X12'-6"
10" Clg.

3-Car Gar
9'-4" Clg.

MstrBed
16X17
Slp. Clg.
9" To 12"

LivRm
16X16
11" Clg.

Kit
14X14
10" Clg.

FmlyRm
18X18
10" Clg.

Mstr Bath
Slp. Clg.
9" To 12"

Shwr

W. I. Clos.

Books

Gallery

Ent

Util

W. I.
Clos.

Bath
#3

Entertainment
Center

Hallway

Bed#4
13X16
9" Clg.

Linen

Study
12X11
9" Clg.

Cov
Por

Ent

FmlDin
12X13
11" Clg.

W. I. Clos.

Bed#2
13X12
10" Clg.

Bed#3
12X11
8" Clg.

Design by
FILLMORE DESIGN GROUP

This home combines the rustic charm of shutters and a random stonework wall with the elegance of molded cornices and arched multi-pane windows to create a look all its own. From the nicely detailed covered porch, enter upon the formal dining room to the right and living room to the rear. The arched gallery leads past the kitchen with island and bar to the family room with fireplace and built-in entertainment center. Adjoining the kitchen and family room is the bay-windowed breakfast nook which looks out onto the rear patio. Three family bedrooms are located to the front. Bedroom 4 offers a private full bath, while Bedrooms 2 and 3 each has its own private vanity in the shared full bath. The left side of the plan is comprised of the master suite and the double-doored, bay-windowed study with built-ins. The master bedroom offers a triple window overlooking the rear property, a private door to the patio, sloped ceiling, walk-in closet, corner garden tub and compartmented toilet.

Width 93'-0"
Depth 65'-0"

Design U208

Square Footage: 2,991

■ Solid-looking stone adds its appeal to the facade of this spacious one-story plan.
Further details include a sheltered covered porch at the left hand corner and a volume
roofline. A brick arch introduces the recessed entry. It opens to a foyer with barrel-
vaulted ceiling. Beyond is the massive great room, also accented with a barrel-vaulted
ceiling, with arched doorways at the hall and connecting to the nook. A U-shaped
kitchen features an island work counter and a planning desk. The den opens through
double doors at the foyer. Enhancing its usefulness are built-in shelves, a window seat
and a door that opens onto the covered porch. Bedroom 2 also has doors to this porch.
The master bedroom sits protected at the rear of the home behind the three-car garage.
A hallway art niche defines its entry. The master bath overlooks an additional, smaller
covered porch at the right side of the plan.

Design by

Ahmann Design, Inc.

Design M157

Square Footage: 3,268

■ Brick, with accents of stone, define the stately facade of this home. It gives some hint of the grand floor plan inside. The entry hall is centrally located to provide convenient access to the study (or make it a bedroom), the formal dining room, the formal living room and the kitchen. Living spaces to the rear include a breakfast nook with snack bar and the angled family room with great views to the rear yard. Across the back and connecting to the formal living room, casual dining area and family room, is a covered porch/patio area. Three family bedrooms dominate the right side of the plan—one has a private bath. The master suite is on the left side and has access to the rear patio and an amenity-filled bath with two walk-in closets, whirlpool tub, shower and double sinks.

Patio Area

Covered Area

Din 14x13 10' Clg. Ht.

FmlyRm 16X21 10' Clg. Ht.

Covered Area

Walk-In Closet

Linen

MstrBed 16x17 Box Ceiling from 9' To 10'

FmlLiv 14x16 10' Clg. Ht.

Kit 14x13 10' Clg. Ht.

Snack Bar

Bed#3 12x13 9' Clg. Ht.

Walk-In Closet

Bed#4 13x12 9' Clg. Ht.

Walk-In Closet

Mstr Bath

Util 9' Clg. Ht.

Linen

Walk-In Closet

Closet

Entry 10' Clg. Ht.

Hallway 9' Clg. Ht.

Study 12-8x13 10' Clg. Ht.

Porch

FmlDin 12x14 10' Clg. Ht.

Bed#2 13x12 9' Clg. Ht.

Closet

3-Car Gar 24x33 8'-4" Clg. Ht.

Width 98'-0"
Depth 67'-3"

Design by
FILLMORE DESIGN GROUP

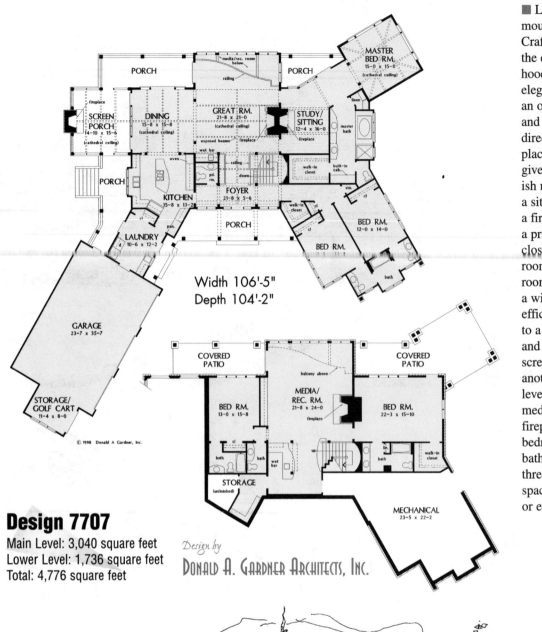

Main Level (upper floor plan):

- PORCH
- media/rec. room below
- railing
- MASTER BED RM. 15-0 x 15-0 (cathedral ceiling)
- PORCH
- linen
- fireplace
- SCREEN PORCH 14-10 x 15-6 (cathedral ceiling)
- DINING 15-8 x 15-8 (cathedral ceiling)
- GREAT RM. 21-8 x 21-0 (cathedral ceiling)
- STUDY/ SITTING 12-4 x 16-0
- master bath
- exposed beams
- fireplace
- fireplace
- wet bar
- oven
- railing
- down
- walk-in closet
- built-in cab.
- sto.
- PORCH
- KITCHEN 15-8 x 13-2
- pd. rm.
- FOYER 21-8 x 5-6
- cl
- cl
- walk-in closet
- cl
- BED RM. 12-0 x 14-0
- pan.
- LAUNDRY 10-6 x 12-2
- PORCH
- BED RM.
- bath

Width 106'-5"
Depth 104'-2"

- GARAGE 23-7 x 35-7
- STORAGE/ GOLF CART 11-4 x 8-0

© 1998 Donald A Gardner, Inc.

Lower Level (lower floor plan):

- COVERED PATIO
- balcony above
- COVERED PATIO
- BED RM. 13-0 x 15-8
- MEDIA/ REC. RM. 21-8 x 24-0
- fireplace
- BED RM. 22-3 x 15-10
- cl
- bath
- bath
- wet bar
- up
- bath
- lin.
- walk-in closet
- STORAGE (unfinished)
- MECHANICAL 23-5 x 22-2

Design 7707

Main Level: 3,040 square feet
Lower Level: 1,736 square feet
Total: 4,776 square feet

Design by
DONALD A. GARDNER ARCHITECTS, INC.

Looking a bit like a mountain resort, this fine Craftsman home is sure to be the envy of your neighborhood. Entering through the elegant front door, one finds an open staircase to the right and a spacious great room directly ahead. Here, a fireplace and a wall of windows give a cozy welcome. A lavish master suite begins with a sitting room complete with a fireplace, and continues to a private porch, large walk-in closet and sumptuous bedroom area. Two family bedrooms share a bath and have a wing to themselves. The efficient kitchen sits adjacent to a large, sunny dining area, and offers access to a screened porch with yet another fireplace! The lower level consists of a huge media room with a fourth fireplace, and two spacious bedrooms, each with private baths and tons of storage. A three-car garage has extra space for storage, a golf cart or even a boat.

© 1998 Donald A. Gardner, Inc.

Design HPTM03012

Square Footage: 2,907

■ Stunning windows and walls of glass enhance the exterior of this contemporary home and provide natural light and wide views to the open interior. The central living room leads to the covered lanai and brings in a wealth of sunlight. Casual living space features a built-in entertainment center and glass doors to the lanai. The gourmet kitchen serves a formal dining room, which has a tray ceiling. The master wing has a walk-in wardrobe, whirlpool tub, two lavatories and access to a private garden.

Design by
©The Sater Design Collection

covered lanai
38'-0" x 10'-0"   butt joint glass

entertainment center
built ins

leisure
17'-0" x 19'-0"
10'-0" clg.

nook
9'-0" x 10'-0"
10'-0" clg.

eating bar

dry bar

server niche

kitchen
14' x 14'

master
17'-0" x 14'-8"
step clg.

living
14'-0" x 14'-0"
step clg.

pantry

arch

gallery

books

arch

art display

arch

arch

br. 2
13'-6" x 10'-10"
10'-0" clg.

walk in wardrobe

dressing

mirror

books

study
10'-0" x 14'-0"
step clg.

foyer

dining
11'-6" x 15'-0"
step clg.

arch

arch

storage

br. 3
13'-6" x 10'-10"
10'-0" clg.

his

hers

covered entry

util.

workbench

privacy wall

private garden

covered entry

Width 65'-0"
Depth 84'-0"

© The Sater Group, Inc.

garage
22'-0" x 23'-8"

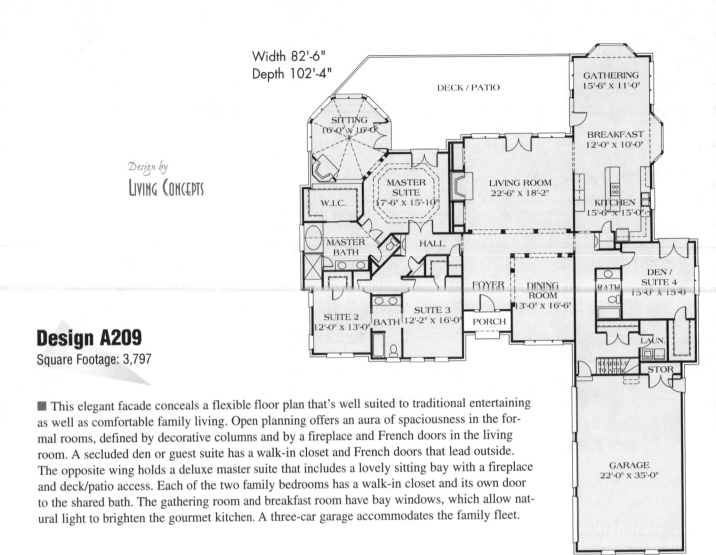

Width 82'-6"
Depth 102'-4"

DECK / PATIO

Design by
LIVING CONCEPTS

GATHERING
15'-6" x 11'-0"

SITTING
16'-0" x 16'-0"

BREAKFAST
12'-0" x 10'-0"

MASTER
SUITE
17'-6" x 15'-10"

LIVING ROOM
22'-6" x 18'-2"

W.I.C.

KITCHEN
15'-6" x 15'-0"

MASTER
BATH

HALL

DEN /
SUITE 4
15'-0" x 15'-0"

BATH

FOYER

DINING
ROOM
13'-0" x 16'-6"

SUITE 2
12'-0" x 13'-0"

BATH

SUITE 3
12'-2" x 16'-0"

PORCH

LAUN.

STAIRS UP
TO ATTIC

STOR

Design A209
Square Footage: 3,797

GARAGE
22'-0" x 35'-0"

■ This elegant facade conceals a flexible floor plan that's well suited to traditional entertaining as well as comfortable family living. Open planning offers an aura of spaciousness in the formal rooms, defined by decorative columns and by a fireplace and French doors in the living room. A secluded den or guest suite has a walk-in closet and French doors that lead outside. The opposite wing holds a deluxe master suite that includes a lovely sitting bay with a fireplace and deck/patio access. Each of the two family bedrooms has a walk-in closet and its own door to the shared bath. The gathering room and breakfast room have bay windows, which allow natural light to brighten the gourmet kitchen. A three-car garage accommodates the family fleet.

Design B502

Main Level: 2,582 square feet
Lower Level: 1,746 square feet
Total: 4,320 square feet

Width 70'-8"
Depth 64'-0"

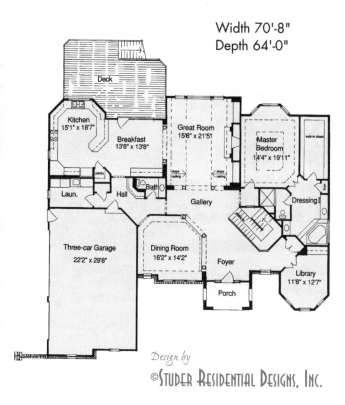

Design by
©Studer Residential Designs, Inc.

■ Stone accents provide warmth and character to the exterior of this home. An arched entry leads to the interior, where elegant window styles and dramatic ceiling treatments create an impressive showplace. The gourmet kitchen and breakfast room offer a spacious area for chores and family gatherings, while providing a striking view through the great room to the fireplace wall. For convenience, the butler's pantry is located in the hall leading to the dining room. An extravagant master suite and a library with built-in shelves round out the main floor. Accented by a wooden rail, an extra-wide stairway leads to the lower level, where two additional bedrooms, a media room, a billiards room and an exercise room complete the home.

This home, as shown in the photograph, may differ from the actual blueprints. For more detailed information, please check the floor plans carefully.

Design 6712

Square Footage: 3,036

■ Here's a coastal cottage with acres of
charm, starting with the covered entry
and glass-paneled front door. An open
interior and walls of glass allow wide
views and plenty of natural light. The
living room opens to a rear lanai, which
features decorative columns and a built-
in grill. Informal entertaining will be a
breeze with the leisure room, kitchen
and breakfast nook. A split sleeping
arrangement places the master suite to
the right of the plan, near the study. The
left side of the plan includes two additional bedrooms and a guest suite.

Design by
©THE SATER DESIGN COLLECTION

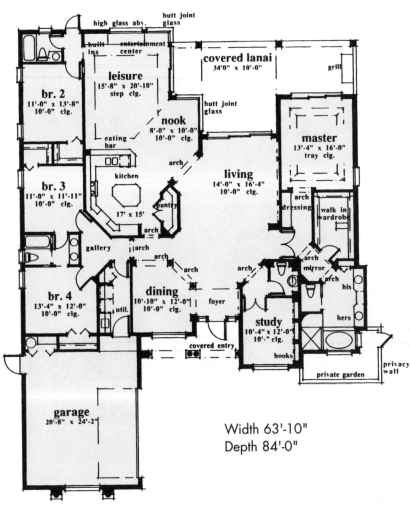

Width 63'-10"
Depth 84'-0"

Design A107

Square Footage: 3,377

■ Traditional in nature, this home is designed with classic embellishments. An arched entry, circle-top windows, corner quoins and a bay window all lend their appeal to the facade. The floor plan is classic in nature, as well. Centered around the family room, additional rooms include a formal living room, formal dining room, home office (or study) and fully windowed breakfast room. The kitchen has an island cooktop and loads of counterspace. You'll love the special appointments in the master suite: tray ceiling, two walk-in closets, nearby study or fourth bedroom and corner whirlpool tub. The two-car garage has extra storage space. Note the covered porch to the rear, with doors leading from the family room and the office to the outside.

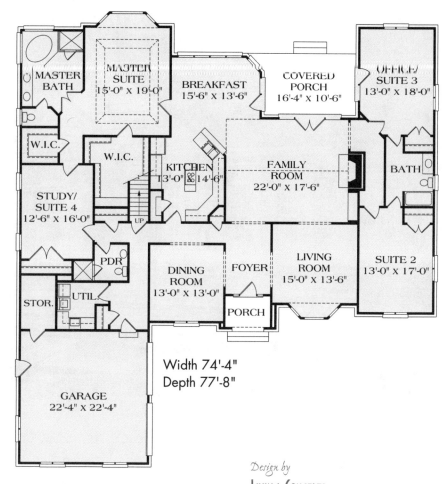

Width 74'-4"
Depth 77'-8"

Design by
Living Concepts

Design T238

Square Footage: 2,814

■ Space to move and room to live well—that's the promise of this elegant one-story design. From the columned entry, the plan opens to a foyer with tray ceiling and extends along a central hallway. The formal dining room, with nearby wet bar, opposes the private study at the other side of the foyer. Both also open to the hallway for easy access. The great room is designed for super gatherings. It is introduced by columns at the hallway entry, has two double-door accesses to the rear covered porch and sports a focal-point fireplace. The breakfast room also accesses the porch and connects to the kitchen (note the island work counter here). Two bedrooms sharing a full bath are on the right side of the plan. The master suite is on the left side. Look for all the best features: walk-in closet, huge shower, whirlpool tub, double sinks and compartmented toilet. This home is designed with a basement foundations

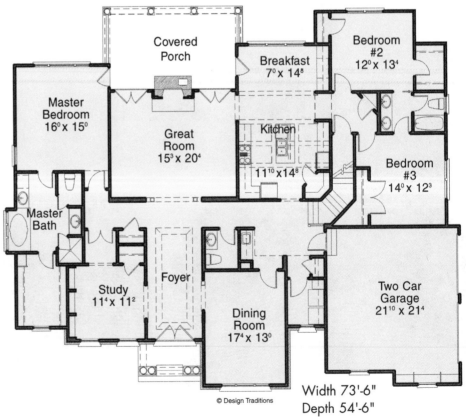

Covered Porch

Master Bedroom
16⁰ x 15⁰

Master Bath

Study
11⁴ x 11²

Foyer

Great Room
15³ x 20⁴

Dining Room
17⁴ x 13⁰

Breakfast
7⁰ x 14⁸

Kitchen
11¹⁰ x 14⁸

Bedroom #2
12⁰ x 13⁴

Bedroom #3
14⁰ x 12³

Two Car Garage
21¹⁰ x 21⁴

© Design Traditions

Width 73'-6"
Depth 54'-6"

Design by
Design Traditions

Width 75'-0"
Depth 70'-0"

Keeping Room 16⁴ x 11²

Breakfast 14⁶ x 13⁸

Covered Porch

Master Bedroom 18⁰ x 15⁴

Kitchen

Dining Room 17⁴ x 12⁵

Great Room 17⁴ x 15³

Master Bath

One Car Garage 17⁴ x 12⁵

Bedroom #2 14⁰ x 11⁴

Two Car Garage 21⁴ x 21⁴

Bedroom #3 12⁸ x 13⁸

Bath

© Design Traditions

Design by
DESIGN TRADITIONS

Design T240

Square Footage: 2,973

■ This home has a rather unique floor plan—and for those who like to entertain in style, it works well. Enter through double doors and find a bedroom or study immediately to the right. Through columns, straight ahead, is a large, open area defined by more columns, that holds the formal dining room and the great room (a fireplace and built-in bookshelves are amenities here). Views here are stunning, past the covered porch and on to the backyard. The kitchen separates this area from the breakfast nook and keeping room—perfect for more casual pursuits. Each bedroom has a private bath and walk-in closet. The master suite has porch access and a lovely tray ceiling. Notice the two separate garages— one a two-car garage and the other a one-car garage. This home is designed with a basement foundation.

Design 6713
Square Footage: 3,036

■ Filled with luxury and special amenities, this stucco beauty offers the best in upscale living. A recessed entry opens to the formal areas: a living room and dining room separated by columns and an arch. For more casual times, look to the leisure room near the island kitchen and nook. A covered lanai lies just outside the living room and the leisure room. The master suite is split from the three family bedrooms on the left side of the plan. It contains outstanding closet space and a fine bath with a garden tub. A nearby study has the use of a half-bath. Note that Bedroom 2 includes a private bath.

Design by
© The Sater Design Collection

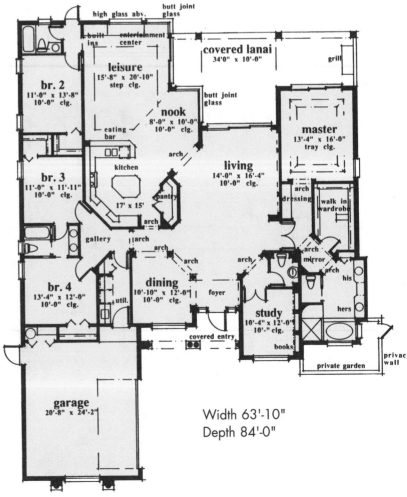

Width 63'-10"
Depth 84'-0"

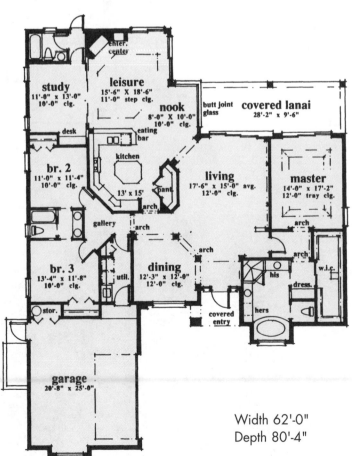

study
11'-0" x 13'-0"
10'-0" clg.

leisure
15'-6" X 18'-6"
11'-0" step clg.

enter.
center

nook
8'-0" X 10'-0"
10'-0" clg.

butt joint
glass

covered lanai
28'-2" x 9'-6"

desk

eating
bar

kitchen

br. 2
11'-0" x 11'-4"
10'-0" clg.

13' x 15'

pant.

arch

living
17'-6" x 15'-0" avg.
12'-0" clg.

master
14'-0" x 17'-2"
12'-0" tray clg.

gallery

arch

arch

br. 3
13'-4" x 11'-8"
10'-0" clg.

util.

arch

arch

w.i.c.

his

dress.

stor.

dining
12'-3" x 12'-0"
12'-0" clg.

covered
entry

hers

garage
20'-8" x 25'-0"

Width 62'-0"
Depth 80'-4"

Design HPTMO3013

Square Footage: 2,802

■ The facade of this contemporary home is clean and elegant with a mix of brick and stucco and high-pitched rooflines. The living room opens to a covered lanai facing the rear yard. The open kitchen, nook and leisure room focus toward the entertainment center. The two secondary bedrooms share a bath while the study accesses the pool. The master suite has a tray ceiling and glass doors to the rear lanai. An oversized walk-in wardrobe closet, a dressing area, His and Hers vanities and a garden tub round out the luxurious master bath.

Design by
©The Sater Design Collection

Design S132

Square Footage: 3,828
Unfinished Bonus Space:
1,018 square feet

■ This Neo-Classical home has plenty to offer! The elegant entrance is flanked by a formal dining room on the left and a beam-ceilinged study—complete with a fireplace—on the right. An angled kitchen is sure to please with a work island, plenty of counter and cabinet space and a snack counter which it shares with the sunny breakfast room. A family room with a second fireplace is nearby. The lavish master bedroom suite features many amenities, including a huge walk-in closet, a three-sided fireplace and a lavish bath. Two secondary bedrooms each have private baths. A three-car garage easily shelters the family fleet.

Design by
ARCHIVAL DESIGNS

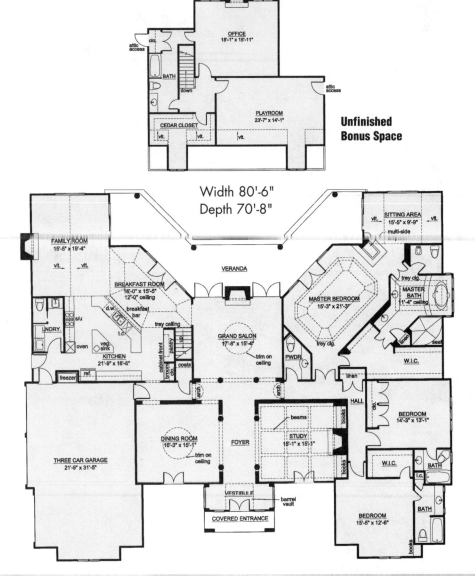

Width 80'-6"
Depth 70'-8"

Design A221

Square Footage: 4,405
Bonus Room: 539 square feet

■ Whoever says luxury can't be found on one level hasn't seen this attractive stucco home. From the high class exterior to the very accommodating interior, this design is sure to please. If entertaining is your forte, this plan is the one for you. Note the way the formal dining room and spacious grand room flow into each other—making formal dinner parties a breeze. If a casual get-together is more your style, take a look at the kitchen/ bayed breakfast area/sun room space. The master retreat is aptly named and includes amenities such as a bayed sitting area, a two-sided fireplace, two closets (one a walk-in), His and Hers bathrooms and direct access to the rear deck. The three secondary bedrooms are complete with their own full baths, providing plenty of room for family and friends.

Design by
LIVING CONCEPTS

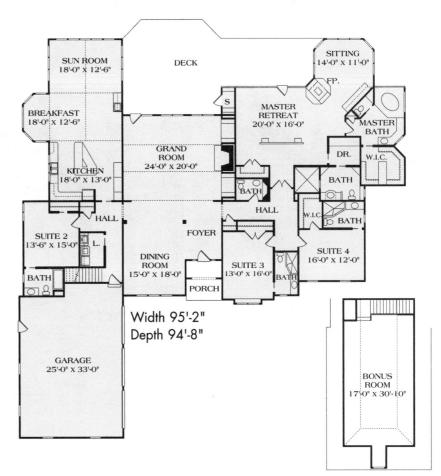

SUN ROOM 18'-0" x 12'-6"

DECK

SITTING 14'-0" x 11'-0"

FP.

BREAKFAST 18'-0" x 12'-6"

S

MASTER RETREAT 20'-0" x 16'-0"

MASTER BATH

KITCHEN 18'-0" x 13'-0"

GRAND ROOM 24'-0" x 20'-0"

DR.

W.I.C.

BATH

BATH

HALL

HALL

W.I.C.

BATH

SUITE 2 13'-6" x 15'-0"

L.

FOYER

BATH

DINING ROOM 15'-0" x 18'-0"

SUITE 3 13'-0" x 16'-0"

SUITE 4 16'-0" x 12'-0"

PORCH

BATH

Width 95'-2"
Depth 94'-8"

GARAGE 25'-0" x 33'-0"

BONUS ROOM 17'-0" x 30'-10"

Design 6604

Square Footage: 2,978

L

■ This Neo-Classic split design exemplifies elegance. Circlehead windows grace the front from the streetscape. A large covered entry leads to a gallery foyer that overlooks the formal living and dining rooms. Informal areas are located in a private wing. A large kitchen, nook and leisure room complete with wet bar overlook the rear veranda and enjoy fantastic views of the backyard. Also on this side are secondary bedrooms. The gallery foyer also leads to the master suite. Its bath features large His and Hers closets and vanities, a garden tub and a glass-enclosed shower. A private study and large utility room round out this very special home.

Design by
THE SATER
DESIGN COLLECTION

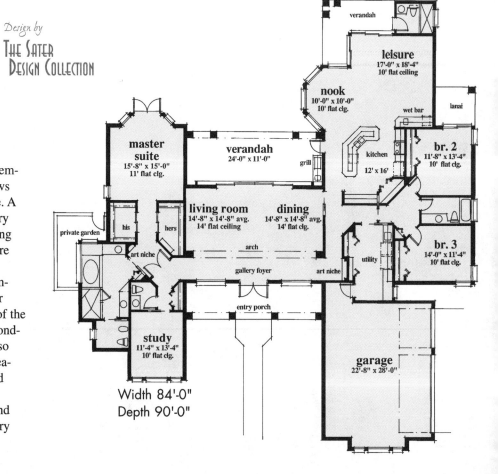

Width 84'-0"
Depth 90'-0"

■ Classic columns, a tiled roof and beautiful arched windows herald a gracious interior for this fine home. Arched windows also mark the entrance into the vaulted living room with a tiled fireplace. The dining room opens off the foyer with vaulted ceiling. Filled with light from a wall of sliding glass doors, the family room leads to the covered patio (note the wet bar and range that enhance outdoor living). The kitchen features a vaulted ceiling and unfolds into the roomy nook which boasts French doors onto the patio. The master bedroom also has patio access and shares a dual fireplace with the master bath. A solarium lights this space. A vaulted study/bedroom sits between two additional bedrooms—all share a full bath.

Width 74'-4"
Depth 82'-4"

Design 8624
Square Footage: 2,987

Design by
HOME DESIGN SERVICES

This home, as shown in the photograph, may differ from the actual blueprints.
For more detailed information, please check the floor plans carefully.

Photo by Peter A. Burg

93

Design HPTM03014

Square Footage: 3,477

L

■ Make dreams come true and vacation in style with this fine sunny design. An octagonal study provides a nice focal point both inside and outside. The living areas remain open to each other and access outdoor areas. A wet bar makes entertaining a breeze, especially with a window pass-through to a grill area on the lanai. The kitchen enjoys shared space with a lovely breakfast nook and a bright leisure room. Two bedrooms are located near the family living center. In the master bedroom suite, luxury abounds with a two-way fireplace, a morning kitchen, two walk-in closets and a compartmented bath. Another full bath accommodates a pool area.

Width 95'-0"
Depth 88'-8"

Design by
©The Sater Design Collection

QUOTE ONE®

Cost to build? See page 434 to order complete cost estimate to build this house in your area!

© The Sater Group, Inc.

Width 90'-0"
Depth 105'-0"

lanai
58'-0" x 10'-0" avg.

master
14'-0" x 18'-2"
13' tray clg.

master garden

atrium

fountain

leisure
20'-0" x 19'-0"
10' clg.

nook
10' x 11'
10' clg.

living
15'-2" x 12'-0"
13' clg.

entertainment
center

arch

arch

gallery

desk

kitchen
13' x 15'

art
niche

dining
15'-0" x 12'-8"
13' clg.

arch

foyer

books

high glass

guest patio

arch

study
13'-8" x 13'-10"
13' clg.

guest
14'-6" x 15'-0"
10' clg.

gallery

art
niche

entry

guest
13'-0" x 14'-4"
10' clg.

garden

util.

Design by
THE SATER
DESIGN COLLECTION

Design 6657
Square Footage: 3,244

garage
22'-0" x 32'-0"

© The Sater Group, Inc.

■ A high, hip roof and contemporary fanlight windows set the tone for this elegant master plan. The grand foyer opens to the formal dining and living rooms that are set apart with arches, highlighted with art niches and framed with walls of windows. Discreetly removed from the entertaining area is the leisure room, where casual living takes precedence. Featuring a gourmet kitchen, breakfast nook and leisure room with built-in entertainment center, this area has full view and access to the lanai. Secondary bedrooms are privately situated through a gallery hall and both have private baths and walk-in closets. The master wing is preceded with a gallery hall and houses a full study and master suite with a private garden. An oversized closet and spa-style bath complete this luxurious retreat.

95

Design 6641

Square Footage: 3,896
Bonus Room: 356 square feet

■ This elegant exterior blends a classical look with a contemporary feel. Corner quoins and round columns highlight the front elevation. The formal living room, complete with a fireplace and a wet bar, and the formal dining room access the lanai through three pairs of French doors. The well-appointed kitchen features an island prep sink, walk-in pantry and a desk. The secondary bedrooms are full guest suites, located away from the private owner's wing. The master suite has enormous His and Hers closets, built-ins, a wet bar and three-sided fireplace that separates the sitting room and the bedroom. The luxurious bath features a stunning, rounded glass-block shower and a whirlpool tub.

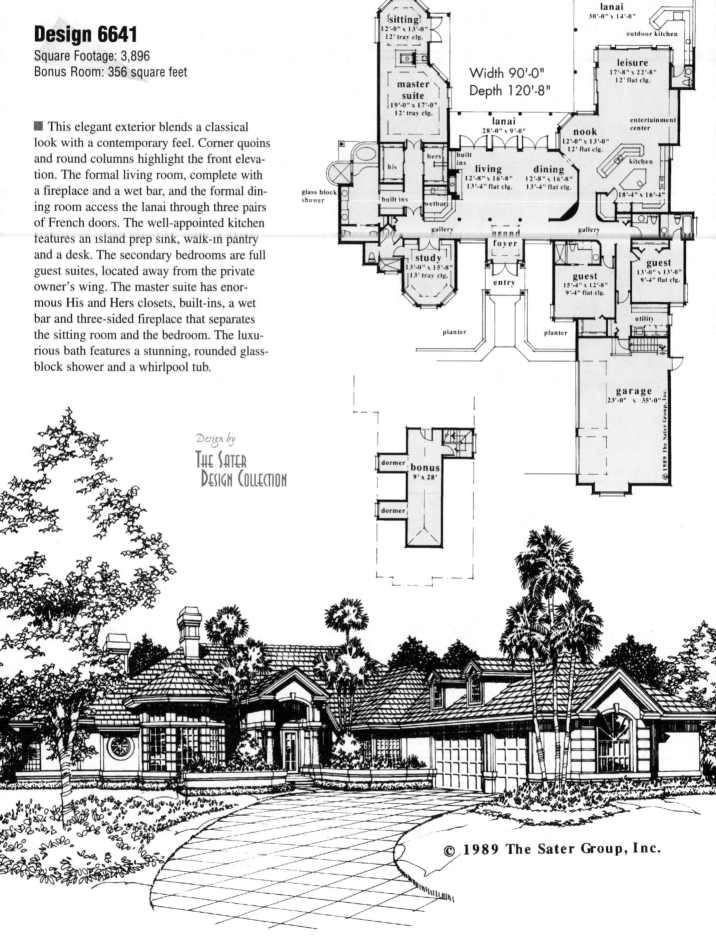

Design by
The Sater
Design Collection

© 1989 The Sater Group, Inc.

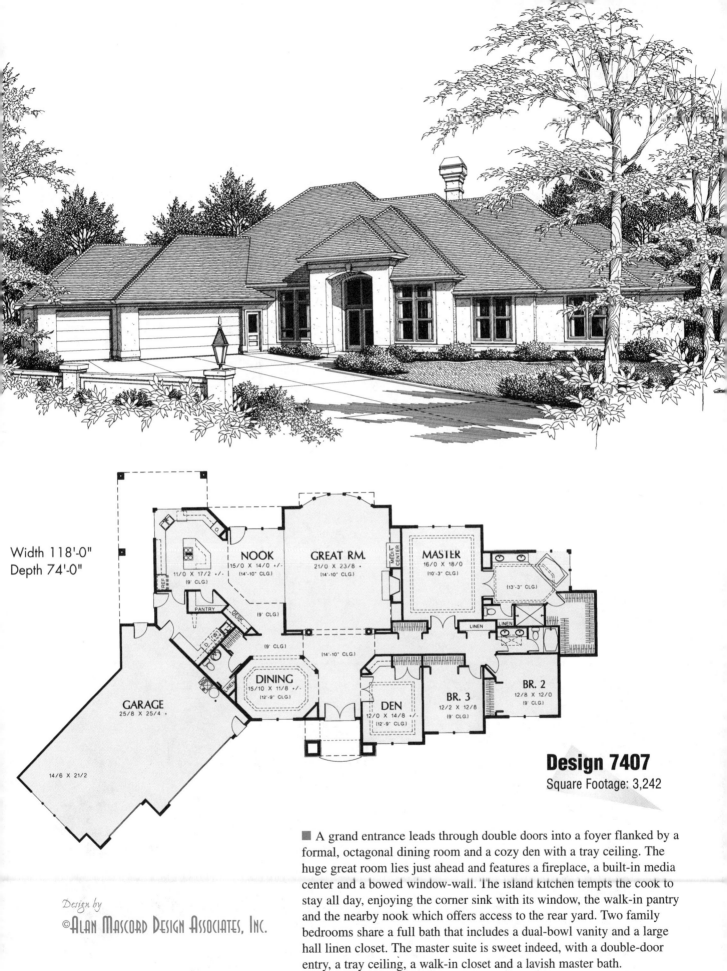

Width 118'-0"
Depth 74'-0"

NOOK
15/0 X 14/0 +/-
(14'-10" CLG.)

GREAT RM.
21/0 X 23/8
(14'-10" CLG.)

MASTER
16/0 X 18/0
(10'-3" CLG.)

(13'-3" CLG.)

PANTRY

DESK

(9' CLG.)

(9' CLG.)

LINEN

LINEN

(14'-10" CLG.)

DINING
15/10 X 11/8 +/-
(12'-9" CLG.)

DEN
12/0 X 14/8
(12'-9" CLG.)

BR. 3
12/2 X 12/8
(9' CLG.)

BR. 2
12/8 X 12/0
(9' CLG.)

GARAGE
25/8 X 25/4 +/-

14/6 X 21/2

Design 7407
Square Footage: 3,242

Design by
©Alan Mascord Design Associates, Inc.

■ A grand entrance leads through double doors into a foyer flanked by a formal, octagonal dining room and a cozy den with a tray ceiling. The huge great room lies just ahead and features a fireplace, a built-in media center and a bowed window-wall. The island kitchen tempts the cook to stay all day, enjoying the corner sink with its window, the walk-in pantry and the nearby nook which offers access to the rear yard. Two family bedrooms share a full bath that includes a dual-bowl vanity and a large hall linen closet. The master suite is sweet indeed, with a double-door entry, a tray ceiling, a walk-in closet and a lavish master bath.

Design 6609

Square Footage: 3,324

L

If spacious, contemporary living sounds like your style, this home may be just the ticket. With gardens on either side, the barrel-ceilinged entry sets the tone for a grand interior. Raised ceilings in the open living and dining rooms—as well as in the study—lend light and air. Through an archway to the right, the gourmet kitchen opens up with an island cooktop and an abundance of storage space. A leisure room here features a tray ceiling and access to a veranda. Nearby, two bedrooms share a full bath with dual lavatories. An archway on the left side of the plan leads to the master bedroom suite where elegance is the byword. His and Hers closets and a lavish bath overlooking a private garden define this room. A study with plenty of built-ins and a full bath with outside access complete the plan.

Design by
THE SATER
DESIGN COLLECTION

Width 74'-0"
Depth 89'-8"

leisure
20'-0" x 24'-0"
tray clg.

verandah
40'-0" x 11'-0"

grill

kitchen
15' x 18'

master
suite
16'-2" x 22'-0"
tray clg.

living
17'-2" x 14'-6"
12' clg.

guest
13'-0" x 13'-6"
10' clg.

hers

desk

his

arch

arch

gallery

guest
13'-0" x 13'-2"
10' clg.

built ins

foyer
barrel clg.

dining
12'-8" x 17'-8"
12' clg.

utility

study
11'-8" x 12'-0"
12' clg.

entry
barrel clg.

© 1991 The Sater Group, Inc.

private garden

garden

garden

garden

garage
22'-0" x 28'-0"

This home, as shown in the photograph, may differ from the actual blueprints. For more detailed information, please check the floor plans carefully.

Photo by Oscar Thompson

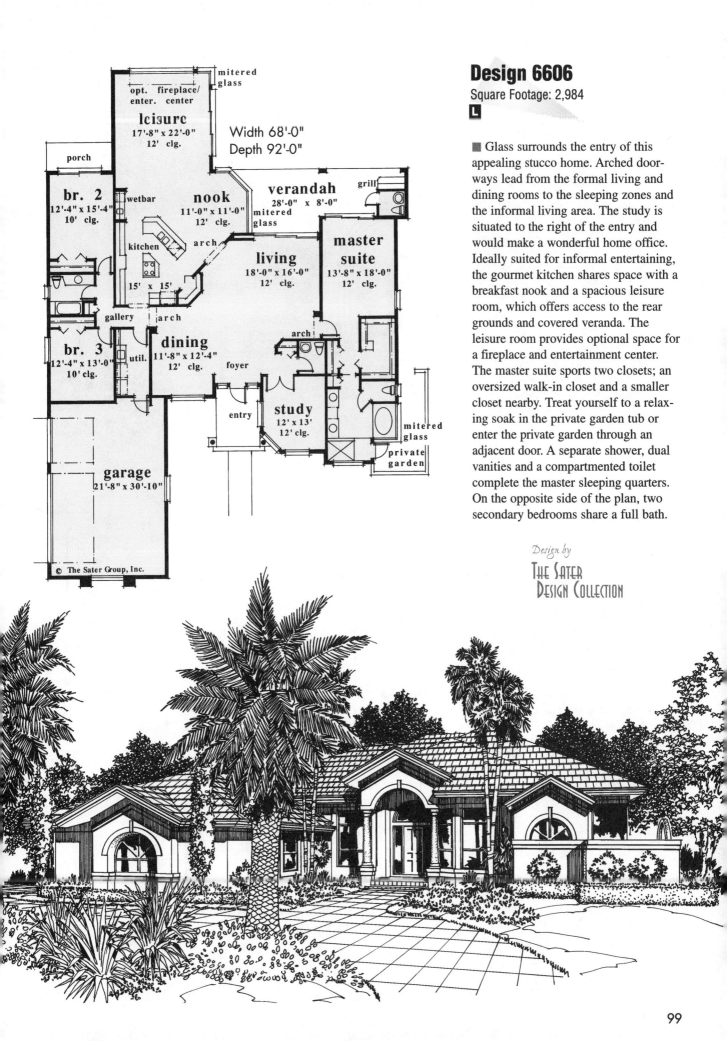

Design 6606

Square Footage: 2,984

L

■ Glass surrounds the entry of this appealing stucco home. Arched doorways lead from the formal living and dining rooms to the sleeping zones and the informal living area. The study is situated to the right of the entry and would make a wonderful home office. Ideally suited for informal entertaining, the gourmet kitchen shares space with a breakfast nook and a spacious leisure room, which offers access to the rear grounds and covered veranda. The leisure room provides optional space for a fireplace and entertainment center. The master suite sports two closets; an oversized walk-in closet and a smaller closet nearby. Treat yourself to a relaxing soak in the private garden tub or enter the private garden through an adjacent door. A separate shower, dual vanities and a compartmented toilet complete the master sleeping quarters. On the opposite side of the plan, two secondary bedrooms share a full bath.

Design by
**The Sater
Design Collection**

Width 68'-0"
Depth 92'-0"

opt. fireplace/ enter. center
mitered glass

leisure
17'-8" x 22'-0"
12' clg.

porch

br. 2
12'-4" x 15'-4"
10' clg.

wetbar

nook
11'-0" x 11'-0"
12' clg.

verandah
28'-0" x 8'-0"

grill

mitered glass

kitchen

arch

living
18'-0" x 16'-0"
12' clg.

master suite
13'-8" x 18'-0"
12' clg.

15' x 15'

gallery

arch

br. 3
12'-4" x 13'-0"
10' clg.

util.

dining
11'-8" x 12'-4"
12' clg.

arch

foyer

arch

entry

study
12' x 13'
12' clg.

mitered glass

private garden

garage
21'-8" x 30'-10"

© The Sater Group, Inc.

Design 6643

Square Footage: 4,028

■ An interesting roofline and custom details add to the charm of this home. The raised entry has a stepped column and arch detail that can be seen throughout the design. The foyer and dining room feature stepped arches and ceiling treatments. Secondary bedrooms provide full guest suites. An arched entryway leads into the master suite highlighted by a bayed sitting area. The bath has a bayed whirlpool tub and a walk-in shower.

Design by

THE Sater DESIGN COLLECTION

Width 80'-0"
Depth 82'-8"

sitting

master suite
16'-8" x 23'-0"
vaulted clg.

lanai
20'-0" x 11'-0"

leisure
22'-8" x 28'-0"
13' flat clg.

nook
10'-8" x 12'-8"
13' flat clg.

entertainment center

arches

living
21'-4" x 16'-4"
14' flat clg.

built ins

skylit atrium

wetbar

bedroom
13'-8" x 13'-4"
9'-4" flat clg.

hers

his

fireplace

built ins

kitchen
19' x 16'

arches

gallery

utility

bedroom
13'-8" x 13'-6"
9'-4" flat clg.

foyer

dining
14'-0" x 16'-0"
stepped clg.

study
12'-8 x 16'-0"
10' flat clg.

private garden

entry

garage
28'-8" x 23'-8"

planter

planter

© 1989 The Sater Group, Inc.

motorcourt

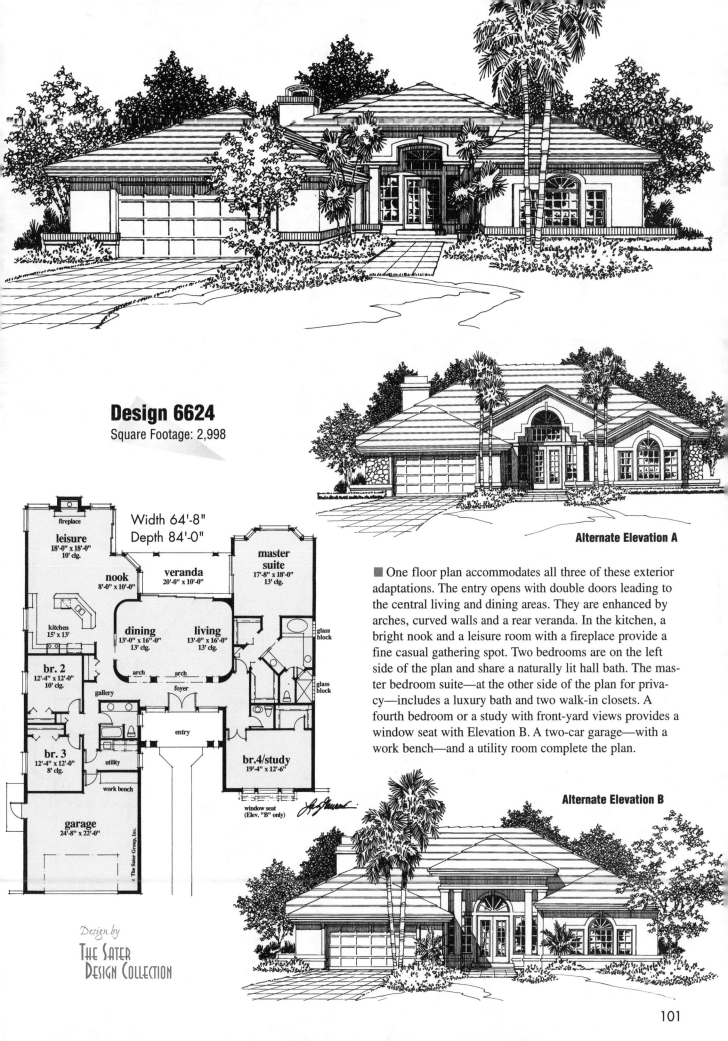

Design 6624
Square Footage: 2,998

Width 64'-8"
Depth 84'-0"

Alternate Elevation A

■ One floor plan accommodates all three of these exterior adaptations. The entry opens with double doors leading to the central living and dining areas. They are enhanced by arches, curved walls and a rear veranda. In the kitchen, a bright nook and a leisure room with a fireplace provide a fine casual gathering spot. Two bedrooms are on the left side of the plan and share a naturally lit hall bath. The master bedroom suite—at the other side of the plan for privacy—includes a luxury bath and two walk-in closets. A fourth bedroom or a study with front-yard views provides a window seat with Elevation B. A two-car garage—with a work bench—and a utility room complete the plan.

Alternate Elevation B

Design by
The Sater Design Collection

Floor plan labels:

fireplace

leisure
18'-0" x 18'-0"
10' clg.

nook
8'-0" x 10'-0"

veranda
20'-0" x 10'-0"

master suite
17'-8" x 18'-0"
13' clg.

kitchen
15' x 13'

dining
13'-0" x 16'-0"
13' clg.

living
13'-0" x 16'-0"
13' clg.

glass block

arch   arch

foyer

glass block

br. 2
12'-4" x 12'-0"
10' clg.

gallery

br. 3
12'-4" x 12'-0"
8' clg.

entry

utility

br.4/study
19'-4" x 12'-6"

work bench

garage
24'-8" x 22'-0"

window seat
(Elev. "B" only)

© The Sater Group, Inc.

101

Design 8087

Square Footage: 5,183
Loft: 238 square feet

■ Contemporary styling coupled with traditional finishes of brick and stucco make this home a stand-out that caters to the discriminating few. The entry, with a two-story ceiling, steps down into an enormous great room with a see-through fireplace. A formal living room is open from the entry and begins one wing of the home. The bedroom wing provides three bedrooms, each with a large amenity-filled bath, as well as a study area and a recreation room. The opposite wing houses the dining room, kitchen, breakfast room and two more bedrooms. The kitchen offers a curved window overlooking the side yard and a cooktop island with a vegetable sink. A stair leads to a loft overlooking the great room and entry.

Design by
LARRY E. BELK
DESIGNS

Width 93'-5"
Depth 113'-0"

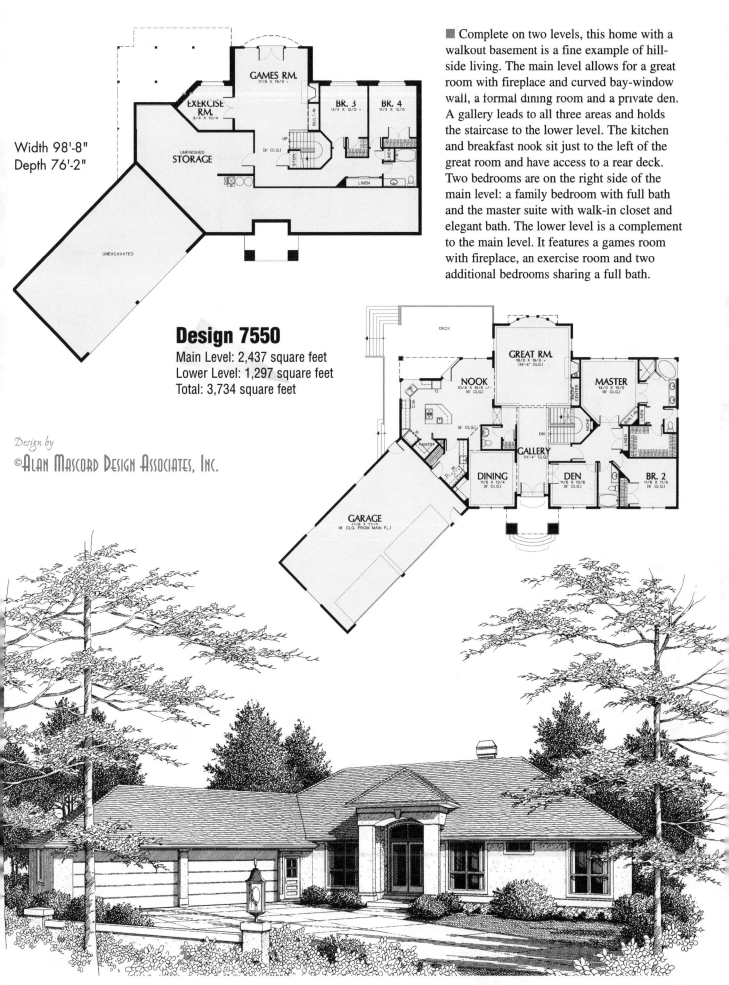

GAMES RM.
17/8 X 19/0 •

EXERCISE RM.
8/4 X 10/4

BR. 3
11/4 X 12/0 •

BR. 4
11/4 X 12/0

UP
(9' CLG.)

BUILT-IN

STOR.

LINEN

UNFINISHED STORAGE

LINEN

UNEXCAVATED

Width 98'-8"
Depth 76'-2"

■ Complete on two levels, this home with a walkout basement is a fine example of hill-side living. The main level allows for a great room with fireplace and curved bay-window wall, a formal dining room and a private den. A gallery leads to all three areas and holds the staircase to the lower level. The kitchen and breakfast nook sit just to the left of the great room and have access to a rear deck. Two bedrooms are on the right side of the main level: a family bedroom with full bath and the master suite with walk-in closet and elegant bath. The lower level is a complement to the main level. It features a games room with fireplace, an exercise room and two additional bedrooms sharing a full bath.

Design 7550

Main Level: 2,437 square feet
Lower Level: 1,297 square feet
Total: 3,734 square feet

Design by
©ALAN MASCORD DESIGN ASSOCIATES, INC.

DECK

GREAT RM.
19/0 X 19/0 •
(14'-4" CLG.)

NOOK
10/4 X 15/6 +/-
(9' CLG.)

MASTER
14/0 X 15/6
(9' CLG.)

NICHE

D.W.

(8' CLG.)

DN.

LINEN

BUILT-IN

LINEN

PANTRY

GALLERY
(14'-4" CLG.)

DINING
11/6 X 13/4
(9' CLG.)

DEN
11/6 X 10/6
(9' CLG.)

BR. 2
11/6 X 11/6
(9' CLG.)

D.W.

GARAGE
21/6 X 22/0
(8' CLG. FROM MAIN FL.)

Design 8665

Square Footage: 2,799

■ An impressive exterior leads to a grand interior. The living areas are highlighted by volume ceilings and double doors. A walk-in closet and nearby full bath add to the utility of the den. The central kitchen with island is convenient to the living, dining, breakfast and family rooms. The family room features a fireplace and access to the covered porch. Double doors lead to the segregated master bedroom with dual walk-in closets and a spacious bath with two vanities, whirlpool tub, separate shower and an attached solarium. Three family bedrooms and a full bath are to the right of the plan.

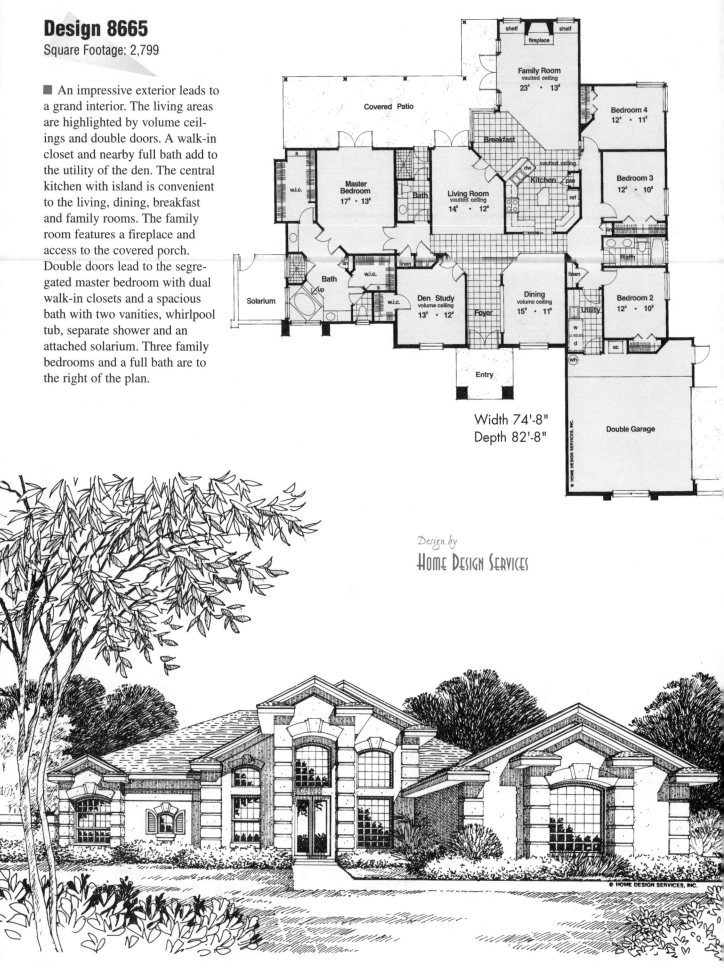

Width 74'-8"
Depth 82'-8"

Design by
HOME DESIGN SERVICES

Design HPTM03015

Square Footage: 3,398

■ Bringing the outdoors in through a multitude of bay windows is what this design is all about. The grand foyer opens to the living room with a magnificent view to the covered lanai. The study and dining room flank the foyer. The master suite is found on the left with an opulent private bath and views of the private garden. To the right, the kitchen adjoins the nook that boasts a mitered-glass bay window overlooking the lanai. Beyond the leisure room are two guest rooms, each with a private bath.

Width 121'-5"
Depth 96'-2"

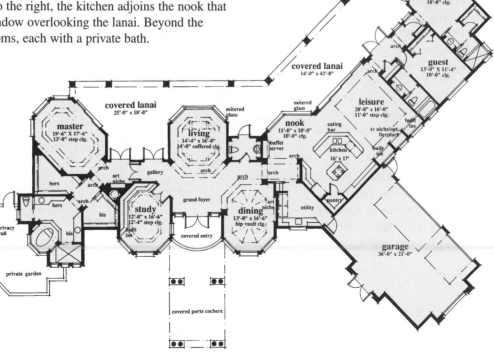

Design HPTM03016

Square Footage: 4,187

L

■ This contemporary masterpiece features many trendsetting details. The exterior lines are clean, but exciting. At the covered entry, a Palladian-style metal grill adds interest. Beyond the foyer, the living room opens up to the lanai through corner glass doors. The doors pocket into the wall, giving the feeling that the outdoors become one with the living area. The informal leisure area is perfect for family gatherings. Full guest suites and an exercise or hobby room are located in the guest wing. The master wing features a study with curved glass, a luxurious bath with His and Hers vanities, a large walk-in closet and a large sleeping area and sitting bay.

Design by
©The Sater Design Collection

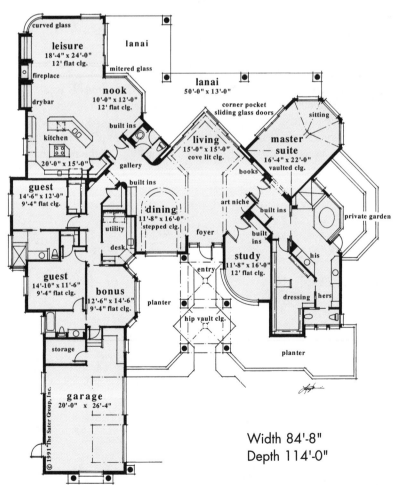

Width 84'-8"
Depth 114'-0"

The Sater Group, Inc.

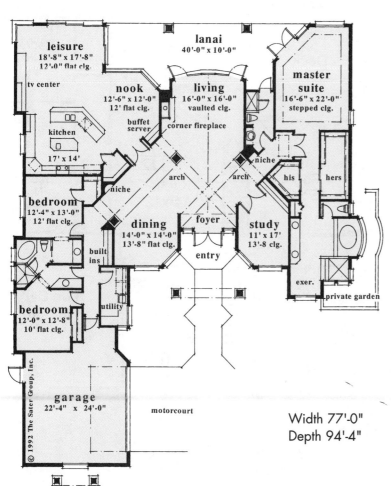

leisure
18'-8" x 17'-8"
12'-0" flat clg.

tv center

lanai
40'-0" x 10'-0"

master suite
16'-6" x 22'-0"
stepped clg.

nook
12'-6" x 12'-0"
12' flat clg.

living
16'-0" x 16'-0"
vaulted clg.

buffet server

kitchen

17' x 14'

corner fireplace

niche

his   hers

arch   arch

niche

bedroom
12'-4" x 13'-0"
12' flat clg.

niche

dining
14'-0" x 14'-0"
13'-8" flat clg.

foyer

study
11' x 17'
13'-8 clg.

built ins

entry

exer.

bedroom
12'-0" x 12'-8"
10' flat clg.

utility

private garden

© 1992 The Sater Group, Inc.

garage
22'-4" x 24'-0"

motorcourt

Width 77'-0"
Depth 94'-4"

Design HPTM03017

Square Footage: 3,743

L

■ An exciting elevation makes the exterior of this home as special as the interior details. A custom grill archway and keystone columns add to the style. The gable roof detail at the entry is carried through to the rear of the house. Columns and archways grace the formal areas of the home. A bow window at the living room overlooks the lanai. A large nook, complete with a buffet server, highlights the family area. The master bedroom has a stepped ceiling and overlooks the lanai. The bath features His and Hers closets, a garden tub and an area for exercise equipment.

Design by
© The Sater Design Collection

Design T157

Square Footage: 2,987

■ Reaching back through the centuries for its inspiration, this home reflects the grandeur that was ancient Rome...as it looked to newly independent Americans in the 1700s. The entry portico provides a classic twist: the balustrade that would have marched across the roof line of a typical Revival home trims to form the balcony outside the French doors of the study. Inside, the foyer opens on the left to a quiet study, on the right to the formal dining room, and straight ahead to a welcoming great room warmed by a fireplace. The left wing is given over to a private master suite with a master bath that offers the ultimate in luxury and a large walk-in closet. On the right side of the house, two additional bedrooms share a full bath. Separating the sleeping wings is the kitchen, with its nearby keeping room/family room. This home is designed with a basement foundation.

Deck

Master Bedroom 15⁰x17⁶

Great Room 15⁰x16⁰

Keeping/ Family Room 18³x14³

Kitchen 14⁹x12⁶

Bedroom No. 2 14⁰x12⁰

Bedroom No. 3 14⁰x12³

Dn

Study 12³x11³

Foyer

Dining Room 12⁹x16³

Two Car Garage 21⁶x21⁹

Width 74'-0"
Depth 62'-0"

Porch

Design by
DESIGN TRADITIONS

108

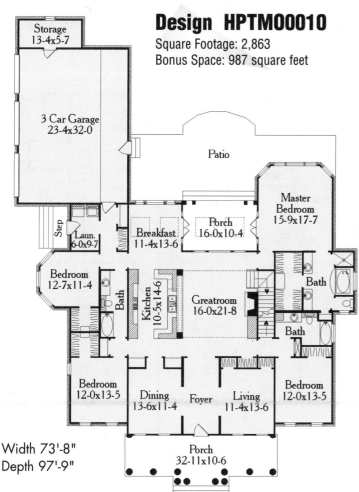

Design HPTM00010

Square Footage: 2,863
Bonus Space: 987 square feet

Storage
13-4x5-7

3 Car Garage
23-4x32-0

Patio

Laun.
6-0x9-7

Step

Breakfast
11-4x13-6

Porch
16-0x10-4

Master
Bedroom
15-9x17-7

Bedroom
12-7x11-4

Bath

Kitchen
10-5x14-6

Greatroom
16-0x21-8

Bath

Bath

Bedroom
12-0x13-5

Dining
13-6x11-4

Foyer

Living
11-4x13-6

Bedroom
12-0x13-5

Width 73'-8"
Depth 97'-9"

Porch
32-11x10-6

Design by
©Larry James & Associates, Inc.

■ A pedimented front porch gives this Southern Colonial home a classic appeal. Inside, the living and dining rooms face each other across the foyer. At the center of the plan is the great room with a fireplace and built-ins. Skylights flood the covered porch and breakfast room with light. Escape the busy world in the master suite with a bay window in the main room and its luxurious bath. Two secondary bedrooms are placed on the opposite side of the home—one with a beautiful bay window—and a third is at the front right. The three-car garage provides plenty of room for family autos and storage area for seasonal items. Expansion is also possible with bonus space on the second floor. Please specify basement, crawlspace or slab foundation when ordering.

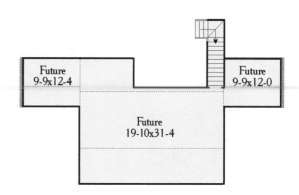

Future
9-9x12-4

Future
9-9x12-0

Future
19-10x31-4

Design T156

Square Footage: 2,998

■ This Colonial adaptation enjoys classic details—like a Palladian window with an arch-top set off by a keystone—but insists on a distinctly contemporary interior. At the heart of this sophisticated floor plan lies a light-hearted spirit, with French doors in the great room to bring in the outdoors. The secluded master suite offers a private bath with twin lavatories and a walk-in closet with its own window. Each of the two family bedrooms offers a private door to a shared full bath. This home is designed with a basement foundation.

Design by
DESIGN TRADITIONS

Width 75'-6"
Depth 57'-0"

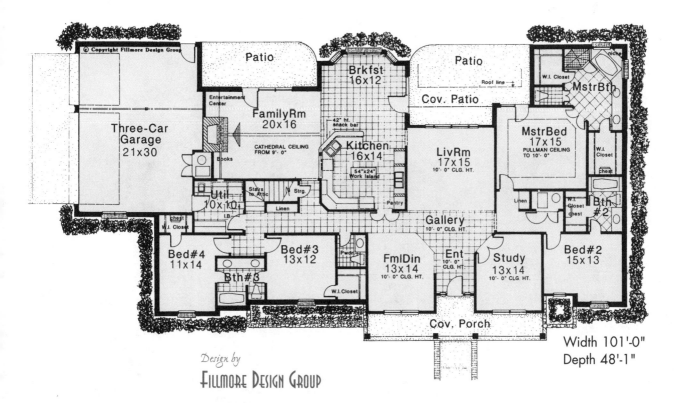

Patio

Brkfst
16x12

Patio

Cov. Patio

Roof line

Entertainment
Center

FamilyRm
20x16

42" ht.
snack bar

MstrBth

niche

W.I. Closet

Three-Car
Garage
21x30

CATHEDRAL CEILING
FROM 9'- 0"

Books

Kitchen
16x14

54"x24"
Work Island

LivRm
17x15
10'- 0" CLG. HT.

MstrBed
17x15
PULLMAN CEILING
TO 10'- 0"

W.I.
Closet

Util
10x10

Stairs
to Attic

Strg

Linen

Pantry

Linen

W.I.
Closet

chest

Bth
#2

chest

chest

L.B.

Gallery
10'- 0" CLG. HT.

W.I. Closet

Bed#4
11x14

Bed#3
13x12

Pwdr

FmlDin
13x14
10'- 0" CLG. HT.

Ent
10'- 0"
CLG. HT.

Study
13x14
10'- 0" CLG. HT.

Bed#2
15x13

Bth#3

W.I. Closet

Cov. Porch

Width 101'-0"
Depth 48'-1"

Design by
FILLMORE DESIGN GROUP

© Copyright Fillmore Design Group

Design M139
Square Footage: 3,270

■ A distinctive exterior, complete with siding, stone and brick, presents a welcoming facade on this four-bedroom home. A cathedral ceiling in the large family room, which includes a fireplace and built-ins, makes this country-style home a great choice. The island kitchen has plenty of work space and direct access to a sunny, bay-windowed breakfast room. A study and formal dining room flank the tiled entryway which leads straight into a formal living room. Three family bedrooms are ranged across the front of the house. The master suite offers plenty of seclusion as well as two walk-in closets, a lavish bath and direct access to the rear patio. A stairway leads to a future upstairs area.

Design T165

Square Footage: 3,066

■ Descended from the architecture that developed in America's Tidewater country, this updated adaptation retains the insouciant charm of a coastal cottage. At the same time, it offers an elegance that is appropriate for any setting in any climate today. Inside, the family living area is concentrated in the center of the house. Central to the social flow in the house, the great room opens to the kitchen, the breakfast room and to the rear porch that runs across the back. The left wing contains a private master suite that includes twin walk-in closets leading into a lavish master bath. Two additional bedrooms share a bath, while Bedroom 4 (located on the right side of the house) enjoys a high level of privacy that makes it an ideal guest room. This home is designed with a basement foundation.

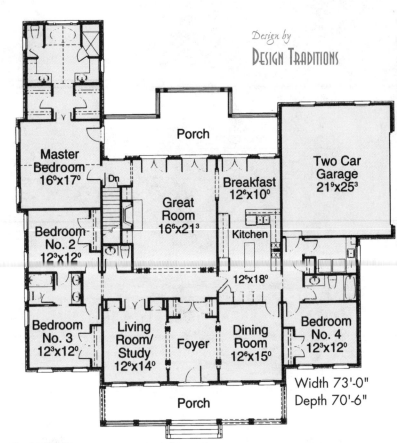

Design by
Design Traditions

Porch

Master Bedroom
16^0x17^0

Two Car Garage
21^9x25^3

Breakfast
12^6x10^0

Dn

Great Room
16^6x21^3

Kitchen

Bedroom No. 2
12^3x12^0

12^6x18^0

Bedroom No. 3
12^3x12^0

Living Room/ Study
12^6x14^0

Foyer

Dining Room
12^6x15^0

Bedroom No. 4
12^3x12^0

Width 73'-0"
Depth 70'-6"

Porch

Porch

Bedroom #2
12⁹ x 12⁶

Master Bedroom
14⁰ x 21³

Great Room
15⁹ x 18⁶

Breakfast
14⁶ x 10⁹

Kitchen

Up

Bedroom #3
13⁹ x 12⁰

12⁹ x 16⁶

Dn

Study
12⁹ x 15⁶

Foyer

Dining Room
14⁰ x 15⁶

Two Car Garage
21³ x 23⁰

Design by
DESIGN TRADITIONS

Width 72'-0"
Depth 64'-0"

Design T239

Square Footage: 2,810

■ Four elegant columns define the front porch of this three-bedroom home. Inside, the foyer is flanked by a cozy study to the left—complete with a fireplace—and a formal dining room to the right. Directly ahead is a spacious great room which features a second fireplace and French doors out to the rear deck. An L-shaped kitchen is complete with a work island and a large pantry and offers easy access to both the formal dining room and the sunny breakfast room. Two family bedrooms each have a walk-in closet and share a full bath. Located on the opposite side of the house for privacy, the master bedroom suite offers many relaxing amenities, including a huge walk-in closet, a lavish bath and access to the rear deck. This home is designed with a basement foundation.

Design M111

Square Footage: 2,539
Bonus Room and Loft: 639 square feet

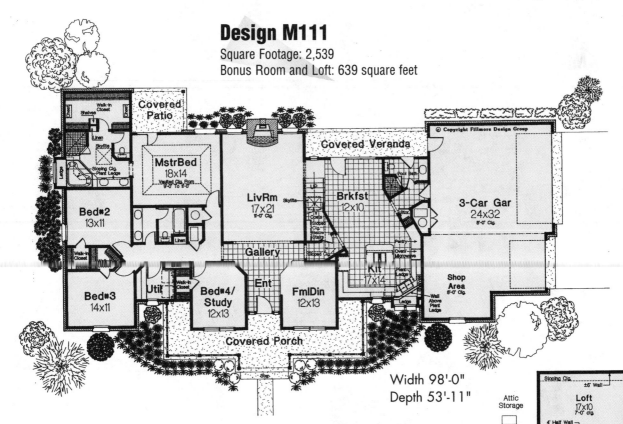

Width 98'-0"
Depth 53'-11"

■ Classic country character complements this one-story home complete with rustic stone corners, a covered front porch and interesting gables. The entry opens onto formal living areas that include a large dining room to the right, and straight ahead to a spacious living room warmed by a fireplace. A gallery leads the way into the efficient kitchen enhanced with a snack bar and large pantry. Casual meals can be enjoyed overlooking the covered veranda and rear grounds from the connecting breakfast room. The other side of the gallery accesses the luxurious master suite and three second bedrooms—all with walk-in closets. A pool bath and a shop area in the three-car garage are welcome amenities to the first floor. For playing, studying, quiet contemplation or relaxing, the second floor contains a loft and an optional bonus room to be developed as needed.

Design by
FILLMORE DESIGN GROUP

114

Design HPTM00011

Square Footage: 1,770

Countryside Classics:
One-story homes with a country flavor

■ This traditional-style home boasts a large receiving porch and free-flowing interior spaces. The spacious living room opens to the adjacent dining room and features a built-in fireplace and entertainment center. The entry, breakfast area, kitchen, plus the dining and living area all have twelve-foot ceilings, while other rooms have traditional eight-foot ceilings. The master suite is isolated for privacy and conveniently located only steps away from the kitchen. Please specify crawlspace or slab foundation when ordering.

Design by
©Breland & Farmer Designers, Inc.

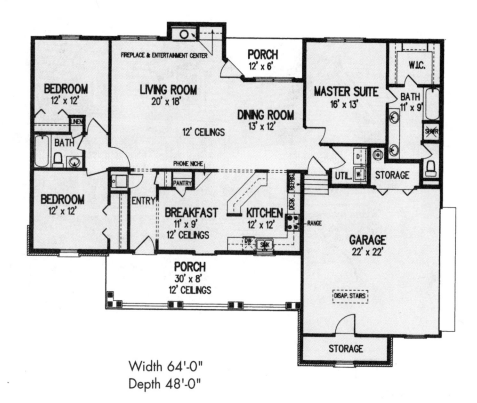

Width 64'-0"
Depth 48'-0"

© 1994 Donald A. Gardner Architects, Inc.

B. NATHAN

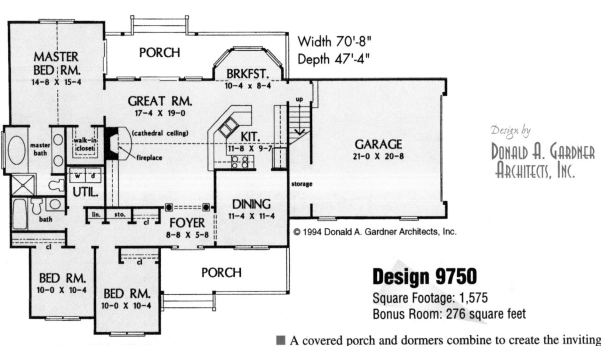

Width 70'-8"
Depth 47'-4"

MASTER BED RM.
14-8 X 15-4

PORCH

BRKFST.
10-4 x 8-4

GREAT RM.
17-4 X 19-0

(cathedral ceiling)

KIT.
11-8 X 9-7

up

GARAGE
21-0 X 20-8

master bath

walk-in closet

fireplace

UTIL.

w d

storage

lin. sto.

DINING
11-4 X 11-4

bath

FOYER
8-8 X 5-8

cl

cl

cl

BED RM.
10-0 X 10-4

BED RM.
10-0 X 10-4

PORCH

Design by
DONALD A. GARDNER
ARCHITECTS, INC.

© 1994 Donald A. Gardner Architects, Inc.

BONUS RM.
24-8 X 11-8

skylights

down

Design 9750
Square Footage: 1,575
Bonus Room: 276 square feet

■ A covered porch and dormers combine to create the inviting exterior on this three-bedroom country home. The foyer leads through columns to an expansive great room with a cozy fireplace, built-in bookshelves and access to the rear covered porch. To the right, an open kitchen is conveniently situated to easily serve the bay-windowed breakfast area and the formal dining room. Sleeping quarters are located on the left, where the master suite enjoys access to the covered porch, a walk-in closet and a relaxing master bath complete with double-bowl vanities, a whirlpool tub and a separate shower. A utility room, two secondary bedrooms and a full bath complete the plan. A bonus room over the garage provides room for future growth.

116

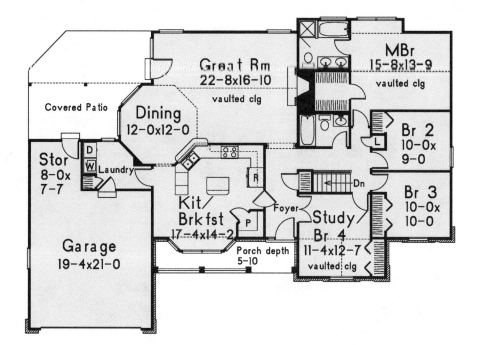

Great Rm
22-8x16-10
vaulted clg

MBr
15-8x13-9
vaulted clg

Covered Patio

Dining
12-0x12-0

Br 2
10-0x
9-0

Stor
8-0x
7-7

D
W
Laundry

**Kit/
Brkfst**
17-4x14-2

Foyer

Dn

**Study
Br 4**
11-4x12-7
vaulted clg

Br 3
10-0x
10-0

P

R

L

Garage
19-4x21-0

Porch depth
5-10

Design HPTM02002
Square Footage: 1,791

Design by
©Home Design Alternatives, Inc.

Width 67'-4"
Depth 48'-0"

■ The two dormers draw attention to this home as well as flood the kitchen and breakfast nook with plenty of natural light. The steep rooflines lend vaulted ceilings to the interior of this home. The great room and octagonal dining room enjoy views of the covered patio. The amazingly well-lit kitchen features a pass-through to the dining room, a center island, a walk-in pantry and a breakfast room with a large bay window. The bedrooms align along the right side of the plan.

Design HPTM02003

Square Footage: 1,761

■ Residing peacefully in a serene country setting, this small family home brings quaint style to an efficient floor plan. The covered porch leads inside to formal vistas from the dining and great rooms. Warmed by a cozy fireplace, the vaulted great room connects to the kitchen/breakfast area, opening onto a rear patio. The master bedroom is vaulted and includes a walk-in closet and private bath. Three additional family bedrooms share a full hall bath. A two-car garage completes this charming plan.

Design by
©Home Design Alternatives, Inc.

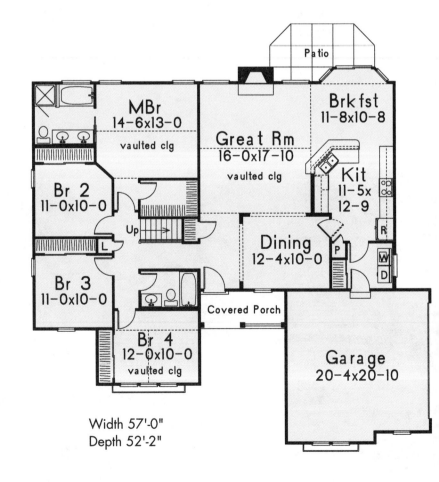

Width 57'-0"
Depth 52'-2"

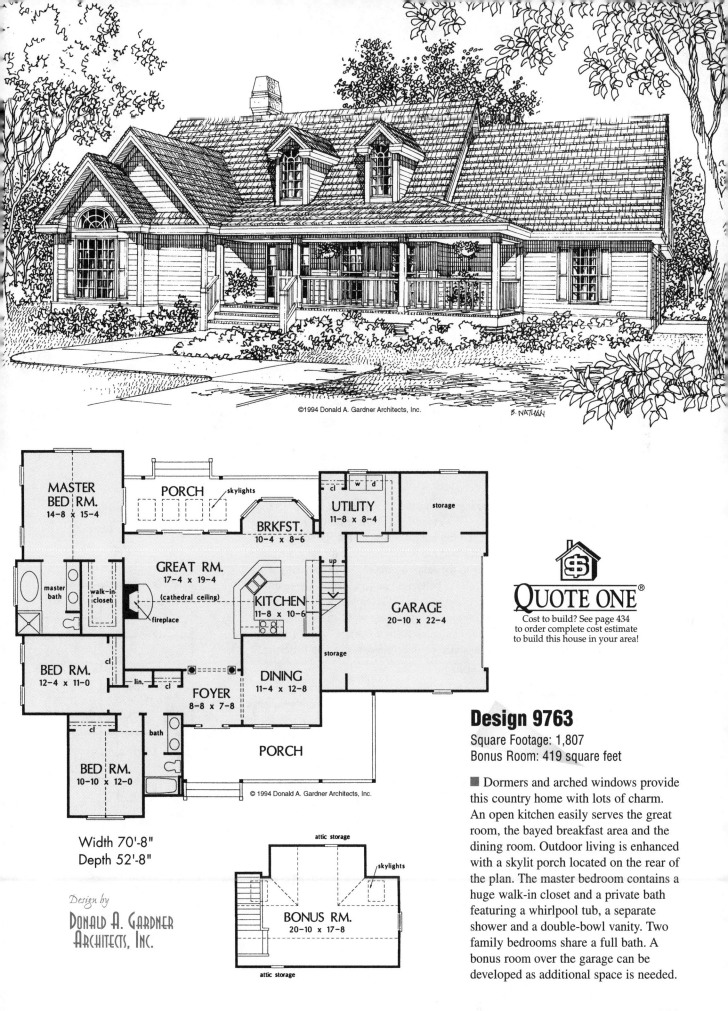

©1994 Donald A. Gardner Architects, Inc.

B. NATHAN

MASTER BED RM.
14-8 x 15-4

PORCH
skylights

UTILITY
11-8 x 8-4

storage

w | d

cl

master bath

walk-in closet

BRKFST.
10-4 x 8-6

GREAT RM.
17-4 x 19-4

(cathedral ceiling)

fireplace

KITCHEN
11-8 x 10-6

up

GARAGE
20-10 x 22-4

BED RM.
12-4 x 11-0

cl

lin.

cl

FOYER
8-8 x 7-8

DINING
11-4 x 12-8

storage

storage

bath

BED RM.
10-10 x 12-0

cl

PORCH

© 1994 Donald A. Gardner Architects, Inc.

Width 70'-8"
Depth 52'-8"

Design by
Donald A. Gardner
Architects, Inc.

attic storage

skylights

BONUS RM.
20-10 x 17-8

attic storage

QUOTE ONE®
Cost to build? See page 434
to order complete cost estimate
to build this house in your area!

Design 9763

Square Footage: 1,807
Bonus Room: 419 square feet

■ Dormers and arched windows provide this country home with lots of charm. An open kitchen easily serves the great room, the bayed breakfast area and the dining room. Outdoor living is enhanced with a skylit porch located on the rear of the plan. The master bedroom contains a huge walk-in closet and a private bath featuring a whirlpool tub, a separate shower and a double-bowl vanity. Two family bedrooms share a full bath. A bonus room over the garage can be developed as additional space is needed.

A porch full of columns gives a relaxing emphasis to this country home. To the right of the foyer, the dining area resides conveniently near the efficient kitchen. The kitchen island, walk-in pantry and serving bar add plenty of work space to the food-preparation zone. Natural light will flood the breakfast nook through a ribbon of windows facing the rear yard. Escape to the relaxing master suite featuring a private sun room/retreat and a luxurious bath set between His and Hers walk-in closets. The great room at the center of this L-shaped plan is complete with a warming fireplace and built-ins. Three family bedrooms enjoy private walk-in closets and share a fully appointed bath. The two-car garage also has a storage area for family treasures. Please specify basement, crawlspace or slab foundation when ordering.

Design by
©Larry James & Associates, Inc.

Design HPTM00012

Square Footage: 2,506

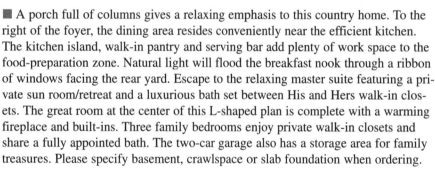

Width 72'-2"
Depth 66'-4"

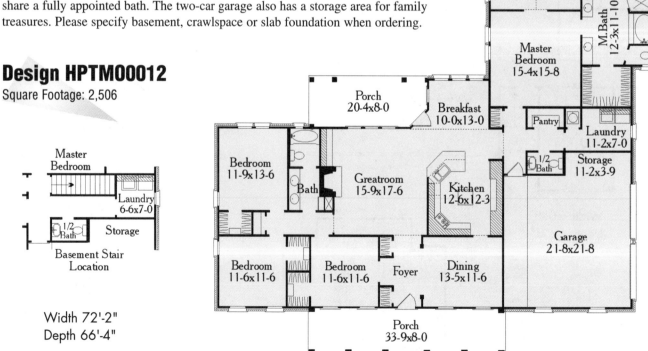

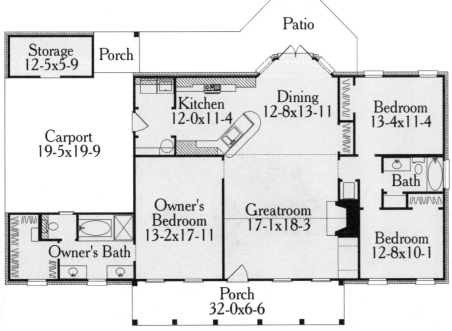

Patio

Storage
12-5x5-9

Porch

Kitchen
12-0x11-4

Dining
12-8x13-11

Bedroom
13-4x11-4

Carport
19-5x19-9

Bath

Owner's
Bedroom
13-2x17-11

Greatroom
17-1x18-3

Owner's Bath

Bedroom
12-8x10-1

Porch
32-0x6-6

Basement
Stair Location

Owner's
Bedroom
13-2x14-3

Design by
©Larry James & Associates, Inc.

Design HPTMO0045

Square Footage: 1,689

■ This attractive facade presents hipped roofs, muntin windows with shutters, and a wide porch—perfect for relaxing or welcoming guests. The fireplace and built-in media center add to the great room. The kitchen and dining room connect by the peninsula with a sink and serving bar. The bay window of the dining area includes French doors that open to a large patio. Two family bedrooms occupy the right side of the plan, and share a full bath that includes a linen closet. Inside the owners bedroom, a private bath includes a garden tub, separate shower and immense walk-in closet. Don't miss the carport and storage space to the rear left of the plan. Please specify basement, crawlspace or slab foundation when ordering.

Width 67'-0"
Depth 43'-0"

Master Bedroom
14'5" x 14'5"

Bath

walk-in closet

Bath

Hall

stairs dn

Bedroom
13'10" x 10'

Bedroom
10'3" x 12'

Foyer

Dining Room
14' 8" x 11'9"

Great Room
19'7" x 18'5"

slope ceiling

slope ceiling

slope ceiling

Breakfast
11'7" x 11'6"

Kitchen
11'6" x 17'9"

slope ceiling

Sun Room
10'10" x 19'6"

Laun.

Two-car Garage
20' x 22'

■ Finished in enduring brick, this one-story home possesses appeal that stands the test of time. Its floor plan is also a classic, with a central great room, formal dining room and breakfast room with sun-room access. The kitchen sits between the dining room and breakfast room and leads to the laundry room and a service entry to the two-car garage. Bedrooms are more privately located on the left side of the plan. The master bedroom features a tray ceiling and has a bath with a corner whirlpool tub and walk-in closet.

Design B584
Square Footage: 2,145

Design by
©Studer Residential Designs, Inc.

Width 71'-2"
Depth 51'-0"

SCREENED PORCH
12-6 X 11-0
10 FT CLG

GREAT ROOM
17-4 X 17-6
12 FT CLG

SITTING
11-2 X 13-6
10 FT CLG

FP

BUILT IN

MASTER BATH
10 FT CLG

K.S.

LEDGE

BRKFST RM
12-6 X 11-0
10 FT CLG

ARCH

PWDR

BUILT IN

MASTER BEDROOM
15-2 X 15-2
10 FT CLG

CHEST

FOYER
10 FT CLG

42" LEDGE

KITCHEN
15-4 X 13-6

10 FT CLG

ARCH

DINING ROOM
15-4 X 13-4
10 FT CLG

ARCH

LIN

BATH 2

PAN

BEDROOM 3
12-4 X 12-0
10 FT CLG

BEDROOM 2
12-6 X 12-6
10 FT CLG

UTIL

RAISED PLANTER

GARAGE

Design by
©Larry E. Belk Designs

Design 8224
Square Footage: 2,439

Width 81'-2"
Depth 67'-10"

■ Graceful arches and columns make a delicate complement to the brick facade of this country house. An extended foyer introduces an exciting interior plan—ten-foot ceilings throughout give a spacious feeling. A cozy fireplace will be appreciated in the great room, as will the nearby screened porch. An efficient kitchen, with cooktop-island counter and an angled sink, serves both the breakfast room and the formal dining room. The master suite, located at the rear of the plan for privacy, offers many amenities. Two family bedrooms are clustered nearby and share a full bath. Please specify crawl-space or slab foundation when ordering.

Width 59'-0"
Depth 58'-0"

Design HPTM00013

Square Footage: 1,955

■ This dynamite brick one-story home holds a floor plan with plenty of space for the family. The great room is the hub of the home and features patio access and a corner fireplace for warmth. A formal dining room, defined by columns, sits at the front of the plan, while a more casual breakfast room connects directly to the gourmet kitchen. The master suite sits behind the two-car garage and contains a walk-in closet and a bath with separate tub and shower. Family bedrooms on the far left side of the plan share a full hall bath.

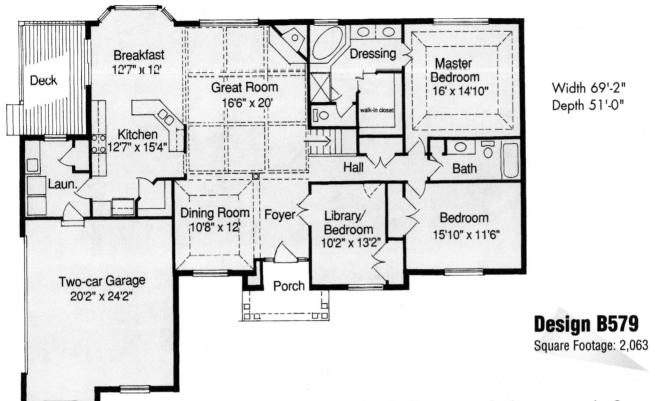

Breakfast
12'7" x 12'

Deck

Great Room
16'6" x 20'

Dressing

Master
Bedroom
16' x 14'10"

walk-in closet

Kitchen
12'7" x 15'4"

Hall

Bath

Laun.

Dining Room
10'8" x 12'

Foyer

Library/
Bedroom
10'2" x 13'2"

Bedroom
15'10" x 11'6"

Two-car Garage
20'2" x 24'2"

Porch

Width 69'-2"
Depth 51'-0"

Design B579
Square Footage: 2,063

Design by
©Studer Residential Designs, Inc.

■ These shadowed gables present a visual treat to passersby. Once inside, you can stand in the foyer and see the delightful open space created by the great room, dining room and breakfast nook. Each room has its own personality, however, with unique ceiling treatments. An optional bedroom/library gives homeowners numerous usage possibilities. Bedrooms are clustered on the right side of the plan and include a master suite with a private bath and two family bedrooms—or one bedroom and a library—that share a full bath.

© 1989 Donald A. Gardner Architects, Inc.

DECK

Width 65'-2"
Depth 74'-8"

cabinets
fireplace

tub

cl

MASTER BED RM.
16-0 × 13-4

GREAT RM.
15-4 × 19-6
(cathedral ceiling)

master bath

lin.

skylights

SUN RM.
12-6 × 9-0

cl   cl

bath

cl

cl   cl   lin.

BRKFST.
9-4 × 9-6

KIT.
12-6 × 13-0

DINING
12-0 × 12-8

FOYER
5-0 × 13-0

optional opening

BED RM./ STUDY
11-4 × 10-4

BED RM.
13-0 × 12-0

UTILITY

wash   dry

PORCH

© 1989 Donald A. Gardner Architects, Inc.

GARAGE
21-10 × 23-0

Design by
DONALD A. GARDNER
ARCHITECTS, INC.

Design 9670
Square Footage: 2,046

■ This three-bedroom country cottage projects an intriguing appearance with its bay windows, dormers and L-shaped layout. The great room has a cathedral ceiling along with an arched window above the exterior door leading to the deck. The sun room with operable skylights is accessible from the great room, kitchen and deck for maximum exposure. The centrally located kitchen allows direct access to eating and living areas. Three bedrooms include a master suite and a bedroom that might also be useful as a study.

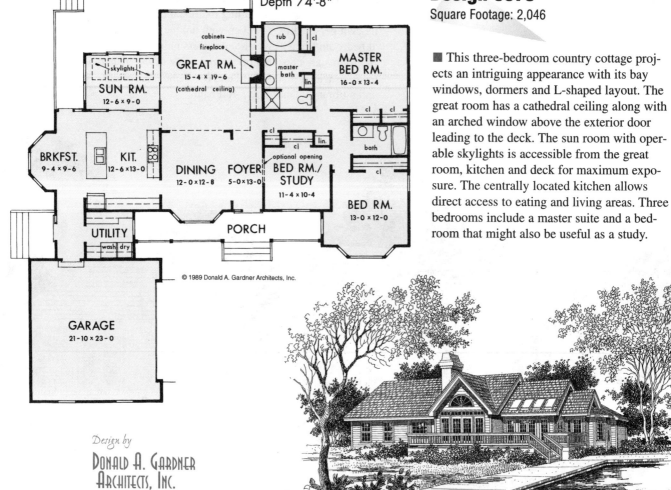

Rear Elevation

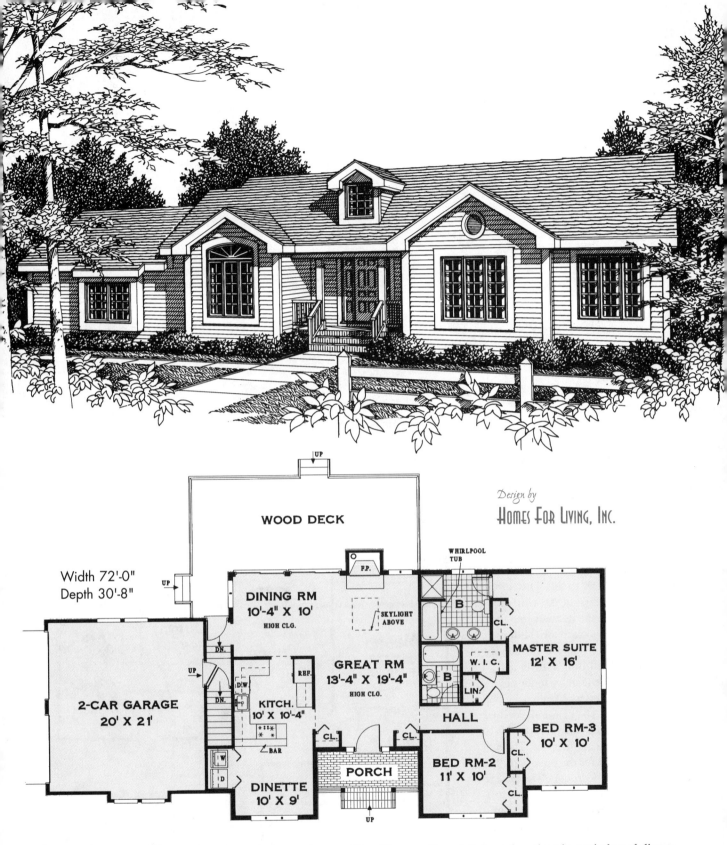

WOOD DECK

Design by
Homes For Living, Inc.

Width 72'-0"
Depth 30'-8"

WHIRLPOOL TUB

DINING RM
10'-4" X 10'
HIGH CLG.

SKYLIGHT ABOVE

F.P.

B

CL.

MASTER SUITE
12' X 16'

REF.

GREAT RM
13'-4" X 19'-4"
HIGH CLG.

W. I. C.

LIN.

2-CAR GARAGE
20' X 21'

DN.

UP

DN.

D/W

KITCH.
10' X 10'-4"

B

HALL

BED RM-3
10' X 10'

BAR

W

CL.

CL.

CL.

D

DINETTE
10' X 9'

PORCH

BED RM-2
11' X 10'

CL.

UP

Design N145
Square Footage: 1,412

■ If traditional exteriors are what you like, this design delivers all the best features: horizontal wood siding, multi-pane windows, a centered dormer and a recessed, raised entry. The great room is the focal point of the plan. It has a fireplace and skylight and overlooks a rear wood deck. The formal dining room is open to the great room and has sliding glass doors to the deck.

Casual dining takes place in a windowed dinette on the opposite side of the U-shaped kitchen. Two family bedrooms have large front-facing windows and share the use of a full bath. The master bedroom features its own bath with whirlpool tub, separate shower and double sinks. A two-car garage is to the left of the plan. Please specify basement or slab foundation when ordering.

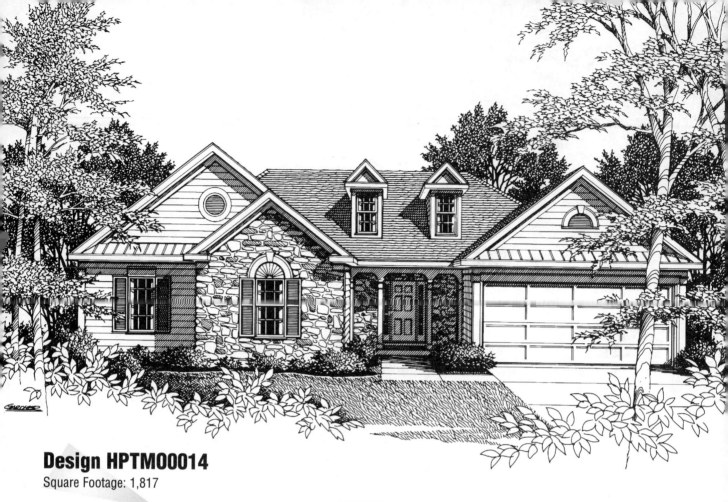

Design HPTM00014

Square Footage: 1,817

■ Stone accents, dormers and a front porch add character to this ranch design. The cathedral design of the main roof draws light from the dormers into the foyer. The ceiling space also allows a plant shelf, which is above the laundry room and visible from the foyer and dining room. The laundry room sits adjacent to the entrance from the garage into the kitchen. The peninsula kitchen makes the breakfast area's two walls of glass light up the entire space. The hall bath is sectioned for the privacy of the three secondary bedrooms. The master bath features a ten-foot vanity and mirror that opens up the entire bathroom. Please specify crawlspace or slab foundation when ordering.

Design by
©Jannis Vann & Associates, Inc.

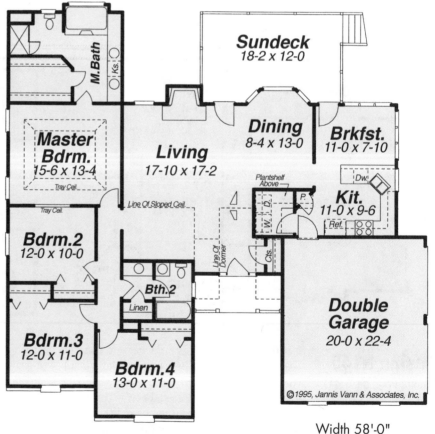

M. Bath

Sundeck
18-2 x 12-0

Master Bdrm.
15-6 x 13-4
Tray Ceil.

Tray Ceil.

Living
17-10 x 17-2

Line Of Sloped Ceil.

Dining
8-4 x 13-0

Brkfst.
11-0 x 7-10

Plantshelf Above

Bdrm.2
12-0 x 10-0

Kit.
11-0 x 9-6

Ref.

Line Of Dormer

Bth.2

Linen

Bdrm.3
12-0 x 11-0

Bdrm.4
13-0 x 11-0

Double Garage
20-0 x 22-4

©1995, Jannis Vann & Associates, Inc.

Width 58'-0"
Depth 55'-5"

NATHAN INC.

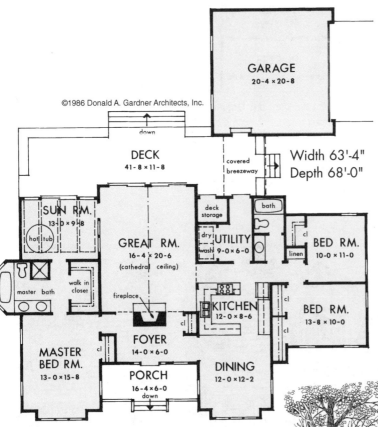

GARAGE
20-4 × 20-8

down

DECK
41-8 × 11-8

Width 63'-4"
Depth 68'-0"

covered breezeway

bath

SUN RM.
13-0 × 9-8

hot tub

deck storage

GREAT RM.
16-4 × 20-6
(cathedral ceiling)

dry
wash

UTILITY
9-0 × 6-0

linen

BED RM.
10-0 × 11-0

master bath

walk in closet

fireplace

KITCHEN
12-0 × 8-6

cl

cl

BED RM.
13-8 × 10-0

MASTER
BED RM.
13-0 × 15-8

cl

FOYER
14-0 × 6-0

cl

PORCH
16-4 × 6-0
down

DINING
12-0 × 12-2

Design by
DONALD A. GARDNER
ARCHITECTS, INC.

Design 9682
Square Footage: 1,826

■ Multi-pane windows, dormers, a covered porch, round gable vents and two projected windows at the dining area add to the flavor of this country-style home. A sun room with hot tub sits adjacent to a deck that is accessed from the great room and master bath. The great room has a fireplace, cathedral ceiling and sliding glass doors with arched windows above to allow for natural light. The kitchen is centrally located between the dining area and the great room for maximum flexibility in layout. A generous master bedroom has a walk-in closet and spacious master bath with double-bowl vanity, shower and garden tub. Two additional bedrooms are located at the other end of the house for privacy.

Rear Elevation

Design 7637

Square Footage: 1,959
Bonus Space: 385 square feet

■ Square columns with chamfered corners set off classic clapboard siding and complement a country-style dormer and twin pediments. The vaulted great room has a focal-point fireplace and access to the rear deck. The well-appointed kitchen opens to a bright breakfast area and enjoys its natural light. The dining room, front bedroom/study and master bedroom feature tray ceilings. The private master suite also includes a skylit bath.

Design by
DONALD A. GARDNER
ARCHITECTS, INC.

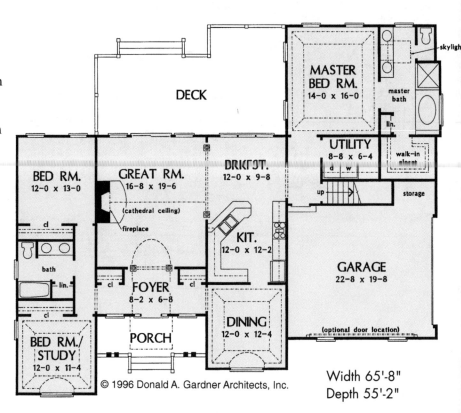

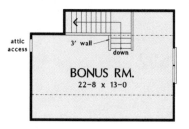

attic access

BONUS RM.
22-8 x 13-0

Width 65'-8"
Depth 55'-2"

© 1996 Donald A. Gardner Architects, Inc.

© 1996 Donald A. Gardner Architects, Inc.

130

Design 9657

Square Footage: 2,165

■ Step into the sun room from the master suite, family room or deck in this sunny, three-bedroom country home—dressed up with dormers, shutters and bay windows. Along with formal living and dining rooms, this home also has a family room flooded with light from a sliding glass door with an arched window above. The kitchen includes an island and an adjacent breakfast area. The ample master suite includes a walk-in closet and a luxurious master bath with dual lavatories, a shower and a whirlpool tub. A separate garage is reached via a covered breezeway across the deck.

Rear Elevation

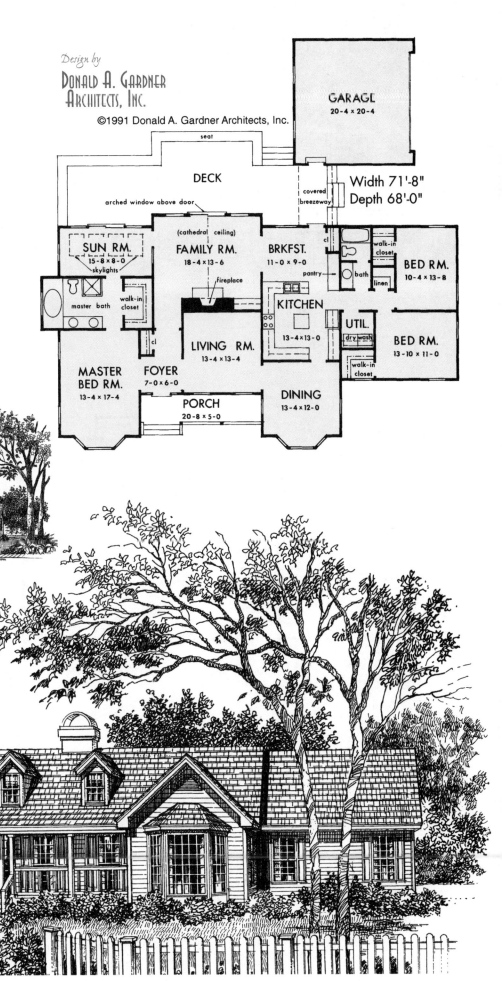

Design by
DONALD A. GARDNER ARCHITECTS, INC.

GARAGE
20-4 × 20-4

DECK

seat

Width 71'-8"
Depth 68'-0"

covered breezeway

arched window above door

SUN RM.
15-8 × 8-0
skylights

(cathedral ceiling)

FAMILY RM.
18-4 × 13-6

BRKFST.
11-0 × 9-0

walk-in closet

BED RM.
10-4 × 13-8

bath

linen

master bath

walk-in closet

fireplace

pantry

KITCHEN
13-4 × 13-0

UTIL.
dry wash

BED RM.
13-10 × 11-0

cl

LIVING RM.
13-4 × 13-4

walk-in closet

MASTER BED RM.
13-4 × 17-4

FOYER
7-0 × 6-0

DINING
13-4 × 12-0

PORCH
20-8 × 5-0

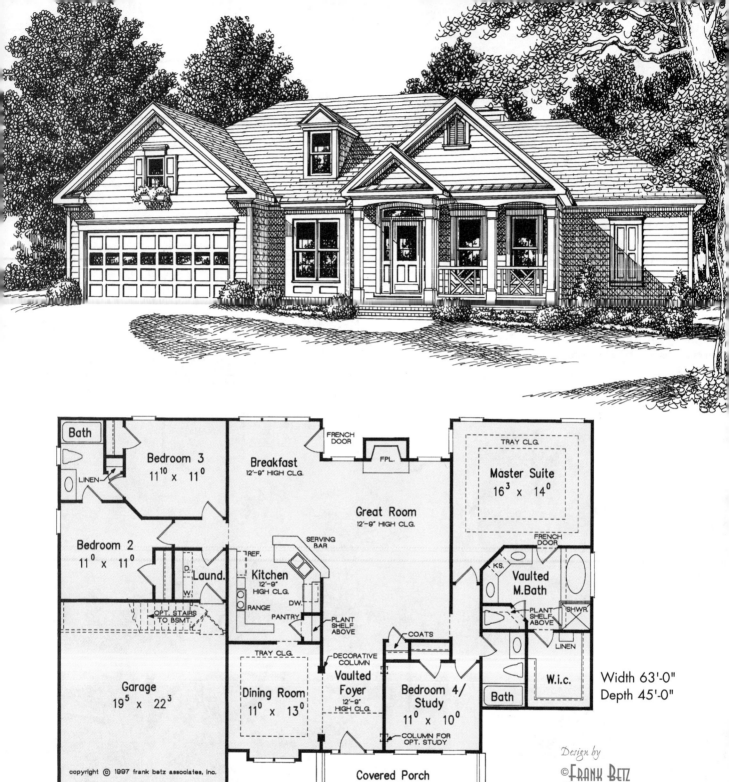

Bath

Bedroom 3
11¹⁰ x 11⁰

LINEN

Bedroom 2
11⁰ x 11⁰

D. W. **Laund.**

OPT. STAIRS TO BSMT.

Garage
19⁵ x 22³

copyright © 1997 frank betz associates, inc.

Breakfast
12'-9" HIGH CLG.

FRENCH DOOR

FPL.

Great Room
12'-9" HIGH CLG.

SERVING BAR

Kitchen
12'-9" HIGH CLG.

REF.

DW.

RANGE

PANTRY

PLANT SHELF ABOVE

TRAY CLG.

Dining Room
11⁰ x 13⁰

DECORATIVE COLUMN

Vaulted Foyer
12'-9" HIGH CLG.

COATS

Bedroom 4/ Study
11⁰ x 10⁰

Bath

COLUMN FOR OPT. STUDY

Covered Porch

TRAY CLG.

Master Suite
16³ x 14⁰

FRENCH DOOR

KS.

Vaulted M.Bath

SHWR.

PLANT SHELF ABOVE

LINEN

W.i.c.

Width 63'-0"
Depth 45'-0"

Design by
© **FRANK BETZ**
ASSOCIATES, INC.

GARAGE LOCATION WITH BASEMENT

Design P296
Square Footage: 1,932

■ Special architectural aspects turn this quaint home into much more than just another one-story ranch design. It is enhanced by a covered, columned front porch, large window areas, a dormer and horizontal wood siding. The floor plan is equally thoughtful in design. A central great room acts as the hub of the plan and is graced by a fireplace flanked on either side by windows. It is separated from the kitchen by a convenient serving bar. Formal dining is accomplished to the front of the plan in a room with a tray ceiling. Casual dining takes place in the breakfast room with its full wall of glass. Two bedrooms are to the left and share a full bath. The master suite and one additional bedroom are to the right. Bedroom 4 would make the perfect study, with the option of a doorway opening directly to the foyer. Please specify basement or crawlspace foundation when ordering.

Width 67'-6"
Depth 63'-6"

Rec. Room

Kitchen

Patio

Bedroom
11'11" x 13'

Bath   Sauna   Basement
Storage

Bath

Exercise
Room
11'11" x 15'2"

Design HPTM00015

Square Footage: 2,041

■ Attention to detail and a touch of luxury create a home that showcases the owners excellent taste while providing an efficient floor plan. From the raised foyer, a striking view is offered through the great room to the elegantly styled windows and beyond to the covered deck. The spacious kitchen offers an abundance of counter space and cabinets and easy access to the dining area and rear yard. Split bedrooms provide privacy to the master suite, where a sitting area is topped by an exciting ceiling treatment. An extra-large garden bath with a spacious walk-in closet and whirlpool tub pampers the homeowner. In the library, a window seat wraps around the tower, providing a point of interest as well as storage. A full walk-out basement is available with this plan, offering additional living space and an extra, large recreation area.

Design by
©Studer Residential Designs, Inc.

Bath

Dressing

walk-in closet

Dining
12'2" x 11'10"

skylight   slope ceiling

Deck

Sitting
Area
11'10" x 11'10"
10'1" ceiling height

9' ceiling height

Master Bedroom
14'4" x 11'10"

Kitchen
11'7" x 14'6"

Great Room
15' x 16'6"

11'7" ceiling height

Bedroom
10'9" x 10'6"

cabinets

Laun.
9'2" x 7'4"

Hall

up 1 riser

Raised
Foyer

up 1 riser

Hall

Bath

Two-car Garage
21' x 25'9"

Porch

Bedroom
/Library
12'10" x 11'6"

window seat w/ storage

133

Design HPTM00016

Square Footage: 2,267

■ Six columns and a steeply pitched roof lend elegance to this four-bedroom home. To the right of the foyer, the dining area sits conveniently near the efficient kitchen. The kitchen island and serving bar add plenty of work space to the food-preparation zone. Natural light will flood the breakfast nook through a ribbon of windows facing the rear yard. Escape to the relaxing master suite, with its luxurious bath set between His and Hers walk-in closets. The great room at the center of this L-shaped plan is complete with a warming fireplace and built-ins. Three family bedrooms enjoy private walk-in closets and share a fully appointed bath. Please specify basement, crawlspace or slab foundation when ordering.

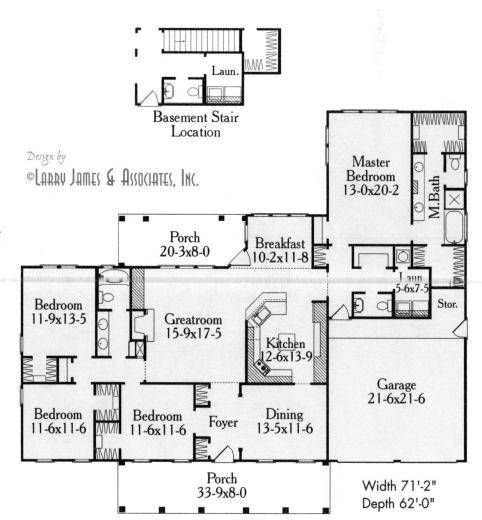

Design by
©Larry James & Associates, Inc.

Basement Stair Location

Laun.

Master Bedroom 13-0x20-2

M.Bath

Porch 20-3x8-0

Breakfast 10-2x11-8

Laun. 5-6x7-5

Stor.

Bedroom 11-9x13-5

Greatroom 15-9x17-5

Kitchen 12-6x13-9

Bedroom 11-6x11-6

Bedroom 11-6x11-6

Foyer

Dining 13-5x11-6

Garage 21-6x21-6

Porch 33-9x8-0

Width 71'-2"
Depth 62'-0"

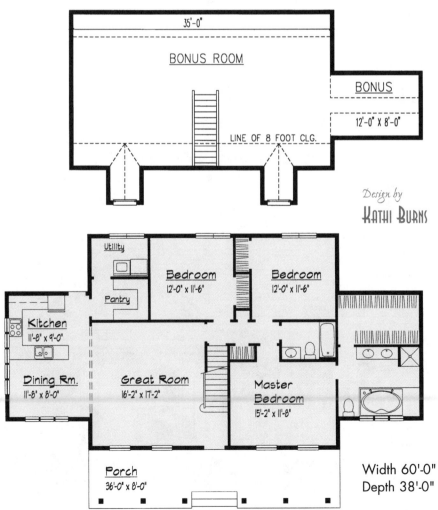

35'-0"

BONUS ROOM

BONUS

12'-0" X 8'-0"

LINE OF 8 FOOT CLG.

Design by
Kathi Burns

Utility

Bedroom
12'-0" x 11'-6"

Bedroom
12'-0" x 11'-6"

Pantry

Kitchen
11'-8" x 9'-0"

Dining Rm.
11'-8" x 8'-0"

Great Room
16'-2" x 17'-2"

Master
Bedroom
15'-2" x 11'-8"

Porch
36'-0" x 8'-0"

Width 60'-0"
Depth 38'-0"

Design W008

Square Footage: 1,512
Bonus Space: 555 square feet

■ Perfectly symmetrical on the outside, this appealing home has an equally classic floor plan on the inside. A covered porch featuring full, multi-paned windows opens directly to the spacious great room. It is open to the dining room and U-shaped kitchen for convenience and gracious entertaining. The kitchen connects to a roomy utility room with loads of counterspace and windows overlooking the rear yard. The master bedroom lies to the front of the plan and has a view of the covered porch. Its bath features a whirlpool tub, separate shower and two sinks. A room-sized walk-in closet is an added amenity. Two family bedrooms reside to the rear of the plan. Each has a window with backyard views. The upstairs is unfinished but can add 555 square feet of usable space when needed. Please specify basement or crawl-space foundation when ordering.

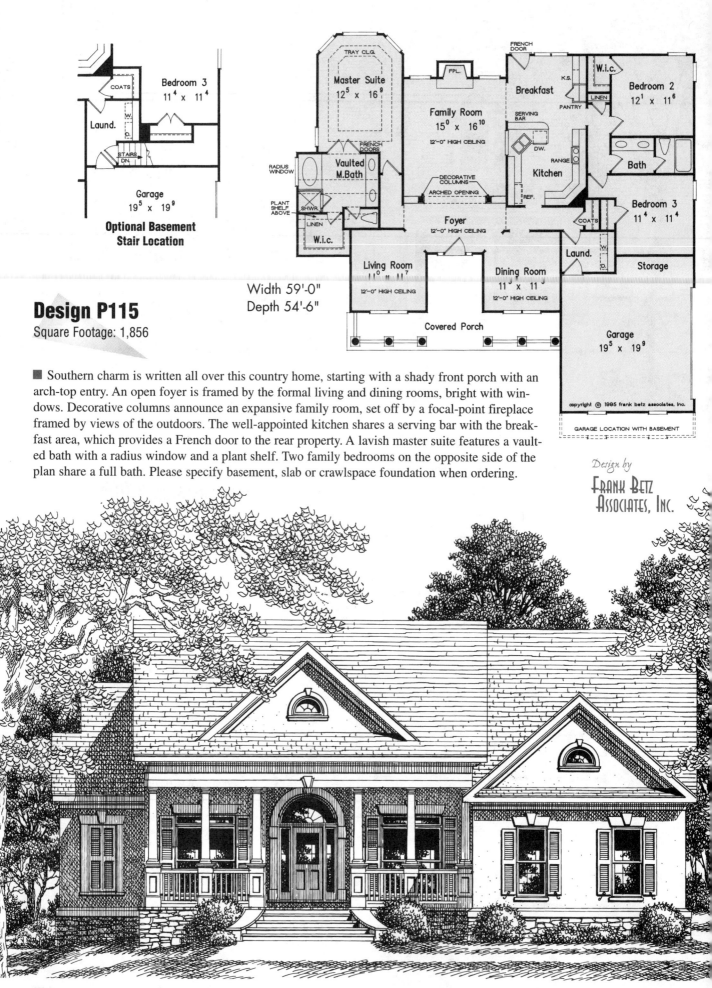

Optional Basement Stair Location

Bedroom 3
11⁴ x 11⁴

COATS

Laund.

Garage
19⁵ x 19⁹

TRAY CLG.

Master Suite
12⁵ x 16⁹

FRENCH DOOR

FPL.

Family Room
15⁰ x 16¹⁰
12'-0" HIGH CEILING

Breakfast

K.S.

W.i.c.

LINEN

PANTRY

Bedroom 2
12¹ x 11⁶

RADIUS WINDOW

Vaulted M.Bath

FRENCH DOORS

SERVING BAR

DW.

Kitchen

RANGE

Bath

PLANT SHELF ABOVE

SHWR.

LINEN

DECORATIVE COLUMNS

ARCHED OPENING

REF.

W.i.c.

Foyer
12'-0" HIGH CEILING

COATS

Bedroom 3
11⁴ x 11⁴

Living Room
11⁰ x 11⁷
12'-0" HIGH CEILING

Dining Room
11 x 11
12'-0" HIGH CEILING

Laund.

W. D.

Storage

Covered Porch

Garage
19⁵ x 19⁹

Width 59'-0"
Depth 54'-6"

copyright © 1995 frank betz associates, inc.

GARAGE LOCATION WITH BASEMENT

Design P115

Square Footage: 1,856

■ Southern charm is written all over this country home, starting with a shady front porch with an arch-top entry. An open foyer is framed by the formal living and dining rooms, bright with windows. Decorative columns announce an expansive family room, set off by a focal-point fireplace framed by views of the outdoors. The well-appointed kitchen shares a serving bar with the breakfast area, which provides a French door to the rear property. A lavish master suite features a vaulted bath with a radius window and a plant shelf. Two family bedrooms on the opposite side of the plan share a full bath. Please specify basement, slab or crawlspace foundation when ordering.

Design by
Frank Betz Associates, Inc.

© 1997 Donald A. Gardner Architects, Inc.

Design 7645
Square Footage: 1,903

■ This symmetrical Folk Victorian combines the charm of yesteryear with a plan designed for today's family. Accented by columns, the great room with a fireplace is vaulted, while the foyer, dining room, kitchen, breakfast bay and bedroom/study boast impressive ten-foot ceilings. With double door entry, the secluded master suite features a tray ceiling, walk-in closet and private, skylit bath. Three additional bedrooms are located on the opposite side of the house and share a full bath with linen closet. Note that the front and back porches extend the living space to the outdoors.

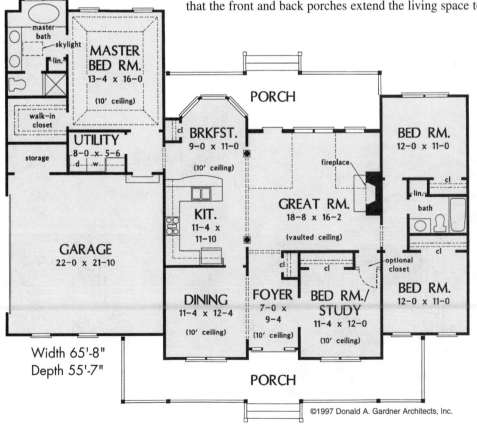

master bath
skylight
lin.

MASTER BED RM.
13-4 x 16-0
(10' ceiling)

walk-in closet

storage

UTILITY
8-0 x 5-6
d — w

cl

BRKFST.
9-0 x 11-0
(10' ceiling)

PORCH

KIT.
11-4 x 11-10

GARAGE
22-0 x 21-10

fireplace

GREAT RM.
18-8 x 16-2
(vaulted ceiling)

BED RM.
12-0 x 11-0

cl
lin.
bath

cl

DINING
11-4 x 12-4
(10' ceiling)

cl

FOYER
7-0 x 9-4
(10' ceiling)

BED RM./ STUDY
11-4 x 12-0
(10' ceiling)

optional closet

BED RM.
12-0 x 11-0

Width 65'-8"
Depth 55'-7"

PORCH

Design by
Donald A. Gardner
Architects, Inc.

©1997 Donald A. Gardner Architects, Inc.

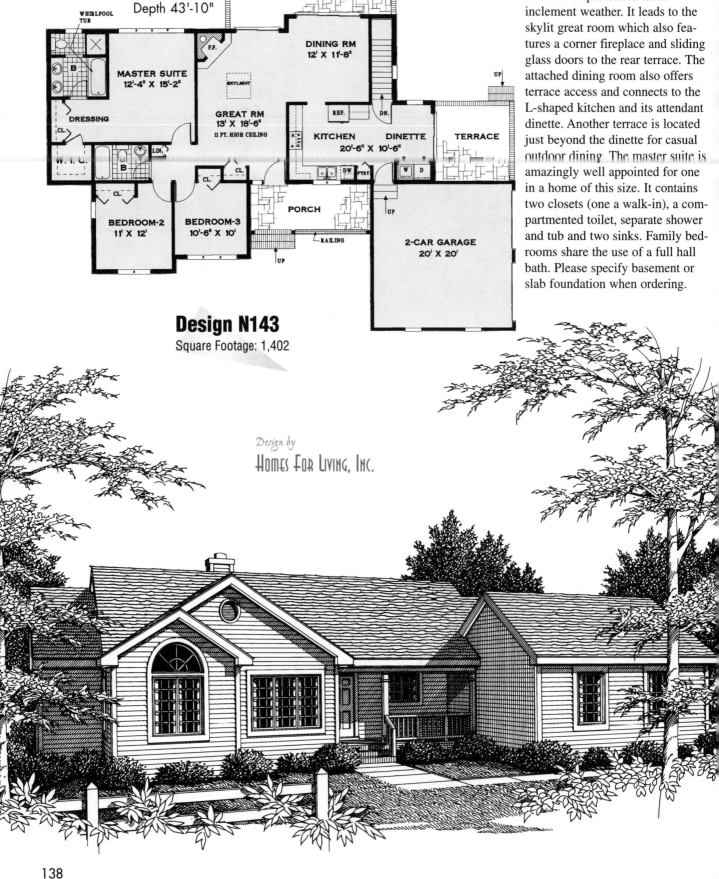

Width 67'-4"
Depth 43'-10"

WHIRLPOOL TUB

B

MASTER SUITE
12'-4" X 15'-2"

F.P.

SKYLIGHT

DINING RM
12' X 11'-8"

DRESSING

GREAT RM
13' X 18'-6"
11 FT. HIGH CEILING

REF.

UP

DN.

CL.

KITCHEN
20'-6" X 10'-6"

DINETTE

TERRACE

W. I. C.

B

LIN.

CL.

CL.

W

D

DW

PTRY.

UP

BEDROOM-2
11' X 12'

BEDROOM-3
10'-6" X 10'

PORCH

UP

2-CAR GARAGE
20' X 20'

RAILING

UP

UP

TERRACE

Design N143

Square Footage: 1,402

Design by
Homes For Living, Inc.

■ Making the most of a smaller floor plan, this one-story has great living areas and indoor/outdoor relationships to boot. The covered, railed porch is quaint and adds a measure of protection from inclement weather. It leads to the skylit great room which also features a corner fireplace and sliding glass doors to the rear terrace. The attached dining room also offers terrace access and connects to the L-shaped kitchen and its attendant dinette. Another terrace is located just beyond the dinette for casual outdoor dining. The master suite is amazingly well appointed for one in a home of this size. It contains two closets (one a walk-in), a compartmented toilet, separate shower and tub and two sinks. Family bedrooms share the use of a full hall bath. Please specify basement or slab foundation when ordering.

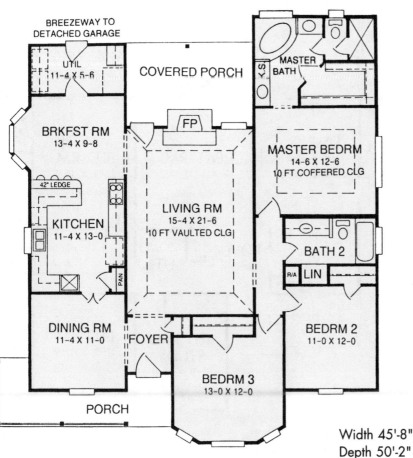

BREEZEWAY TO
DETACHED GARAGE

UTIL
11-4 X 5-6

COVERED PORCH

MASTER
BATH

BRKFST RM
13-4 X 9-8

FP

MASTER BEDRM
14-6 X 12-6
10 FT COFFERED CLG

42" LEDGE

KITCHEN
11-4 X 13-0

LIVING RM
15-4 X 21-6
10 FT VAULTED CLG

BATH 2

PAN

R/A   LIN

DINING RM
11-4 X 11-0

FOYER

BEDRM 2
11-0 X 12-0

BEDRM 3
13-0 X 12-0

PORCH

Design HPTM03018

Square Footage: 1,772

■ A Folk Victorian flair gives this home
its curb appeal. Inside, a large living
room boasts a centerpiece fireplace and
a coffered ceiling. The kitchen has a 42-
inch-high breakfast bar and a pantry.
The master suite includes a ten-foot coffered ceiling and a luxury bath with a
corner whirlpool tub, separate shower,
His and Hers vanities and a roomy
walk-in closet. Two additional bedrooms and a bath are nearby. A two-car
garage plan is included with this design
and can be connected to the home with
a breezeway. Please specify crawlspace
or slab foundation when ordering.

Design by
©Larry E. Belk Designs

Width 45'-8"
Depth 50'-2"

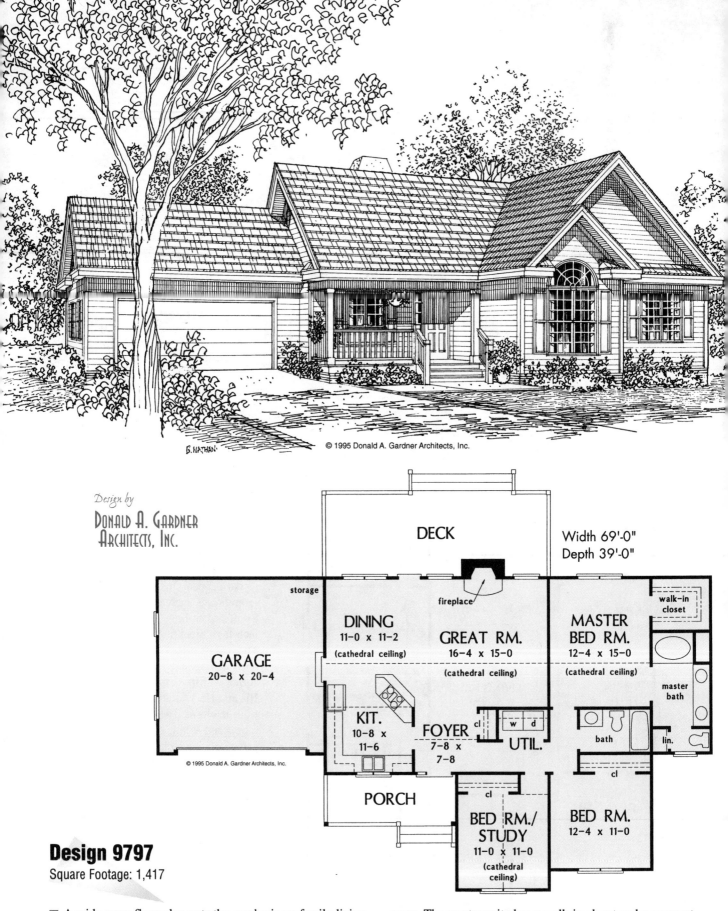

Design by
Donald A. Gardner
Architects, Inc.

© 1995 Donald A. Gardner Architects, Inc.

DECK

Width 69'-0"
Depth 39'-0"

storage

fireplace

walk-in
closet

GARAGE
20-8 x 20-4

DINING
11-0 x 11-2
(cathedral ceiling)

GREAT RM.
16-4 x 15-0
(cathedral ceiling)

MASTER
BED RM.
12-4 x 15-0
(cathedral ceiling)

master
bath

KIT.
10-8 x
11-6

FOYER
7-8 x
7-8

cl
w d
UTIL.

bath

lin.

© 1995 Donald A. Gardner Architects, Inc.

PORCH

cl

cl

BED RM./
STUDY
11-0 x 11-0
(cathedral
ceiling)

BED RM.
12-4 x 11-0

B. NATHAN

© 1995 Donald A. Gardner Architects, Inc.

Design 9797
Square Footage: 1,417

■ A wide-open floor plan puts the emphasis on family living in this modest, single-story home. A cathedral ceiling stretches the length of the plan, stylishly topping the dining room, great room and master bedroom. Cooks will enjoy working in the presentation kitchen that's open to the dining room and great room. The master suite has a walk-in closet and a compartmented bath with a garden tub and twin vanities. One of the two family bedrooms has a cathedral ceiling as well, making it an optional study. A full hall bath and a convenient hallway laundry center complete this plan.

Width 62'-0"
Depth 61'-6"

BEDROOM NO. 3
11'-6" X 11'-0"

BATH

BEDROOM NO. 2
11'-4" X 11'-0"

SUN ROOM
12'-0" X 13'-8"

PORCH

MASTER
BATH

W.I.C.

MASTER BEDROOM
13'-4" X 15'-6"

PORCH

BREAKFAST
10'-0" X 9'-0"

FAMILY ROOM
18'-0" X 14'-0"

LAUNDRY

KITCHEN
12'-0" X 13'-2"

BATH

STORAGE

DN

TWO CAR GARAGE
20'-4" X 19'-8"

DINING ROOM
11'-4" X 11'-4"

FOYER
6'-8" X 11'-10"

DEN/GUEST
BEDROOM
11'-4" X 14'-0"

PORCH

Design HPTM03019

Square Footage: 2,170

■ This classic cottage features a stone
and wooden exterior with an arch-
detailed porch. From a hallway off the
foyer, double doors open to the den with
a box-bay window and a fireplace. A
full bath is situated next to the den,
allowing for an optional guest room.
The family room is centrally located,
just beyond the foyer. Its hearth is
framed by windows overlooking the
porch at the rear of the home. A breakfast area complements the attractive and
efficiently designed kitchen. The master
bedroom includes a private bath with a
large walk-in closet, double vanities, a
corner tub and separate shower. Two
secondary bedrooms with large closets
share a full bath featuring double vanities. This home is designed with a walkout basement foundation.

Design by
©Stephen Fuller, Inc.

Quote One®

Cost to build? See page 434
to order complete cost estimate
to build this house in your area!

141

© 1994 Donald A. Gardner Architects, Inc.

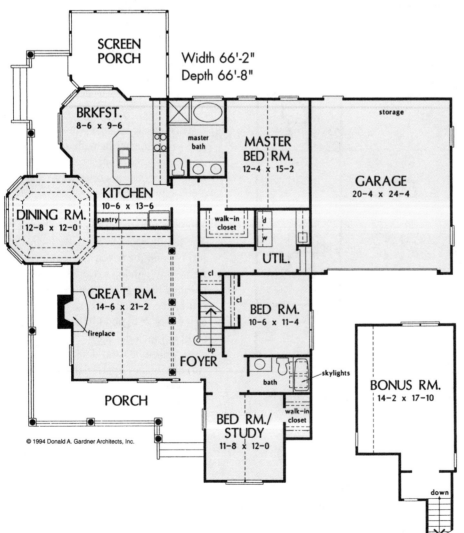

SCREEN PORCH

Width 66'-2"
Depth 66'-8"

BRKFST.
8-6 x 9-6

master bath

MASTER BED RM.
12-4 x 15-2

storage

KITCHEN
10-6 x 13-6

GARAGE
20-4 x 24-4

DINING RM.
12-8 x 12-0

pantry

walk-in closet

d w

UTIL.

GREAT RM.
14-6 x 21-2

fireplace

cl

cl

BED RM.
10-6 x 11-4

FOYER

up

bath

skylights

BONUS RM.
14-2 x 17-10

PORCH

© 1994 Donald A. Gardner Architects, Inc.

BED RM./ STUDY
11-8 x 12-0

walk-in closet

down

Design 7601

Square Footage: 1,787
Bonus Room: 326 square feet

■ A neighborly porch as friendly as a handshake wraps around this charming country home, warmly greeting family and friends alike. Inside, cathedral ceilings promote a feeling of spaciousness. To the left of the foyer, the great room is enhanced with a fireplace and built-in bookshelves. A uniquely shaped formal dining room separates the kitchen and breakfast area. Outdoor pursuits—rain or shine—will be enjoyed from the screen porch. The master suite is located at the rear of the plan for privacy and features a walk-in closet and a luxurious bath. Two additional bedrooms, one with a walk-in closet, share a skylit bath. A second-floor bonus room is available to develop later as a study, home office or play area.

Design by
DONALD A. GARDNER
ARCHITECTS, INC.

142

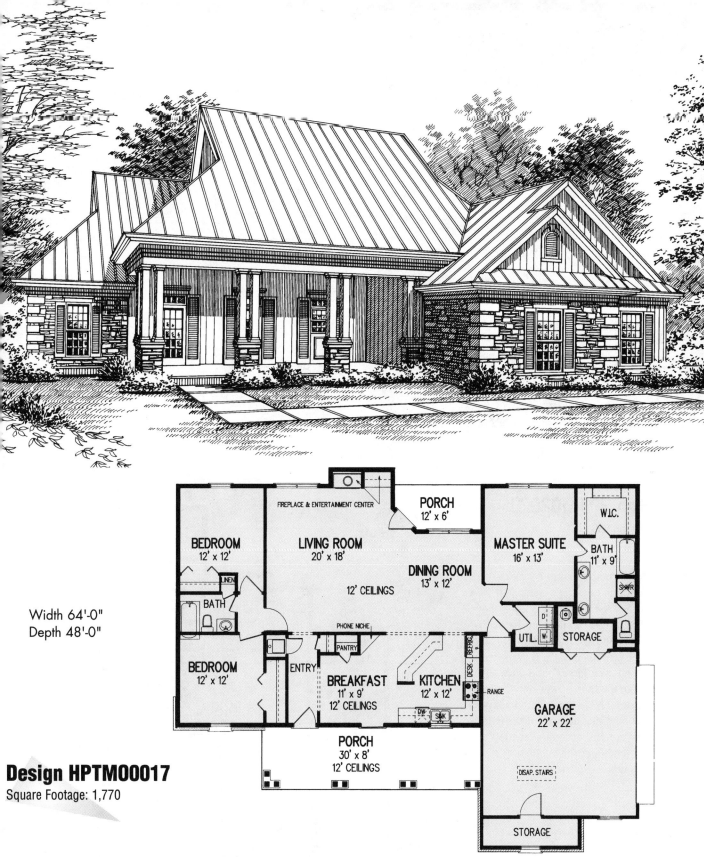

Width 64'-0"
Depth 48'-0"

Design HPTM00017
Square Footage: 1,770

Using wood and stone for the exterior facade, this traditional Prairie-style home boasts a large receiving porch and free-flowing interior spaces. The spacious living room is open to the adjacent dining room and has a built-in fireplace and entertainment center. Two secondary bedrooms share a full bath along the left of the plan, while the master suite is isolated to the right of the dining room and features a bath with a separate tub and shower and a liberal-size walk-in closet. Two storage closets are available in the garage to protect all the family treasures. Please specify crawlspace or slab foundation when ordering.

Design by
©Breland & Farmer Designers, Inc.

Design HPTM03020

Square Footage: 1,673

■ Quaint country charm pervades the facade of this one-story home. The living room at the heart of the floor plan features a fireplace and a ten-foot ceiling. The island kitchen and dining area are nearby. A covered patio to the back leads to an even larger patio area, accessible from the living room and the master bedroom. Note the coffered ceiling and fine bath that are part of the master suite. Twin family rooms in the left wing of the home share a bath that includes double sinks.

Design by
©Fillmore Design Group

Width 48'-0"
Depth 63'-1"

Design HPTM00018

Square Footage: 1,772

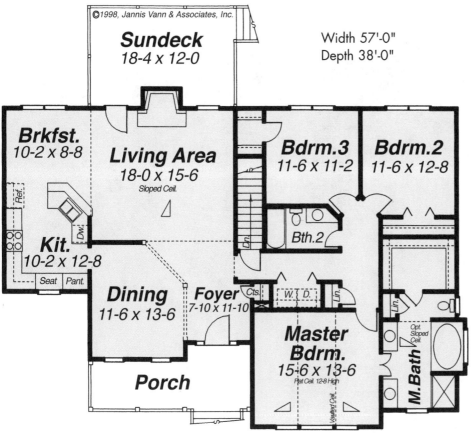

©1998, Jannis Vann & Associates, Inc.

Sundeck
18-4 x 12-0

Width 57'-0"
Depth 38'-0"

Brkfst.
10-2 x 8-8

Living Area
18-0 x 15-6
Sloped Ceil.

Bdrm.3
11-6 x 11-2

Bdrm.2
11-6 x 12-8

Ref.

Kit.
10-2 x 12-8

Bth.2

Seat | Pant.

Dining
11-6 x 13-6

Foyer
7-10 x 11-10

Cts.

W. D.

Lin.

Lin.

Porch

Master Bdrm.
15-6 x 13-6
Flat Ceil. 12-8 High

Opt.
Sloped
Ceil.

M.Bath

Vaulted Ceil.

■ A beautiful Palladian window and the arched porch add an elegant style to this charming one-story home. Inside, the foyer opens directly to the formal dining room and living area. A fireplace, framed by a window and a door, is the focus of the living room. Nearby, the breakfast area joins the kitchen with a serving bar. The master bedroom features the Palladian window of the front exterior, and a well-appointed bath includes a large walk-in closet, oversized soaking tub, separate shower and twin vanity sinks. Two family bedrooms share a full bath and complete this simple design.

Design HPTM03021

Square Footage: 1,822

■ A quaint mix of materials and an enticing floor plan lend this home modern interest with traditional perks. Inside, the foyer is flanked by a dining room and a study/office. The vaulted living room is warmed by a fireplace and connects to the kitchen/nook area. The secluded master suite includes a private bath and walk-in closet. Family bedrooms located on the opposite side of the home share a hall bath that accesses the rear porch. Grilling and seasonal activities will be enjoyed on the porch.

Design by
© THE SATER DESIGN COLLECTION

Width 58'-0"
Depth 66'-8"

Bedroom 1
11'-10" x 11'-4"
9'-0" Flat Clg.

Bath 2

Porch
39'-6" x 10'-0"
9'-0" Flat Clg.

Nook
9'-4" x 9'-4"
9'-0" Flat Clg.

built-ins

fireplace

Kit.
9'-4" x
8'-6"
9' Clg.

Master Suite
13'-2" x 15'-2"
Tray Clg.

Bedroom 2
11'-10" x 10'-8"
9'-0" Flat Clg.

Living Room
16'-0" x 14'-8"
Vaulted Clg.

WIC

WIC

Study/Office
12'-6" x 11'-0"
Tray Ceiling

Foyer

Dining
11'-8" x 10'-4"
Vaulted Clg.

Utility
6'-10" x
10'-10"

WIC

M. Bath

bench
Dn.

Porch
31'-8" x 7'-0"

2 Car Garage
20'-4' x 23'-10"

146

Design HPTM00019

Square Footage: 1,925

■ This three-bedroom farmhouse offers classic style and an up-to-date floor plan. The slope-ceilinged living room provides a fireplace and French-door access to a covered rear porch. The kitchen features a large pantry and is located between the casual eating area and the formal dining room. Two family bedrooms, one with built-in bookshelves and a walk-in closet, share a full bath to the left of the living room. To the right, the master suite includes a dressing room and a full bath with a walk-in closet. Please specify crawlspace or slab foundation when ordering.

Design by
©Breland & Farmer Designers, Inc.

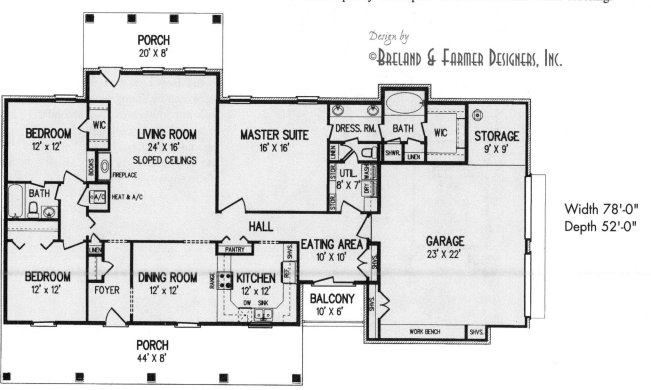

PORCH
20' X 8'

BEDROOM
12' X 12'

WIC

LIVING ROOM
24' X 16'
SLOPED CEILINGS

BOOKS

FIREPLACE

HEAT & A/C

A/C

MASTER SUITE
16' X 16'

DRESS. RM.

BATH

WIC

STORAGE
9' X 9'

LINEN

STOR.

UTIL.
8' X 7'

SHWR.

LINEN

BATH

LINEN

BEDROOM
12' X 12'

LINEN

FOYER

DINING ROOM
12' X 12'

PANTRY

RANGE

KITCHEN
12' X 12'

DW   SINK

HALL

SHVS.

EATING AREA
10' X 10'

BALCONY
10' X 6'

SHVS.

GARAGE
23' X 22'

WORK BENCH   SHVS.

PORCH
44' X 8'

Width 78'-0"
Depth 52'-0"

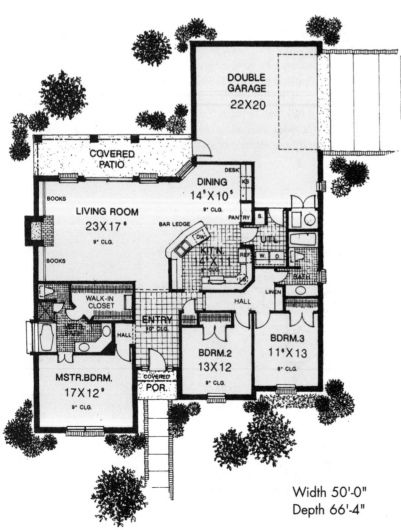

DOUBLE GARAGE
22X20

COVERED PATIO

DINING
14⁵X10⁵
9" CLG.

DESK

KS

PANTRY

S.

LIVING ROOM
23X17⁶
9" CLG.

BOOKS

BOOKS

BAR LEDGE

KIT'N
14'X11
9" CLG.

DW

REF

UTIL

W. D.

BATH

LINEN

WALK-IN CLOSET

HALL

HALL

ENTRY
10' CLG.

MSTR.BDRM.
17X12⁹
9" CLG.

COVERED POR.

BDRM.2
13X12
9" CLG.

BDRM.3
11⁶X13
8" CLG.

Width 50'-0"
Depth 66'-4"

Design HPTM03022

Square Footage: 1,862

■ Stone and brick give this home a solid look and make it an attractive addition to any neighborhood. The tiled entry opens to joined living and dining rooms. Both areas can enjoy the fire-place, and the living room features built-in bookshelves. Two secondary bedrooms share a full hall bath while the master suite, with a walk-in closet and dual vanities, is off to the left side of the home.

Design by
©FILLMORE DESIGN GROUP

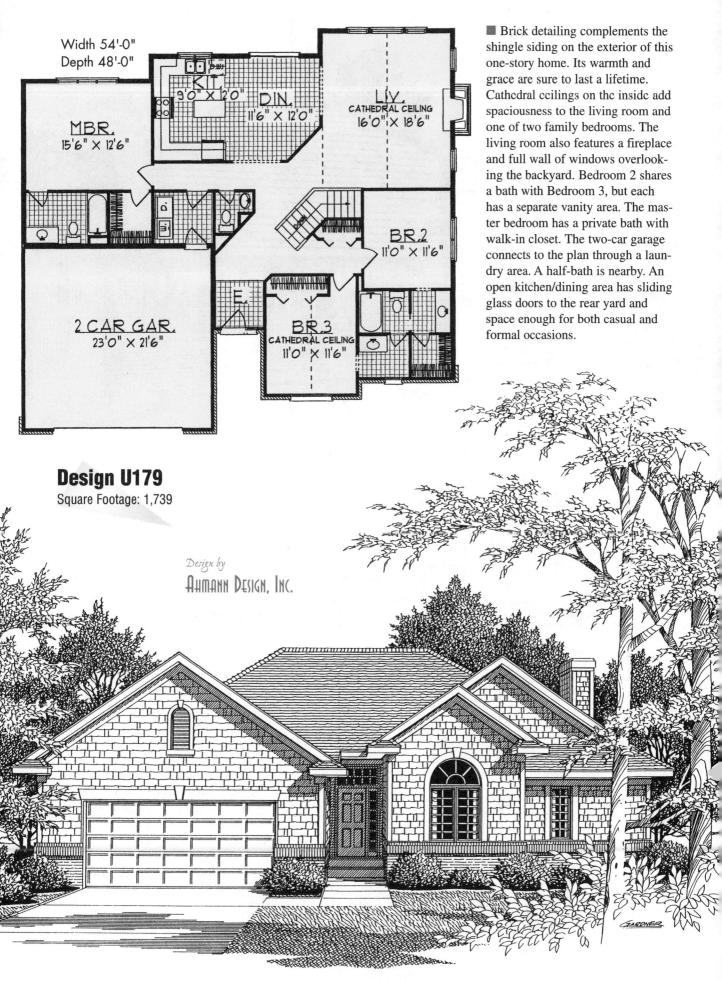

Width 54'-0"
Depth 48'-0"

MBR.
15'6" X 12'6"

KIT.
9'0" X 12'0"

DIN.
11'6" X 12'0"

LIV.
CATHEDRAL CEILING
16'0" X 18'6"

BR.2
11'0" X 11'6"

2 CAR GAR.
23'0" X 21'6"

BR.3
CATHEDRAL CEILING
11'0" X 11'6"

Design U179

Square Footage: 1,739

Design by
Ahmann Design, Inc.

■ Brick detailing complements the shingle siding on the exterior of this one-story home. Its warmth and grace are sure to last a lifetime. Cathedral ceilings on the inside add spaciousness to the living room and one of two family bedrooms. The living room also features a fireplace and full wall of windows overlooking the backyard. Bedroom 2 shares a bath with Bedroom 3, but each has a separate vanity area. The master bedroom has a private bath with walk-in closet. The two-car garage connects to the plan through a laundry area. A half-bath is nearby. An open kitchen/dining area has sliding glass doors to the rear yard and space enough for both casual and formal occasions.

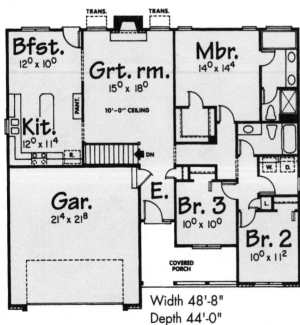

Width 48'-8"
Depth 44'-0"

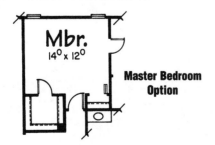

Master Bedroom Option

Design by
DESIGN BASICS, INC.

Design 7373

Square Footage: 1,453

■ With two gables, a hip roof and a covered front porch, this petite three bedroom home is sure to please. A spacious great room features a warming fireplace flanked by transom windows. In the kitchen, an island counter is available for added space to prepare meals. A large breakfast area is adjacent to this room. Two secondary bedrooms share a full bath as well as easy access to the laundry room. The master bedroom offers a walk-in closet and a private bath. Note the option for a second closet in the bedroom.

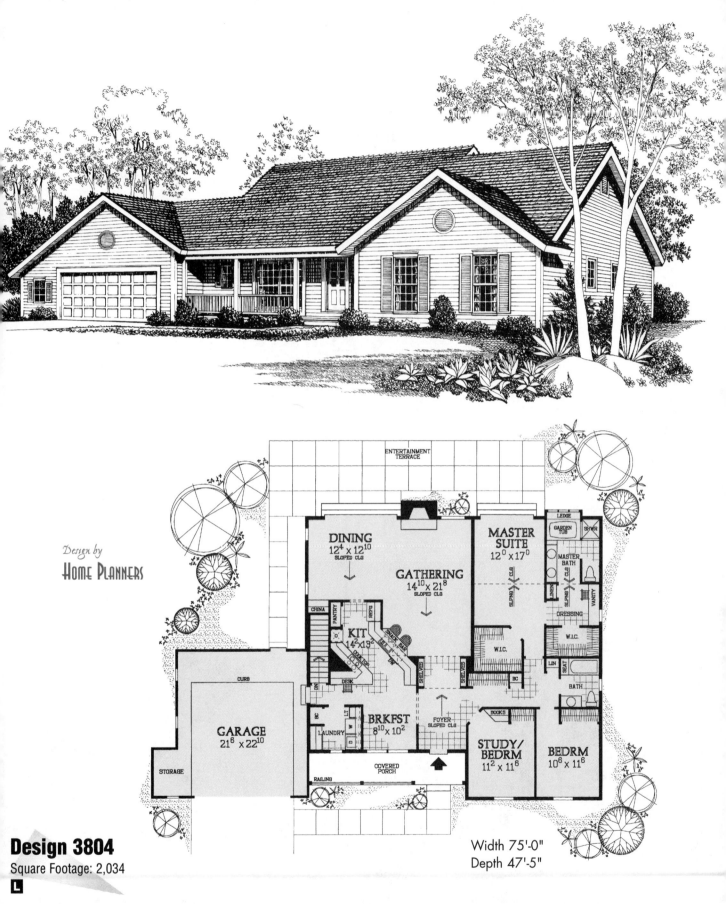

Design 3804

Square Footage: 2,034

L

■ Horizontal siding, multi-pane windows and a simple balustrade lend a Prairies 'N' Plains flavor to this traditional, three bedroom home. A roomy foyer with a sloped ceiling leads through a tiled vestibule with built-in shelves to the spacious gathering room, complete with a warming fireplace. An angled kitchen with a snack bar easily serves the formal dining room, which leads outdoors to the rear entertainment terrace. The luxurious master suite has its own door to the terrace as well as a fabulous private bath with a windowed whirlpool tub. Two additional bedrooms share a full bath and a hall that offers more wardrobe space.

Width 75'-0"
Depth 47'-5"

A porch with column detailing covers the entry to this single-story American classic. Inside, the foyer opens to the living room with a wall of windows and French doors that lead outside. A splendid colonnade defines the banquet-sized dining room. To the right, the spacious kitchen with work island opens to a sunlit breakfast area and a keeping room featuring a warming hearth and doors to the rear deck. A hallway just off the foyer leads to the double doors of the master suite. Inside, the special shape of the suite and mirrored ceiling detail make this room unique. The bath accommodates every need with His and Hers vanities, a garden tub and walk-in closet. Two additional bedrooms with spacious closets, common bath with dual vanities, and individual tub and water closet complete the main level. This home is designed with a basement foundation.

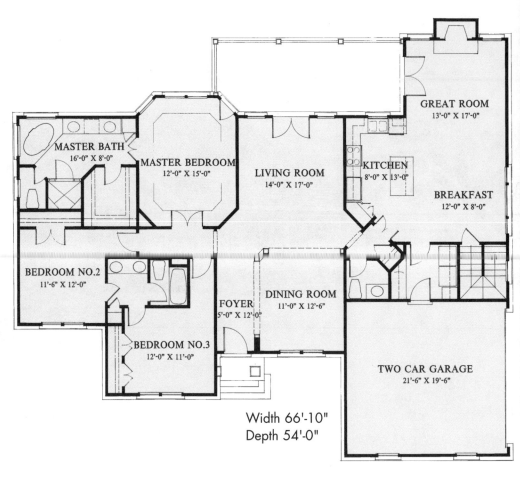

MASTER BATH
16'-0" X 8'-0"

MASTER BEDROOM
12'-0" X 15'-0"

LIVING ROOM
14'-0" X 17'-0"

GREAT ROOM
13'-0" X 17'-0"

KITCHEN
8'-0" X 13'-0"

BREAKFAST
12'-0" X 8'-0"

BEDROOM NO.2
11'-6" X 12'-0"

BEDROOM NO.3
12'-0" X 11'-0"

FOYER
5'-0" X 12'-0"

DINING ROOM
11'-0" X 12'-6"

TWO CAR GARAGE
21'-6" X 19'-6"

Width 66'-10"
Depth 54'-0"

Design T072
Square Footage: 2,077

Design by
DESIGN TRADITIONS

© Design Traditions

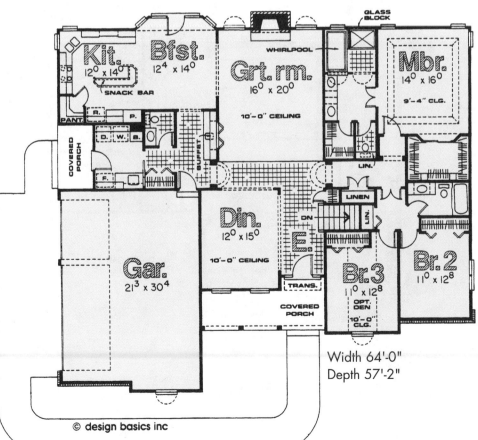

Kit.
12⁰ x 14⁰

Bfst.
12⁴ x 14⁰

SNACK BAR

PANT.

COVERED PORCH

R.
P.
D.
W.
B.
F.

Grt. rm.
16⁰ x 20⁰

10'-0" CEILING

BUFFET

WHIRLPOOL

GLASS BLOCK

Mbr.
14⁰ x 16⁰

9'-4" CLG.

LIN.

Gar.
21³ x 30⁴

Din.
12⁰ x 15⁰

10'-0" CEILING

TRANS.

COVERED PORCH

DN
E.

LINEN

LIN.

Br.3
11⁰ x 12⁸

OPT. DEN

10'-0" CLG.

Br.2
11⁰ x 12⁸

Width 64'-0"
Depth 57'-2"

Design 7332

Square Footage: 2,311

■ Interesting details on the front porch add to the appeal of this ranch home. The great room is highlighted by a pass-through wet bar/buffet and sits just across the hall from the formal dining room. A well-planned kitchen features a walk-in pantry and L-shaped island snack bar. The bedrooms are found in a cluster to the right of the home; a master suite, and two family bedrooms sharing a full bath. The master suite has a shower with glass-block detailing, a whirlpool tub and dual vanities. A three-car garage attaches to the main house via a service entrance.

Design by
Design Basics, Inc.

Design HPTM03023

Square Footage: 2,260

■ A charming facade with a European flavor graces the exterior of this county home that offers a three-car garage. Inside, the entry leads to the gallery that opens to the spacious living room with its cathedral ceiling, fireplace, built-ins and wonderful window wall looking out to the covered patio. The angled kitchen sits to the right with an adjoining breakfast nook. The family bedrooms reside on the far right sharing a full bath while the lavish master suite rests on the far left. Finishing out the floor plan are the study and the formal dining room which flank the entry.

Design by
© FILLMORE DESIGN GROUP

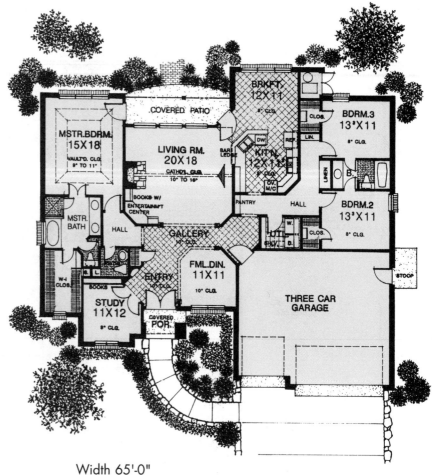

Width 65'-0"
Depth 57'-10"

154

Design HPTM03024
Square Footage: 2,570

■ A European country flair is evident in this rustic one-story home. The three-car garage allows room for a golf cart, making this home an ideal choice for a golf course lot. Inside, the entry opens to the gallery that separates the spacious living room from the formal dining room. The bedrooms are clustered creatively on the left with the master suite in the rear with its private bath and patio area. On the right, the island kitchen and breakfast nook lead to the family room—perfect for more casual entertaining with a cathedral ceiling, centered fireplace and access to the second covered patio and lanai. A fourth bedroom rests at the end of a hallway on the right, creating seclusion for overnight guests.

Design by
©FILLMORE DESIGN GROUP

Width 70'-0"
Depth 64'-10"

Design HPTM00020

Square Footage: 2,053

■ Shutters, multi-pane glass windows
and cross-hatched railing on the front
porch make this a beautiful country
cottage. To the left of the foyer is a
roomy great room and a warming fireplace, framed by windows. To the right
of the foyer, two family bedrooms feature walk-in closets and share a fully
appointed bath. The efficient kitchen
centers around a long island workstation and opens to the large dining/sit-
ting room. The rear porch adds living
space to view the outdoors. French
doors, a fireplace and columns complete this three-bedroom design. Please
specify basement, crawlspace or slab
foundation when ordering.

Design by
©Larry James & Associates, Inc.

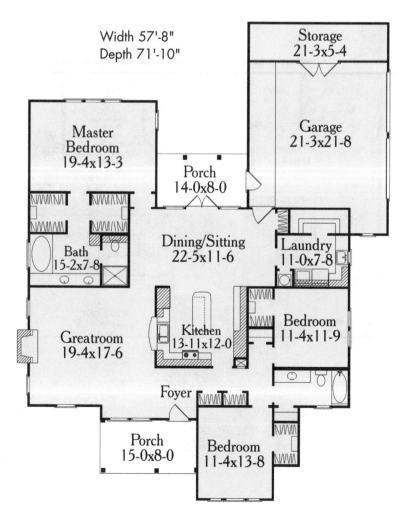

Width 57'-8"
Depth 71'-10"

Storage
21-3x5-4

Garage
21-3x21-8

Master
Bedroom
19-4x13-3

Porch
14-0x8-0

Dining/Sitting
22-5x11-6

Laundry
11-0x7-8

Bath
15-2x7-8

Greatroom
19-4x17-6

Kitchen
13-11x12-0

Bedroom
11-4x11-9

Foyer

Porch
15-0x8-0

Bedroom
11-4x13-8

156

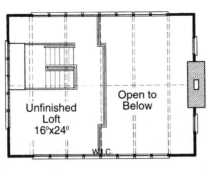

Unfinished Loft
$16^0 \times 24^0$

Open to Below

W.I.C.

Design T183

Square Footage: 2,019
Loft: 384 square feet

■ This design takes inspiration from the casual fishing cabins of the Pacific Northwest and interprets it for modern livability. It offers three options for a main entrance. One door opens onto a mud porch, where a small hall leads to a galley kitchen and the vaulted great room. Two French doors on the side porch open into a dining room with bay-window seating. Another porch entrance opens directly into the great room. The great room is centered around a massive stone fireplace and is accented with a beautiful wall of windows. The secluded master bedroom features a master bath with a claw-foot tub and twin pedestal sinks, as well as a separate shower and walk-in closet. Two more bedrooms share a spacious bath. Ideal for a lounge or extra sleeping space, an unfinished loft looks over the great room.

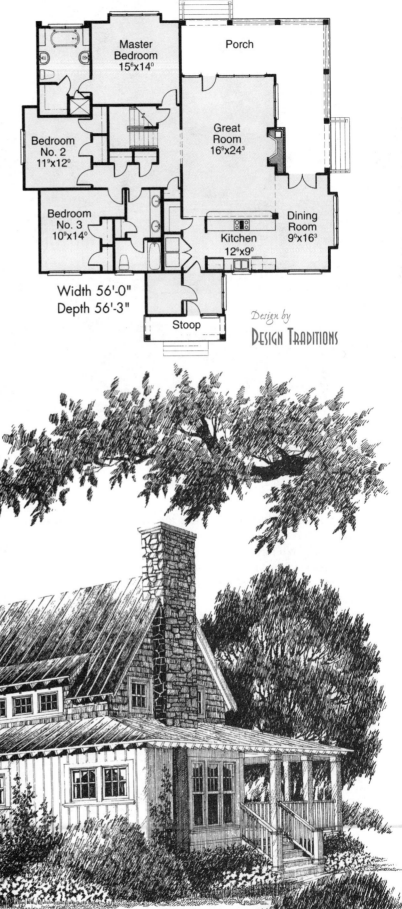

Master Bedroom
$15^6 \times 14^0$

Porch

Bedroom No. 2
$11^9 \times 12^0$

Great Room
$16^9 \times 24^3$

Bedroom No. 3
$10^9 \times 14^0$

Kitchen
$12^6 \times 9^0$

Dining Room
$9^0 \times 16^3$

Width 56'-0"
Depth 56'-3"

Stoop

Design by Design Traditions

© Design Traditions

Design HPTM03025

Square Footage: 2,745

■ A gentle European charm flavors the facade of this ultra-modern home. The foyer opens to a formal dining room, which leads to the kitchen through privacy doors. Here, a center cooktop island complements wrapping counter space, a walk-in pantry and a snack counter. Casual living space shares a through-fireplace with the formal living room and provides its own access to the rear porch. Clustered sleeping quarters include a well-appointed master suite, two family bedrooms and an additional bedroom which could double as a study. Please specify basement, crawlspace or slab foundation when ordering.

Design by
©Larry E. Belk Designs

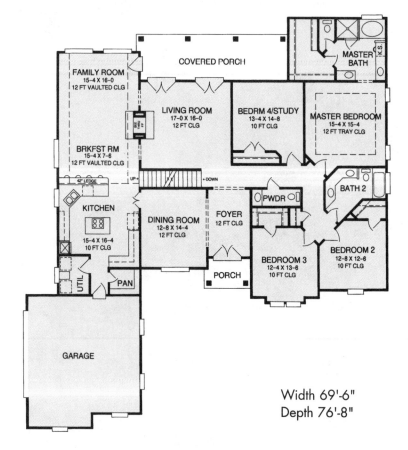

Width 69'-6"
Depth 76'-8"

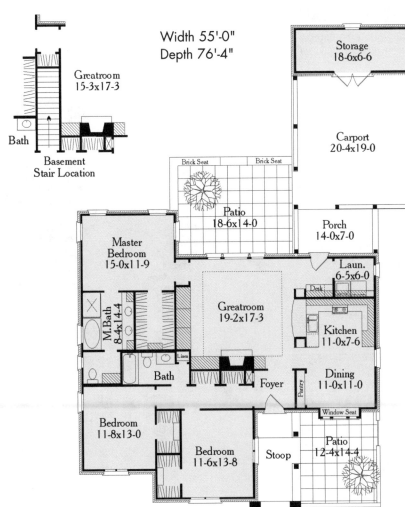

Width 55'-0"
Depth 76'-4"

Greatroom
15-3x17-3

Bath

Basement
Stair Location

Storage
18-6x6-6

Carport
20-4x19-0

Brick Seat   Brick Seat

Patio
18-6x14-0

Porch
14-0x7-0

Master
Bedroom
15-0x11-9

M.Bath
8-4x14-4

Greatroom
19-2x17-3

Laun.
6-5x6-0

Desk

Kitchen
11-0x7-6

Bath

Linen

Foyer

Pantry

Dining
11-0x11-0

Window Seat

Bedroom
11-8x13-0

Bedroom
11-6x13-8

Stoop

Patio
12-4x14-4

Design HPTM00021

Square Footage: 1,702

■ Arched lintels, shutters and a welcoming covered entryway lend this three-bedroom home country charm. Inside, the foyer leads directly to the great room with a fireplace and built-ins along two walls. Nearby, the kitchen joins the dining area, which contains a built-in pantry and window seat. Keeping household records organized will be easy with the built-in desk by the laundry room. The sleeping quarters all reside on the left of this design. The master suite includes a lavish bath with a garden tub, separate shower, dual vanity sinks and compartmented toilet. Two secondary bedrooms share a bath. Homeowners will sigh with relief when they see the large storage off the carport. Please specify basement, crawlspace or slab foundation when ordering.

Design by
©Larry James & Associates, Inc.

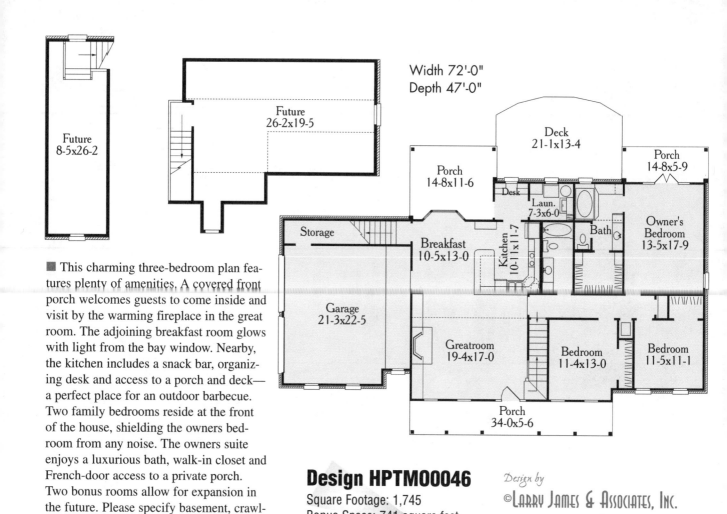

Future
8-5x26-2

Future
26-2x19-5

Width 72'-0"
Depth 47'-0"

Deck
21-1x13-4

Porch
14-8x11-6

Porch
14-8x5-9

Desk

Laun.
7-3x6-0

Bath

Owner's
Bedroom
13-5x17-9

Storage

Breakfast
10-5x13-0

Kitchen
10-11x11-7

Garage
21-3x22-5

Greatroom
19-4x17-0

Bedroom
11-4x13-0

Bedroom
11-5x11-1

Porch
34-0x5-6

■ This charming three-bedroom plan features plenty of amenities. A covered front porch welcomes guests to come inside and visit by the warming fireplace in the great room. The adjoining breakfast room glows with light from the bay window. Nearby, the kitchen includes a snack bar, organizing desk and access to a porch and deck—a perfect place for an outdoor barbecue. Two family bedrooms reside at the front of the house, shielding the owners bedroom from any noise. The owners suite enjoys a luxurious bath, walk-in closet and French-door access to a private porch. Two bonus rooms allow for expansion in the future. Please specify basement, crawlspace or slab foundation when ordering.

Design HPTM00046

Square Footage: 1,745
Bonus Space: 741 square feet

Design by
©Larry James & Associates, Inc.

Design 9686

Square Footage: 1,980

■ Providing the utmost in flexible outdoor living, this home is graced with a covered front porch and generous rear deck. On the interior is a floor plan that is a pleasure to live in. The great room has a fireplace, cathedral ceiling and sliding glass doors with an arched window above to admit natural light. Impressive round columns promote a sense of elegance in the dining room. The master suite boasts a large master bedroom with two walk-in closets and a well-organized master bath with double-bowl vanity and a whirlpool tub. Two more bedrooms are located at the opposite end of the house for privacy. The garage is connected to the house with a breezeway.

Width 63'-10"
Depth 73'-4"

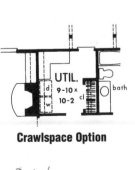

Crawlspace Option

Design by
Donald A. Gardner
Architects, Inc.

Design HPTM00022

Square Footage: 2,465

■ This home boasts a well-laid-out design that promotes comfort and flow. The great room offers two sets of French doors to the rear porch, a fireplace and a spacious layout perfect for entertaining. The owners suite delights in a room-size sitting area, His and Her walk-in closets and vanities, compartmented toilet, and separate tub and shower. Please specify basement, crawlspace or slab foundation when ordering

Design by
©Larry James & Associates, Inc.

Width 65'-1"
Depth 73'-7"

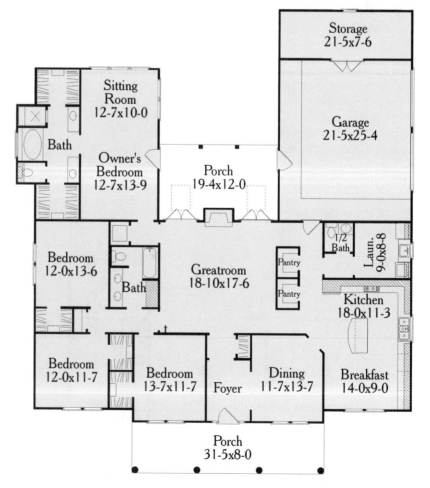

Storage
21-5x7-6

Garage
21-5x25-4

Sitting
Room
12-7x10-0

Bath

Owner's
Bedroom
12-7x13-9

Porch
19-4x12-0

1/2
Bath

Laun.
9-0x8-8

Bedroom
12-0x13-6

Bath

Greatroom
18-10x17-6

Pantry

Pantry

Kitchen
18-0x11-3

Bedroom
12-0x11-7

Bedroom
13-7x11-7

Foyer

Dining
11-7x13-7

Breakfast
14-0x9-0

Porch
31-5x8-0

Design 7616

Square Footage: 2,450
Bonus Room: 423 square feet

■ A handsome display of columns frames the porch of this gracious Southern home. The foyer opens to the dining room and to a study, which could also be an additional bedroom. The open living room and family room are joined under a dramatic cathedral ceiling, divided with a showpiece fireplace that opens to both rooms. The efficient corner kitchen has a handy breakfast nook that opens to a morning porch and a work island with a cooktop and curved snack bar. The master suite has a stylish tray ceiling, twin walk-in closets and a compartmented bath with an elegant bumped-out tub.

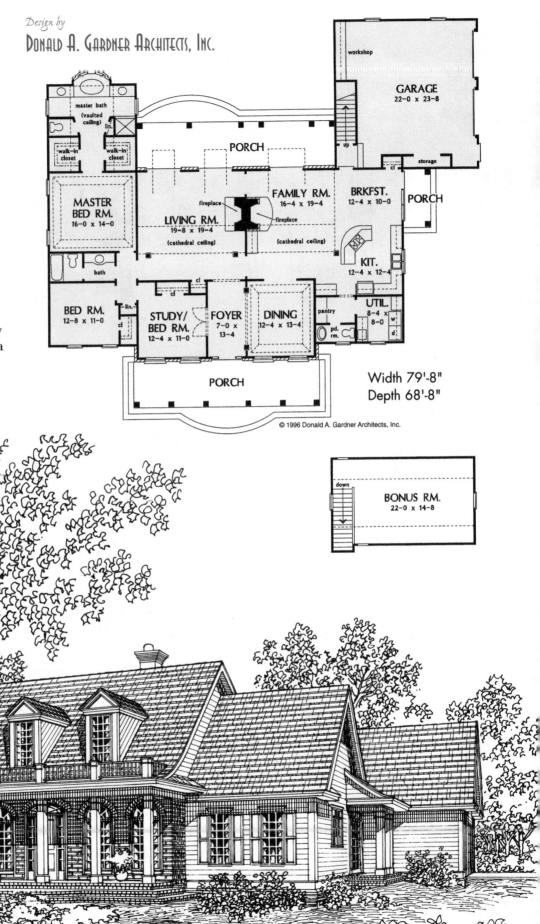

Design by
DONALD A. GARDNER ARCHITECTS, INC.

Width 79'-8"
Depth 68'-8"

© 1996 Donald A. Gardner Architects, Inc.

163

Design B585

Square Footage: 2,278

■ This three-bedroom, one-level plan offers an exciting exterior of brick and stone coupled with a floor plan designed to offer the comfort of informal living with the amenities to create an artful showplace. The formal dining room adjacent to the foyer is defined with columns and a dropped soffit. Columns repeat at the entrance to the great room, where a dramatic fireplace decorates one wall and dual windows offer a view to the rear yard. A grand opening between the breakfast room and kitchen adds to the spacious feeling of the defined living space. An oversized island with a sink shapes the kitchen and separates it from the roomy breakfast area. Split stairs lead to a lower level that can be accessed for additional square footage. The master bedroom suite with vaulted ceiling and large bath and walk-in closet becomes a quiet retreat with two secondary bedrooms located to the front of the house.

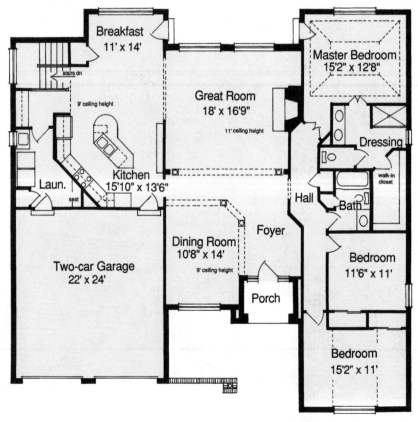

Width 59'-0"
Depth 57'-0"

Design by
©Studer Residential Designs, Inc.

164

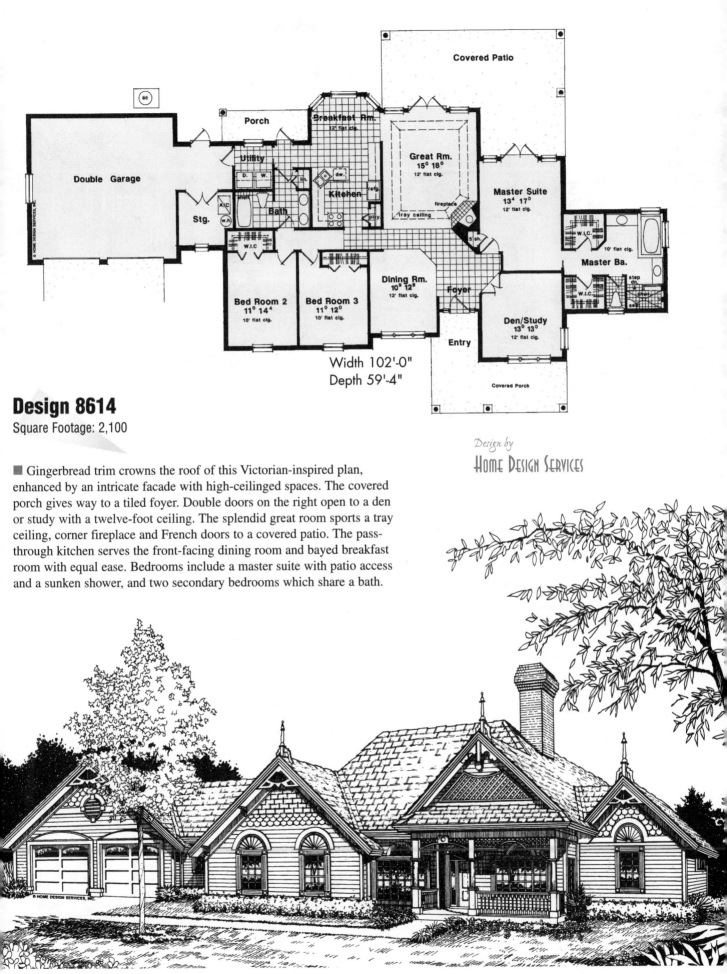

Covered Patio

Porch

Breakfast Rm.
12' flat clg.

Great Rm.
15⁰ 18⁰
12' flat clg.

Utility

D. | W.

Double Garage

Master Suite
13⁴ 17⁰
12' flat clg.

Kitchen

Bath

Stg.

W.I.C

W.I.C.

Master Ba.
10' flat clg.

tray ceiling

fireplace

W.I.C.

Bed Room 2
11⁰ 14⁴
10' flat clg.

Bed Room 3
11⁰ 12⁰
10' flat clg.

Dining Rm.
10⁹ 12⁸
12' flat clg.

Foyer

Den/Study
13⁰ 13⁰
12' flat clg.

Entry

Width 102'-0"
Depth 59'-4"

Covered Porch

Design 8614
Square Footage: 2,100

■ Gingerbread trim crowns the roof of this Victorian-inspired plan, enhanced by an intricate facade with high-ceilinged spaces. The covered porch gives way to a tiled foyer. Double doors on the right open to a den or study with a twelve-foot ceiling. The splendid great room sports a tray ceiling, corner fireplace and French doors to a covered patio. The pass-through kitchen serves the front-facing dining room and bayed breakfast room with equal ease. Bedrooms include a master suite with patio access and a sunken shower, and two secondary bedrooms which share a bath.

Design by
HOME DESIGN SERVICES

■ Simply country describes this front-porch, split-bedroom drive-under design. The living area is highlighted by a modified cathedral ceiling framing the mantle of the fire-place at the a opposite side of the entry to this room. A spacious breakfast room with bay window opens to the kitchen, which features a peninsula counter to separate the areas and even has room for a desk and pantry. Bay windows give additional light and space to the master bedroom and the front bedroom on the opposite side of the house. Another bay window gives extra space and light to the breakfast room. The master bath features a dramatic corner garden tub flanked by a glassed shower and double vanity. The secondary bedrooms share a compartmented hall bath and are conveniently near the laundry closet.

Design HPTM00023
Square Footage: 1,778

Design by
© Jannis Vann & Associates, Inc.

Width 62'-0"
Depth 48'-0"

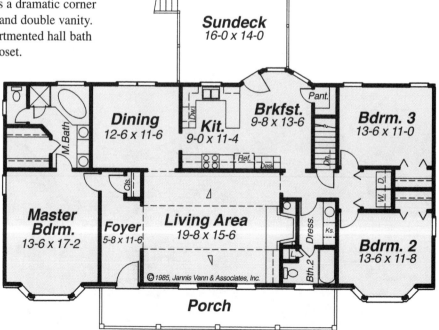

Sundeck
16-0 x 14-0

M. Bath

Dining
12-6 x 11-6

Kit.
9-0 x 11-4

Brkfst.
9-8 x 13-6

Pant.

Bdrm. 3
13-6 x 11-0

Ref.

Desk

W. D.

Master Bdrm.
13-6 x 17-2

Foyer
5-8 x 11-6

Living Area
19-8 x 15-6

Dress.

Ks.

Bth.2

Bdrm. 2
13-6 x 11-8

© 1985, Jannis Vann & Associates, Inc.

Porch

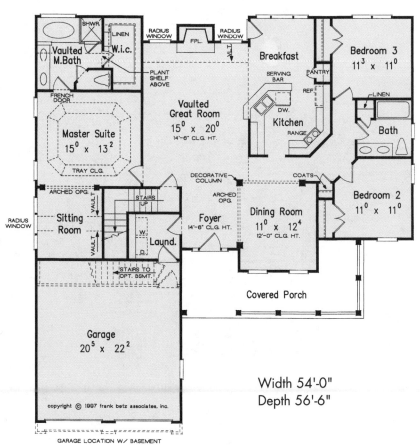

Vaulted M.Bath
SHWR.
LINEN
W.i.c.
RADIUS WINDOW
FPL.
RADIUS WINDOW

PLANT SHELF ABOVE

Breakfast
SERVING BAR
PANTRY

Bedroom 3
11³ x 11⁰

REF.
LINEN

FRENCH DOOR

Master Suite
15⁰ x 13²
TRAY CLG.

Vaulted Great Room
15⁰ x 20⁰
14'-6" CLG. HT.

Kitchen
DW.
RANGE

Bath

ARCHED OPG.
VAULT.

DECORATIVE COLUMN

COATS

RADIUS WINDOW

Sitting Room
VAULT.
STAIRS UP
W. D.
Laund.

ARCHED OPG.

Foyer
14'-6" CLG. HT.

Dining Room
11⁰ x 12⁴
12'-0" CLG. HT.

Bedroom 2
11⁰ x 11⁰

STAIRS TO OPT. BSMT.

Covered Porch

Garage
20⁵ x 22²

copyright © 1997 frank betz associates, inc.

GARAGE LOCATION W/ BASEMENT

Width 54'-0"
Depth 56'-6"

Design HPTMO3026

Square Footage: 1,692
Bonus Space: 358 square feet

■ This cozy country cottage is enhanced with a front-facing planter box above the garage and a charming covered porch. The foyer leads to a vaulted great room, complete with a fireplace and radius windows. Decorative columns complement the entrance to the dining room, as does a decorative arch. On the left side of the plan resides the master suite, which is resplendent with amenities including a vaulted sitting room, tray ceiling, French doors to the vaulted full bath and an arched opening to the sitting room. On the right side, two additional bedrooms share a full bath. Please specify basement or crawlspace foundation when ordering.

Design by
© Frank Betz Associates, Inc.

167

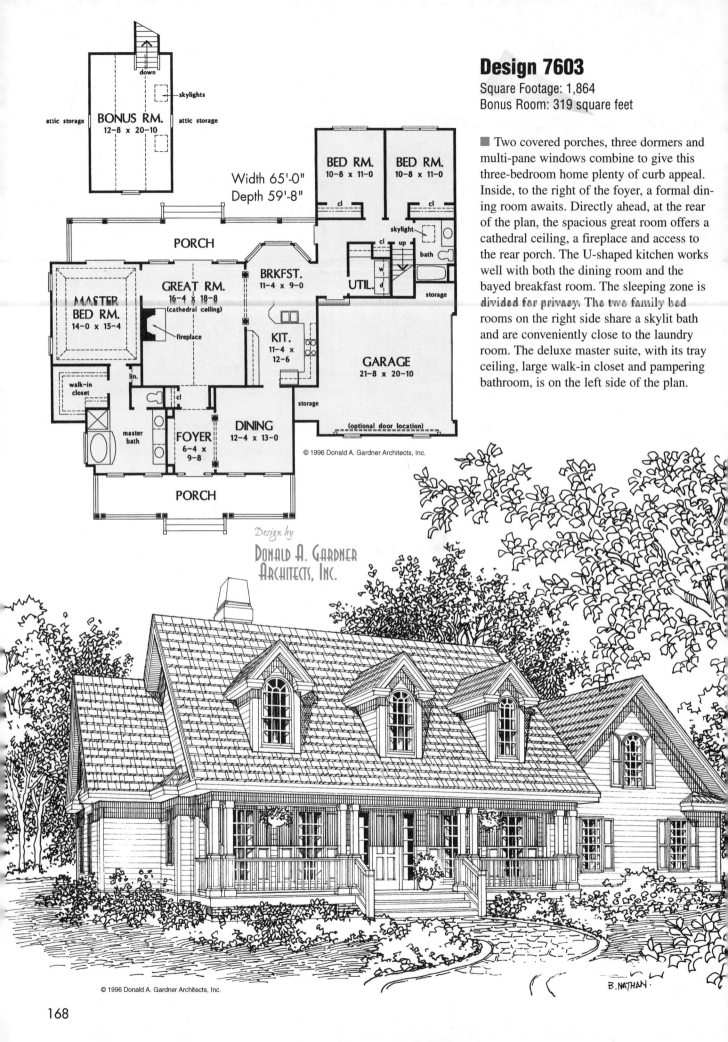

Design 7603

Square Footage: 1,864
Bonus Room: 319 square feet

■ Two covered porches, three dormers and multi-pane windows combine to give this three-bedroom home plenty of curb appeal. Inside, to the right of the foyer, a formal dining room awaits. Directly ahead, at the rear of the plan, the spacious great room offers a cathedral ceiling, a fireplace and access to the rear porch. The U-shaped kitchen works well with both the dining room and the bayed breakfast room. The sleeping zone is divided for privacy. The two family bedrooms on the right side share a skylit bath and are conveniently close to the laundry room. The deluxe master suite, with its tray ceiling, large walk-in closet and pampering bathroom, is on the left side of the plan.

Width 65'-0"
Depth 59'-8"

BONUS RM.
12–8 x 20–10

attic storage

attic storage

skylights

down

PORCH

GREAT RM.
16–4 x 18–8
(cathedral ceiling)

fireplace

MASTER
BED RM.
14–0 x 15–4

walk-in closet

master bath

lin.

cl

FOYER
6–4 x 9–8

DINING
12–4 x 13–0

BRKFST.
11–4 x 9–0

KIT.
11–4 x 12–6

UTIL.

w d

cl

up

skylight

bath

BED RM.
10–8 x 11–0

BED RM.
10–8 x 11–0

cl

cl

storage

GARAGE
21–8 x 20–10

storage

(optional door location)

PORCH

© 1996 Donald A. Gardner Architects, Inc.

Design by
**DONALD A. GARDNER
ARCHITECTS, INC.**

B. NATHAN

B. NATHAN

Design 7658

Square Footage: 1,899
Bonus Room: 315 square feet

■ Country charm in a one-story home—but it looks like a two-story. The upper-level dormers provide light to the floor plan and add detailing to the exterior. A covered porch wraps around three sides of the plan and is accessed at two separate points. Both the great room and the master bedroom have cathedral ceilings, while the formal dining room has a vaulted ceiling. A screen porch to the rear can be reached from the breakfast room (note the bay window here). The plan calls for three bedrooms, but one may be used as a study or home office if you choose. The two-car garage sits to the rear of the plan, taking nothing away from the beauty of the facade. Appointments in the master suite include a bath with vaulted ceiling, garden whirlpool and compartmented toilet. A bonus room over the garage allows space to expand.

Design by

DONALD A. GARDNER
ARCHITECTS, INC.

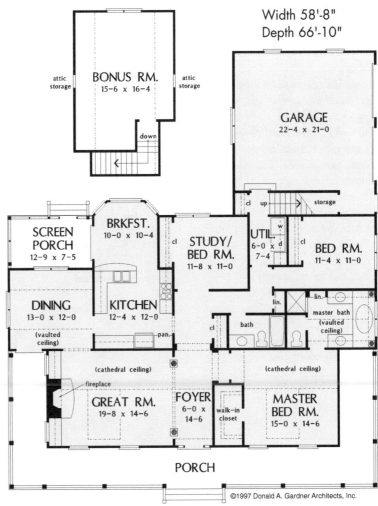

Width 58'-8"
Depth 66'-10"

attic storage

BONUS RM.
15-6 x 16-4

attic storage

down

GARAGE
22-4 x 21-0

cl | up | storage

SCREEN PORCH
12-9 x 7-5

BRKFST.
10-0 x 10-4

STUDY/ BED RM.
11-8 x 11-0

UTIL.
6-0 x 7-4

w
d

BED RM.
11-4 x 11-0

DINING
13-0 x 12-0
(vaulted ceiling)

KITCHEN
12-4 x 12-0

pan.

lin.

lin.

master bath
(vaulted ceiling)

cl

bath

(cathedral ceiling)

fireplace

GREAT RM.
19-8 x 14-6

FOYER
6-0 x 14-6

walk-in closet

(cathedral ceiling)

MASTER BED RM.
15-0 x 14-6

PORCH

169

Design HPTM03027

Square Footage: 2,308

■ Corner quoins combined with arch-top windows and a columned entry lend an exciting facade to this four-bedroom home. The foyer is entered through double doors and introduces the open dining and family room area. The master suite occupies the left side of the plan and enjoys a sun-strewn sitting room, two walk-in closets and a luxurious bath complete with a garden tub and separate shower. The kitchen sits conveniently near the dining room and features a pantry, desk and view through the breakfast-nook windows. Two family bedrooms, sharing a full bath, reside near the kitchen. A fourth bedroom or guest suite is located by the family room. The family room contains a warming fireplace and media wall, which will make it a wonderful gathering place for the family.

Width 67'-0"
Depth 56'-8"

Design by
© HOME DESIGN SERVICES, INC.

170

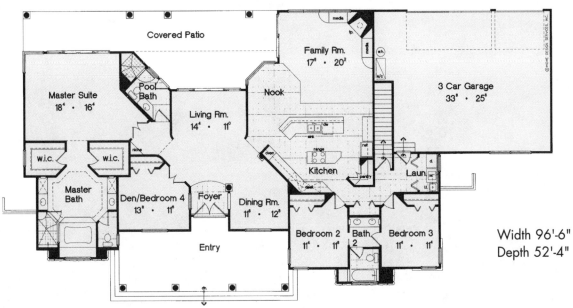

Covered Patio

Master Suite
18⁴ · 16⁴

Pool Bath

Living Rm.
14⁴ · 11⁰

Nook

Family Rm.
17⁸ · 20²

3 Car Garage
33⁸ · 25⁸

w.i.c. w.i.c.

niche

Master Bath

Den/Bedroom 4
13⁸ · 11⁰

Foyer

Dining Rm.
11⁸ · 12⁸

Kitchen

Laun.

Bedroom 2
11⁴ · 11⁰

Bath 2

Bedroom 3
11⁰ · 11⁰

Entry

Width 96'-6"
Depth 52'-4"

Design HPTM03028
Square Footage: 2,636

■ This home makes a commanding presence with its country porch and stone veneer accents. Upon entering, views throughout the home are possible as this home reaches out in all directions. The living room has a wall of glass to the covered patio, and the dining room, with its decorative columns and angular wall, creates an impressive space. Enter the master suite through double doors with a decorative niche nearby. The family living area of this home is just as impressive, with a massive island kitchen serving as the centerpiece. The generous nook can accommodate a large family, as can the family room with its a media/fireplace wall.

Design Z026

Square Footage: 1,091

Width 31'-8"
Depth 40'-0"

■ Small but commodious living
abounds in this delightful one-story
home. A cathedral ceiling lends an aura
of spaciousness to the living/dining
area. The front bay window adds charm
outside and allows natural light inside.
The breakfast area is brightened by sliding glass doors to a side patio. A full
bath with a double-bowl vanity and a
separate shower is thoughtfully placed
between the two bedrooms. This home
is designed with a basement foundation.

Design by
©DRUMMOND DESIGNS, INC.

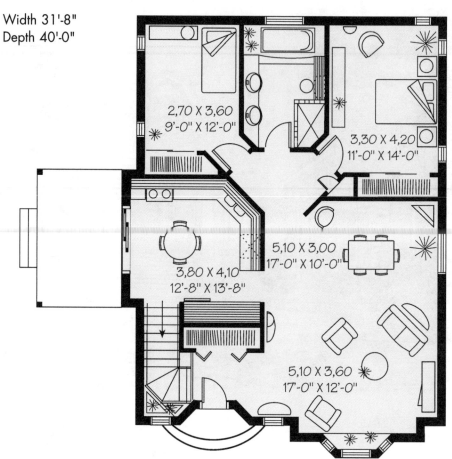

2,70 X 3,60
9'-0" X 12'-0"

3,30 X 4,20
11'-0" X 14'-0"

3,80 X 4,10
12'-8" X 13'-8"

5,10 X 3,00
17'-0" X 10'-0"

5,10 X 3,60
17'-0" X 12'-0"

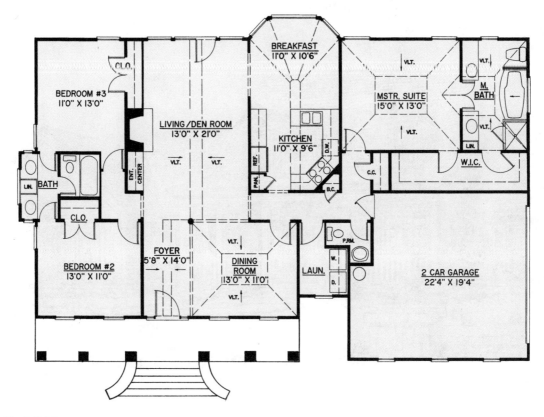

BREAKFAST
11'0" X 10'6"

BEDROOM #3
11'0" X 13'0"

CLO.

LIVING/DEN ROOM
13'0" X 21'0"

VLT. VLT.

MSTR. SUITE
15'0" X 13'0"

M. BATH

VLT. VLT. VLT.

KITCHEN
11'0" X 9'6"

REF.

PAN.

D.W.

B.C.

C.C.

W.I.C.

LIN.

ENT. CENTER

BATH

LIN.

CLO.

FOYER
5'8" X 14'0"

DINING ROOM
13'0" X 11'0"

VLT.

VLT.

VLT.

P. RM.

W.

D.

LAUN.

2 CAR GARAGE
22'4" X 19'4"

BEDROOM #2
13'0" X 11'0"

Width 64'-0"
Depth 40'-6"

Design by
ARCHIVAL DESIGNS

Design S126

Square Footage: 1,751

■ This raised-porch farmhouse holds all the charisma of others of its style, but boasts a one-story floor plan. A huge living area dominates the center of the plan. It features a vaulted ceiling, built-ins and a warming fireplace. The formal dining room is across the hall and open to the foyer and the living area, defined by a single column at its corner. Casual dining takes place in a light-filled breakfast room, attached to the designer kitchen. A spectacular master suite sits behind the two-car garage. It has a tray ceiling, enormous walk-in closet and well-appointed bath. Family bedrooms are at the other end of the hallway and share a jack-and-jill bath with separate vanity area.

Design HPTM03029

Square Footage: 2,342
Bonus Space: 452 square feet

■ Double dormers, a covered front porch and the stone facade give this country farmhouse a warm feeling of home. Inside, to the right is a dining area greeted by French doors and an island kitchen with lots of counter space and a convenient pantry. A gallery is just steps away, leading to the great room which boasts an optional sloped ceiling, a cozy fireplace and access to the rear covered patio. Secluded to the rear right is the sumptuous master bedroom with a bayed sitting area, private access to the rear patio, a pampering master bath with a large soaking tub, and a walk-in closet. To the opposite end are three additional bedrooms with plenty of space sharing a full dual-vanity bath. This plan is complete with a three-car garage.

Design by
©FILLMORE DESIGN GROUP

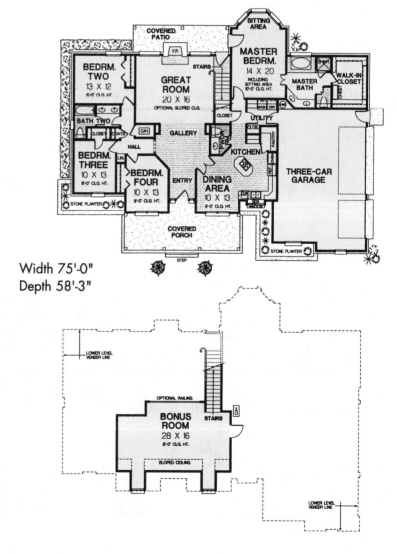

Width 75'-0"
Depth 58'-3"

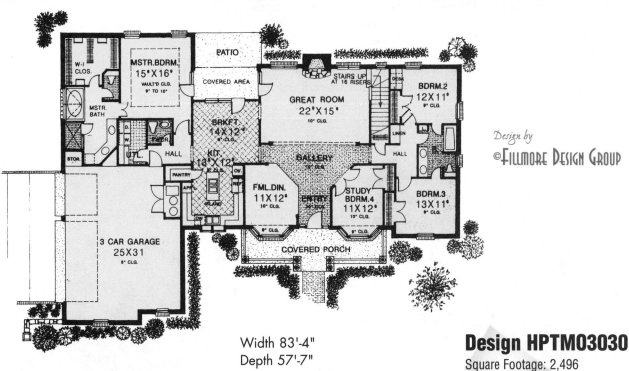

Width 83'-4"
Depth 57'-7"

Design HPTM03030

Square Footage: 2,496
Bonus Space: 483 square feet

■ This countryside estate boasts a quaint rustic charm. Inside, the dining room and study can be found on either side of the entryway—both feature bayed windows. A gallery separates the formal rooms from the great room, which offers a country fireplace. The master suite is enhanced by a vaulted ceiling and features a private master bath. The right side of the home hosts two additional family bedrooms. Upstairs, an unfinished bonus room with a sloped ceiling is reserved for future use.

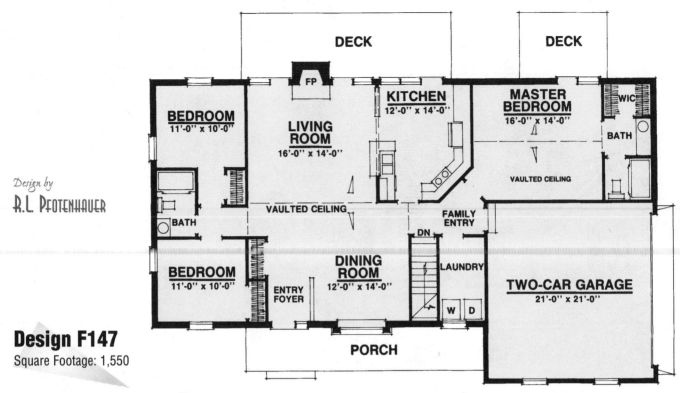

DECK   DECK

BEDROOM
11'-0'' x 10'-0''

FP

LIVING ROOM
16'-0'' x 14'-0''

KITCHEN
12'-0'' x 14'-0''

MASTER BEDROOM
16'-0'' x 14'-0''

WIC

BATH

VAULTED CEILING

Design by
R.L. Pfotenhauer

BATH

VAULTED CEILING

FAMILY ENTRY

BEDROOM
11'-0'' x 10'-0''

DN

DINING ROOM
12'-0'' x 14'-0''

LAUNDRY

TWO-CAR GARAGE
21'-0'' x 21'-0''

ENTRY FOYER

W   D

PORCH

Design F147
Square Footage: 1,550

Width 62'-9"
Depth 36'-1"

■ If you like the rustic appeal of ranch-style homes, you'll love this version. Both horizontal and vertical siding appear on the exterior and are complemented by a columned covered porch and a delightful cupola as accent. The entry opens to a huge open living/dining room combination. A fireplace in the living area is flanked by windows and doors to one of two rear decks. A vaulted ceiling runs the width of this area. The kitchen also accesses the deck and features counterspace galore. Look for a private deck behind the master suite. A vaulted ceiling graces the master bedroom. Two family bedrooms have good closet space and share a full bath at the opposite end of the hall.

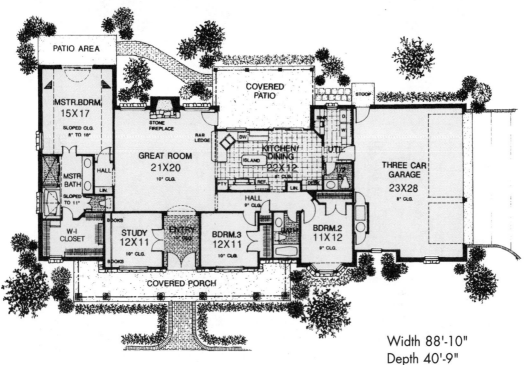

Width 88'-10"
Depth 40'-9"

■ This amazing home is detailed with sloped roofs, a stone facade and muntin windows. Enjoy the stone fireplace whether relaxing in the great room or sipping a drink at the bar extended from the kitchen. Adjacent to the kitchen, a dining area includes sliding glass doors leading to a covered patio. A private patio area is available to the master bedroom, as well as a spacious private bath, which includes a double-bowl sink and a vast walk-in closet. Two family bedrooms each have double-door closets and share a full bath. A three-car garage resides to the far right of the plan, with an entryway opening to the utility room.

Design HPTM03031
Square Footage: 2,061

Design by
©FILLMORE DESIGN GROUP

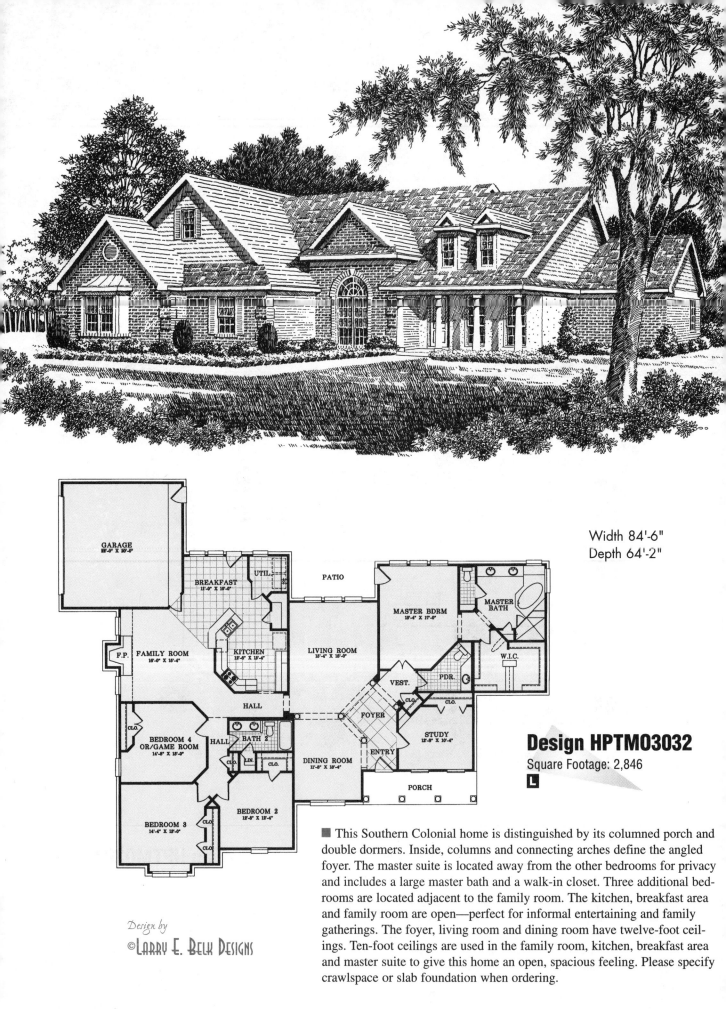

Width 84'-6"
Depth 64'-2"

GARAGE
22'-0" X 20'-0"

BREAKFAST
11'-0" X 10'-0"

UTIL.

PATIO

MASTER BDRM
15'-4" X 17'-0"

MASTER BATH

F.P.

FAMILY ROOM
16'-0" X 18'-4"

KITCHEN
13'-8" X 13'-4"

LIVING ROOM
15'-4" X 18'-0"

W.I.C.

HALL

VEST.

PDR.

CLO.

BEDROOM 4
OR/GAME ROOM
14'-8" X 18'-0"

HALL

BATH 2

LIN.

CLO.

FOYER

ENTRY

STUDY
12'-8" X 10'-4"

CLO.

DINING ROOM
11'-8" X 18'-4"

BEDROOM 2
13'-8" X 12'-4"

PORCH

BEDROOM 3
14'-4" X 12'-0"

CLO.

CLO.

Design HPTM03032
Square Footage: 2,846
L

Design by
©**Larry E. Belk Designs**

■ This Southern Colonial home is distinguished by its columned porch and double dormers. Inside, columns and connecting arches define the angled foyer. The master suite is located away from the other bedrooms for privacy and includes a large master bath and a walk-in closet. Three additional bedrooms are located adjacent to the family room. The kitchen, breakfast area and family room are open—perfect for informal entertaining and family gatherings. The foyer, living room and dining room have twelve-foot ceilings. Ten-foot ceilings are used in the family room, kitchen, breakfast area and master suite to give this home an open, spacious feeling. Please specify crawlspace or slab foundation when ordering.

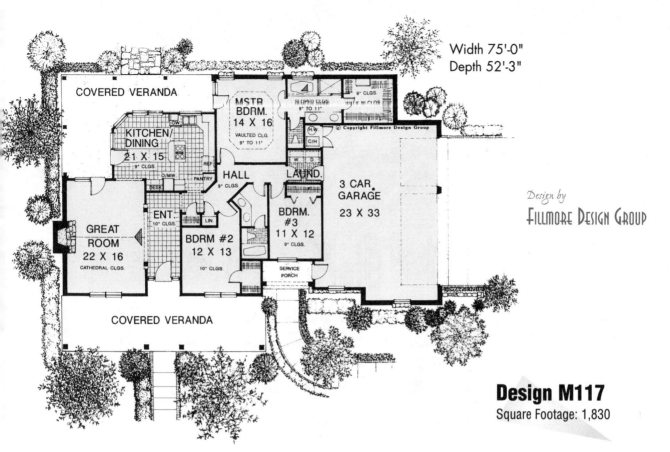

Width 75'-0"
Depth 52'-3"

COVERED VERANDA

MSTR. BDRM.
14 X 16
VAULTED CLG.
9" TO 11"

KITCHEN/ DINING
21 X 15
9" CLGS.

SLOPED CLGS
9" TO 11"

9" CLGS.

© Copyright Fillmore Design Group

HALL
9" CLGS.

LAUND.

3 CAR GARAGE
23 X 33

GREAT ROOM
22 X 16
CATHEDRAL CLGS.

ENT.
10" CLGS.

PANTRY

DESK

LIN.

BDRM #2
12 X 13
10" CLGS.

BDRM. #3
11 X 12
9" CLGS.

SERVICE PORCH

COVERED VERANDA

Design by
FILLMORE DESIGN GROUP

Design M117
Square Footage: 1,830

■ Characteristics that include a cupola, shutters, arched transoms and an exterior of combined stone and lap siding give this one-story home its country identity. To the left of the entry is the great room. Here, a cathedral ceiling and a fireplace extend an invitation for family and friends alike to relax and enjoy themselves. The kitchen and dining room are located nearby. Kitchen amenities include an island cooktop, a built-in planning desk and a pantry, while the multi-windowed dining room overlooks and provides access to the covered veranda. A hall leads to sleeping quarters that include two secondary bedrooms and a luxurious master suite. Conveniently situated to serve the entire household is a laundry room. Room for the family fleet is provided by the three-car garage. Details for both a crawlspace and a slab foundation are included in the blueprints.

Design HPTM03033

Square Footage: 1,997
Bonus Space: 310 square feet

Design by
©Home Design Services, Inc.

🖿 The hub of this charming plan is the spacious kitchen with an island and serving bar. The nearby breakfast nook accesses the greenhouse with its wall of windows and three large skylights. A built-in media center and a warming fireplace are the focal point of the family room. Bedroom 2 shares a full bath with the den/study, which might also be a third bedroom. The master suite features large His and Hers vanity sinks, a corner tub with an open walk-in shower, and a supersized walk-in closet. Future space over the garage can expand the living space as your family grows. Please specify basement, crawlspace or slab foundation when ordering.

Width 64'-4"
Depth 63'-0"

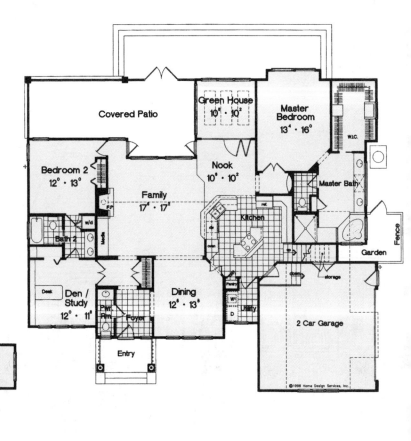

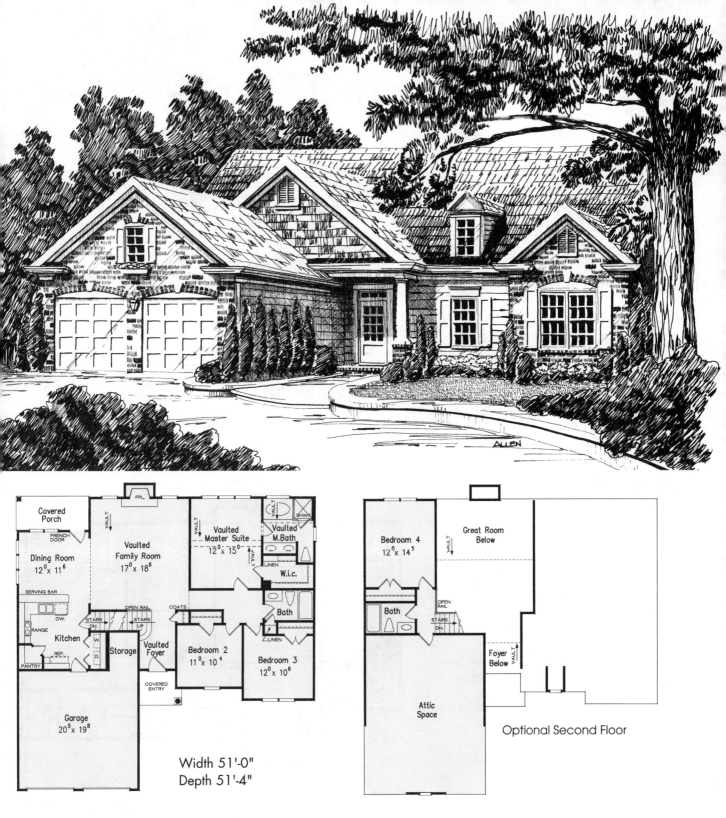

Width 51'-0"
Depth 51'-4"

Optional Second Floor

Design HPTM03034

Square Footage: 1,477
Bonus Space: 283 square feet

Design by
© Frank Betz Associates, Inc.

■ This adorable four-bedroom home will provide a pleasant atmosphere for your family. The communal living areas reside on the left side of the plan. The L-shaped kitchen includes a serving bar which opens to the dining area. The vaulted family room features a fireplace and leads to the sleeping quarters. A master suite and vaulted master bath will pamper homeowners. Two family bedrooms reside across the hall and share a full hall bath. Upstairs, a fourth bedroom and a full bath are perfect for guests. Please specify basement or crawlspace foundation when ordering.

© design basics inc.

Design 7333

Square Footage: 1,554

■ A lovely corner wrapping porch provides a focal point for this cozy ranch design. The entry opens to a great room with cathedral ceiling and to a formal dining room with a ten-foot-high ceiling. The spacious kitchen features a corner sink and a built-in bookcase and shares a snack bar with the breakfast area. The bedroom wing has convenient laundry access. Choose the formal dining room or, if needed, make this room into a third bedroom. The master suite opens with French doors. Amenities here include a volume ceiling, mirrored walk-in closet doors and a sunny whirlpool bath.

Optional Layout

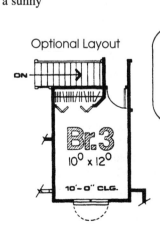

Design by
DESIGN BASICS, INC.

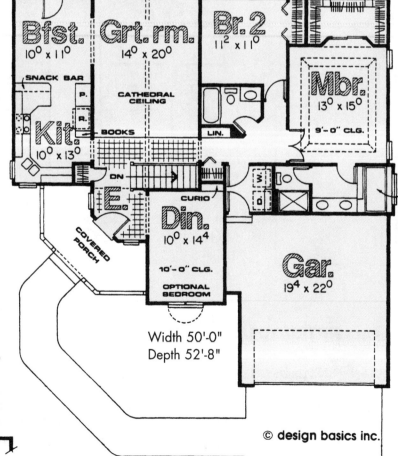

Width 50'-0"
Depth 52'-8"

© design basics inc.

Traditional Americana:

One-story homes found in your neighborhood

Design HPTM03035

Square Footage: 1,322

■ This traditional-style homestead is a delight, with clapboard siding, classic shutters and a box-paneled door. A columned covered porch leads the way through a gallery foyer to wide-open living space with a centered fireplace flanked by windows. The gourmet kitchen boasts wrapping counters, a walk-in pantry, a work island and casual dining space with interior vistas to the living room and fireplace. Clustered sleeping quarters offer a master suite with a walk-in closet and twin vanities. Two family bedrooms share a full bath and include plenty of closet space. A utility area, set off by double doors, offers room for a full-size washer and dryer, while a service entrance leads to additional storage space in the garage. Please specify crawlspace or slab foundation when ordering.

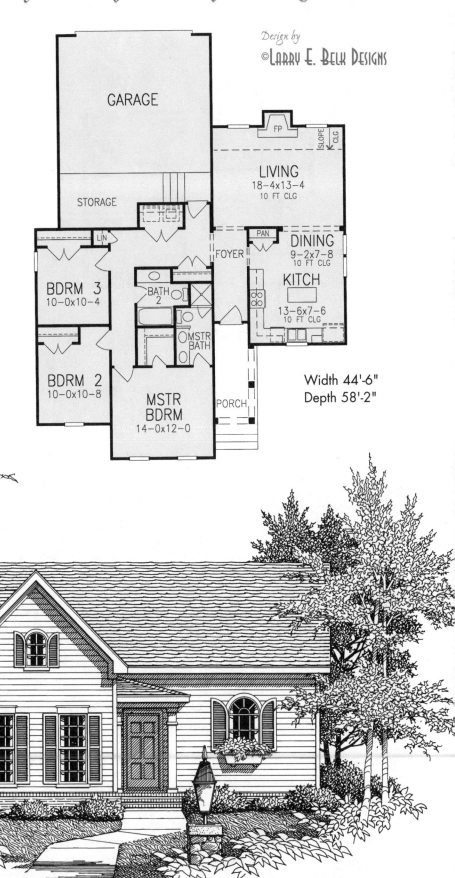

Design by
©Larry E. Belk Designs

GARAGE

STORAGE

LIVING
18-4x13-4
10 FT CLG

FP

SLOPE CLG

FOYER

DINING
9-2x7-8
10 FT CLG

PAN

KITCH
13-6x7-6
10 FT CLG

LIN

BDRM 3
10-0x10-4

BATH 2

MSTR BATH

BDRM 2
10-0x10-8

MSTR BDRM
14-0x12-0

PORCH

Width 44'-6"
Depth 58'-2"

4,80 X 3,60
16'-0" X 12'-0"

5,20 X 3,90
17'-4" X 13'-0"

3,70 X 3,20
12'-4" X 10'-8"

3,00 X 3,00
10'-0" X 10'-0"

3,70 X 3,00
12'-4" X 10'-0"

3,30 X 4,70
11'-0" X 15'-8"

6,10 X 6,20
20'-4" X 20'-8"

Width 55'-8"
Depth 44'-4"

Design Z029
Square Footage: 1,504

■ A quaint covered porch and large, arched windows add to the appeal of this cottage. The entry hall opens to a living area on the right side, which is open to the dining room and kitchen. A closet in the entry hall is perfect for storing coats and hats. The bedrooms on the left side of the plan include two family bedrooms and a master bedroom. The shared hall bath contains a large corner tub with a window above. Reach the two-car garage via a service entry at the end of the center hall. This home is designed with a basement foundation.

Design 9567

Square Footage: 1,644
Lower Level: 1,012 square feet

■ The character of this home is purely traditional. At the forefront is an elegant dining room open to the great room. The spacious kitchen is centered around a cooktop island. Double doors lead to a rear deck. The main-level master suite also opens to this area. A den or bedroom faces the front and is not far from a full bath, making it an ideal guest room. On the lower level, a games room and two more bedrooms reside. Built-ins and outdoor access make the games room versatile.

MASTER
13/0 X 16/0
(10'-4" CLG.)

GREAT RM.
17/2 X 16/0
(10'-4" CLG.)

18/6 X 13/8

SPA

DN.

DINING
10/8 X 13/2
(10'-4" CLG.)

LIN.

GARAGE
19/4 X 21/8 +/-

DEN/ BR. 2
13/0 X 10/0 +

Width 52'-0"
Depth 55'-0"

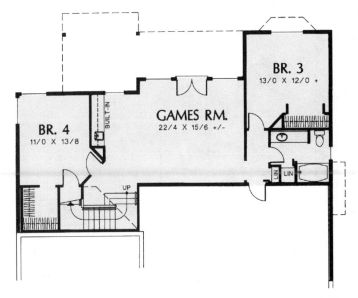

BR. 3
13/0 X 12/0 +

BUILT-IN

GAMES RM.
22/4 X 15/6 +/-

BR. 4
11/0 X 13/8

UP

LIN LIN

Design by
ALAN MASCORD
DESIGN ASSOCIATES, INC.

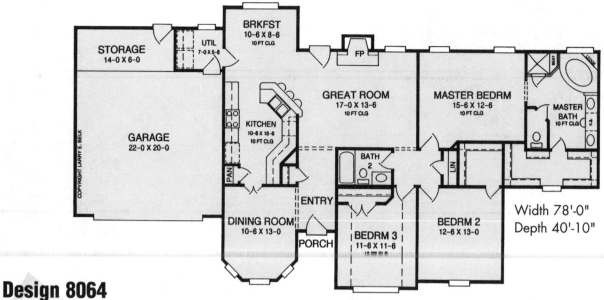

STORAGE
14-0 X 6-0

UTIL
7-0 X 5-6

BRKFST
10-6 X 8-6
10 FT CLG

FP

GARAGE
22-0 X 20-0

KITCHEN
10-6 X 16-6
10 FT CLG

PAN

GREAT ROOM
17-0 X 13-6
10 FT CLG

MASTER BEDRM
15-6 X 12-6
10 FT CLG

MASTER
BATH
10 FT CLG

COPYRIGHT LARRY E. BELK

BATH
2

ENTRY

LIN

DINING ROOM
10-6 X 13-0

PORCH

BEDRM 3
11-6 X 11-6

BEDRM 2
12-6 X 13-0

Width 78'-0"
Depth 40'-10"

Design 8064

Square Footage: 1,742

■ This traditional design warmly welcomes both family and visitors with a delightful bay window, a Palladian window and shutters. The entry introduces a beautiful interior plan, starting with the formal dining room and the central great room with fireplace, and views and access to outdoor spaces. Ten-foot ceilings in the major living areas give the home an open, spacious feel. The kitchen features an angled eating bar, a pantry and lots of cabinet and counter space. Comfort and style abound in the distinctive master suite, offering a high ceiling, corner whirlpool tub, knee-space vanity and compartmented toilet. An ample walk-in closet with a window for natural light completes this owner's retreat. Bedrooms 2 and 3 are nearby and share a hall bath, and Bedroom 3 offers a raised ceiling. Please specify basement or crawlspace foundation when ordering.

Design by
Larry E. Belk
Designs

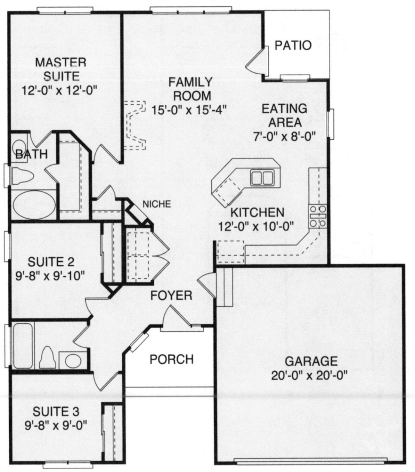

PATIO

MASTER
SUITE
12'-0" x 12'-0"

FAMILY
ROOM
15'-0" x 15'-4"

EATING
AREA
7'-0" x 8'-0"

BATH

NICHE

KITCHEN
12'-0" x 10'-0"

SUITE 2
9'-8" x 9'-10"

FOYER

SUITE 3
9'-8" x 9'-0"

PORCH

GARAGE
20'-0" x 20'-0"

Design HPTM03036

Square Footage: 1,204

■ This delightful home packs quite a
punch. The welcoming porch leads to
an entry that features a sidelight and
transom. Inside, the foyer carries guests
past a utility closet and niche, to the
island kitchen with a snack bar. The
kitchen opens to the eating area and the
family room (with an optional fireplace)
accessible to the rear patio. The secluded master suite provides privacy and
features a master bath and walk-in closet. Suites 2 and 3 are separated from the
living area and share a full hall bath.
The well-placed garage entrance opens
to the foyer.

Design by
©Living Concepts Home Planning

Width 43'-1"
Depth 47'-1"

Width 47'-7"
Depth 46'-5"

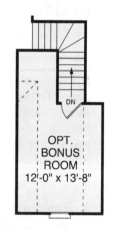

OPT. BONUS ROOM
12'-0" x 13'-8"

DN

Design HPTM03037

Square Footage: 1,458
Bonus Space: 256 square feet

■ This cozy home gives a warming appeal with its great attention to detail. As you enter the home you will find two family bedrooms to the left that share a full bath. Nearby a spacious kitchen opens to the formal dining room and massive living room. To the far right is the elegant master suite, which enjoys a private bath and boasts a pampering garden tub and spacious walk-in closet. An optional bonus room is available with this plan.

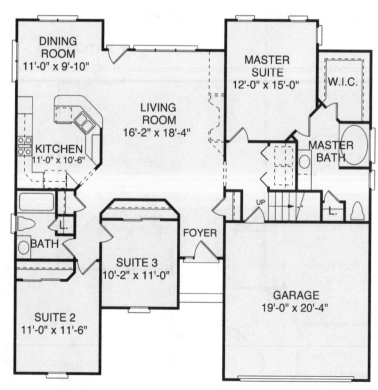

DINING ROOM
11'-0" x 9'-10"

MASTER SUITE
12'-0" x 15'-0"

W.I.C.

LIVING ROOM
16'-2" x 18'-4"

KITCHEN
11'-0" x 10'-6"

MASTER BATH

UP

BATH

L.

SUITE 3
10'-2" x 11'-0"

FOYER

L.

GARAGE
19'-0" x 20'-4"

SUITE 2
11'-0" x 11'-6"

Design by
©Living Concepts Home Planning

Design T235

Square Footage: 3,063

■ Though all on one level, the floor plan for this home defines masterful design. Open planning is evident, though there are spaces for privacy as well. The great room and dining room are separated only by well-placed columns, yet each is distinct in its purpose and structure. Similarly, the keeping room is open to the breakfast area and kitchen, but retains a sense of solitude with a cozy fireplace and built-ins. The kitchen is all a gourmet might ever ask for, with a huge storage pantry, butler's pantry connecting it to the dining room and an island cooktop. Each bedroom has its own bath—take a close look at the master bath and its superb amenities. A rear covered porch is accessed through the great room, the keeping room and the master bedroom. The two-car garage holds a bit of extra space for storage or a workshop bench.

Master Bedroom
13⁸ x 17²

Covered Porch

Great Room
15⁸ x 11⁴

Great Room
15⁸ x 18⁶

Breakfast
16⁰ x 11⁸

Kitchen
16⁸ x 11⁸

Bedroom #2
12⁰ x 14⁶

Bedroom #3
14⁶ x 13²

Foyer

Dining Room
13⁴ x 13⁷

Width 68'-0"
Depth 80'-0"

Two Car Garage
24⁴ x 23²

Design by
DESIGN TRADITIONS

Design P294

Square Footage: 1,232

■ Gabled rooflines, shutters and siding—all elements of a fine facade, and the floor plan inside equals this quality. The foyer opens directly into the vaulted great room, where a fireplace waits to warm cool winter evenings. Nearby, the efficient kitchen has easy access to the dining room. Two secondary bedrooms share a full hall bath with a linen closet nearby. The deluxe master bedroom suite, with a tray ceiling, offers a vaulted master bath and a spacious walk-in closet. A laundry room is located in between the master suite and the two-car garage. Please specify basement or crawlspace foundation when ordering.

Design by
Frank Betz Associates, Inc.

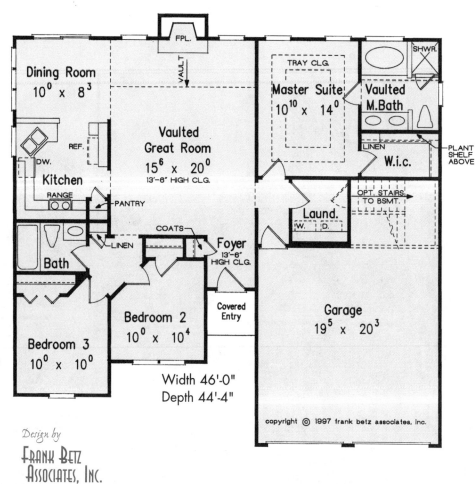

FPL.

VAULT

Dining Room
10⁰ x 8³

REF.

DW.

Kitchen

RANGE

PANTRY

Vaulted
Great Room
15⁶ x 20⁰
13'-6" HIGH CLG.

TRAY CLG.

Master Suite
10¹⁰ x 14⁰

SHWR.

Vaulted
M.Bath

LINEN

W.i.c.

PLANT
SHELF
ABOVE

OPT. STAIRS
TO BSMT.

LINEN

Bath

COATS

Foyer
13'-6"
HIGH CLG.

Laund.

W. D.

Bedroom 3
10⁰ x 10⁰

Bedroom 2
10⁰ x 10⁴

Covered
Entry

Garage
19⁵ x 20³

Width 46'-0"
Depth 44'-4"

copyright © 1997 frank betz associates, inc.

Design S131

Square Footage: 1,670

■ With an offset entrance, this home adds interest and charm to any neighborhood. Enter into a spacious family room, with a galley kitchen nearby offering easy access to the sunny breakfast room. Bedrooms 2 and 3 each have walk-in closets and share a full hall bath. Bedroom 2, which opens off the family room, could also be used as a den. The formal dining room separates the master bedroom from the rest of the home, providing pleasant privacy. The master suite features many amenities, including a walk-in closet, a private bath and access to a private courtyard.

Design by
ARCHIVAL DESIGNS

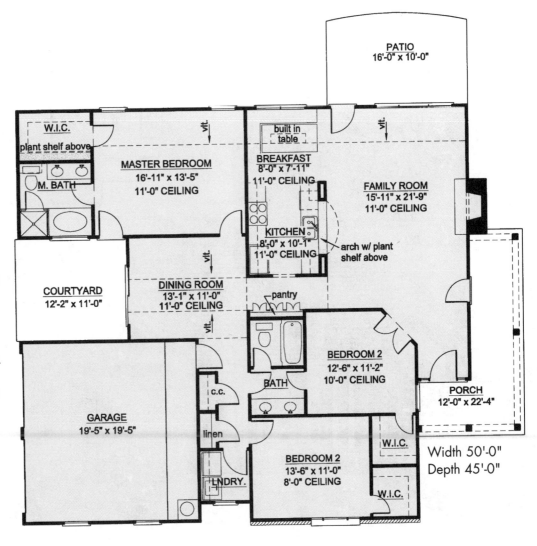

Width 50'-0"
Depth 45'-0"

Design 9735

Square Footage: 2,625
Bonus Room: 447 square feet

■ This stately brick facade features a columned, covered porch that ushers visitors in to the large foyer. An expansive great room with a fireplace and access to a covered rear porch awaits. The centrally located kitchen is within easy reach of the great room, formal dining room and skylit breakfast area. Split-bedroom planning places the master bedroom and elegant master bath to the right of the home. Two bedrooms with abundant closet space are placed to the left, while an optional bedroom or study with a Palladian window faces the front. A large bonus room is located above the garage.

Design by
DONALD A. GARDNER ARCHITECTS, INC.

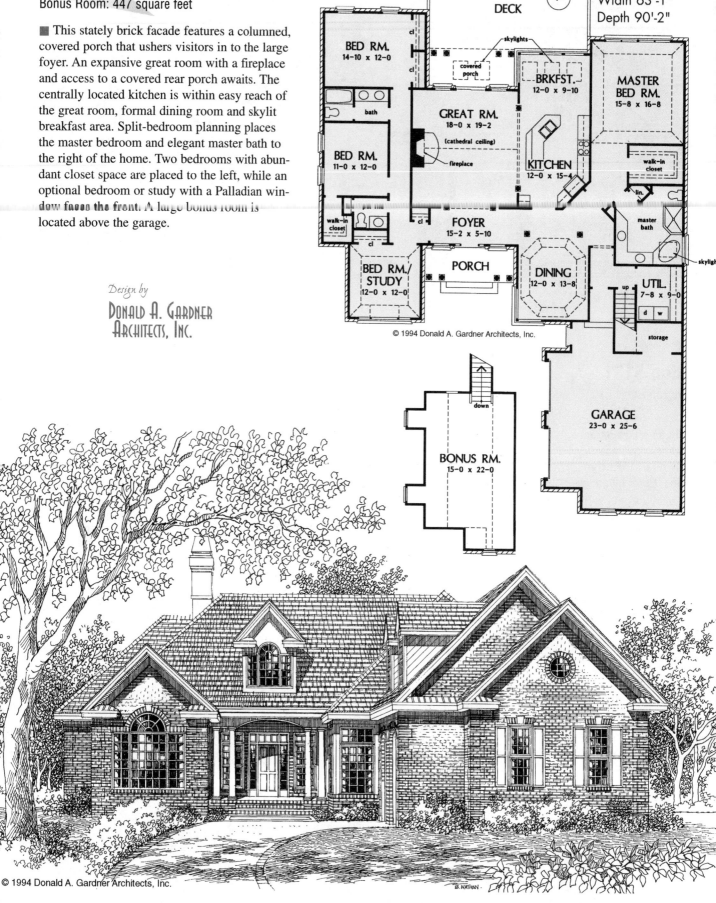

Width 63'-1"
Depth 90'-2"

DECK
spa

BED RM.
14-10 x 12-0

skylights
covered porch

BRKFST.
12-0 x 9-10

MASTER BED RM.
15-8 x 16-8

bath

GREAT RM.
18-0 x 19-2
(cathedral ceiling)
fireplace

KITCHEN
12-0 x 15-4

walk-in closet

BED RM.
11-0 x 12-0

lin.

walk-in closet

master bath

FOYER
15-2 x 5-10

cl

skylight

BED RM./STUDY
12-0 x 12-0

PORCH

DINING
12-0 x 13-8

up
UTIL.
7-8 x 9-0
d w

storage

© 1994 Donald A. Gardner Architects, Inc.

down

GARAGE
23-0 x 25-6

BONUS RM.
15-0 x 22-0

B. NATHAN

Design 7009

Square Footage: 1,806

■ This is up-to-date floor planning at its best—open, airy and allowing for plenty of options. The main living area is casual, but is complemented by a formal dining room for special occasions. Both rooms sport ten-foot ceilings. The great room has a focal-point fireplace. To make serving easy, the dining room connects to the kitchen via a servery. You'll also appreciate the peninsula snack bar in the kitchen that divides it from the breakfast room. A door here leads to a covered porch for outdoor meals. The master suite also has a ten-foot ceiling. Its bath is complete with a corner whirlpool tub, separate shower, compartmented toilet and walk-in closet. Family bedrooms share the use of a full bath with double sinks. A three-car garage guarantees you never lack for vehicle parking space again.

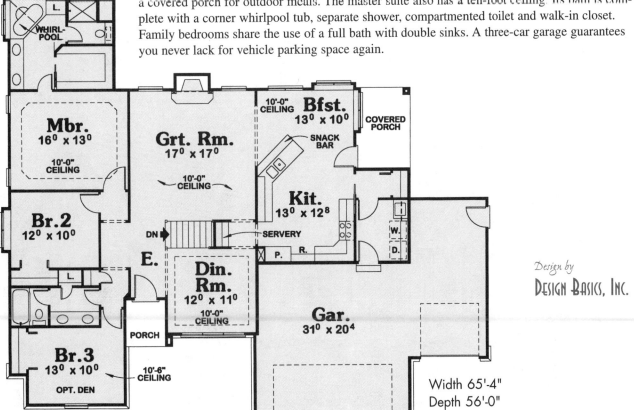

Design by
Design Basics, Inc.

Width 65'-4"
Depth 56'-0"

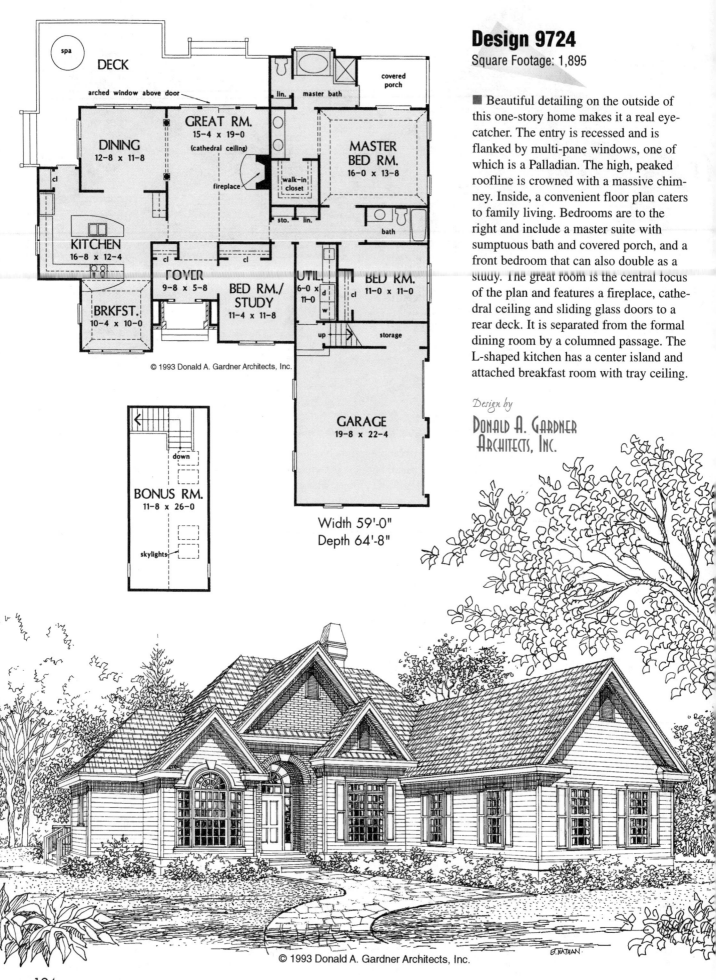

Design 9724
Square Footage: 1,895

■ Beautiful detailing on the outside of this one-story home makes it a real eye-catcher. The entry is recessed and is flanked by multi-pane windows, one of which is a Palladian. The high, peaked roofline is crowned with a massive chimney. Inside, a convenient floor plan caters to family living. Bedrooms are to the right and include a master suite with sumptuous bath and covered porch, and a front bedroom that can also double as a study. The great room is the central focus of the plan and features a fireplace, cathedral ceiling and sliding glass doors to a rear deck. It is separated from the formal dining room by a columned passage. The L-shaped kitchen has a center island and attached breakfast room with tray ceiling.

Design by
DONALD A. GARDNER
ARCHITECTS, INC.

DECK
spa

arched window above door
GREAT RM.
15-4 x 19-0
(cathedral ceiling)
fireplace
DINING
12-8 x 11-8
cl

master bath
lin.
covered porch

MASTER BED RM.
16-0 x 13-8
walk-in closet
sto.   lin.
bath

KITCHEN
16-8 x 12-4
FOYER
9-8 x 5-8
cl   cl
BED RM./STUDY
11-4 x 11-8

UTIL.
6-0 x 11-0
d
w

BED RM.
11-0 x 11-0

BRKFST.
10-4 x 10-0

up   storage

© 1993 Donald A. Gardner Architects, Inc.

GARAGE
19-8 x 22-4

Width 59'-0"
Depth 64'-8"

down

BONUS RM.
11-8 x 26-0

skylights

© 1993 Donald A. Gardner Architects, Inc.

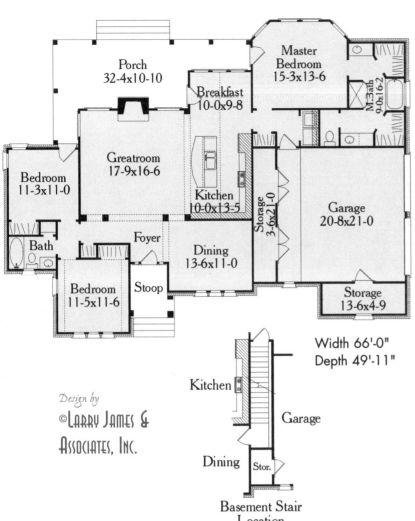

Porch
32-4x10-10

Breakfast
10-0x9-8

Master
Bedroom
15-3x13-6

M. Bath
9-0x16-2

Greatroom
17-9x16-6

Bedroom
11-3x11-0

Kitchen
10-0x13-5

Storage
3-6x21-0

Garage
20-8x21-0

Bath

Foyer

Dining
13-6x11-0

Bedroom
11-5x11-6

Stoop

Storage
13-6x4-9

Width 66'-0"
Depth 49'-11"

Kitchen

Garage

Dining

Stor.

Basement Stair
Location

Design by
©Larry James &
Associates, Inc.

Design HPTM00028

Square Footage: 1,698

■ Gables, columns and multi-pane windows give this ranch-style home great curb appeal. A columned foyer branches off into the great room, formal dining area and two family bedrooms. A fireplace warms the great room and is visible from the kitchen. The adjoining kitchen and breakfast area enjoy an island/snack bar and a ribbon of windows facing the rear yard. The master suite is privately tucked behind the kitchen and accesses the rear deck. Please specify basement, crawlspace or slab foundation when ordering.

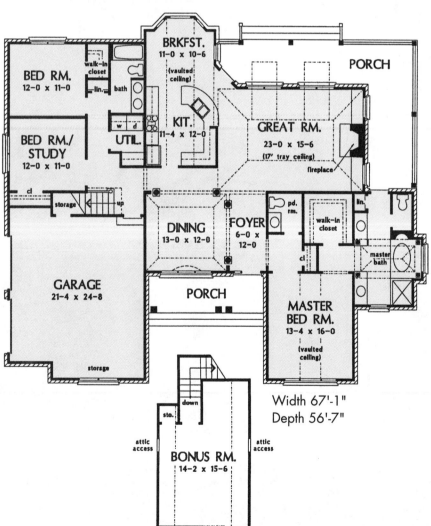

BED RM.
12-0 x 11-0

walk-in closet
lin.   bath

BRKFST.
11-0 x 10-6
(vaulted ceiling)

PORCH

BED RM./
STUDY
12-0 x 11-0

w d
UTIL.

KIT.
11-4 x 12-0

GREAT RM.
23-0 x 15-6
(17' tray ceiling)

fireplace

cl
storage   up

DINING
13-0 x 12-0

FOYER
6-0 x 12-0

pd. rm.

walk-in closet

lin.

cl

master bath

GARAGE
21-4 x 24-8

PORCH

MASTER BED RM.
13-4 x 16-0
(vaulted ceiling)

storage

Width 67'-1"
Depth 56'-7"

down
sto.

attic access   attic access

BONUS RM.
14-2 x 15-6

seat

Design 7657

Square Footage: 2,198
Bonus Room: 325 square feet

■ If you find that the great livability in this one-story home is not quite enough, you can develop the bonus room into a home office, guest suite or hobby room, how and when you choose. In the meantime, you'll find that the main floor plan holds superior spaces: a formal dining room, a great room (both with tray ceilings), a gourmet-style kitchen with attached breakfast room, and three bedrooms with two full baths. The comfortable wrap-around porch at the rear of the plan extends its invitation to the master suite, great room and breakfast room, for all to enjoy. Vaulted ceilings in the breakfast room and master bedroom open these areas to new heights. One of the family bedrooms sports a walk-in closet.

Design by
Donald A. Gardner
Architects, Inc.

Design 7624

Square Footage: 1,800

Design by
DONALD A. GARDNER ARCHITECTS, INC.

■ A covered front porch and plenty of windows give this elevation a lot of charm. The floor plan is attractive, too, for empty-nesters or those just starting out. A front bedroom could serve as a study, leaving another family bedroom and, on the other side of the house, a secluded master suite. With a tray ceiling, skylit bath and walk-in closet, this bedroom is sure to please. The spacious foyer provides two closets and an arched opening into the great room that fills the middle of the home. Highlighted by a fireplace and cathedral ceiling, this room offers access to the back patio and opens into the breakfast room/kitchen area. Located at the front of the house, the charming dining room is also easily accessible from the kitchen.

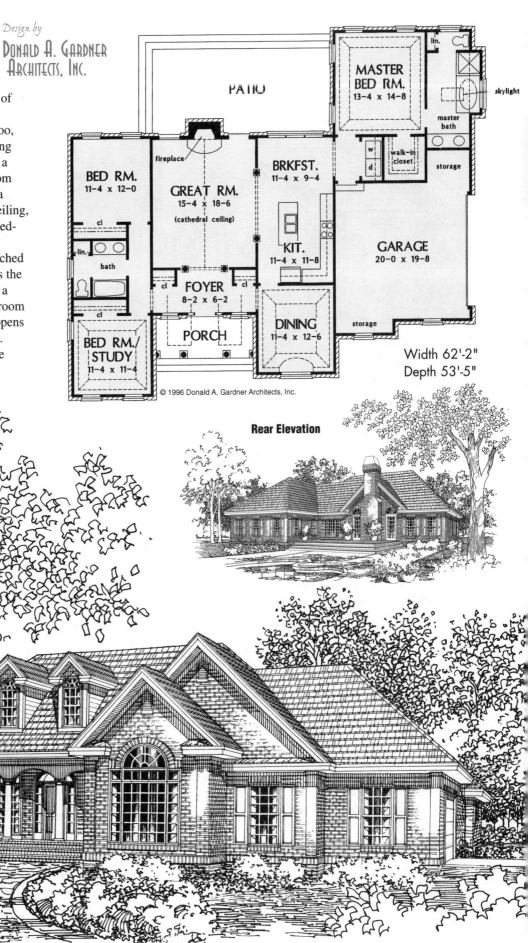

PATIO

MASTER BED RM.
13-4 x 14-8

skylight

master bath

lin.

walk-in closet

storage

w / d

fireplace

BED RM.
11-4 x 12-0

GREAT RM.
15-4 x 18-6
(cathedral ceiling)

BRKFST.
11-4 x 9-4

KIT.
11-4 x 11-8

GARAGE
20-0 x 19-8

cl

lin.

bath

cl

FOYER
8-2 x 6-2

cl

BED RM./ STUDY
11-4 x 11-4

PORCH

DINING
11-4 x 12-6

storage

Width 62'-2"
Depth 53'-5"

© 1996 Donald A. Gardner Architects, Inc.

Rear Elevation

Design 7004

Square Footage: 2,750

■ This is a grand design—much more than the typical ranch-style home. It speaks of tradition and classic planning. First is the quaint covered porch with an elegant entry and sidelites. The main foyer opens on the right to a dining room with tray ceiling or straight ahead to the spacious great room with fireplace. The kitchen has more-than-adequate details: a snack bar, walk-in pantry, planning desk and attached breakfast room with extended ceiling. Choose three family bedrooms or two and a den. Two full baths are found here. The master suite is at the opposite end of the plan for privacy. A massive walk-in closet, corner whirlpool tub and compartmented toilet are among its many appointments. Don't miss the convenience of the three-car garage.

Design by
DESIGN BASICS, INC.

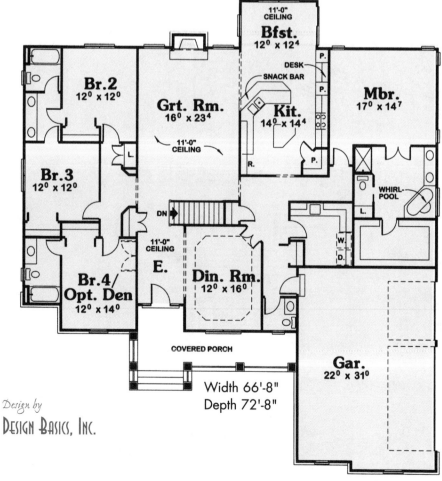

Width 66'-8"
Depth 72'-8"

Rear Elevation

Design 7308
Square Footage: 2,186

■ Brick columns and a tall, gabled entry create a prominent elevation with brick-and-siding accents. A bright twelve-foot entry enjoys interior vistas of the expansive great room, which offers a fireplace with an extended hearth and opens to the formal dining room. The nearby gourmet island kitchen with a service bar and lots of wrapping counters is well integrated with the bayed breakfast and dining areas. A spacious and secluded master suite boasts a lavish whirlpool bath, a U-shaped walk-in closet and ten-foot ceilings. The utility corridor leads to a laundry and to a convenient computer area, which could also be developed as an oversized walk-in pantry. A sunlit shop area highlights the three-car garage.

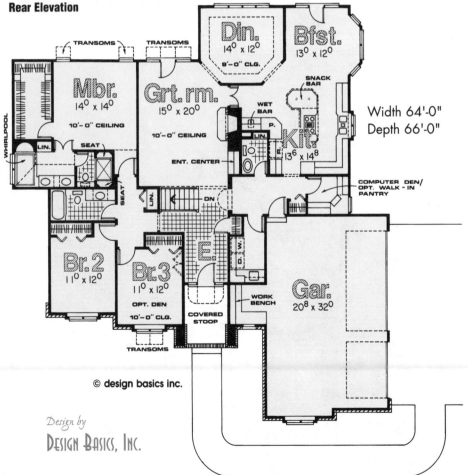

Width 64'-0"
Depth 66'-0"

© design basics inc.

Design by
DESIGN BASICS, INC.

199

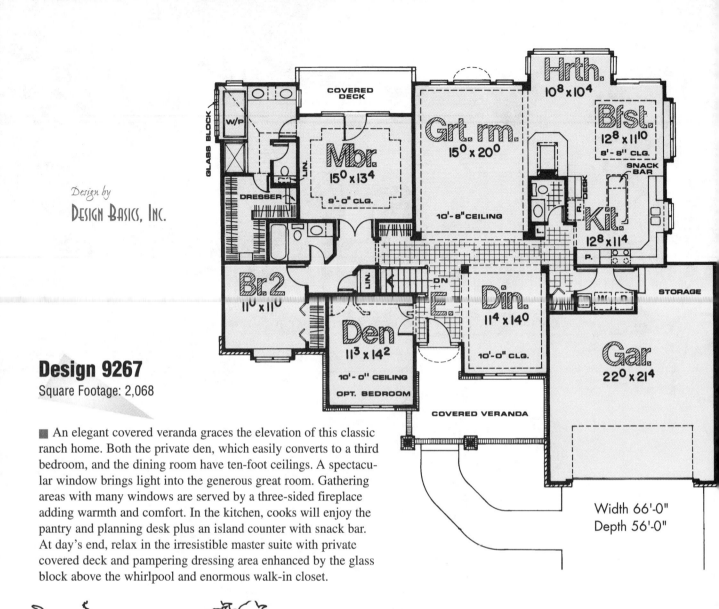

Design by
DESIGN BASICS, INC.

COVERED DECK

Mbr.
15⁰ x 13⁴
9'-0" CLG.

Grt. rm.
15⁰ x 20⁰
10'-8" CEILING

Hrth.
10⁸ x 10⁴

Bfst.
12⁸ x 11¹⁰
8'-8" CLG.

SNACK BAR

Kit.
12⁸ x 11⁴

Br. 2
11⁰ x 11⁰

LIN.

Den
11³ x 14²
10'-0" CEILING
OPT. BEDROOM

Din.
11⁴ x 14⁰
10'-0" CLG.

STORAGE

Gar.
22⁰ x 21⁴

COVERED VERANDA

GLASS BLOCK

W/P

DRESSER

Design 9267
Square Footage: 2,068

■ An elegant covered veranda graces the elevation of this classic ranch home. Both the private den, which easily converts to a third bedroom, and the dining room have ten-foot ceilings. A spectacular window brings light into the generous great room. Gathering areas with many windows are served by a three-sided fireplace adding warmth and comfort. In the kitchen, cooks will enjoy the pantry and planning desk plus an island counter with snack bar. At day's end, relax in the irresistible master suite with private covered deck and pampering dressing area enhanced by the glass block above the whirlpool and enormous walk-in closet.

Width 66'-0"
Depth 56'-0"

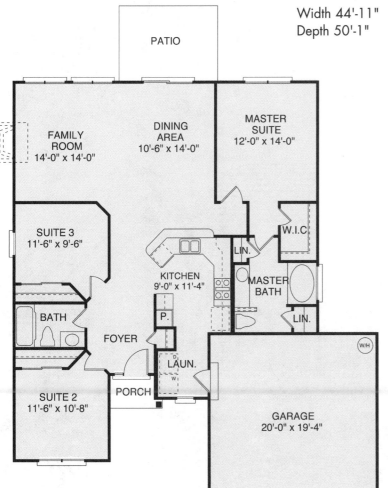

Width 44'-11"
Depth 50'-1"

PATIO

FAMILY ROOM
14'-0" x 14'-0"

DINING AREA
10'-6" x 14'-0"

MASTER SUITE
12'-0" x 14'-0"

SUITE 3
11'-6" x 9'-6"

W.I.C

LIN.

KITCHEN
9'-0" x 11'-4"

MASTER BATH

BATH

LIN.

FOYER

P.

LAUN.

PORCH

SUITE 2
11'-6" x 10'-8"

W/H

GARAGE
20'-0" x 19'-4"

Design HPTMO3038

Square Footage: 1,395

■ A combination of muntin windows with lintels, side paneling and brick adds flavor to this traditional home. Surrounding the foyer is a full hall bath separating two family suites. The master bedroom is located to the rear of the plan and boasts a private bath, linen closet and a huge walk-in closet. The self-sufficient kitchen includes plenty of work space, a breakfast bar and a pantry. Adjacent to the dining room, the family room provides an area for an optional fireplace. The garage entrance is conveniently placed near the laundry room and the kitchen.

Design by
© Living Concepts Home Planning

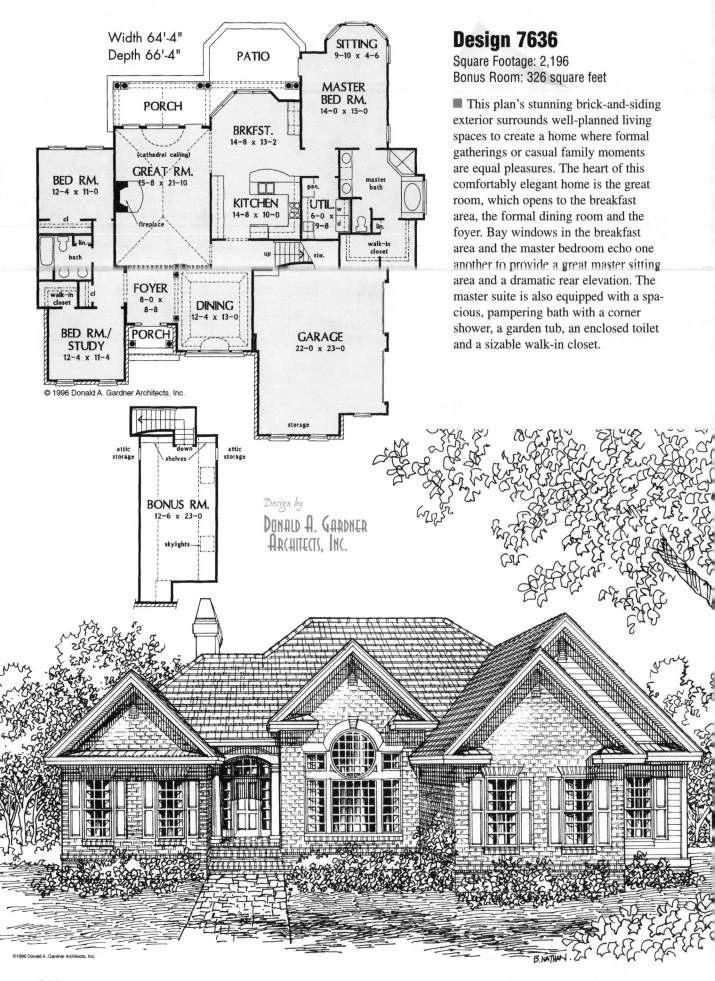

Width 64'-4"
Depth 66'-4"

PATIO

SITTING
9-10 x 4-6

Design 7636

Square Footage: 2,196
Bonus Room: 326 square feet

PORCH

MASTER
BED RM.
14-0 x 15-0

BRKFST.
14-8 x 13-2

(cathedral ceiling)

GREAT RM.
15-8 x 21-10

KITCHEN
14-8 x 10-0

pan.

master
bath

UTIL.
6-0 x
9-8

w
d

lin.

fireplace

BED RM.
12-4 x 11-0

cl

lin.

bath

walk-in
closet

up

sto.

walk-in
closet

walk-in
closet

cl

FOYER
8-0 x
8-8

DINING
12-4 x 13-0

GARAGE
22-0 x 23-0

BED RM./
STUDY
12-4 x 11-4

PORCH

storage

© 1996 Donald A. Gardner Architects, Inc.

attic
storage

down
shelves

attic
storage

BONUS RM.
12-6 x 23-0

skylights

Design by

DONALD A. GARDNER
ARCHITECTS, INC.

■ This plan's stunning brick-and-siding exterior surrounds well-planned living spaces to create a home where formal gatherings or casual family moments are equal pleasures. The heart of this comfortably elegant home is the great room, which opens to the breakfast area, the formal dining room and the foyer. Bay windows in the breakfast area and the master bedroom echo one another to provide a great master sitting area and a dramatic rear elevation. The master suite is also equipped with a spacious, pampering bath with a corner shower, a garden tub, an enclosed toilet and a sizable walk-in closet.

©1996 Donald A. Gardner Architects, Inc.

B. NATHAN

202

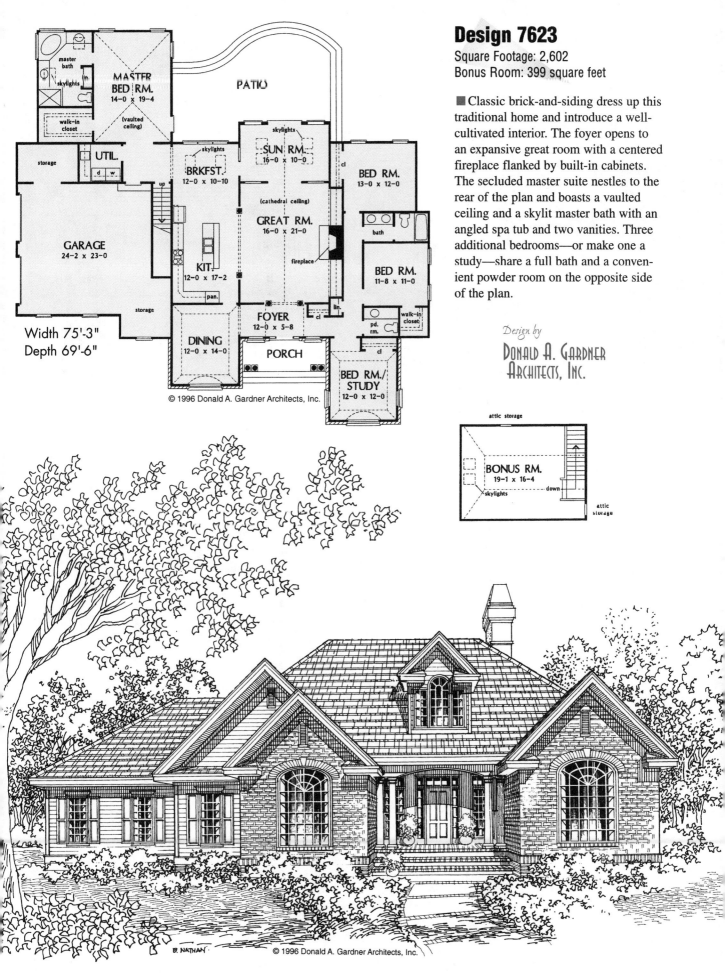

Design 7623

Square Footage: 2,602
Bonus Room: 399 square feet

■ Classic brick-and-siding dress up this traditional home and introduce a well-cultivated interior. The foyer opens to an expansive great room with a centered fireplace flanked by built-in cabinets. The secluded master suite nestles to the rear of the plan and boasts a vaulted ceiling and a skylit master bath with an angled spa tub and two vanities. Three additional bedrooms—or make one a study—share a full bath and a convenient powder room on the opposite side of the plan.

Design by
Donald A. Gardner
Architects, Inc.

master bath
skylights
lin.
MASTER BED RM.
14-0 x 19-4
(vaulted ceiling)
walk-in closet
storage
UTIL.
d w
GARAGE
24-2 x 23-0
storage
PATIO
skylights
BRKFST.
12-0 x 10-10
up
KIT.
12-0 x 17-2
pan.
SUN RM.
16-0 x 10-0
(cathedral ceiling)
GREAT RM.
16-0 x 21-0
fireplace
DINING
12-0 x 14-0
FOYER
12-0 x 5-8
PORCH
cl
BED RM.
13-0 x 12-0
bath
BED RM.
11-8 x 11-0
lin.
pd. rm.
walk-in closet
BED RM./ STUDY
12-0 x 12-0
cl

Width 75'-3"
Depth 69'-6"

© 1996 Donald A. Gardner Architects, Inc.

attic storage
BONUS RM.
19-1 x 16-4
down
skylights
attic storage

B. NATHAN
© 1996 Donald A. Gardner Architects, Inc.

203

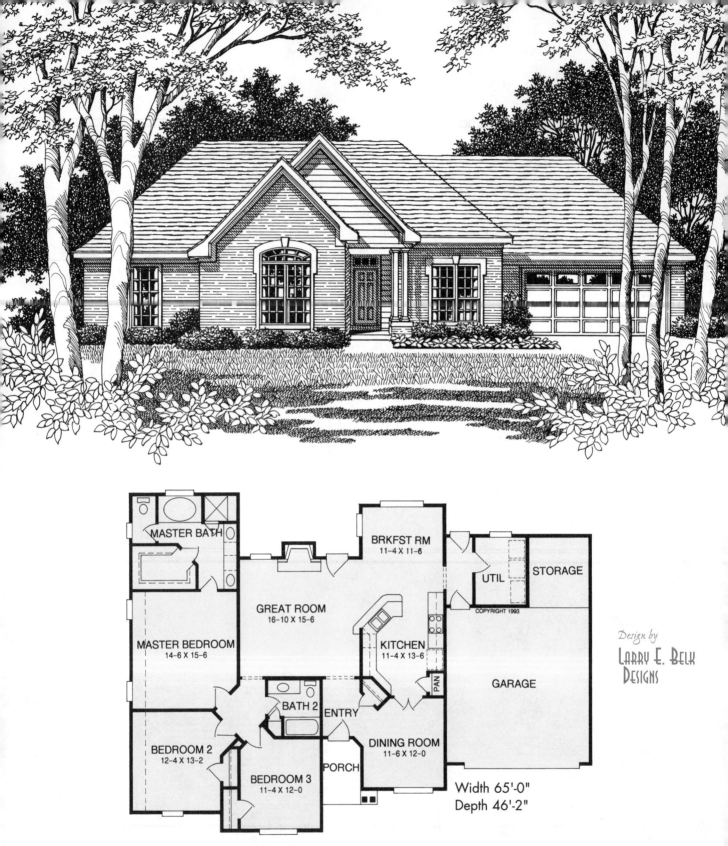

MASTER BATH

BRKFST RM
11-4 X 11-6

UTIL

STORAGE

COPYRIGHT 1993

GREAT ROOM
16-10 X 15-6

MASTER BEDROOM
14-6 X 15-6

KITCHEN
11-4 X 13-6

Design by
LARRY E. BELK
DESIGNS

PAN

GARAGE

BATH 2

ENTRY

DINING ROOM
11-6 X 12-0

BEDROOM 2
12-4 X 13-2

PORCH

Width 65'-0"
Depth 46'-2"

BEDROOM 3
11-4 X 12-0

Design 8180
Square Footage: 1,862

■ This charming traditional has all the amenities of a larger plan in a compact layout. Ten-foot ceilings give this home an expansive feel. An angled eating bar separates the kitchen and great room while leaving these areas open to one another for family gatherings and entertaining. The master bedroom includes a huge walk-in closet and a superior master bath with a whirlpool tub and separate shower. A large utility room and an oversized storage area are located near the secondary entrance to the home. Two additional bedrooms and a bath finish the plan. Please specify crawlspace or slab foundation when ordering.

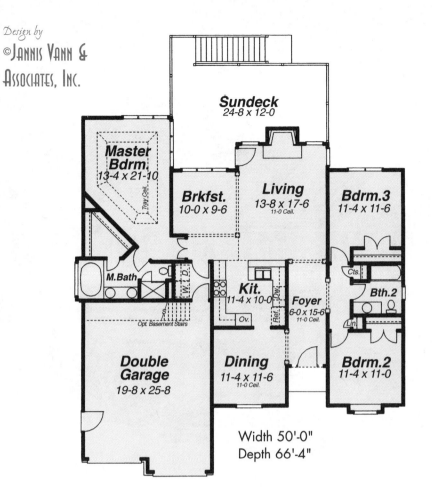

Design by
©Jannis Vann & Associates, Inc.

Sundeck
24-8 x 12-0

Master Bdrm.
13-4 x 21-10
Tray Ceil.

Brkfst.
10-0 x 9-6

Living
13-8 x 17-6
11-0 Ceil.

Bdrm.3
11-4 x 11-6

M.Bath

W.D.

Cts.

Kit.
11-4 x 10-0

Foyer
6-0 x 15-6
11-0 Ceil.

Bth.2

Ref. Dw.

Ov.

S

Opt. Basement Stairs

Lin

Double Garage
19-8 x 25-8

Dining
11-4 x 11-6
11-0 Ceil.

Bdrm.2
11-4 x 11-0

Width 50'-0"
Depth 66'-4"

Design X066
Square Footage: 1,635

■ Just the perfect size, this one-story home is great for families. A central foyer allows passage to the formal dining room and the living room, which features a fireplace flanked by windows. Access the sun deck in the rear from the living room, allowing expansion of entertaining options. The breakfast room is nearby, close to the work-savvy kitchen. Two family bedrooms line the right side of the home, separated by a full, shared bath. The master bedroom sits behind the garage and holds a tray ceiling and private bath with whirlpool tub. Please specify basement, crawlspace or slab foundation when ordering.

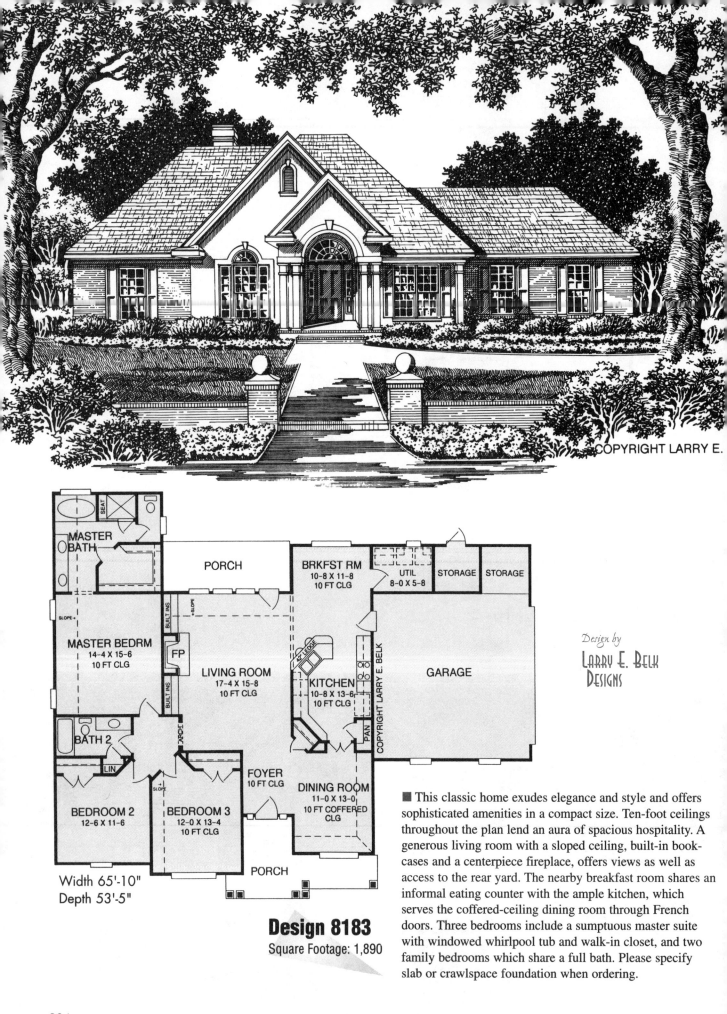

COPYRIGHT LARRY E.

MASTER BATH

PORCH

BRKFST RM
10-8 X 11-8
10 FT CLG

UTIL
8-0 X 5-8

STORAGE

STORAGE

Design by
LARRY E. BELK
DESIGNS

MASTER BEDRM
14-4 X 15-6
10 FT CLG

FP

LIVING ROOM
17-4 X 15-8
10 FT CLG

KITCHEN
10-8 X 13-6
10 FT CLG

GARAGE

COPYRIGHT LARRY E. BELK

BATH 2

LIN

FOYER
10 FT CLG

BEDROOM 2
12-6 X 11-6

BEDROOM 3
12-0 X 13-4
10 FT CLG

DINING ROOM
11-0 X 13-0
10 FT COFFERED CLG

Width 65'-10"
Depth 53'-5"

PORCH

Design 8183
Square Footage: 1,890

■ This classic home exudes elegance and style and offers sophisticated amenities in a compact size. Ten-foot ceilings throughout the plan lend an aura of spacious hospitality. A generous living room with a sloped ceiling, built-in bookcases and a centerpiece fireplace, offers views as well as access to the rear yard. The nearby breakfast room shares an informal eating counter with the ample kitchen, which serves the coffered-ceiling dining room through French doors. Three bedrooms include a sumptuous master suite with windowed whirlpool tub and walk-in closet, and two family bedrooms which share a full bath. Please specify slab or crawlspace foundation when ordering.

Design by
©Larry E.
Belk Designs

HER BATH

MASTER BEDROOM
17-6 X 17-6
10 FT CEILING

FAMILY ROOM/BRKFST
19-6 X 14-6
10 FT CEILING

PORCH

BUILT INS

LIN

HIS BATH

PORCH

BEDRM 2
12-4 X 13-4

EXERCISE

UTIL

PWDR

KITCHEN
13-4 X 12-6
10 FT CEILING

GREAT ROOM
15-0 X 15-0
12 FT CEILING

LIN

PAN

BATH 2
10 FT CEILING

DRSSNG

STEP

LIN

GARAGE

DINING ROOM
12-6 X 12-6
10 FT CEILING

ENTRY
12 FT CEILING

Width 89'-6"
Depth 54'-2"

PORCH

BEDRM 3
12-4 X 11-4

STORAGE

Design 8053
Square Footage: 2,506

■ A traditional exterior accented by triple gables introduces this well-appointed one-story home. Columns with connecting arched openings define the formal dining room and create a dramatic entrance. An efficiently planned kitchen faces the spacious family room and breakfast room. The corner fireplace with a raised hearth bids a warm welcome, making this a splendid area for informal entertaining. The romantic master suite is designed with a fireplace and an exercise room that includes space for a tanning bed. The master bath has large His and Hers walk-in closets as well as His and Hers baths with separate entrances to a shared shower. Two additional bedrooms featuring walk-in closets are located on the opposite side of the home. Please specify crawl-space or slab foundation when ordering.

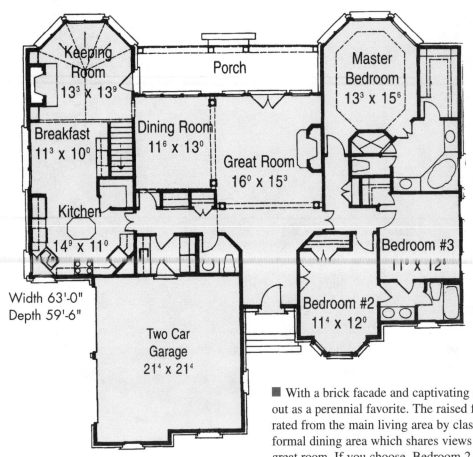

Keeping Room
13³ x 13⁹

Porch

Master Bedroom
13³ x 15⁶

Breakfast
11³ x 10⁰

Dining Room
11⁶ x 13⁰

Great Room
16⁰ x 15³

Kitchen
14⁹ x 11⁰

Bedroom #3
11⁰ x 12⁰

Width 63'-0"
Depth 59'-6"

Bedroom #2
11⁴ x 12⁰

Two Car Garage
21⁴ x 21⁴

Design by
DESIGN TRADITIONS

■ With a brick facade and captivating adornments, this one-story plan stands out as a perennial favorite. The raised front porch opens to an entry hall separated from the main living area by classic columns. Columns also define the formal dining area which shares views of the covered rear porch with the great room. If you choose, Bedroom 2 might become a den—change its entry from the secluded hall to the entry hall. A grand kitchen features an island workspace and attaches to a breakfast room and hearth-warmed keeping room beyond. Bedrooms are to the right of the plan and include a master suite with a tray ceiling, walk-in closet and corner whirlpool tub. The two-car garage protects the main house from street noise and traffic. This home is designed with a basement foundation.

Design T213
Square Footage: 2,150

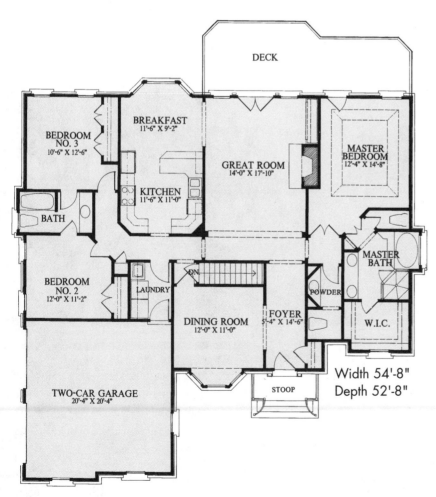

DECK

BREAKFAST
11'-6" X 9'-2"

BEDROOM
NO. 3
10'-6" X 12'-6"

GREAT ROOM
14'-0" X 17'-10"

MASTER
BEDROOM
12'-4" X 14'-8"

KITCHEN
11'-6" X 11'-0"

BATH

MASTER
BATH

BEDROOM
NO. 2
12'-0" X 11'-2"

LAUNDRY

DN

POWDER

FOYER
5'-4" X 14'-6"

W.I.C.

DINING ROOM
12'-0" X 11'-0"

TWO-CAR GARAGE
20'-4" X 20'-4"

STOOP

Width 54'-8"
Depth 52'-8"

Design T091

Square Footage: 1,850

■ A side-loaded garage helps maintain a beautiful facade for this brick one-story. The recessed entry opens to a central foyer that leads to the dining room on the left and the great room to the rear. A lovely deck is found beyond the great room and is also accessed from the master suite. The large kitchen has an attached breakfast room with bay window and is just across the hall from the service entrance with laundry. Two secondary bedrooms have plenty of closet space and share a compartmented full bath. This home is designed with a basement foundation.

Design by
DESIGN TRADITIONS

Design T215

Square Footage: 1,733

■ Count on the center-hall design and open floor planning of this design to meet your livability needs for years to come. The great room serves both informal and formal occasions and is close enough to the formal dining room and the less formal breakfast room to make entertaining easy. Further enhancements in the great room include a fireplace and double doors opening to the rear deck. The breakfast room has a bay-style window for sunny morning coffee. Bedrooms are split with two family bedrooms and a full bath on the left and the master suite on the right. The master bedroom features a tray ceiling and a bath with plenty of closet space, a garden whirlpool and double sinks. The two-car garage has extra room for storage or a workbench. This home is designed with a basement foundation.

Design by
DESIGN TRADITIONS

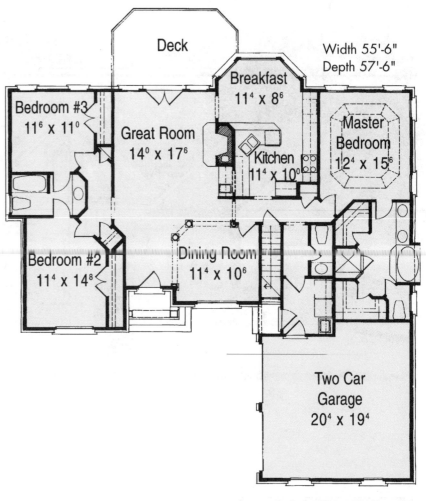

Deck

Width 55'-6"
Depth 57'-6"

Bedroom #3
11⁶ x 11⁰

Great Room
14⁰ x 17⁶

Breakfast
11⁴ x 8⁶

Kitchen
11⁴ x 10⁰

Master Bedroom
12⁴ x 15⁶

Bedroom #2
11⁴ x 14⁸

Dining Room
11⁴ x 10⁶

Two Car Garage
20⁴ x 19⁴

Design T110

Square Footage: 1,815

Floor Plan Labels

PORCH

BREAKFAST
10'-0" X 10'-0"

GREAT ROOM
16'-0" X 18'-0"

MASTER BEDROOM
15'-0" X 14'-0"

W.I.C.

MASTER BATH

POWDER

KITCHEN
14'-0" X 11'-4"

DINING ROOM
10'-6" X 13'-0"

FOYER
5'-0" X 9'-0"

BEDROOM NO. 2
11'-2" X 11'-0"

BEDROOM
NO. 3
10'-6" X 10'-0"

BATH

LAUND
5'-2" X
10'-6"

DN

TWO CAR GARAGE
20'-4" X 19'-4"

Width 60'-0"
Depth 60'-6"

Design by
DESIGN TRADITIONS

■ With zoned living at the core of this floor plan, livability takes a convenient turn. Living areas are to the left of the plan; sleeping areas to the right. The formal dining room is open to the central hallway and foyer, and features graceful columned archways to define its space. The great room has angled corners and a magnificent central fireplace and offers ample views to the rear grounds. Steps away is a well-lit breakfast room with private rear-porch access and an adjoining U-shaped kitchen with unique angled counter space and sink. Sleeping quarters are clustered around a private hallway which offers a guest bath. The master suite includes a resplendent bath with garden tub, dual lavatories and walk-in closet. Two family bedrooms share a full bath with compartmented toilet and tub. This home is designed with a basement foundation.

Porch
17-10x10-0

Master
Bedroom
13-0x17-1

M.Bath

Greatroom
21-0x16-3

Breakfast
13-3x8-11

Desk

Laun.
6-0x7-1

Stor.
8-1x7-1

Bath

Kitchen
13-0x14-0

Garage
20-11x21-5

Bedroom
13-0x11-3

Bedroom
13-1x14-1

Foyer

Dining
13-0x10-11

Porch
22-11x5-10

Width 74'-11"
Depth 49'-2"

Design by
©Larry James &
Associates, Inc.

Design HPTM00029
Square Footage: 2,018

■ A Palladian window set into a front-facing gable highlights this ranch home. The dining room, on the right, includes accent columns and convenient kitchen service. The great room offers twin French doors that access the rear porch. Meal preparation will be easy in the kitchen with a work island and cheerful light streaming in from the bay-windowed breakfast nook. The master suite is set to the rear and features a walk-in closet made for two, dual vanities and a compartment toilet. Two family bedrooms near the front of the plan share a full bath. Please specify basement, crawlspace or slab foundation when ordering.

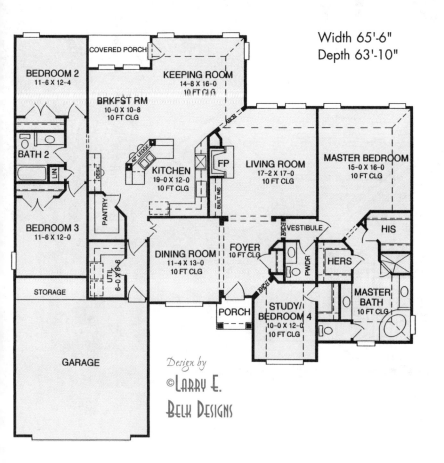

Width 65'-6"
Depth 63'-10"

BEDROOM 2
11-6 X 12-4

COVERED PORCH

KEEPING ROOM
14-8 X 16-0
10 FT CLG

BRKFST RM
10-0 X 10-8
10 FT CLG

BATH 2

KITCHEN
19-0 X 12-0
10 FT CLG

FP

LIVING ROOM
17-2 X 17-0
10 FT CLG

MASTER BEDROOM
15-0 X 16-0
10 FT CLG

PANTRY

DESK

BUILT INS

BEDROOM 3
11-6 X 12-0

LIN

VESTIBULE

HIS

DINING ROOM
11-4 X 13-0
10 FT CLG

FOYER
10 FT CLG

PWDR

HERS

UTIL
6-0 X 8-6

STORAGE

PORCH

STUDY/
BEDROOM 4
10-0 X 12-0
10 FT CLG

MASTER
BATH
10 FT CLG

GARAGE

Design by
©Larry E.
Belk Designs

Design 8140

Square Footage: 2,559

■ Traditional in character, this efficiently designed one-story home comes with all the amenities. Ten-foot ceilings in all major living areas give the plan a big-home feel. The kitchen, breakfast room and keeping room are adjacent and open to one another for family gatherings. The kitchen features a large walk-in pantry, desk and snack bar. Family bedrooms are located away from the master suite. A private study is situated off the foyer and could be used for an in-home office or nursery. Please specify crawl-space or slab foundation when ordering.

Design P295

Square Footage: 1,425

■ The floor plan of this beautifully styled traditional home leaves room for many options. For instance, Bedroom 2, with its vaulted ceiling, would make a fine home office or den. Plant shelves throughout the plan allow you to indulge your hobby as an indoor gardener, or to display fine collectibles or art objects. Living spaces are open and graced with extended ceilings. The family room features a corner fireplace and shares with the dining room a serving bar in the kitchen. A nearby breakfast room has a vaulted ceiling also and a wall of windows overlooking the rear yard. The master suite is truly luxurious. It is appointed with a tray ceiling and has a vaulted master bath with a huge whirlpool tub, walk-in closet with built-in linen storage and double sink. The two-car garage contains extra storage space.

Design by
Frank Betz
Associates, Inc.

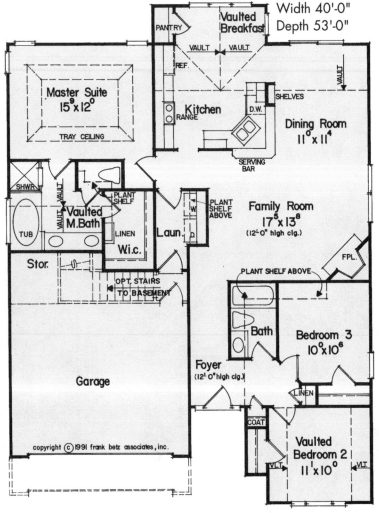

Width 40'-0"
Depth 53'-0"

Design A246

Square Footage: 1,913

■ This traditional home begins with a
stylish columned lanai, which leads to a
spacious foyer and hall that opens to all
areas. The kitchen overlooks a central formal dining room with views and access to
the rear deck. An open, spacious gathering room shares the glow of an extended-
hearth fireplace with the dining area and
kitchen. The master suite opens from a
private vestibule and offers a deluxe bath
with a garden tub, a separate shower and
a U-shaped walk-in closet. Two additional
suites share a full bath on the other side
of the plan. One of these rooms could
serve as a den or study. A service entrance
from the two-car garage leads to a pantry
area and to the laundry.

Design by
Living Concepts

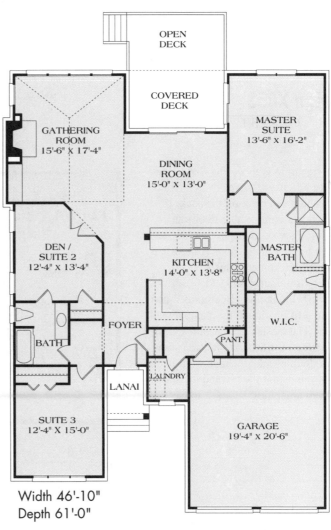

Width 46'-10"
Depth 61'-0"

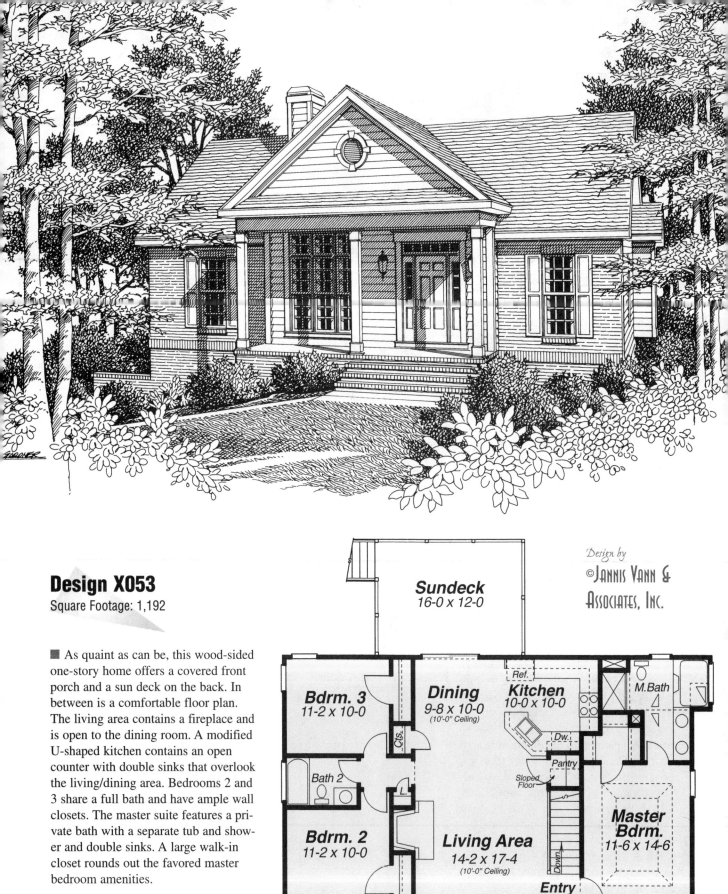

Design X053

Square Footage: 1,192

■ As quaint as can be, this wood-sided one-story home offers a covered front porch and a sun deck on the back. In between is a comfortable floor plan. The living area contains a fireplace and is open to the dining room. A modified U-shaped kitchen contains an open counter with double sinks that overlook the living/dining area. Bedrooms 2 and 3 share a full bath and have ample wall closets. The master suite features a private bath with a separate tub and shower and double sinks. A large walk-in closet rounds out the favored master bedroom amenities.

Design by
©Jannis Vann & Associates, Inc.

Sundeck
16-0 x 12-0

Bdrm. 3
11-2 x 10-0

Dining
9-8 x 10-0
(10'-0" Ceiling)

Kitchen
10-0 x 10-0

Ref.

M.Bath

Cts.

Bath 2

Dw.

Pantry

Sloped Floor

Bdrm. 2
11-2 x 10-0

Living Area
14-2 x 17-4
(10'-0" Ceiling)

Down

Master Bdrm.
11-6 x 14-6

Entry

Sh.

Width 46'-0"
Depth 33'-0"

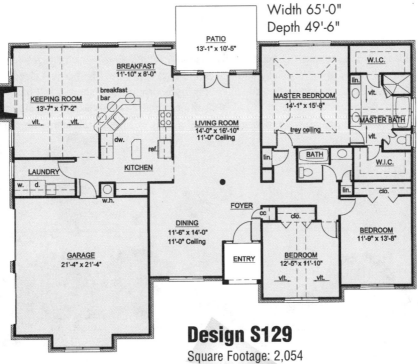

Width 65'-0"
Depth 49'-6"

PATIO
13'-1" x 10'-5"

BREAKFAST
11'-10" x 8'-0"

breakfast
bar

KEEPING ROOM
13'-7" x 17'-2"

vlt.   vlt.

dw.

ref.

LAUNDRY

w.   d.

KITCHEN

w.h.

GARAGE
21'-4" x 21'-4"

LIVING ROOM
14'-0" x 16'-10"
11'-0" Ceiling

DINING
11'-6" x 14'-0"
11'-0" Ceiling

FOYER

cc   clo.

ENTRY

MASTER BEDROOM
14'-1" x 15'-8"

trey ceiling

lin.

BATH

lin.

lin.

BEDROOM
12'-5" x 11'-10"

vlt.   vlt.

W.I.C.

lin.   vlt.

MASTER BATH

vlt.

W.I.C.

clo.

BEDROOM
11'-9" x 13'-8"

Design S129
Square Footage: 2,054

■ Defined by an elegant column, the covered entrance to this three bedroom home welcomes friends and family. Inside, a formal dining room and formal living room, also defined by a graceful column, are open to one another, providing a wonderful entertaining area. The kitchen, enhanced by angles, features a work island and a breakfast bar. The nearby keeping room offers a vaulted ceiling and a warming fireplace. Two secondary bedrooms share a hall bath, while the master bedroom is complete with many amenities. Here, a tray ceiling, two walk-in closets and a vaulted bath are sure to please.

Design by
ARCHIVAL DESIGNS

Design 9264

Square Footage: 2,355

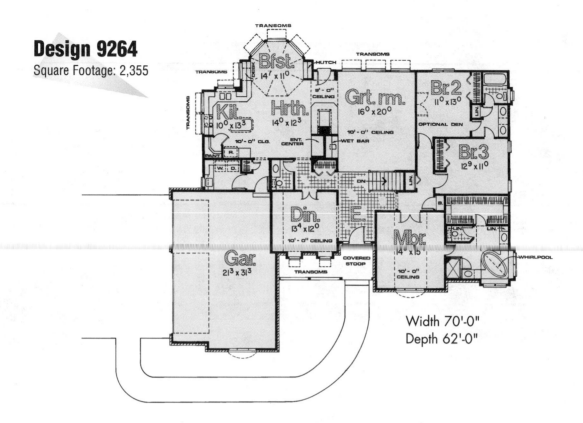

Width 70'-0"
Depth 62'-0"

■ This home presents a facade of simple, timeless elegance. The vaulted entry paves the way to views of the stairway and great room beyond. The three-sided fireplace serves as a focal point for both the great room and the adjacent hearth room. The formal dining room has ten-foot ceilings and boxed windows. A breakfast room with gazebo ceiling is convenient for more casual dining. The home's sleeping wing includes two family bedrooms that share a full bath. A luxurious master suite is highlighted by a dressing area with twin vanities, an angled oval whirlpool tub and a large walk-in closet.

Design by
DESIGN BASICS, INC.

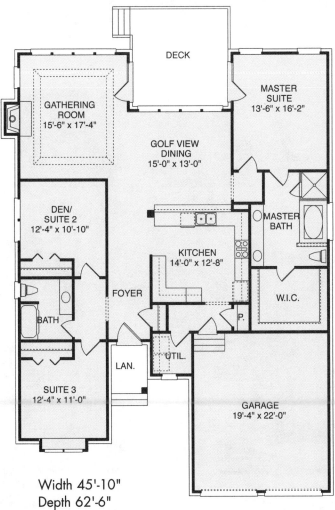

DECK

GATHERING
ROOM
15'-6" x 17'-4"

MASTER
SUITE
13'-6" x 16'-2"

GOLF VIEW
DINING
15'-0" x 13'-0"

DEN/
SUITE 2
12'-4" x 10'-10"

MASTER
BATH

KITCHEN
14'-0" x 12'-8"

FOYER

W.I.C.

BATH

P.

LAN.

UTIL.

SUITE 3
12'-4" x 11'-0"

GARAGE
19'-4" x 22'-0"

Width 45'-10"
Depth 62'-6"

Design HPTM03039

Square Footage: 1,915

■ Choose three bedrooms or two bedrooms plus a den in this contemporary single-level design. The well-equipped kitchen has a pass-through to a large dining room that overlooks the deck just beyond. The gathering room with a sloped ceiling highlights a wall of windows across the back and a fireplace in the side wall. The master suite features twin basins and a walk-in closet. Two other bedrooms with an adjoining bath reside off the entry foyer. One of these bedrooms may be used as a den.

Design by
© Living Concepts Home Planning

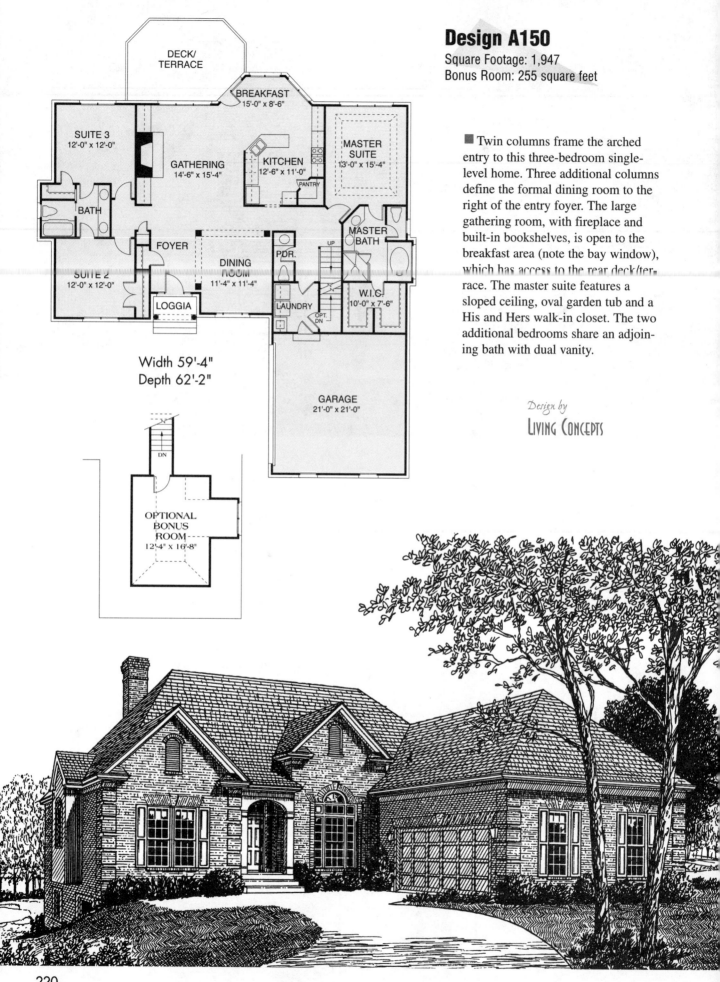

Design A150

Square Footage: 1,947
Bonus Room: 255 square feet

DECK/TERRACE

BREAKFAST
15'-0" x 8'-6"

SUITE 3
12'-0" x 12'-0"

GATHERING
14'-6" x 15'-4"

KITCHEN
12'-6" x 11'-0"

MASTER SUITE
13'-0" x 15'-4"

PANTRY

BATH

FOYER

DINING ROOM
11'-4" x 11'-4"

PDR.

UP

MASTER BATH

SUITE 2
12'-0" x 12'-0"

LOGGIA

LAUNDRY

OPT. DN

W.I.C.
10'-0" x 7'-6"

Width 59'-4"
Depth 62'-2"

GARAGE
21'-0" x 21'-0"

DN

OPTIONAL BONUS ROOM
12'-4" x 16'-8"

■ Twin columns frame the arched entry to this three-bedroom single-level home. Three additional columns define the formal dining room to the right of the entry foyer. The large gathering room, with fireplace and built-in bookshelves, is open to the breakfast area (note the bay window), which has access to the rear deck/terrace. The master suite features a sloped ceiling, oval garden tub and a His and Hers walk-in closet. The two additional bedrooms share an adjoining bath with dual vanity.

Design by
Living Concepts

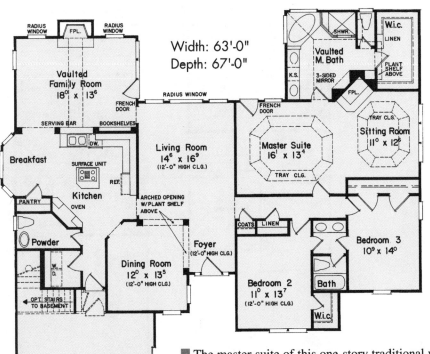

Width: 63'-0"
Depth: 67'-0"

RADIUS WINDOW

FPL.

RADIUS WINDOW

Vaulted Family Room
18⁰ x 13⁶

SERVING BAR

BOOKSHELVES

FRENCH DOOR

DW.

Breakfast

SURFACE UNIT

Kitchen
OVEN

REF.

PANTRY

Powder

W. D.

OPT. STAIRS TO BASEMENT

Garage

copyright (c) 1993 frank betz associates, inc.

RADIUS WINDOW

Living Room
14⁶ x 16⁹
(12'-0" HIGH CLG.)

ARCHED OPENING W/PLANT SHELF ABOVE

Dining Room
12⁰ x 13⁵
(12'-0" HIGH CLG.)

Foyer
(12'-0" HIGH CLG.)

W.i.c.

LINEN

SHWR.

Vaulted M. Bath

K.S.

3-SIDED MIRROR

PLANT SHELF ABOVE

FPL.

FRENCH DOOR

Master Suite
16¹ x 13⁴

TRAY CLG.

TRAY CLG.

Sitting Room
11⁰ x 12⁸

COATS

LINEN

Bedroom 3
10⁹ x 14⁰

Bedroom 2
11⁰ x 13⁷
(12'-0" HIGH CLG.)

Bath

W.i.c.

Design P126
Square Footage: 2,236

Design by
Frank Betz Associates, Inc.

■ The master suite of this one-story traditional will be a haven for any homeowner. Separate tray ceilings split a generous sitting room from the main bedroom while a fireplace warms both areas. The vaulted master bath includes a three-sided mirror, a corner whirlpool tub, His and Hers sinks and a walk-in closet with built-in linen storage. The master suite also includes French-door access to the rear yard. The rest of the home is equally impressive. Radius windows highlight the central living room, arches create a dramatic entrance to the dining room and the open kitchen area includes a cooktop island, a sunny breakfast area and a serving bar to the vaulted family room with its cozy fireplace. Two bedrooms and a full bath with dual basins complete this amenity-filled design. Please specify basement or crawlspace foundation when ordering.

Design HPTM03040

Square Footage: 1,430

■ Gables and a combination of brick-and-siding make this fine three-bedroom home perfect for any neighborhood. Inside, a vaulted family room is the center of attention with a warming fireplace to gather around. The angled kitchen easily serves both the dining room and the bayed breakfast area. Three bedrooms include a deluxe master suite that's complete with a walk-in closet and a vaulted bath. Please specify basement, crawlspace or slab foundation when ordering.

Design by
© Frank Betz Associates, Inc.

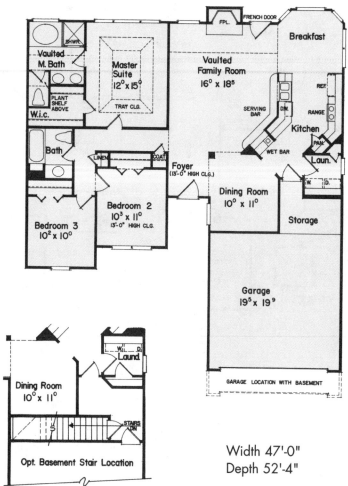

Width 47'-0"
Depth 52'-4"

Design 7315

Square Footage: 1,782

■ Symmetrical gables offset a hip roof and arch-top windows and complement a stately brick exterior with this traditional design. Inside, the formal dining room opens from an elegant tiled entry and offers space for quiet, planned occasions as well as traditional festivities. The casual living area shares a three-sided fireplace with the breakfast area and hearth room, while the kitchen offers a convenient snack bar for easy meals. A nine-foot ceiling enhances the master suite, which features a whirlpool tub, twin vanities, an ample walk-in closet and a compartmented toilet. Split sleeping quarters offer privacy to both the master and the family bedrooms, which share a full bath.

Design by
Design Basics, Inc.

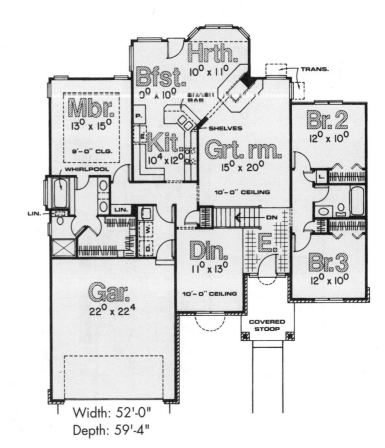

Width: 52'-0"
Depth: 59'-4"

Rear Elevation

Design 7345

Square Footage: 2,504

■ Brick detail and interesting window treatments create a dramatic exterior on this traditional one-story home. Inside, formal living and dining rooms share a through-fireplace. Additionally, transom windows and French doors open the formal living area to the outside. A nearby kitchen provides a snack bar, an island counter, easy access to the dining room and a cathedral ceiling. A perfect retreat, the master suite is highlighted by French doors, matching vanities, a walk-in closet and an oval whirlpool tub.

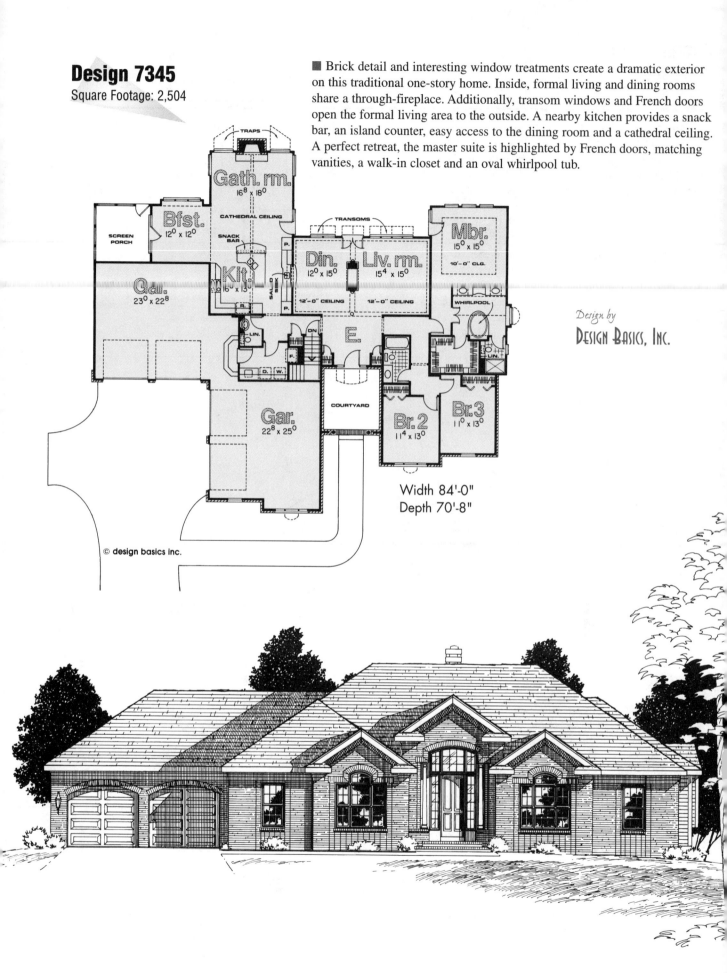

Gath. rm.
16⁸ x 18⁰

CATHEDRAL CEILING

Bfst.
12⁰ x 12⁰

SCREEN PORCH

SNACK BAR

Kit.
16⁰ x 13⁰

Gar.
23⁰ x 22⁸

TRANSOMS

Din.
12⁰ x 15⁰

Liv. rm.
15⁴ x 15⁰

Mbr.
15⁰ x 15⁰

10'-0" CLG.

12'-0" CEILING   12'-0" CEILING

WHIRLPOOL

LIN.

E.

Gar.
22⁸ x 25⁰

COURTYARD

Br. 2
11⁴ x 13⁰

Br. 3
11⁰ x 13⁰

Width 84'-0"
Depth 70'-8"

Design by
DESIGN BASICS, INC.

© design basics inc.

224

Design 9396

Square Footage: 2,775

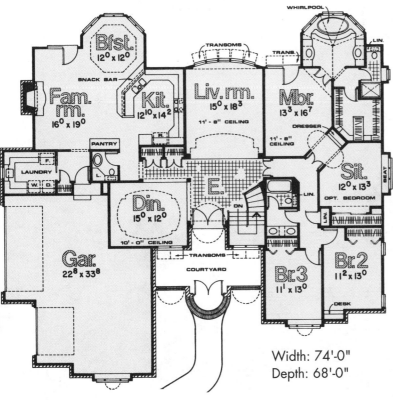

Bfst.
$12^0 \times 12^0$

Fam. rm.
$16^0 \times 19^0$

Kit.
$12^{10} \times 14^2$

Liv. rm.
$15^0 \times 18^3$
11'-8" CEILING

Mbr.
$13^3 \times 16^7$
11'-8" CEILING
DRESSER

SNACK BAR

TRANSOMS

WHIRLPOOL

TRANS.

LIN.

PANTRY

LAUNDRY

E.

DN

Sit.
$12^0 \times 13^3$
OPT. BEDROOM

SEAT

LIN.

Din.
$15^0 \times 12^0$
10'-0" CEILING

Gar.
$22^8 \times 33^8$

TRANSOMS

COURTYARD

Br. 3
$11^1 \times 13^0$

Br. 2
$11^2 \times 13^0$

DESK

Width: 74'-0"
Depth: 68'-0"

Design by
DESIGN BASICS, INC.

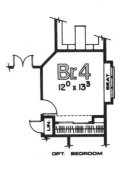

Br. 4
$12^0 \times 13^3$

SEAT

LIN.

OPT. BEDROOM

■ An impressive wrought iron-accented entry introduces a captivating courtyard. The dignified surroundings of the formal dining room enhance entertaining. Family living is highlighted in the integrated design of the kitchen, breakfast bay and family room. The huge laundry room is well planned and placed for efficiency and convenience. For maximum privacy, double doors seclude the bedroom wing from the rest of the house. The master suite includes a built-in dresser, outdoor access and a private sitting room. The master bath with dual lavatories and an extra-large oval whirlpool is distinguished by a multi-faceted sloped ceiling.

■ Stately brick detailing embellishes this European-style ranch home. The entry allows a lovely view of the fireplace in the great room, framed by handsome windows and transoms. The living room offers a ten-foot ceiling and is located conveniently across the foyer from the formal dining room. If you choose, the living room may be made into a fourth bedroom. Bowed windows in the breakfast area and a snack bar peninsula in the kitchen serve to dress up this casual living space. The master suite features a ten-foot ceiling and access to a private deck. Look for a corner whirlpool tub, His and Hers vanities and a large walk-in closet in the master bath. Secondary bedrooms are in a separate wing for privacy. They share a full bath. The three-car garage is a side-load style.

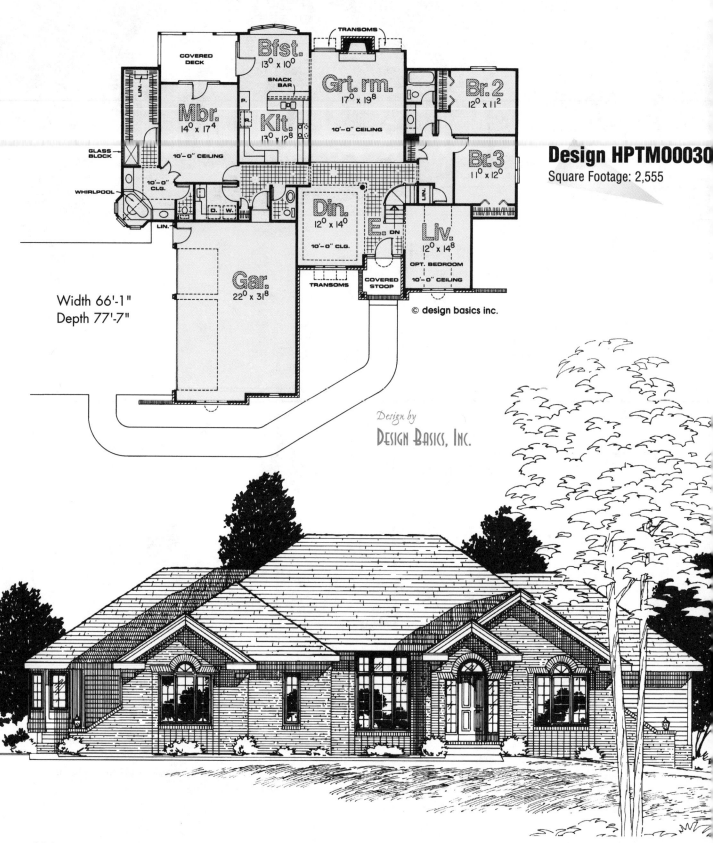

Design HPTM00030

Square Footage: 2,555

Width 66'-1"
Depth 77'-7"

© design basics inc.

Design by
DESIGN BASICS, INC.

Design 7318

Square Footage: 2,187

Design by
DESIGN BASICS, INC.

■ Multiple arches adorn the covered front porch of this volume three-bedroom home. Inside, an elegant formal dining room is located immediately to the right of the foyer, separated from the large and inviting great room by graceful columns. The great room and the hearth room share a through-fireplace. The large island kitchen is a gourmet's delight, with plenty of cabinet and counter space available. The adjacent bayed breakfast nook offers direct access to the rear yard and is sure to please. The sleeping zone consists of two secondary bedrooms (or make one a cozy study with built-ins) that share a full hall bath, and a lavish master bedroom suite. The amenities are many in this sumptuous suite, ranging from a tray ceiling, a large walk-in closet and a luxurious bath, to a private covered deck.

Bfst.
11⁰ x 11⁰

Mbr.
14⁰ x 15⁰
9'-0" CEILING

COVERED DECK

ENT. CENTER

Grt. rm.
18⁰ x 15⁰
10'-0" CEILING

Hrth.
11⁰ x 15⁰

SNACK BAR

Kit.
11⁰ x 13²

WET BAR

LIN.

Din.
11⁴ x 15⁰
10'-0" CLG.

Br.3
11⁰ x 12⁰

Br.2
11⁴ x 12⁰
10'-6" CEILING
OPTIONAL DEN

Gar.
22⁰ x 31⁸

COVERED PORCH

© design basics inc.

Den
11⁴ x 13⁰
10'-6" CEILING

BOOKS

Optional Den

Width 64'-0"
Depth 66'-0"

Rear Elevation

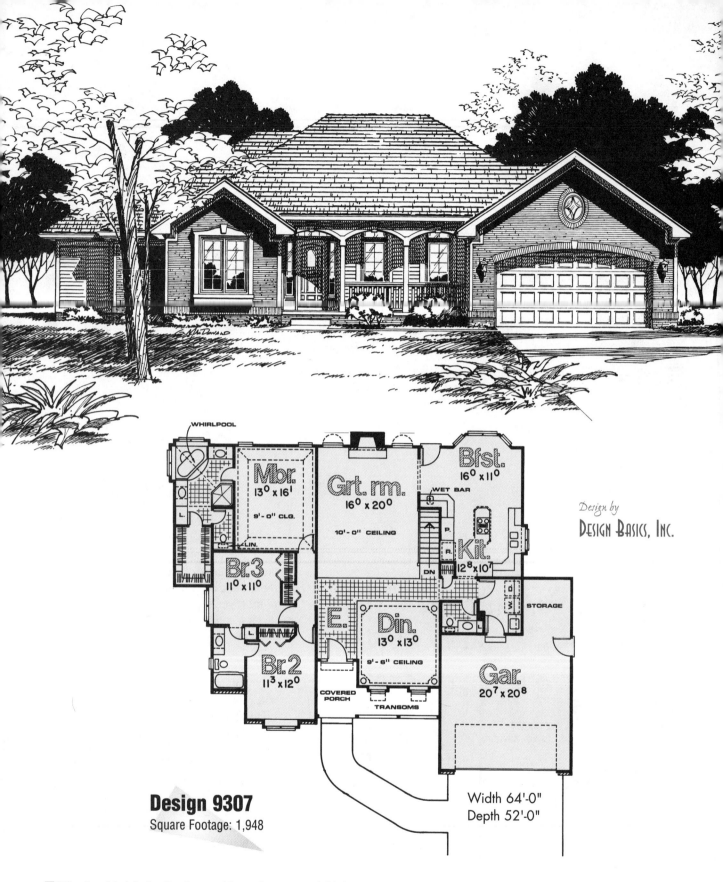

WHIRLPOOL

Mbr.
13⁰ x 16¹

9'-0" CLG.

Grt. rm.
16⁰ x 20⁰

10'-0" CEILING

Bfst.
16⁰ x 11⁰

WET BAR

LIN.

Br.3
11⁰ x 11⁰

DN

Kit.
12⁸ x 10⁷

P.

R.

STORAGE

E.

Din.
13⁰ x 13⁰

9'-6" CEILING

Br.2
11³ x 12⁰

Gar.
20⁷ x 20⁸

COVERED PORCH

TRANSOMS

Design by
DESIGN BASICS, INC.

Design 9307
Square Footage: 1,948

Width 64'-0"
Depth 52'-0"

■ Wood and brick details along with an elegant porch highlight the elevation of this special design. A ten-foot-high entry views the open dining room with tapered columns. Gourmet cooks will delight in the island kitchen with pantry and wrapping wet bar/servery. Outdoor access is available from the sunny bayed dinette. In the great room, a cozy fireplace is flanked by large windows with arched transoms above. Two secondary bedrooms share a Hollywood bath with a linen cabinet. At night, the lucky homeowners can retreat to the elegant master suite complete with vaulted ceilings and a pampering master bath. Special amenities include His and Hers vanities, linen closet, corner whirlpool, special shower and roomy walk-in closet. Truly, this home is delightful inside and out.

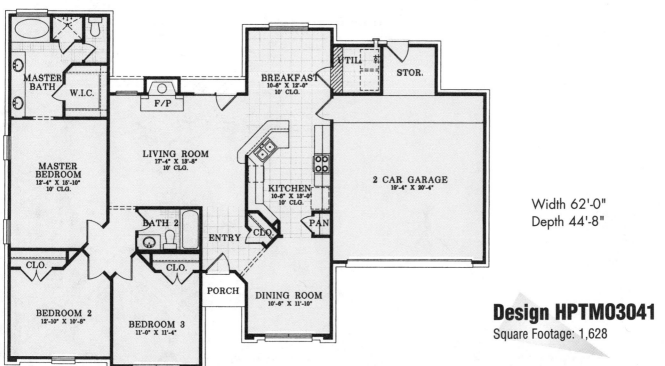

MASTER
BATH

W.I.C.

MASTER
BEDROOM
12'-4" X 15'-10"
10' CLG.

F/P

LIVING ROOM
17'-4" X 18'-8"
10' CLG.

BREAKFAST
10'-6" X 12'-0"
10' CLG.

UTIL.

STOR.

KITCHEN
10'-6" X 13'-0"
10' CLG.

2 CAR GARAGE
19'-4" X 20'-4"

PAN.

CLO.

BATH 2

ENTRY

CLO.

CLO.

CLO.

BEDROOM 2
12'-10" X 10'-8"

BEDROOM 3
11'-0" X 11'-4"

PORCH

DINING ROOM
10'-6" X 11'-10"

Width 62'-0"
Depth 44'-8"

Design HPTM03041
Square Footage: 1,628

Design by
©Larry E. Belk Designs

A lovely traditional facade complements this up-to-date floor plan.
Inside, the open angled breakfast bar connects the kitchen and breakfast
room to the main living area beyond. Ten-foot ceilings give the home a
spacious feel. The master suite features a roomy walk-in closet, double
vanities and a separate shower and whirlpool tub. Two family bedrooms
have stylish angled entries and share a hall bath. Please specify crawlspace or slab foundation when ordering.

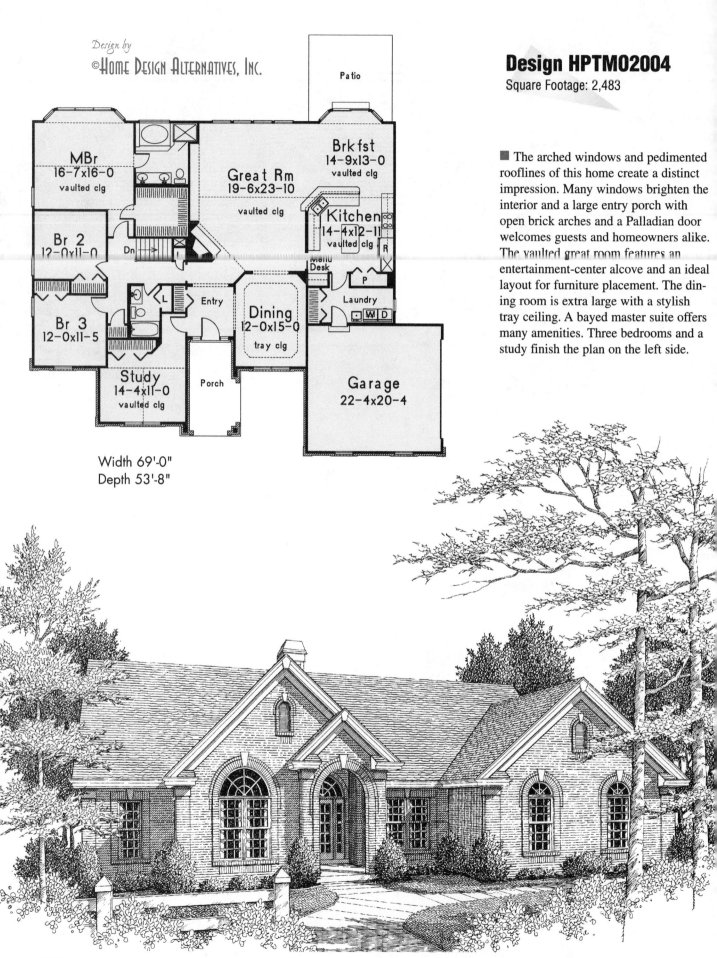

Design by
©HOME DESIGN ALTERNATIVES, INC.

Patio

MBr
16-7x16-0
vaulted clg

Great Rm
19-6x23-10

Brk fst
14-9x13-0
vaulted clg

vaulted clg

Kitchen
14-4x12-11
vaulted clg

Br 2
12-0x11-0

Dn

Menu
Desk

R

P

Br 3
12-0x11-5

Entry

Dining
12-0x15-0

Laundry

W D

tray clg

Study
14-4x11-0
vaulted clg

Porch

Garage
22-4x20-4

Width 69'-0"
Depth 53'-8"

Design HPTM02004

Square Footage: 2,483

■ The arched windows and pedimented rooflines of this home create a distinct impression. Many windows brighten the interior and a large entry porch with open brick arches and a Palladian door welcomes guests and homeowners alike. The vaulted great room features an entertainment-center alcove and an ideal layout for furniture placement. The dining room is extra large with a stylish tray ceiling. A bayed master suite offers many amenities. Three bedrooms and a study finish the plan on the left side.

Design 9328
Square Footage: 1,496

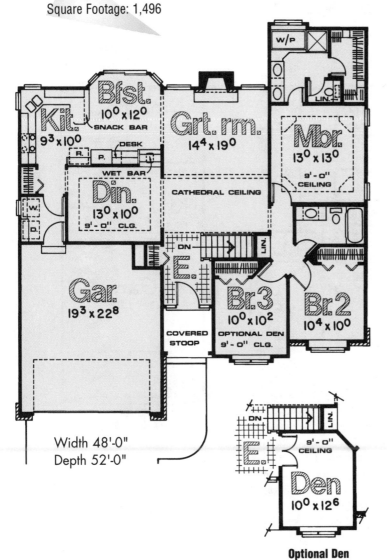

Bfst. $10^0 \times 12^0$

SNACK BAR

Kit. $9^3 \times 10^0$

DESK

R. P.

WET BAR

Dn. $13^0 \times 10^0$ 9'-0" CLG.

W. D.

Grt. rm. $14^4 \times 19^0$

CATHEDRAL CEILING

W/P LIN.

Mbr. $13^0 \times 13^0$ 9'-0" CEILING

Gar. $19^3 \times 22^8$

DN E. LIN.

Br.3 $10^0 \times 10^2$ OPTIONAL DEN 9'-0" CLG.

Br.2 $10^4 \times 10^0$

COVERED STOOP

Width 48'-0"
Depth 52'-0"

DN LIN.

E. 9'-0" CEILING

Den $10^0 \times 12^6$

Optional Den

■ Sleek rooflines, lap siding and brick accents highlight the exterior of this three-bedroom ranch home. A tiled entry views the spacious great room featuring a sloping cathedral ceiling and window-framed fireplace. Note the strategic location of the dining room (with nine-foot boxed ceiling and wet bar/servery) which accommodates formal entertaining and family gatherings. Natural light and warmth add comfort to the bayed breakfast area with pantry, handy planning desk and the peninsula kitchen. Well-segregated sleeping quarters add to the flexibility of this modern floor plan. Both secondary bedrooms share a full bath and linen closet. Bedroom 3 is easily converted to a den or home office. With the nine-foot high boxed ceiling, walk-in closet, sunlit whirlpool tub and double vanities, the master suite is soothing and luxurious.

Design by
Design Basics, Inc.

231

Design 7365

Square Footage: 1,729

Design by
Design Basics, Inc.

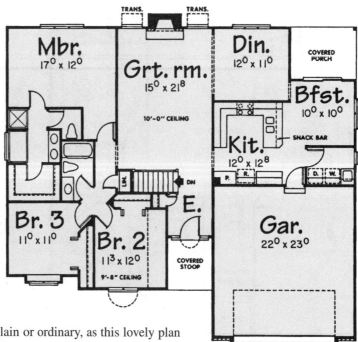

Width 55'-4"
Depth 48'-4"

■ Simple, single-level design need not be plain or ordinary, as this lovely plan proves. Its facade is well managed, with horizontal wood siding, brick accents and an arched window under a gabled pediment. The floor plan is accommodating, with well-defined living and sleeping areas. A large great room with ten-foot ceiling dominates the center of the plan, with a smaller dining room, a light-filled breakfast room and a U-shaped kitchen falling to the right. On the left are two family bedrooms which have use of a full bath. The master suite stands alone and is graced by a walk-in closet, separate shower and tub and dual lavatories. A two-car garage is the icing on this ranch-style cake.

232

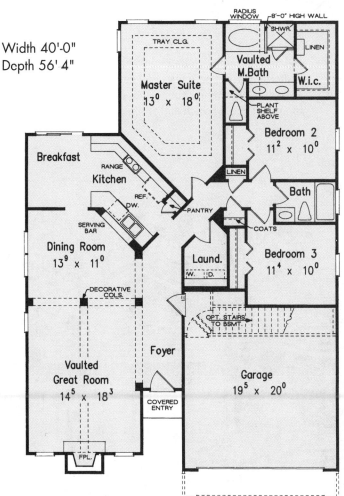

Width 40'-0"
Depth 56' 4"

RADIUS WINDOW
8'-0" HIGH WALL

TRAY CLG.

SHWR.

Vaulted M.Bath

LINEN

Master Suite
13⁰ x 18⁰

W.i.c.

PLANT SHELF ABOVE

Bedroom 2
11² x 10⁰

LINEN

Breakfast

RANGE

Kitchen

REF.

DW.

PANTRY

Bath

SERVING BAR

COATS

Dining Room
13⁹ x 11⁰

Laund.
W. D.

Bedroom 3
11⁴ x 10⁰

DECORATIVE COLS.

OPT. STAIRS TO BSMT.

Foyer

Vaulted Great Room
14⁵ x 18³

Garage
19⁵ x 20⁰

COVERED ENTRY

FPL.

Design HPTM03042

Square Footage: 1,573

■ Charm the neighborhood with the unique exterior on this three-bedroom cottage—the fireplace is set between two front windows. Inside, a vaulted great room boasts a centerpiece fireplace, decorative columns and an open layout. The dining room can enjoy the fireplace display while receiving convenient service from the pass-through bar of the nearby galley kitchen. A tray ceiling adorns the master suite and the luxurious bathroom features a radius window by the oval tub. Two family bedrooms share a full hall bath. Please specify basement or crawlspace foundation when ordering.

Design by
©Frank Betz Associates, Inc.

233

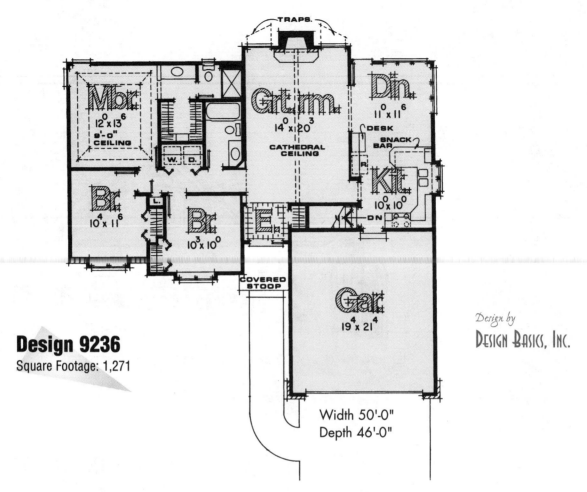

Design 9236
Square Footage: 1,271

Design by
DESIGN BASICS, INC.

Width 50'-0"
Depth 46'-0"

■ This charmingly snug three-bedroom home offers all the features you've been looking for in a family home. The great room has a lovely cathedral ceiling and a fireplace surrounded by windows. Nearby is the dining area and efficient kitchen with a window box, planning desk, Lazy Susan and snack bar counter. Intriguing ceiling treatment dominates the master bedroom where you'll also find corner windows, a dressing area with large vanity and a walk-in closet. Two family bedrooms share a full bath and are located near the laundry room.

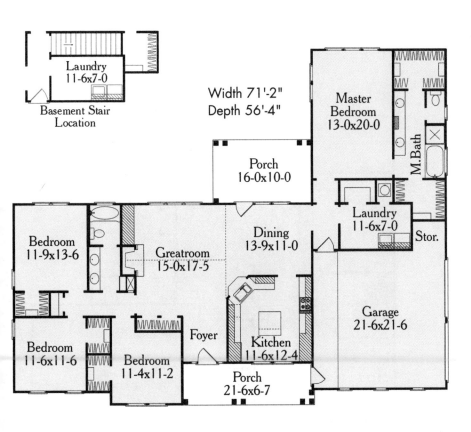

Laundry
11-6x7-0

**Basement Stair
Location**

Width 71'-2"
Depth 56'-4"

Porch
16-0x10-0

Master
Bedroom
13-0x20-0

M.Bath

Dining
13-9x11-0

Greatroom
15-0x17-5

Bedroom
11-9x13-6

Laundry
11-6x7-0

Stor.

Bedroom
11-6x11-6

Foyer

Kitchen
11-6x12-4

Bedroom
11-4x11-2

Garage
21-6x21-6

Porch
21-6x6-7

Design HPTM00032

Square Footage: 2,093

■ Welcome your family home to this wonderful four-bedroom cottage. Step through the entry door with its transom and sidelights to a well-lit foyer. A ribbon of windows greets the eye in the great room, and a warming fireplace spreads comfort. A pass-through window to the kitchen is an added convenience. The master suite enjoys a private wing, luxurious bath and His and Hers walk-in closets. On the opposite side of the plan, three secondary bedrooms—all with walk-in closets!—share a full bath. Please specify basement, crawlspace or slab foundation when ordering.

Design by
©Larry James &
Associates, Inc.

235

Design HPTM03043

Square Footage: 1,395

■ A double-gabled roof and garage lead
you to admire the welcoming porch and
front muntin window with shutters of
this cozy cottage. Inside, two bedroom
suites are divided by a full hall bath.
The L-shaped kitchen includes a pantry
and snack bar and opens to the family
room with an optional fireplace. The
dining area provides sliding glass doors
to the rear patio. The master suite boasts
a vast walk-in closet and a grand private
bath. The garage entrance is located in
the utility room.

Design by
© LIVING CONCEPTS HOME PLANNING

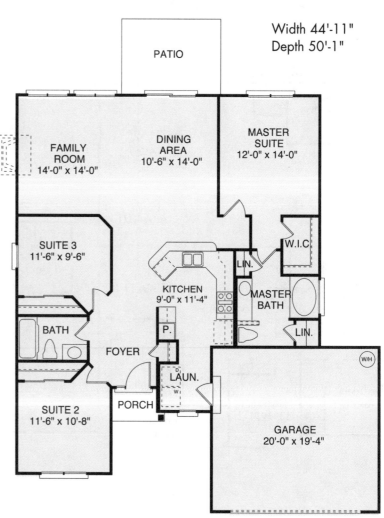

Width 44'-11"
Depth 50'-1"

Design P233

Square Footage: 1,671

■ Asymmetrical gables, a columned porch and an abundance of windows brighten the exterior of this compact home. An efficient kitchen boasts a pantry and a serving bar that it shares with the formal dining room and the vaulted family room. A sunny breakfast room and nearby laundry room complete the living zone. Be sure to notice extras such as the focal-point fireplace in the family room and a plant shelf in the laundry room. The sumptuous master suite offers a door to the backyard, a vaulted sitting area and a pampering bath. Two family bedrooms share a hall bath. Please specify basement, crawlspace or slab foundation when ordering.

QUOTE ONE®

Cost to build? See page 434
to order complete cost estimate
to build this house in your area!

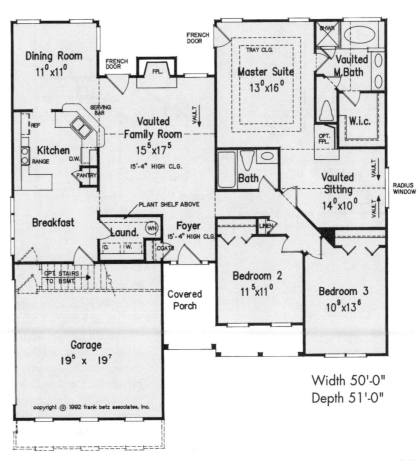

Dining Room
11⁰x11⁰

Master Suite
13⁰x16⁰

Vaulted M. Bath

W.i.c.

Vaulted
Family Room
15⁵x17⁵
15'-4" HIGH CLG.

Kitchen

PANTRY

Bath

Vaulted
Sitting
14⁰x10⁰

RADIUS
WINDOW

Breakfast

Laund.

Foyer
15'-4" HIGH CLG.

PLANT SHELF ABOVE

Bedroom 2
11⁵x11⁰

Bedroom 3
10⁹x13⁶

Covered
Porch

OPT. STAIRS
TO BSMT.

Garage
19⁵ x 19⁷

copyright © 1992 frank betz associates, inc.

Width 50'-0"
Depth 51'-0"

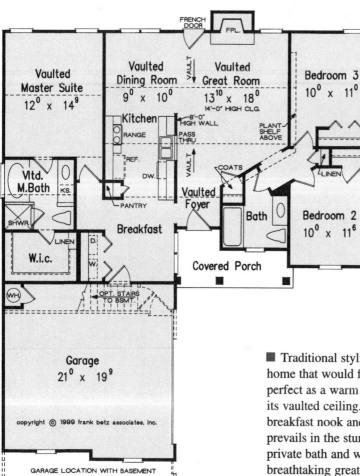

FRENCH DOOR

FPL.

Vaulted Master Suite
12⁰ x 14⁹

Vaulted Dining Room
9⁰ x 10⁰

Vaulted Great Room
13¹⁰ x 18⁰
14'-0" HIGH CLG.

Bedroom 3
10⁰ x 11⁰

VAULT

8'-0" HIGH WALL

PLANT SHELF ABOVE

Kitchen
RANGE

PASS THRU

REF.

VAULT

COATS

LINEN

DW.

Vtd. M.Bath
KS.

PANTRY

Vaulted Foyer

Bath

Bedroom 2
10⁰ x 11⁶

SHWR.

LINEN

Breakfast

W.i.c.
D.
W.

Covered Porch

WH

OPT. STAIRS TO BSMT.

Garage
21⁰ x 19⁹

copyright © 1999 frank betz associates, inc.

GARAGE LOCATION WITH BASEMENT

Design by
© FRANK BETZ ASSOCIATES, INC.

Width 46'-0"
Depth 53'-4"

Design HPTM03044
Square Footage: 1,290

■ Traditional stylings and an efficient floor plan create this charming home that would fit splendidly in any neighborhood. The covered porch—perfect as a warm summer evening retreat—opens to the grand foyer with its vaulted ceiling. The central galley kitchen sits between the sunny breakfast nook and the formal dining room for ease of service. Privacy prevails in the stunning master suite, on the left, complete with a lavish private bath and walk-in closet. The vaulted ceiling presides over the breathtaking great room with its warming fireplace. The two family bedrooms are tucked away on the right where they share a full bath. Please specify basement, crawlspace or slab foundation when ordering.

Design 7619

Square Footage: 1,912
Bonus Room: 398 square feet

■ An appealing blend of stone, siding and stucco announces a 21st-Century floor plan. A formal dining area defined by decorative columns opens to a grand great room with a centered hearth. The gourmet kitchen overlooks the great room, and enjoys natural light brought in by the bayed breakfast nook. The sleeping wing, to the right of the plan, includes a sumptuous master suite with a tray ceiling and a skylit bath with twin vanities. A secluded study is near a family bedroom and shares its bath.

Design by
Donald A. Gardner Architects, Inc.

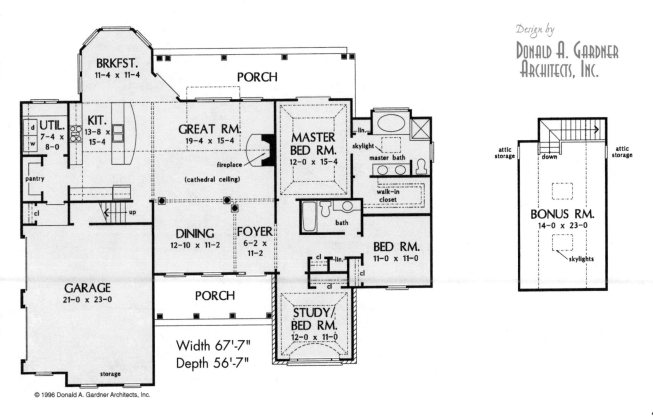

Width 67'-7"
Depth 56'-7"

Rear Elevation

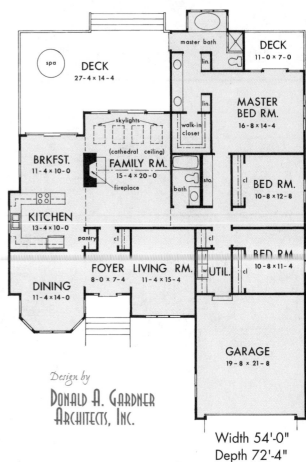

Design 9716
Square Footage: 2,097

■ A bank of ventilating skylights flood the large family room with natural light and fresh air in this three-bedroom ranch. Many other special features—uncommon in a home this size—make an appearance. For example, the breakfast area, family room and master bath open to a spacious deck with a spa area. In the family room you'll find a cathedral ceiling and a fireplace. The plan provides both formal living and dining rooms. The U-shaped kitchen epitomizes the best in efficiency. The large master bedroom has a private deck and pampers with a whirlpool tub, a separate shower and a double-bowl vanity. Two secondary bedrooms each find ample closet space and share a full hall bath.

Design by
Donald A. Gardner Architects, Inc.

Width 54'-0"
Depth 72'-4"

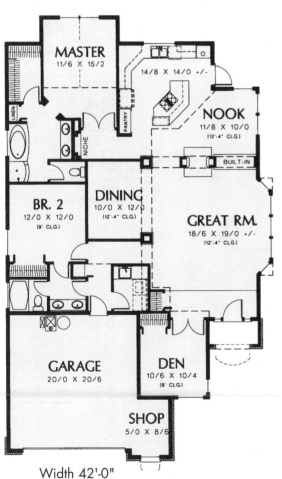

MASTER
11/6 X 15/2

14/8 X 14/0 +/-

NOOK
11/8 X 10/0
(12'-4" CLG.)

LINEN

PANTRY

NICHE

BUILT-IN

BR. 2
12/0 X 12/0
(9' CLG.)

DINING
10/0 X 12/0
(12'-4" CLG.)

GREAT RM.
18/6 X 19/0 +/-
(12'-4" CLG.)

GARAGE
20/0 X 20/6

DEN
10/6 X 10/4
(9' CLG.)

SHOP
5/0 X 8/6

Width 42'-0"
Depth 68'-0"

Design 7449
Square Footage: 1,864

■ With an offset front entry and brick-and-siding detail, this home is the model of sheltered style. The entry opens directly into the large great room, but a secluded den is just to the left through double doors. A through-fireplace serves both the great room and nook; columns separate the formal dining room from the great room. A lovely island kitchen features everything the gourmet might request: pantry, abundant counterspace, an over-the-sink window and outdoor access. Both bedrooms have private baths. The master bath is a study in indulgence with a whirlpool tub, separate shower, compartmented toilet, double sink and huge walk-in closet. The two-car garage has space enough for a work-shop.

Design by
Alan Mascord
Design Associates, Inc.

Design 3345
Square Footage: 1,738

L

■ This quaint shingled cottage offers an unexpected amount of living space in just over 1,700 square feet. The large gathering room with fireplace, dining room with covered porch, and kitchen with breakfast room handle formal parties as easily as they do the casual family get-together. Three bedrooms, one that could also serve as a study, are found in a separate wing of the house. Special note should be taken of all the storage space provided in this home as well as the extra touches that set it apart from many homes of equal size.

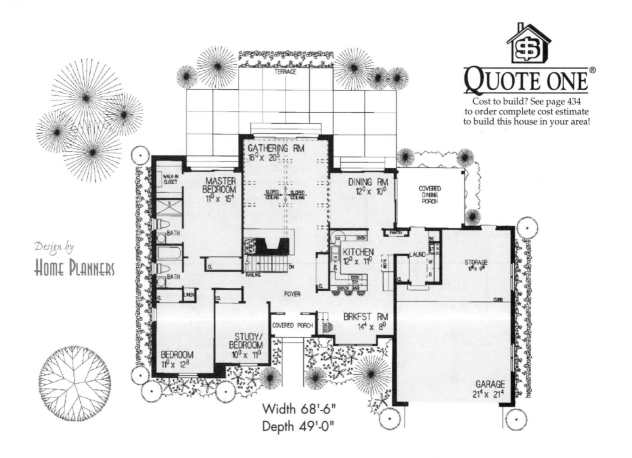

Quote One®
Cost to build? See page 434
to order complete cost estimate
to build this house in your area!

Design by
Home Planners

TERRACE

GATHERING RM
16⁰ x 20⁵

MASTER BEDROOM
11⁰ x 15⁴

WALK-IN CLOSET

SLOPED CEILING SLOPED CEILING

DINING RM
12⁰ x 10⁰

COVERED DINING PORCH

BATH

BATH

PANTRY

KITCHEN
12⁰ x 11⁰

LAUND

STORAGE
12⁴ x 9⁰

RAILING

DN

FOYER

SNACK BAR

LINEN

BEDROOM
11⁰ x 12⁸

STUDY/ BEDROOM
10⁰ x 11⁰

COVERED PORCH

BRKFST RM
14⁴ x 8⁰

GARAGE
21⁴ x 21⁴

Width 68'-6"
Depth 49'-0"

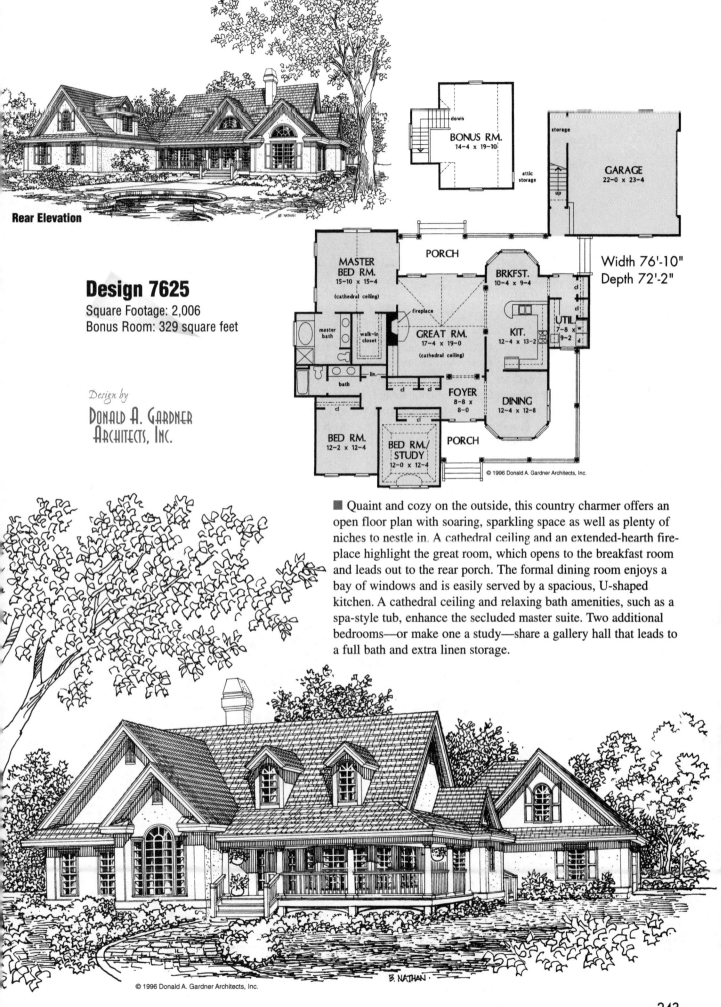

Rear Elevation

BONUS RM.
14-4 x 19-10

down

attic storage

storage

GARAGE
22-0 x 23-4

up

Design 7625

Square Footage: 2,006
Bonus Room: 329 square feet

Design by
Donald A. Gardner
Architects, Inc.

MASTER BED RM.
15-10 x 15-4
(cathedral ceiling)

PORCH

BRKFST.
10-4 x 9-4

Width 76'-10"
Depth 72'-2"

master bath

walk-in closet

fireplace

GREAT RM.
17-4 x 19-0
(cathedral ceiling)

KIT.
12-4 x 13-2

UTIL.
7-8 x 9-2

bath

lin.

FOYER
8-8 x 8-0

DINING
12-4 x 12-8

BED RM.
12-2 x 12-4

BED RM./ STUDY
12-0 x 12-4

PORCH

© 1996 Donald A. Gardner Architects, Inc.

■ Quaint and cozy on the outside, this country charmer offers an open floor plan with soaring, sparkling space as well as plenty of niches to nestle in. A cathedral ceiling and an extended-hearth fireplace highlight the great room, which opens to the breakfast room and leads out to the rear porch. The formal dining room enjoys a bay of windows and is easily served by a spacious, U-shaped kitchen. A cathedral ceiling and relaxing bath amenities, such as a spa-style tub, enhance the secluded master suite. Two additional bedrooms—or make one a study—share a gallery hall that leads to a full bath and extra linen storage.

© 1996 Donald A. Gardner Architects, Inc.

B. NATHAN.

Design T233
Square Footage: 2,204

Design by
DESIGN TRADITIONS

Width 71'-2"
Depth 49'-7"

■ A bay window is accented by a gracefully covered porch on this three bedroom home. If entertaining is your hobby, note how the great room and the formal dining room are only separated by elegant columns, providing ease for any gathering you wish. The large U-shaped kitchen is sure to please also, with a worktop island, plenty of counter and cabinet space and an adjacent breakfast room. Two secondary bedrooms—one with a bay window—share a full bath, while the master suite is full of amenities. From the two walk-in closets, the lavish bath and the bayed sitting area, this room is a haven for any homeowner. This home is designed with a basement foundation.

244

Design 3487

Square Footage: 1,835

Design by
HOME PLANNERS

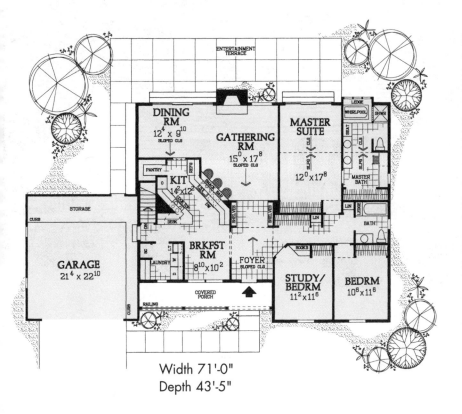

Width 71'-0"
Depth 43'-5"

■ Country living is the focus of this charming design. A cozy covered porch invites you into the foyer with the sleeping area on the right and the living area straight ahead. From the windowed front-facing breakfast room, enter the efficient kitchen with its corner laundry room, large pantry, snack-bar pass-through to the gathering room, and passage to the dining room. The massive gathering room and dining room feature sloped ceilings, an impressive fireplace and access to the rear terrace. Terrace access is also available from the master bedroom with its sloped ceiling and a master bath that includes a whirlpool tub, a separate shower and a separate vanity area. A study at the front of the house can also be converted into a third bedroom.

KOIZUMI/BUTLER

Design 3489

Square Footage: 2,415

L D

■ This traditional design incorporates the perfect floor plan for a large family. Privacy is assured with three family bedrooms and a strategically placed laundry on the left side of the home, and a large master bedroom with a luxurious bath and spacious walk-in closet on the right side. A comfortable covered porch welcomes you to the living areas. The family room looks out to the covered porch and continues on to the efficient kitchen with a writing desk, a large pantry and access to the dining room. The kitchen also features a snack bar that provides a perfect opportunity to chat with folks in the large gathering room with its warming fireplace and access to the backyard terrace. Sloped ceilings in the living areas and the master bedroom, and nine-foot ceilings in the other bedrooms, give this home a spacious, airy feel.

Width 74'-0"
Depth 54'-0"

QUOTE ONE®

Cost to build? See page 434
to order complete cost estimate
to build this house in your area!

Design by
Home Planners

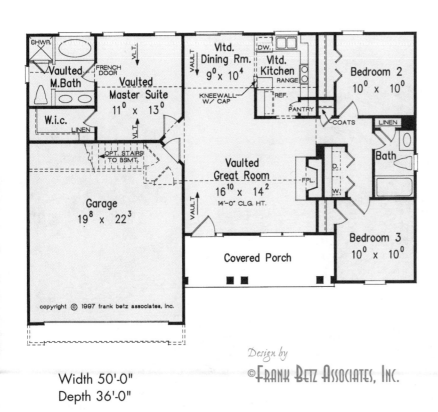

Width 50'-0"
Depth 36'-0"

Design by
©FRANK BETZ ASSOCIATES, INC.

Design HPTM03045

Square Footage: 1,080

■ The two front-facing gables on this home border an expansive covered porch that shelters the entry from the elements. Inside, the great room is crowned with a vaulted ceiling accented by the fireplace. The formal dining room, angled kitchen and master bedroom also enjoy the elegance of vaulted ceilings. Split-bedroom planning puts the family bedrooms on the right, where they share a full bath, while the master suite resides on the left with a lavish private bath that includes a double-sink vanity, garden tub, compartmented toilet and shower. This plan offers an optional basement staircase and mudroom. Please specify basement or crawlspace foundation when ordering.

Design HPTM00033

Square Footage: 2,177

■ A commodious covered porch
fronts the entry to this ranch-style
home. The entry door opens to a
central foyer, separated from the
dining room by columns. The
great room to the back features a
fireplace and built-in bookshelves.
An island kitchen complements
the bayed breakfast nook. The
laundry and a half-bath flank the
hall that leads to the carport in the
rear. Family bedrooms share a hall
bath, while the master bedroom
has a private bath and two walk-in
closets. Please specify basement,
crawlspace or slab foundation
when ordering.

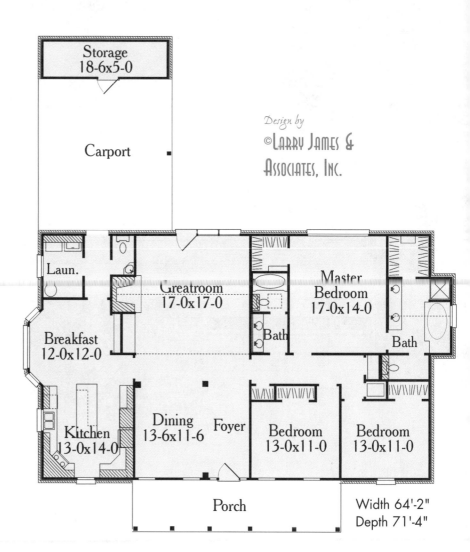

Storage
18-6x5-0

Carport

Design by
©Larry James &
Associates, Inc.

Laun.

Greatroom
17-0x17-0

Master
Bedroom
17-0x14-0

Bath

Bath

Breakfast
12-0x12-0

Kitchen
13-0x14-0

Dining
13-6x11-6

Foyer

Bedroom
13-0x11-0

Bedroom
13-0x11-0

Porch

Width 64'-2"
Depth 71'-4"

248

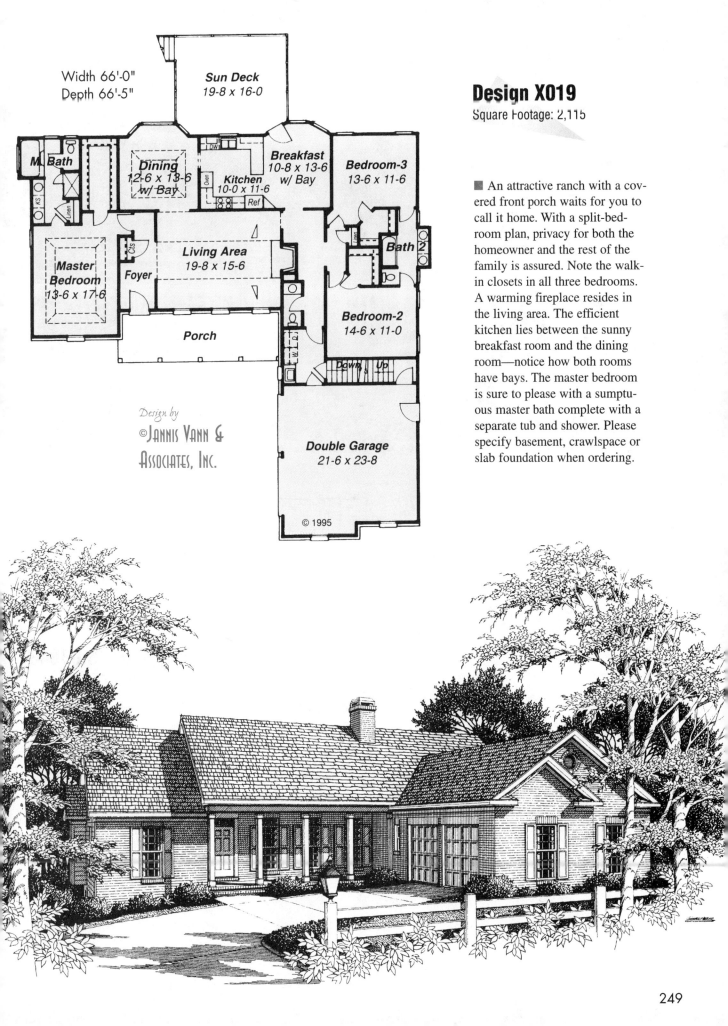

Width 66'-0"
Depth 66'-5"

Sun Deck
19-8 x 16-0

Dining
12-6 x 13-6
w/ Bay

Kitchen
10-0 x 11-6

Breakfast
10-8 x 13-6
w/ Bay

Bedroom-3
13-6 x 11-6

M. Bath

Master Bedroom
13-6 x 17-6

Foyer

Living Area
19-8 x 15-6

Bath 2

Porch

Bedroom-2
14-6 x 11-0

Down   Up

Design by
© Jannis Vann &
Associates, Inc.

Double Garage
21-6 x 23-8

© 1995

Design X019

Square Footage: 2,115

■ An attractive ranch with a covered front porch waits for you to call it home. With a split-bedroom plan, privacy for both the homeowner and the rest of the family is assured. Note the walk-in closets in all three bedrooms. A warming fireplace resides in the living area. The efficient kitchen lies between the sunny breakfast room and the dining room—notice how both rooms have bays. The master bedroom is sure to please with a sumptuous master bath complete with a separate tub and shower. Please specify basement, crawlspace or slab foundation when ordering.

DECK

SITTING
12'-0"x 12'-0"

W.I.C.

MASTER
BATH

BREAKFAST
12'-0"x 13'-6"

DN.

GREAT ROOM
20'-6"x 18'-6"

MASTER SUITE
16'-6"x 15'-0"

W.I.C.

KITCHEN
14'-13"x 13'-6"

POWDER

BEDROOM NO.3
12'-0"x 12'-0"

LAUNDRY
9'-0" X 8'-6"

DINING ROOM
13'-6" X 14'-6"

FOYER

STORAGE

STOOP

BEDROOM NO.2
12'-3"x 14'-0"

BATH

TWO CAR GARAGE
21'-6"X 27'-6"

Width 73'-6"
Depth 78'-0"

Design by
©Stephen Fuller, Inc.

Design HPTM03046
Square Footage: 2,770

■ This English cottage with a cedar shake exterior displays the best qualities of traditional design. The foyer opens to both the dining room and the great room with its fireplace and built-in cabinetry. Surrounded by windows, the breakfast room opens to a gourmet kitchen. Two bedrooms with large closets are joined by a full bath with individual vanities and a window seat. Through double doors at the end of a short hall, the master suite awaits with a tray ceiling and an adjoining sunlit sitting room. This home is designed with a walkout basement foundation.

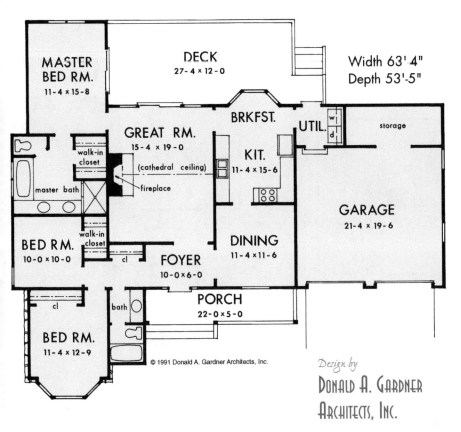

MASTER BED RM.
11- 4 x 15-8

DECK
27- 4 × 12- 0

Width 63' 4"
Depth 53'-5"

walk-in closet

master bath

GREAT RM.
15- 4 x 19- 0

(cathedral ceiling)

fireplace

BRKFST.

KIT.
11- 4 x 15- 6

UTIL.
w/d

storage

BED RM.
10- 0 x 10- 0

walk-in closet

cl

FOYER
10- 0×6- 0

DINING
11- 4 ×11- 6

GARAGE
21- 4 × 19- 6

BED RM.
11- 4 x 12- 9

cl

bath

PORCH
22- 0 ×5- 0

© 1991 Donald A. Gardner Architects, Inc.

Design by

DONALD A. GARDNER
ARCHITECTS, INC.

Design 9679

Square Footage: 1,512

■ A multi-pane bay window, dormers, a cupola, a covered porch and a variety of building materials all combine to dress up this intriguing country cottage. The generous entry foyer leads to a formal dining room and an impressive great room with a cathedral ceiling and fireplace. The kitchen includes a breakfast area with a bay window overlooking the deck. The great room and master bedroom also access the deck. An amenity-filled master suite is highlighted by a private bath that includes a double-bowl vanity, a shower and a garden tub. Two additional bedrooms located at the front of the house share a full bath.

Design HPTM00035

Square Footage: 1,894

■ Elegant pillars and multi-pane windows below two gabled dormers give this design classy curb appeal. Inside, the foyer is connected to the dining room with columns. The convenient galley kitchen leads to a breakfast area with a ribbon of windows. The living room will draw people in to watch a crackling fire or look out the two windows framing the fireplace. Walk-in closets and extra storage space provide plenty of room for the family belongings. The split-bedroom floor plan allows for privacy. The two covered porches extend the living area outside. Please specify basement, crawlspace or slab foundation when ordering.

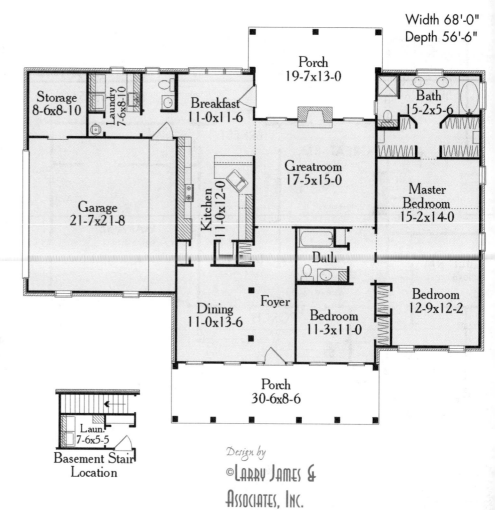

Width 68'-0"
Depth 56'-6"

Storage
8-6x8-10

Laundry
7-6x8-10

Breakfast
11-0x11-6

Porch
19-7x13-0

Bath
15-2x5-6

Garage
21-7x21-8

Kitchen
11-0x12-0

Greatroom
17-5x15-0

Master Bedroom
15-2x14-0

Bath

Dining
11-0x13-6

Foyer

Bedroom
11-3x11-0

Bedroom
12-9x12-2

Porch
30-6x8-6

Laun.
7-6x5-5

Basement Stair Location

Design by
© Larry James & Associates, Inc.

252

Design 8229

Square Footage: 1,955

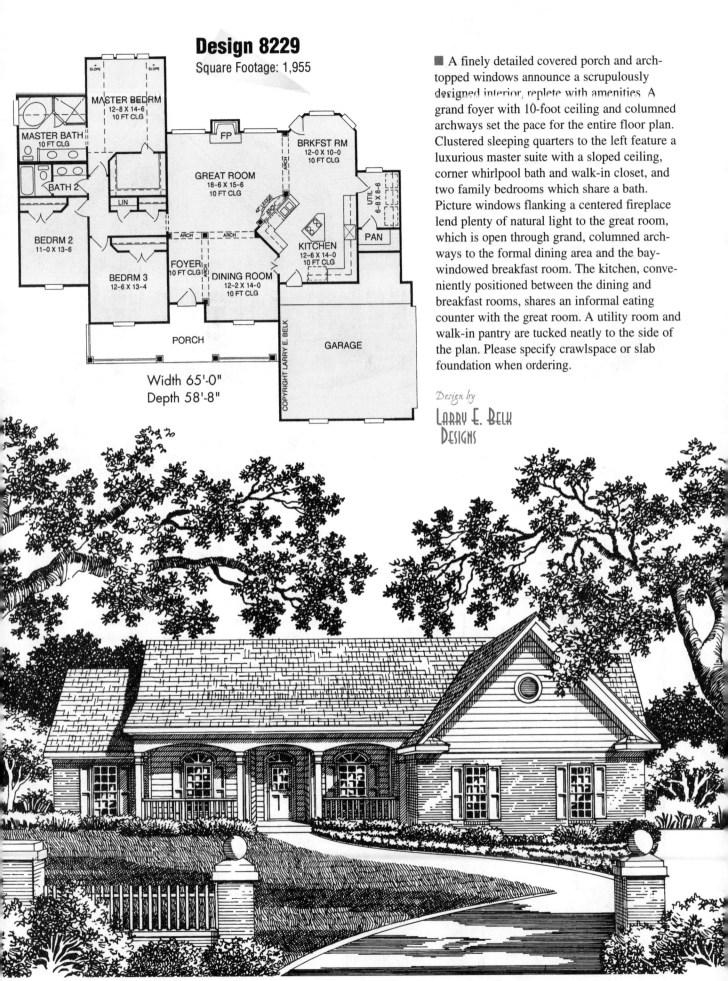

Width 65'-0"
Depth 58'-8"

COPYRIGHT LARRY E. BELK

■ A finely detailed covered porch and arch-topped windows announce a scrupulously designed interior, replete with amenities. A grand foyer with 10-foot ceiling and columned archways set the pace for the entire floor plan. Clustered sleeping quarters to the left feature a luxurious master suite with a sloped ceiling, corner whirlpool bath and walk-in closet, and two family bedrooms which share a bath. Picture windows flanking a centered fireplace lend plenty of natural light to the great room, which is open through grand, columned archways to the formal dining area and the bay-windowed breakfast room. The kitchen, conveniently positioned between the dining and breakfast rooms, shares an informal eating counter with the great room. A utility room and walk-in pantry are tucked neatly to the side of the plan. Please specify crawlspace or slab foundation when ordering.

Design by
Larry E. Belk
Designs

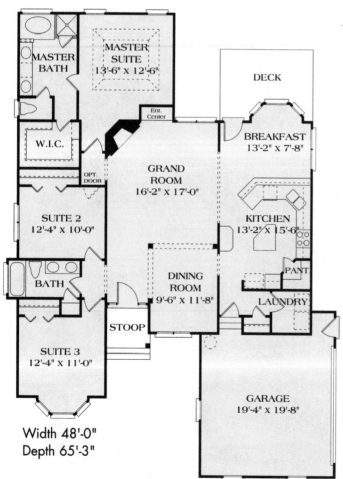

MASTER
BATH

MASTER
SUITE
13'-6" x 12'-6"

DECK

W.I.C.

Ent.
Center

BREAKFAST
13'-2" x 7'-8"

GRAND
ROOM
16'-2" x 17'-0"

OPT.
DOOR

KITCHEN
13'-2" x 15'-6"

SUITE 2
12'-4" x 10'-0"

BATH

DINING
ROOM
9'-6" x 11'-8"

PANT.

LAUNDRY

STOOP

SUITE 3
12'-4" x 11'-0"

GARAGE
19'-4" x 19'-8"

Width 48'-0"
Depth 65'-3"

Design A245
Square Footage: 1,734

■ Master planning makes the most of the smaller square footage of this one-story home. The raised porch allows entry to a short hallway, open through columns to the formal dining room and the large grand room beyond. The grand room is graced by a corner fireplace and entertainment center built right in. On the right is the island kitchen and bay-windowed breakfast nook with deck access. At the other end, the kitchen connects to the two-car garage through a laundry area with broom closet. The master suite is at the rear of the plan for privacy. Its tray ceiling and elegant bath make it a standout. You may wish to include a door from the master suite directly into Suite 2 (perfect for a nursery) or choose the more private option, with both family suites opening from their own hallway. Suite 3 has a lovely bay window overlooking the front yard.

Design by
LIVING CONCEPTS

Design by
DESIGN TRADITIONS

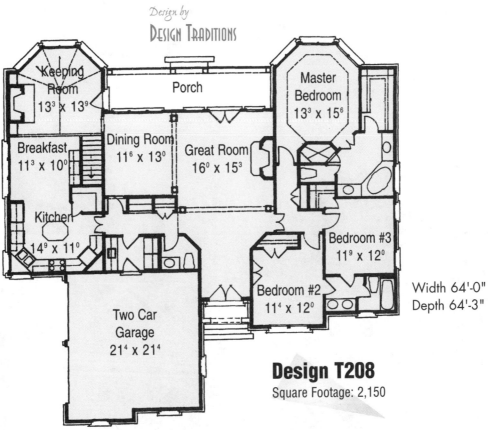

Keeping Room
13³ x 13⁹

Porch

Master Bedroom
13³ x 15⁶

Breakfast
11³ x 10⁰

Dining Room
11⁶ x 13⁰

Great Room
16⁰ x 15³

Kitchen
14⁹ x 11⁰

Bedroom #3
11⁹ x 12⁰

Width 64'-0"
Depth 64'-3"

Two Car Garage
21⁴ x 21⁴

Bedroom #2
11⁴ x 12⁰

Design T208
Square Footage: 2,150

■ This attractive brick cottage home with an arched covered entry makes visitors feel warmly welcomed. The jack-arch window detailing adds intrigue to the exterior. The foyer, dining room and great room are brought together, defined by decorative columns. To the right of the foyer, a bedroom with a complete bath could double as a home office or children's den. The spacious kitchen has a centered work island and an adjacent keeping room with a fireplace—ideal for families that like to congregate at meal times. The abundance of windows throughout the back of the home provides a grand view of the back property. The master suite enjoys privacy to the rear of the home. A garden tub, large walk-in closet and two vanities make a perfect homeowner retreat. This home is designed with a basement foundation.

Design T237

Square Footage: 2,919

■ This plan was made for entertaining. Its entry and center hall are lined with columns that help define, but not limit, the great room, dining room and bedroom wing. A beamed ceiling, a fireplace and covered rear porch access are highlights in the great room. It also is open to a sun room and the bay-windowed breakfast room. A large, gourmet-styled kitchen is a great work center. Bedrooms include two family suites with shared bath and private vanity areas and a master suite with tray ceiling in the bedroom. The master bath has His and Hers walk-in closets, a garden whirlpool, separate shower, compartmented toilet and make-up vanity. A powder room in the central hall and a convenient laundry room round out the interior spaces. The two-car garage sits to the front to screen street noise. It features storage or work-bench space. This home is designed with a basement foundation.

Design by
DESIGN TRADITIONS

Width 70'-10"
Depth 66'-6"

© Design Traditions

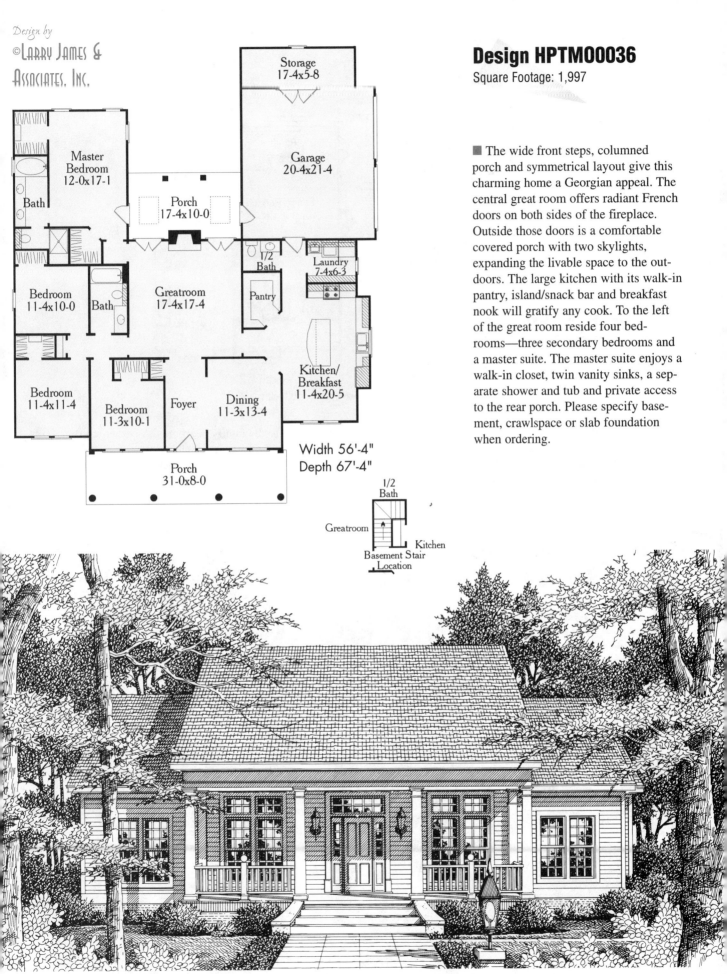

Design by
©Larry James &
Associates, Inc.

Storage
17-4x5-8

Garage
20-4x21-4

Master
Bedroom
12-0x17-1

Bath

Porch
17-4x10-0

1/2
Bath

Laundry
7-4x6-3

Bedroom
11-4x10-0

Bath

Greatroom
17-4x17-4

Pantry

Bedroom
11-4x11-4

Foyer

Bedroom
11-3x10-1

Dining
11-3x13-4

Kitchen/
Breakfast
11-4x20-5

Porch
31-0x8-0

Width 56'-4"
Depth 67'-4"

1/2
Bath

Greatroom

Kitchen

Basement Stair
Location

Design HPTM00036

Square Footage: 1,997

■ The wide front steps, columned
porch and symmetrical layout give this
charming home a Georgian appeal. The
central great room offers radiant French
doors on both sides of the fireplace.
Outside those doors is a comfortable
covered porch with two skylights,
expanding the livable space to the outdoors. The large kitchen with its walk-in
pantry, island/snack bar and breakfast
nook will gratify any cook. To the left
of the great room reside four bedrooms—three secondary bedrooms and
a master suite. The master suite enjoys a
walk-in closet, twin vanity sinks, a separate shower and tub and private access
to the rear porch. Please specify basement, crawlspace or slab foundation
when ordering.

257

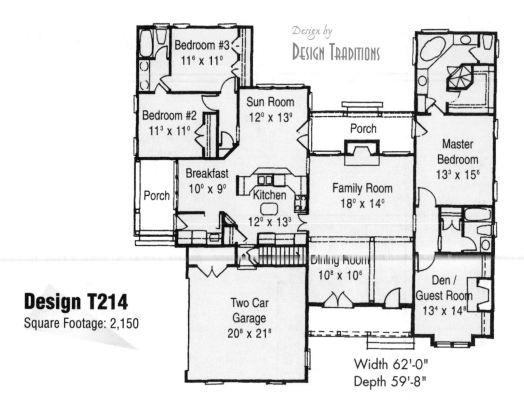

Design by
DESIGN TRADITIONS

Bedroom #3
11⁶ x 11⁰

Bedroom #2
11³ x 11⁰

Sun Room
12⁰ x 13⁹

Porch

Master
Bedroom
13³ x 15⁶

Porch

Breakfast
10⁰ x 9⁰

Kitchen
12⁰ x 13³

Family Room
18⁰ x 14⁰

Dining Room
10⁸ x 10⁶

Den /
Guest Room
13⁴ x 14⁸

Two Car
Garage
20⁸ x 21⁸

Design T214
Square Footage: 2,150

Width 62'-0"
Depth 59'-8"

■ Open, casual living space is offset by a quiet den or study with its own fireplace in this casual Colonial-style home. A bright sunroom opens to the covered rear porch through French doors. The gourmet kitchen enjoys a breakfast area convenient to the family bedrooms. A corner whirlpool tub and an angled shower highlight the master suite, which also has a walk-in closet and separate lavatories. This home is designed with a basement foundation.

© Design Traditions

Width 48'-0"
Depth 44'-0"

Design by
© Frank Betz Associates, Inc.

Design HPTM03047
Square Footage: 1,198

■ The well-planned interior of this cozy home allows it to live larger than its 1,198 square feet. Vaulted ceilings add space to the family room, dining room, kitchen and master bath, while a tray ceiling accents the master bedroom. A fireplace warms the family room; nearby, the dining room opens to the rear yard. Two family bedrooms, each naturally lit by large windows, share a full hall bath. The master suite includes a walk-in closet and a private bath with dual vanities, a whirlpool tub and separate shower.

Design HPTM00037

Square Footage: 2,360

■ Columns, transom windows and an eyebrow dormer lend this house a stylish country charm. Inside, a built-in media center, fireplace, skylights and columns add to the wonderful livability of this home. The modified galley kitchen features a serving bar and an island workstation. Escape to the relaxing owners suite featuring a private sitting room and a luxurious bath set between His and a Hers walk-in closets. Three bedrooms share a bath on the other side of the plan, ensuring privacy. Please specify basement, crawlspace or slab foundation when ordering.

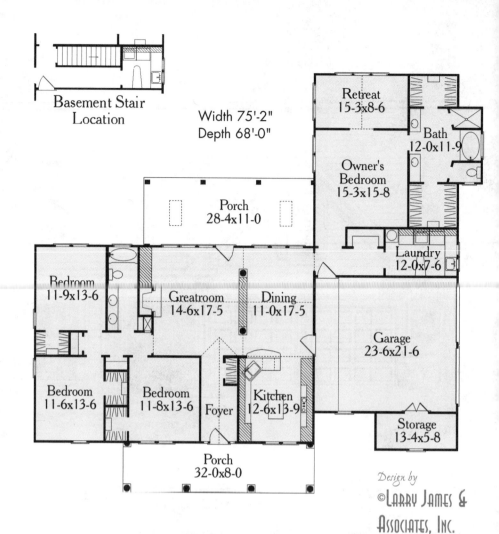

Basement Stair Location

Width 75'-2"
Depth 68'-0"

Retreat
15-3x8-6

Bath
12-0x11-9

Owner's
Bedroom
15-3x15-8

Porch
28-4x11-0

Laundry
12-0x7-6

Bedroom
11-9x13-6

Greatroom
14-6x17-5

Dining
11-0x17-5

Garage
23-6x21-6

Bedroom
11-6x13-6

Bedroom
11-8x13-6

Foyer

Kitchen
12-6x13-9

Storage
13-4x5-8

Porch
32-0x8-0

Design by
©Larry James &
Associates, Inc.

260

Design 9205

Square Footage: 2,254

Width 64'-0"
Depth 69'-4"

■ Richly dressed with special detail, this three-bed-room ranch makes a beautiful home. Visible from the entry, the great room features a cathedral ceiling, floor-to-ceiling windows overlooking the backyard and a through-fireplace to the kitchen. Also off the entry is the formal dining room with arched window and ten-foot detailed ceiling. The sumptuous master suite features an arched ceiling and window, and a bath with a dressing area and corner whirlpool. Two family bedrooms are to the rear—one could easily serve as a den.

Design by
DESIGN BASICS, INC.

Width 63'-10"
Depth 77'-5"

Ext. Storage

Garage
22'-11" x 20'-0"

Patio

Utility

Cov. Porch
19'-10" x 8'-0"

Bath

Study
15'-4" x 13'-0"

Bath

Bedroom
16'-10" x 15'-0"

Kitchen
10'-6" x 11'-0"

Living
21'-8" x 19'-6"

Bath

Breakfast
13'-1" x 8'-4"

Dining
11'-11" x 13'-6"

Foyer

Hall

Bedroom
13'-1" x 12'-0"

Bedroom
11'-11" x 11'-0"

Porch
32'-0" x 6'-0"

Design by
CHATHAM HOME
PLANNING, INC.

Design E112
Square Footage: 2,547

■ This stately Southern exterior welcomes guests in style with a raised porch displaying decorative columns and lovely arched windows. Ten-foot ceilings prevail downstairs, enhancing the foyer and the formal dining room, as well as the central living area with a welcoming fireplace and views to the rear yard. The magnificent foyer announces the living and dining areas with stunning decorative columns. The perfect marriage of style and comfort was made in the plush master suite, highlighted by a raised ceiling and voluminous bath with twin corner walk-in closets and separate dual lavatories. The spacious kitchen shares a corner of the plan with a sunlit informal eating area and allows access to the rear of the home, where a quiet study and guest bath await. Please specify crawlspace or slab foundation when ordering.

European Inspiration:
One-story homes with Old World influence

Design M104
Square Footage: 2,696

■ A brick archway covers the front porch of this European-style home, creating a truly grand entrance. Situated beyond the entry, the living room takes center-stage with a fireplace flanked by tall windows that overlook the backyard. To the right is a bayed eating area, reserved for casual meals, and an efficient kitchen. Steps away is the formal dining room for holidays and special occasions. Skillful planning creates flexibility for the master suite. If you wish, use Bedroom 2 as a secondary bedroom or guest room with the adjacent study accessible to everyone. Or if you prefer, combine the master suite with the study, using it as a private retreat and Bedroom 2 as a nursery, creating a wing that provides complete privacy. Completing this clever plan are two family bedrooms—each with a walk-in closet—a powder room and a utility room.

Width 80'-0"
Depth 64'-1"

Design by
FILLMORE DESIGN GROUP

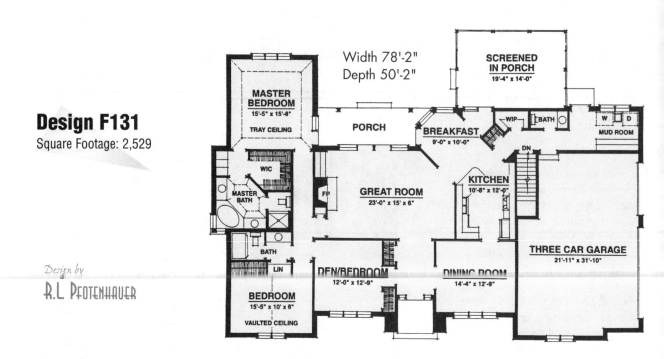

Design F131

Square Footage: 2,529

Width 78'-2"
Depth 50'-2"

SCREENED IN PORCH
19'-4" x 14'-0"

MASTER BEDROOM
15'-5" x 15'-8"

TRAY CEILING

PORCH

BREAKFAST
9'-0" x 10'-0"

WIP

BATH

W D

MUD ROOM

WIC

MASTER BATH

FP

GREAT ROOM
23'-0" x 15'-6"

KITCHEN
10'-8" x 12'-0"

DN

THREE CAR GARAGE
21'-11" x 31'-10"

BATH

LIN

DEN/BEDROOM
12'-0" x 12'-9"

DINING ROOM
14'-4" x 12'-9"

BEDROOM
15'-5" x 10'-6"

VAULTED CEILING

Design by
R.L Pfotenhauer

■ This charming home grabs attention with a beautiful facade including corner quoins, symmetrical design and a lovely roofline. The floor plan holds great livability. A central great room connects to the breakfast room and galley-style kitchen. A formal dining room, just off the foyer, has a huge wall of windows for elegant dining. A complementary room to the left of the foyer serves as a den or guest bedroom as needed. The master bedroom features a tray ceiling and wonderfully appointed bath. A family bedroom to the front of the plan has a vaulted ceiling. Don't miss the screened porch to the rear of the plan.

Design HPTM02005

Square Footage: 2,723

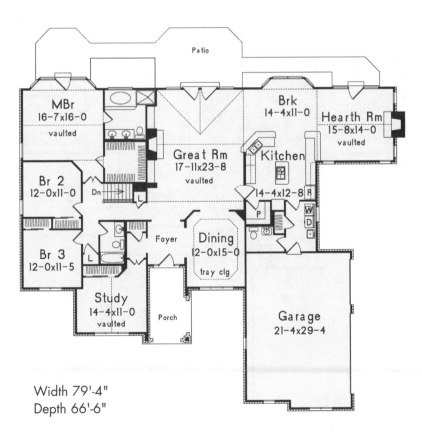

Width 79'-4"
Depth 66'-6"

■ Corner quoins and pedimented arches make this home a delight to view and visit. The great room features a vaulted ceiling and French doors leading to the rear patio. A tray ceiling accents the sophisticated dining room nicely. Light is shed into the kitchen and onto the snack bar from the bayed breakfast nook. A fireplace becomes the focal point in the vaulted hearth room. Two family bedrooms and the master bedroom are located on the left of the plan for optimum privacy. The vaulted master bedroom features an expansive master bath and a private exit onto the rear patio.

Design by
© HOME DESIGN ALTERNATIVES, INC.

265

Design HPTM03048

Square Footage: 1,688

■ Contrasting shapes and textures add
interest to the exterior of this home.
Warmth from the fireplace in the family
room will spread throughout the open
living area, which includes a dining
room, kitchen and breakfast room. Extra
amenities such as a serving bar, pantry
and plant shelf abound. The master suite
boasts access to the rear property, as
well as a luxurious bath with a vaulted
ceiling and a garden tub. Please specify
slab, crawlspace or basement foundation
when ordering.

Design by
© Frank Betz Associates, Inc.

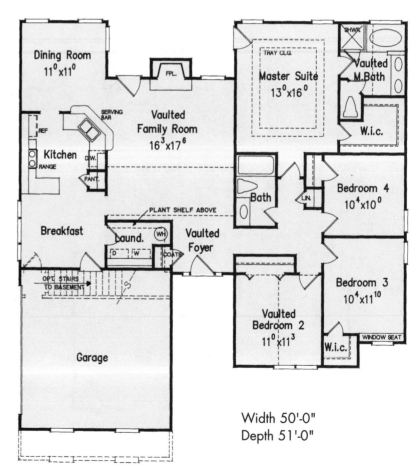

Width 50'-0"
Depth 51'-0"

Width 61'-0"
Depth 73'-8"

Porch

Master
Bedroom
16³ x 13⁶

Bedroom
Office
10³ x 11⁰

Breakfast
13³ x 9⁰

Kitchen
13³ x 10⁶

Great
Room
17⁰ x 17⁹

Bedroom
No. 2
10³ x 12⁰

Dining
Room
11³ x 12⁹

Bedroom
No. 3
11³ x 12⁰

Two Car
Garage
20⁶ x 19⁶

Dn

Design HPTM03049

Square Footage: 2,127

■ The foyer of this quaint French cottage is set apart from the formal dining room with stately columns. The great room will accommodate easy living with a grand fireplace and doors to the rear porch. A gourmet-style kitchen has a cooktop island and a bayed breakfast nook. The master suite provides twin walk-in closets and a luxury bath. Two secondary bedrooms share a hall bath. An additional bedroom and bath off the kitchen would make a nice guest suite or a home office. This house is designed with a walkout basement foundation.

Design by
©STEPHEN FULLER, INC.

Design 9734

Square Footage: 1,977
Bonus Room: 430 square feet

■ A two-story foyer with a Palladian window above sets the tone for this sunlit home. Columns mark the passage from the foyer to the great room, where a centered fireplace and built-in cabinets are found. A screened porch with four skylights above and a wet bar provides a pleasant place to start the day or wind down after work. Just a few steps away is the deck with a spa. The kitchen is flanked by the formal dining room and the breakfast room with sliding glass doors to the large, rear deck. Hidden quietly in the rear, the owners suite includes a bath with dual vanities and skylights. Two family bedrooms—one an optional study—share a bath that has twin sinks.

QUOTE ONE®

Cost to build? See page 434 to order complete cost estimate to build this house in your area!

Design by
DONALD A. GARDNER ARCHITECTS, INC.

Width 69'-8"
Depth 59'-6"

© 1994 Donald A. Gardner Architects, Inc.

Design 9656

Square Footage: 2,099

Design by
DONALD A. GARDNER
ARCHITECTS, INC.

Rear Elevation

■ By putting the garage to the rear of this plan, nothing is taken away from the beautiful stone and stucco facade. Access from the garage is enhanced by a covered breezeway which passes the rear covered porch and connects to the home at the utility room. A great room with cathedral ceiling and fireplace has sliding glass doors to the rear deck and access to the skylit sunroom which also opens to the deck. The master bath connects to the sunroom as well. It is the perfect complement to the private master bedroom. Choose two styles of dining: the formal dining room with columned entrance to the great room, or the sunny breakfast room, attached to the U-shaped kitchen. Two additional bedrooms are at the right side of the plan and share a full bath with linen storage.

Width 68'-4"
Depth 68'-7"

GARAGE
20-4 × 20-4

DECK
43-0 × 10-0

covered breezeway

SUN RM.
15-8 × 7-10

GREAT RM.
20-0 × 15-6
(cathedral ceiling)

fireplace

UTILITY
8-10 × 5-4

powder rm.

bath

BED RM.
11-4 × 13-8

hot tub

skylights

master bath

walk-in closet

MASTER BED RM.
13-4 × 18-8

FOYER
6-10 × 5-4

DINING
12-0 × 12-0

KITCHEN
14-4 × 12-0

BRKFST.
13-4 × 9-8

BED RM.
14-8 × 11-0

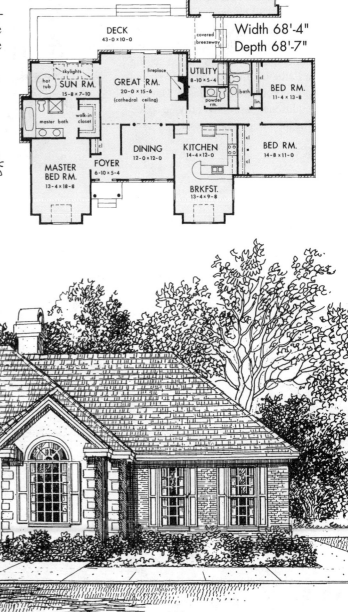

Design M132

Square Footage: 2,026

■ The graceful high roofline, brick gables and arch-top windows balance this outstanding traditional. A colonnaded formal dining room and gallery add an atmosphere of luxury. The great room features a wide brick fireplace and a full-height window, which looks out to a private patio surrounded by brick seating. A tiled kitchen and breakfast area enjoy wonderful views of the rear gardens. The master bedroom suite contains a high sloped ceiling, a Palladian-influenced window and a generous walk-in closet. Three additional bedrooms provide space for the family and guests.

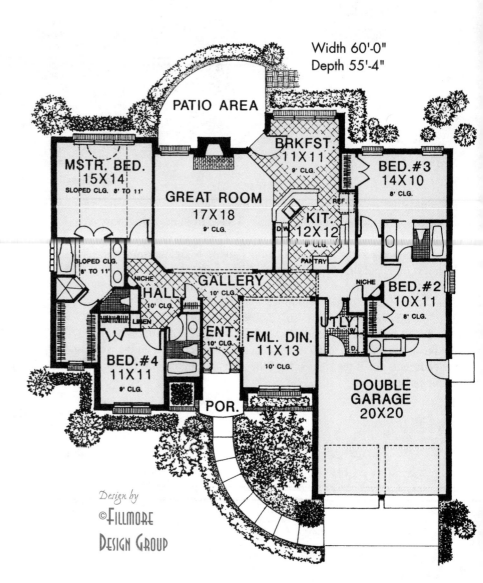

Width 60'-0"
Depth 55'-4"

PATIO AREA

MSTR. BED.
15X14
SLOPED CLG. 8' TO 11'

GREAT ROOM
17X18
9' CLG.

BRKFST.
11X11
9' CLG.

BED. #3
14X10
8' CLG.

KIT.
12X12

HALL
10' CLG.

GALLERY
10' CLG.

NICHE

BED. #2
10X11
8' CLG.

ENT.
10' CLG.

FML. DIN.
11X13
10' CLG.

UTLY.

BED. #4
11X11
9' CLG.

POR.

DOUBLE GARAGE
20X20

Design by
©FILLMORE
DESIGN GROUP

Design M102

Square Footage: 2,888

■ Alternate exteriors—both European style! Stone quoins and shutters give one elevation the appearance of a French country cottage. The other, with keystone window treatment and a copper roof over the bay window creates the impression of a stately French chateau. From the entry, formal living areas are accessed through graceful columned openings—living room to the left and dining room to the right. Straight ahead, the comfortable family room awaits with its warming fireplace and cathedral ceiling, offering room to relax and enjoy casual gatherings. The private master suite features a pullman ceiling, a luxurious bath and twin walk-in closets. A private lanai is accessed from the master bath. Located nearby, Bedroom 2 serves nicely as a guest room or easily converts to a nursery or study. Two family bedrooms with a connecting bath, a handy kitchen and breakfast room, and a utility room complete the floor plan.

Width 68'-6"
Depth 78'-1"

© Copyright Fillmore Design Group

Design by
FILLMORE DESIGN GROUP

Alternate Elevation

Design HPTM03050

Square Footage: 2,757

■ French country appointments lend an elegant Old World look to this design. The foyer opens to the well-proportioned dining room, which boasts a twelve-foot ceiling. Two sets of French doors with transoms open off the living room to the rear porch. The kitchen, breakfast room and family room are open to one another. The fireplace is visible from all these areas and provides a lovely focal point for the room. The master suite features a tray ceiling and a luxury master bath. Please specify basement, crawlspace or slab foundation when ordering.

Design by
©Larry E. Belk Designs

Width 69'-6"
Depth 68'-8"

Design M505

Square Footage: 2,322

m bath

mbr
14-10 X 14

laundry

pantry

brkfst
10-10 X 12-6

porch

br.2
11 X 11

family
18 X 19-4

dining
11 X 13

foyer

kit
16 X 9

loggia

br.3
11 X 11

br.4
(opt. study)
11 X 11

garage
20 X 23

Width 68'-11"
Depth 74'-0"

■ A stucco and brick facade declares the Old World influence used in this design. The steeply pitched roofline adds airiness to the interior spaces. The central entry opens to living spaces: a dining room on the left and the family room with fireplace on the right. The kitchen and breakfast nook sit nearby. The kitchen features an island cooktop and a huge pantry. A door in the breakfast room leads out to the rear porch. The bedrooms include three family bedrooms—one of which could be used as a study—and a master suite. Note the double closets in the master bath.

Design A157

Square Footage: 2,500

■ Triple dormers highlight the roofline of this distinctive single-level French country design. Double doors enhance the covered entryway leading to a grand open area with graceful columns outlining the dimensions of the formal living room and dining room. The large family room with fireplace opens through double doors to the rear terrace. An L-shaped island kitchen opens into a breakfast area with bay window. The master bedroom suite fills one wing and features a bay window, vaulted ceilings and access to the terrace. Two additional bedrooms on the opposite side of the house share a full bath.

BREAKFAST
12'-6" x 10'-0"

DECK/
TERRACE

SUITE 2
13'-0" x 10'-6"

KITCHEN
15'-0" x 14'-0"

MASTER
SUITE
14'-0" x 18'-0"

BATH

FAMILY ROOM
20'-6" x 15'-0"

LAUN.

PDR.

SUITE 3
12'-0" x 11'-6"

W.I.C.

W.I.C.

LIVING
ROOM
12'-0" x 12'-6"

FOYER

DINING
ROOM
11'-6" x 12'-6"

MASTER
BATH

LOGGIA

GARAGE
22'-0" x 30'-0"

Width 73'-0"
Depth 65'-10"

Design by
LIVING CONCEPTS

porch

sitting

keeping
16-2 x 18-2

brkfst
12-8 x 15

mbr
18 x 21

family
20-5 x 14

kit
16-6 x 11-8

br.2
14-8 x 11

m bath

study
12-6 x 14

foyer

dining
12-6 x 14

desk

laundry

br.3
12 x 11

Width 73'-0"
Depth 87'-8"

garage
31-9 x 20-10

Design M518

Square Footage: 3,032

■ This country estate is bedecked
with all the details that pronounce
its French origins. The roofline, in
particular, is an outstanding feature
and allows high ceilings for interi-
or spaces. Gathering areas are varied and large and include a study, a
family room and a keeping room.
Dine in one of two areas—the formal dining room or the casual
breakfast room. A large porch to
the rear can be reached through the
breakfast room or the master suite
sitting area. All three bedrooms in
the plan hold walk-in closets. Bedrooms 2 and 3 share a full bath
that includes private vanities.

Design by
©ANDY McDONALD
DESIGN GROUP

Design HPTM00039

Square Footage: 1,730
Bonus Room: 520 square feet

■ A well-balanced exterior with stately columns and hipped roof-lines is just the beginning of the appeal of this home. The porch offers three French-door entries to the great room, which features a fireplace and rear-porch access. Two family bedrooms and a bath can be found to the left. The owners suite enjoys views of the front property, a sumptuous bath and a spacious walk-in closet. The gourmet kitchen offers plenty of counter and cabinet space and serves the breakfast area with ease. A bonus room is perfect for future expansion. Please specify basement, crawlspace or slab foundation when ordering.

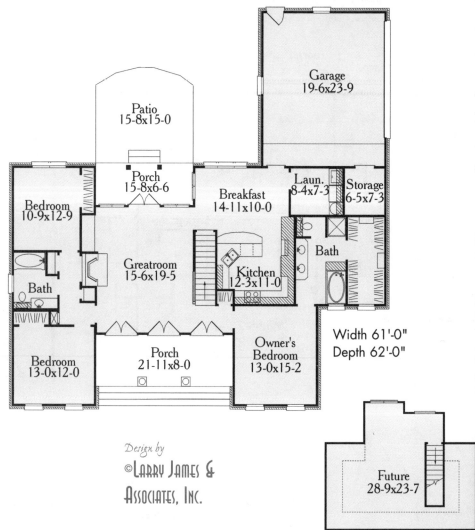

Garage
19-6x23-9

Patio
15-8x15-0

Porch
15-8x6-6

Breakfast
14-11x10-0

Laun.
8-4x7-3

Storage
6-5x7-3

Bedroom
10-9x12-9

Greatroom
15-6x19-5

Kitchen
12-3x11-0

Bath

Bath

Bedroom
13-0x12-0

Porch
21-11x8-0

Owner's
Bedroom
13-0x15-2

Width 61'-0"
Depth 62'-0"

Future
28-9x23-7

Design by
©Larry James &
Associates, Inc.

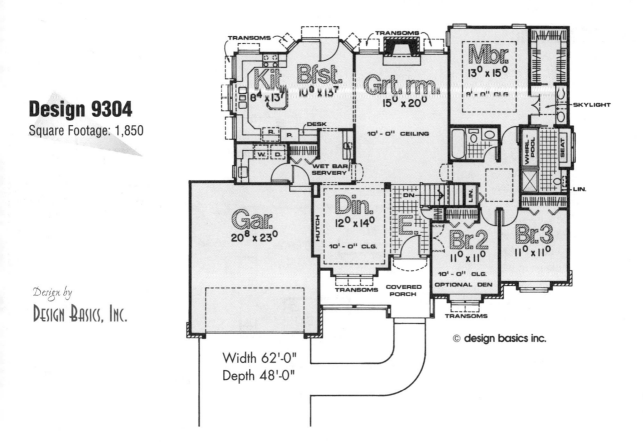

Design 9304

Square Footage: 1,850

Design by
Design Basics, Inc.

Width 62'-0"
Depth 48'-0"

■ European style influences the elevation of this distinctive ranch home. Appealing rooflines and a covered porch with repeating arches provide stunning curb appeal. Inside, an impressive ten-foot-high entry greets family and friends. An open concept pervades the kitchen/dinette area. Picture your family enjoying the bayed eating area, wrapping counters, desk, island and wet bar/servery ideal for entertaining. The decorative hutch space adds appeal to a formal dining room.

Bright windows frame a fireplace in the great room. Sure to please is the service entry to the laundry/mud room with soaking sink and counter space. Bedroom 2 can easily be converted into a private den. A boxed ceiling decorates the master suite, while three windows provide natural lighting. Dual lavs, a walk-in closet, whirlpool and cedar-lined window seat enhance the master bath.

Design HPTM00040

Square Footage: 2,200

■ A versatile swing room is a highlight of this compact and charming French-style home. Using the optional door opening to the entry, the swing room makes a perfect office, or it can be used as a bedroom or study. The king-size master suite is isolated for privacy and sports a spacious bath and walk-in closet with passage to the utility room. The open and spacious living room features twelve-foot ceilings. Two secondary bedrooms offer walk-in closets and private baths. Please specify crawlspace or slab foundation when ordering.

Design by
©Breland & Farmer
Designers, Inc.

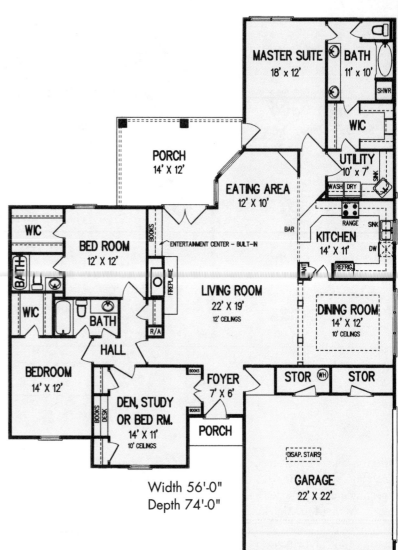

MASTER SUITE 18' x 12'
BATH 11' x 10'
WIC
PORCH 14' X 12'
EATING AREA 12' X 10'
UTILITY 10' X 7'
WASH DRY
RANGE SINK
KITCHEN 14' X 11'
REFRIG.
BAR
WIC
BED ROOM 12' X 12'
BOOKS
ENTERTAINMENT CENTER – BUILT-IN
BATH
WIC
FIREPLACE
LIVING ROOM 22' X 19' 12' CEILINGS
DINING ROOM 14' X 12' 10' CEILINGS
BATH
HALL
R/A
BEDROOM 14' X 12'
BOOKS DESK
DEN, STUDY OR BED RM. 14' X 11' 10' CEILINGS
BOOKS
FOYER 7' X 6'
BOOKS
STOR WH STOR
PORCH
DISAP. STAIRS
GARAGE 22' X 22'

Width 56'-0"
Depth 74'-0"

Design 7447

Square Footage: 1,790

■ With horizontal wood siding and brick accents, this clever design offers exterior charm. The floor plan is practical, but contains many amenities to boost livability, as well. A central hall unites the living areas and defines formal from informal spaces. The living and dining rooms are graced with columns and ten-foot ceilings. The family room also has a ten-foot ceiling, plus it features a warming fireplace and media center. An island kitchen and breakfast nook are close by. The nook has sliding glass doors to the rear yard. The bedrooms are aligned along the left side of the plan, behind the two-car garage. One of the family bedrooms sports a walk-in closet. The master suite is to the rear and has a tray ceiling and walk-in closet. Its bath bows to graciousness with a large spa tub, separate shower and double sinks.

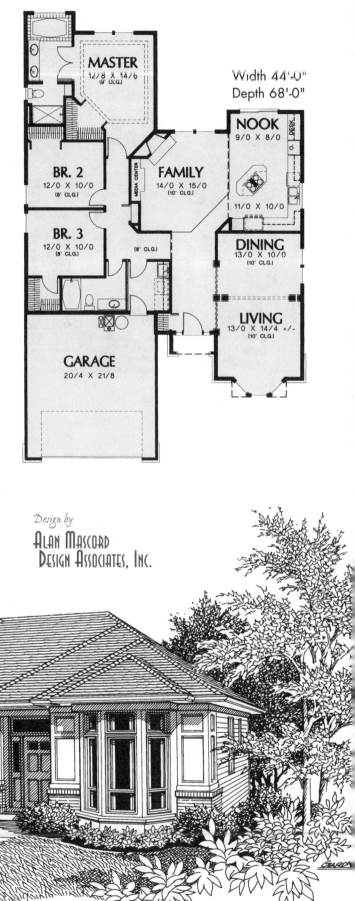

Width 44'-0"
Depth 68'-0"

MASTER
12/8 X 14/6
(9' CLG.)

NOOK
9/0 X 8/0

BR. 2
12/0 X 10/0
(8' CLG.)

FAMILY
14/0 X 15/0
(10' CLG.)

11/0 X 10/0

BR. 3
12/0 X 10/0
(8' CLG.)

(8' CLG.)

DINING
13/0 X 10/0
(10' CLG.)

LIVING
13/0 X 14/4 +/-
(10' CLG.)

GARAGE
20/4 X 21/8

Design by
Alan Mascord
Design Associates, Inc.

279

Design HPTM03051

Square Footage: 2,403
Bonus Space: 285 square feet

■ Asymmetrical gables, pediments and tall arch-top windows accent a European-style exterior, while inside, an unrestrained floor plan expresses its independence. A spider-beam ceiling and a centered fireplace framed by shelves redraw the open space of the family room to cozy dimensions. The vaulted breakfast nook enjoys a radius window and a French door that leads outside. Split sleeping quarters lend privacy to the luxurious master suite. Please specify basement or crawlspace foundation when ordering.

Optional Basement Stair Location

Width 60'-0"
Depth 67'-0"

Design by
© Frank Betz Associates, Inc.

Sitting Area

TRAY CEILING

FRENCH DOOR

Master Suite
16⁰ x 14⁰

RAD. WDW.

RAD. WDW.

RAD. WDW.

Breakfast
11'-0" HIGH CLG.

FRENCH DOOR

ACTIVE DORMER W/ RAD. WDW.

VAULT

VAULT

W.i.c.

SHWR

Vaulted M.Bath

RAD. WDW.

LINEN

FPL

COATS

Vaulted Family Room
15⁸ x 20²

DBL OVEN

DW.

Kitchen
11'-0" HIGH CLG.

RANGE

ISLAND

REF.

PANTRY

Bedroom 2
11⁰ x 13⁰

Bath

W.i.c.

LINEN

W.i.c.

Pwdr.

PLANT SHELF ABOVE

DECORATIVE COLUMNS

ARCHED OPENINGS

VAULT

SINK

W.H.

W

D

Bedroom 3
12¹⁰ x 11⁶

Foyer
14'-0" HIGH CLG.

Dining Room
12⁰ x 14⁰
14'-0" HIGH CLG.

Laund.

Living Room
13⁵ x 14⁰

FRENCH DOORS

COVERED ENTRY

OPT. STAIR TO BSMT.

Garage
20⁵ x 20⁹

copyright © 1995 frank betz associates, inc.

GARAGE LOCATION WITH BASEMENT

Width 62'-0"
Depth 61'-0"

Design by

© FRANK BETZ ASSOCIATES, INC.

Design HPTMO3052

Square Footage: 2,322

■ An eclectic mix of building materials—stone, stucco and siding—sings in tune with the European charm of this one-story home. Within, decorative columns set off the formal dining room and the foyer from the vaulted family room, while the formal living room is quietly tucked behind French doors. The gourmet kitchen provides an angled snack bar and a sunny breakfast room. Two family bedrooms each have a walk-in closet and private access to a shared bath. The master suite holds an elegant tray ceiling, a bay sitting area and a lush bath. Please specify basement, crawlspace or slab foundation when ordering.

Width 74'-0"
Depth 44'-0"

Design HPTMO3053

Square Footage: 1,807

Design by
©FILLMORE DESIGN GROUP

■ The striking European facade of this home presents a beautiful stone exterior, complete with stone quoins, a shingled rooftop and French-style shutters on the front windows. Step inside the great room where a ten-foot ceiling and fireplace will greet you. A large island in the kitchen provides plenty of much-needed counter space for the cook of the family. An element of privacy is observed with the master suite separated from the other two bedrooms, which share a full bath. An oversized two-car garage and a covered patio are just some of the added amenities.

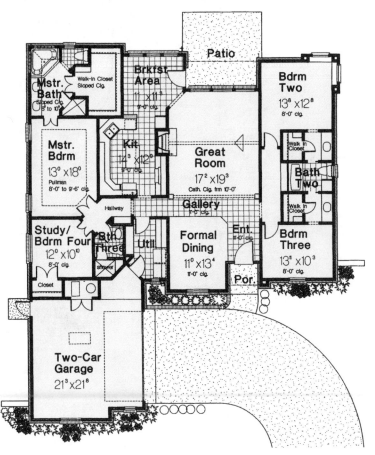

Width 57'-5"
Depth 57'-10"

Design HPTM03054

Square Footage: 2,288

■ Steeply pitched gables resemble a quaint country church. This home takes quaint and pushes it to comfortable luxury. The formal dining room sits across the tiled gallery from the spacious great room. Plenty of natural light filters in from the wall of windows in the great room. To the right, two family bedrooms share a Jack-and-Jill bath and feature walk-in closets. A large kitchen, breakfast area and utitlity room serve both casual and formal areas. The master suite enjoys a roomy bath and walk-in closet. An extra bedroom or study resides just down the hall, close to a full bath.

Design by
©FILLMORE DESIGN GROUP

Design HPTM03055

Square Footage: 2,391

■ Tall, narrow windows, an arched entry and a uniquely shaped dormer window add European style to this sturdy brick home. The interior, fit for royalty, includes a formal dining room and a distinguished study that can double as an extra bedroom. The central great room, serving as the heart of the home, offers a fireplace and windows that overlook the covered rear patio. To the right of the great room, a lavish master suite provides lots of much-desired amenities—spacious walk-in closet, private dual-vanity bath and access to the patio. Family bedrooms to the left of the plan—one with a walk-in closet—share a full bath.

Design by
©FILLMORE DESIGN GROUP

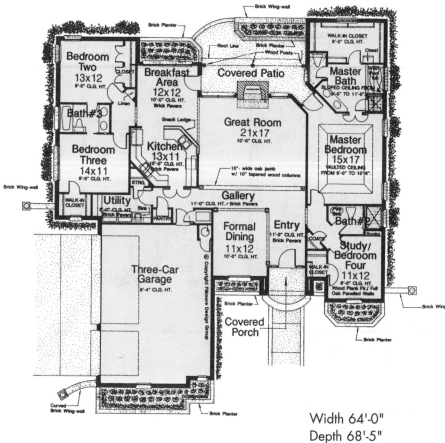

Width 64'-0"
Depth 68'-5"

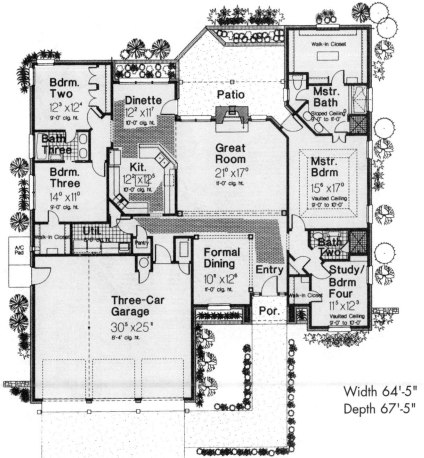

Design HPTM03056

Square Footage: 2,483

■ This country cottage estate offers a fine picture of comfort and luxury within 2,500 square feet. A formal dining room is accented by columns and sits across a gallery from the great room. A large fireplace provides a warm visual display for this area and the dining room. To the right, the master suite is provided with privacy and the convenient comforts of a full bath and oversized walk-in closet. Across the short hall is a study or extra bedroom. To the left, two family bedrooms share a compartmented bath. The kitchen is a grand amenity for the gourmet. A three-car garage completes this design.

Width 64'-5"
Depth 67'-5"

Design by
©FILLMORE DESIGN GROUP

Design M171

Square Footage: 2,526

Walk-in Closet
9'-0" Clg
Shelves

Whirl Pool Tub

Covered Patio

Covered Patio

Din
10x15
9'-0" Clg
Brick Pavers

Kit
12⁵x12⁵
Brick Pavers

FamilyRm
16x16³
Cathedral Ceiling

Walk in Closet

Bed#3
12x13³
8'-0" Clg

Linen

MstrBed
15x17
Vaulted Ceiling
9'-0" To 10'-6"

FmlLiv
14x14
9'-0" Clg

Display

Utll

Pantry

Hall
9'-0" Clg

Linen

Bed#2
12x13
8'-0" Clg

Gallery
9'-0" Clg
Brick Pavers

Brick Pavers

Walk-in Closet

Hall
Clg

Ent
9'-0" Clg
Brick Pavers

FmlDin
10⁵x12
9'-0" Clg

Coats

Bed#4
/Study
11x12
9'-0" Clg

Walk-in Closet

Cov Por

3-Car·Gar
22⁵x30
9'-4" Clg

Width 64'-0"
Depth 81'-7"

Interesting angles and creative detailing characterize the exterior of this brick cottage. Inside, the formal dining room is just off the foyer for ease in entertaining. A gallery hall leads to the island kitchen, which opens to an informal dining area with access to two covered patios. Sleeping quarters include two family bedrooms to the right of the plan and another bedroom, which could be used as a study, on the left. The left wing is dedicated to a lavish master suite complete with a vaulted ceiling and sumptuous bath with a whirlpool tub and separate shower.

Design by
©FILLMORE
DESIGN GROUP

Width 66'-6"
Depth 62'-0"

Porch

Bedroom
No. 2
11³ x 13⁰

Breakfast
13⁰ x 10⁰

Master
Bedroom
15³ x 16³

Family
Room
16³ x 20⁰

Bedroom
No. 3
11³ x 13⁰

Kitchen
13⁶ x 12³

Dining
Room
11⁹ x 17⁶

Foyer

Study
12⁶ x 13⁶

Two Car
Garage
22⁰ x 23⁶

Design by
DESIGN TRADITIONS

Design T236

Square Footage: 2,648

■ With brick and siding, a hipped roofline, a covered porch accented by columns and two fireplaces, this three-bedroom home is a perfect example of Old-World class. Inside, the foyer is flanked by a formal dining room and a cozy study. Directly ahead is the family room, complete with a fireplace, built-ins and French doors to the rear deck. Nearby, the elegant kitchen is full of amenities, including a snack bar, a pantry and the adjacent bayed breakfast area. Sleeping quarters consist of two family bedrooms which share a bath, and a deluxe master suite. Here, the homeowner will relish such amenities as a large walk-in closet, a separate tub and shower and direct access to the rear deck. This home is designed with a basement foundation.

© Design Traditions

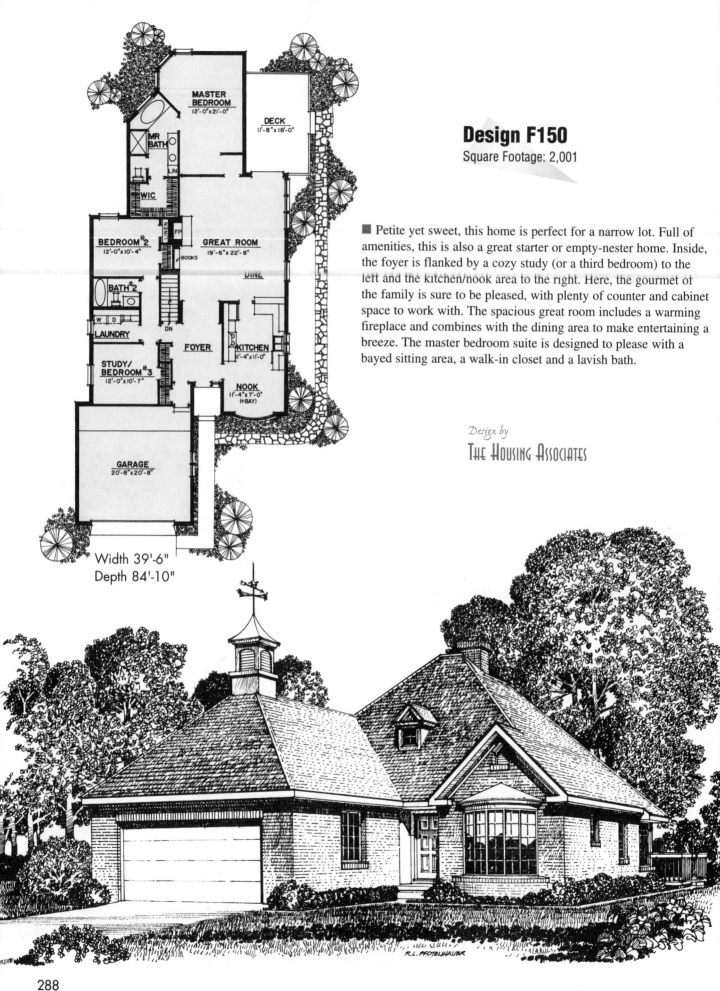

MASTER BEDROOM
12'-0"x21'-0"

DECK
11'-8"x16'-0"

MR BATH

WIC

LIN

BEDROOM #2
12'-0"x10'-4"

GREAT ROOM
19'-6"x22'-8"

FP

BOOKS

LINEN

DINE

BATH #2

W D

LAUNDRY

DN

FOYER

KITCHEN
11'-4"x11'-0"

STUDY/ BEDROOM #3
12'-0"x10'-7"

NOOK
11'-4"x7'-0"
(+BAY)

GARAGE
20'-8"x20'-8"

Width 39'-6"
Depth 84'-10"

Design F150

Square Footage: 2,001

■ Petite yet sweet, this home is perfect for a narrow lot. Full of amenities, this is also a great starter or empty-nester home. Inside, the foyer is flanked by a cozy study (or a third bedroom) to the left and the kitchen/nook area to the right. Here, the gourmet of the family is sure to be pleased, with plenty of counter and cabinet space to work with. The spacious great room includes a warming fireplace and combines with the dining area to make entertaining a breeze. The master bedroom suite is designed to please with a bayed sitting area, a walk-in closet and a lavish bath.

Design by
THE HOUSING ASSOCIATES

R.L. PFOTENHAUER

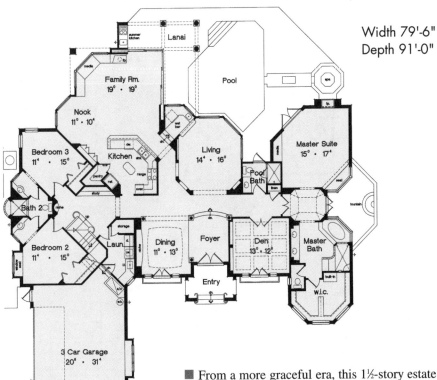

Width 79'-6"
Depth 91'-0"

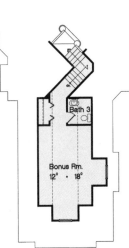

Design HPTM03057

Square Footage: 3,064
Bonus Space: 366 square feet

■ From a more graceful era, this 1½-story estate evokes the sense of quiet refinement. Exquisite exterior detailing makes it a one-of-a-kind. Inside are distinctive treatments that make the floor plan unique and functional. The central foyer is enhanced with columns that define the dining room and formal living room. A beam ceiling complements the den. An indulgent master suite includes a fountain in a private garden, pool access, a large walk-in closet and a fireplace to the outdoor spa. Family bedrooms share an unusual compartmented bath. The kitchen and family room are completed with a breakfast nook. Pool access and a lanai with a summer kitchen make this area a natural for casual lifestyles. A bonus area over the garage can become a home office or game room.

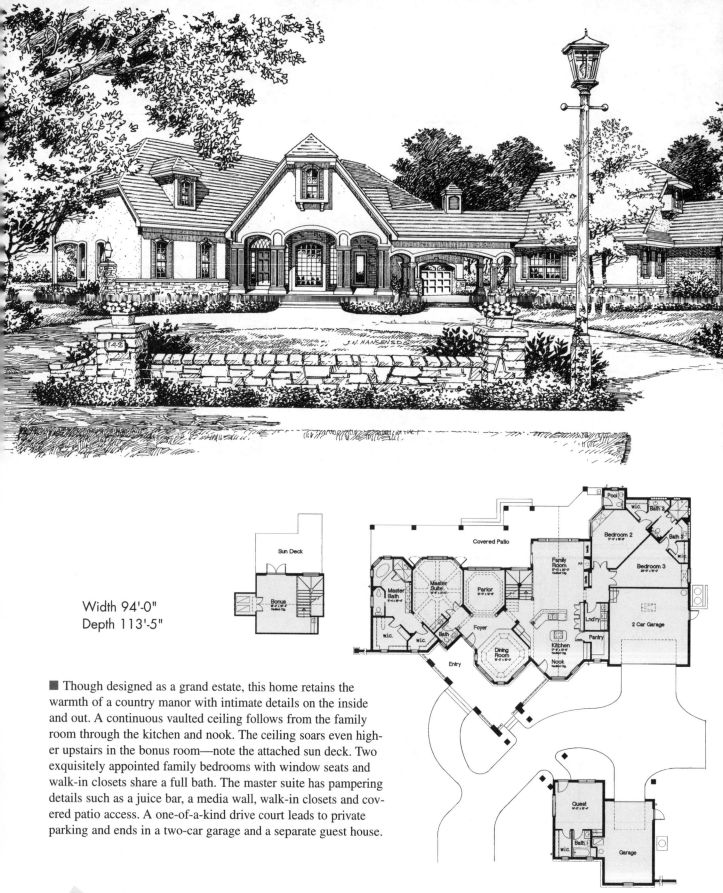

Width 94'-0"
Depth 113'-5"

■ Though designed as a grand estate, this home retains the warmth of a country manor with intimate details on the inside and out. A continuous vaulted ceiling follows from the family room through the kitchen and nook. The ceiling soars even higher upstairs in the bonus room—note the attached sun deck. Two exquisitely appointed family bedrooms with window seats and walk-in closets share a full bath. The master suite has pampering details such as a juice bar, a media wall, walk-in closets and covered patio access. A one-of-a-kind drive court leads to private parking and ends in a two-car garage and a separate guest house.

Design HPTM03058

Square Footage: 2,816
Bonus Space: 290 square feet

Design by
©Home Design Services, Inc.

Design 9203
Square Footage: 2,422

■ You can't help but feel spoiled by this amenity-filled plan. A tiled entry and open stairwell with dome ceiling greet visitors to this unusual home. Just off the entry is a den or optional bedroom, an open dining room with hutch space and an enormous great room with arched windows. An open-hearth fireplace serves both the great room and kitchen, creating a hearth room on the kitchen side. A large work area in the kitchen caters to the resident gourmet. The spacious master suite includes ten-foot ceilings, a whirlpool with dome ceiling and an enormous walk-in closet.

Bfst.
11x11
DOME
SNACK BAR
Kit.
12x12
Hrth.
13x14
DESK
WET BAR
Grt. rm.
19x17
10'-0" CEILING
Mbr.
13x17
10'-0" CEILING
TRANS.
WHIRL POOL
DOME
DRESSING
LIN.
Br.
13x11
DOME
Gar
30x22
10'-0" CEILING
Dn.
12x13
OPT. BEDROOM
Den
12x12
COVERED STOOP

Width 72'-0"
Depth 55'-8"

Design by
DESIGN BASICS, INC.

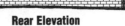

Rear Elevation

■ Tall hipped rooflines, corner quoins and brick detailing are just the beginning of class for this three-bedroom home. Inside, compact doesn't mean cramped, with the living room opening to the dining area, giving a spacious feeling to the layout. Here also is a warming fireplace, waiting to add cheer to chilly winter evenings. Two family bedrooms—or make one a comfortable study—share a full hall bath. The master bedroom suite is full of amenities, including a large walk-in closet, a lavish bath and direct access to the rear covered patio. A two-car garage easily shelters the family fleet. Please specify basement or crawlspace foundation when ordering.

Design F149

Square Footage: 1,527

Design by
©R.L Pfotenhauer

Width 55'-1"
Depth 51'-1"

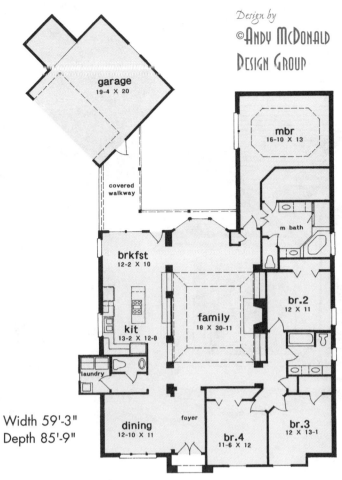

Design by
©ANDY MCDONALD
DESIGN GROUP

Design M507
Square Footage: 2,451

■ Quaint French country design makes an appealing facade for this home. The combination of stucco, brick and double front doors spells classic design. On the inside, the family room dominates the center of the plan and features built-ins, a fireplace and a tray ceiling. The dining room is to the front of the plan, while the more casual breakfast room resides to the back, near a covered walkway to the two-car garage. Four bedrooms and two full baths include a master bedroom with a tray ceiling.

garage
19-4 X 20

covered walkway

mbr
16-10 X 13

m bath

brkfst
12-2 X 10

br.2
12 X 11

family
18 X 30-11

kit
13-2 X 12-8

laundry

dining
12-10 X 11

foyer

br.4
11-6 X 12

br.3
12 X 13-1

Width 59'-3"
Depth 85'-9"

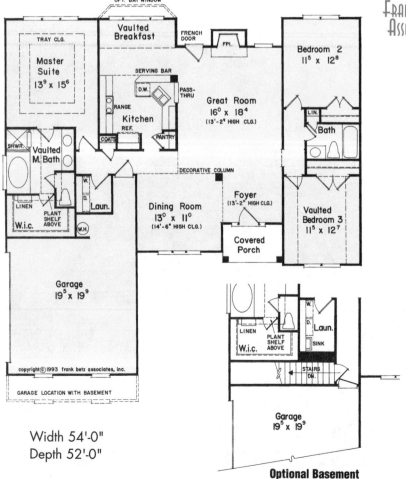

Width 54'-0"
Depth 52'-0"

**Optional Basement
Stair Location**

Design by
Frank Betz
Associates, Inc.

Design P109
Square Footage: 1,670

■ A grand front window display illuminates the formal dining room and the great room in this country French charmer. Open planning allows for easy access between the formal dining room, great room, vaulted breakfast nook and kitchen. Extra amenities include a decorative column, fireplace and an optional bay window in the breakfast nook. The elegant master suite is fashioned with a tray ceiling in the bedroom, a vaulted master bath and a walk-in closet. Two family bedrooms are designated in a pocket-door hall and share a large hall bath. Please specify basement, crawlspace or slab foundation when ordering.

QUOTE ONE®
Cost to build? See page 434
to order complete cost estimate
to build this house in your area!

Design E120

Square Footage: 2,434

Design by

CHITHILL HUITL
PLANNING, INC.

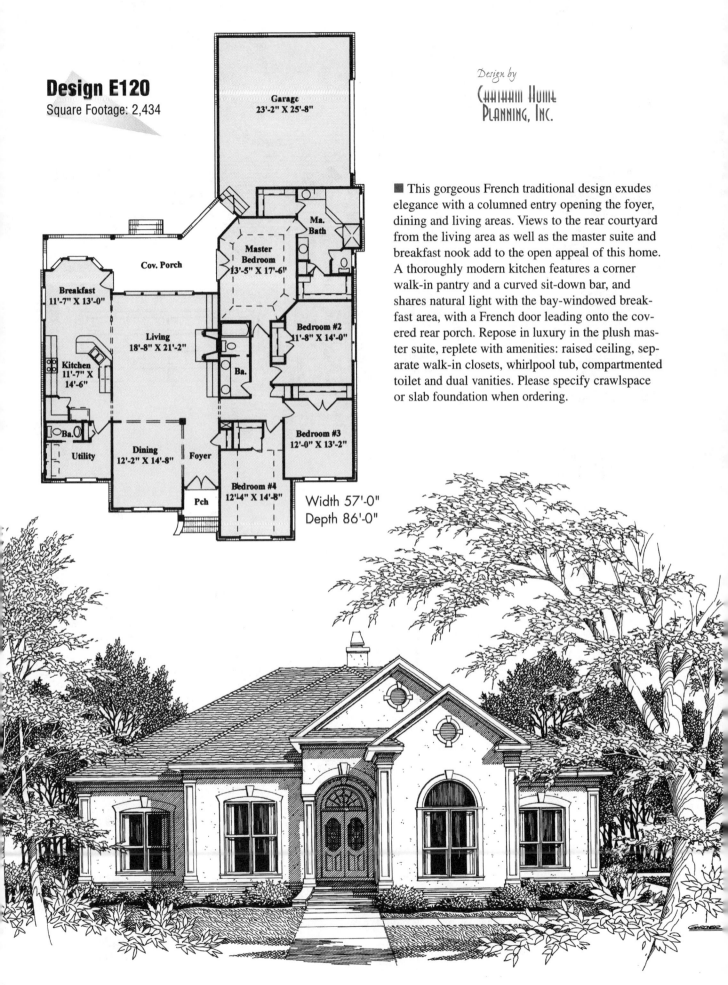

Garage
23'-2" X 25'-8"

Ma. Bath

Master Bedroom
13'-5" X 17'-6"

Cov. Porch

Breakfast
11'-7" X 13'-0"

Living
18'-8" X 21'-2"

Bedroom #2
11'-8" X 14'-0"

Kitchen
11'-7" X 14'-6"

Ba.

Ba.

Utility

Dining
12'-2" X 14'-8"

Foyer

Bedroom #3
12'-0" X 13'-2"

Bedroom #4
12'4" X 14'-8"

Pch

Width 57'-0"
Depth 86'-0"

■ This gorgeous French traditional design exudes elegance with a columned entry opening the foyer, dining and living areas. Views to the rear courtyard from the living area as well as the master suite and breakfast nook add to the open appeal of this home. A thoroughly modern kitchen features a corner walk-in pantry and a curved sit-down bar, and shares natural light with the bay-windowed breakfast area, with a French door leading onto the covered rear porch. Repose in luxury in the plush master suite, replete with amenities: raised ceiling, separate walk-in closets, whirlpool tub, compartmented toilet and dual vanities. Please specify crawlspace or slab foundation when ordering.

Design by

Frank Betz
Associates, Inc.

Quote One®

Cost to build? See page 434
to order complete cost estimate
to build this house in your area!

Design P123

Square Footage: 1,715

■ A grand double bank of windows looking in on the formal dining room mirrors the lofty elegance of the extra-tall vaulted ceiling inside. From the foyer, an arched entrance to the great room visually frames the fireplace on the back wall. The wraparound kitchen has plenty of counter and cabinet space, along with a handy serving bar. The luxurious master suite features a front sitting room for quiet times and a large spa-style bath. Two family bedrooms are split from the master for privacy and share a hall bath. Please specify basement, crawlspace or slab foundation when ordering.

Width 55'-0"
Depth 49'-0"

Design P129

Square Footage: 1,845
Bonus Room: 409 square feet

copyright © 1994 frank betz associates, inc.

Design by

FRANK BETZ ASSOCIATES, INC.

Master Suite 14⁰ x 17⁰
TRAY CEILING

Breakfast
DESK
K.S.
PANTRY
REF.
SERVING BAR
Kitchen
RANGE
DW

Vaulted M.Bath
K.S.
PLANT SHELF ABOVE
SHWR
LINEN
W.i.c.
Pwdr.
COATS
Laund.
W. D.
Stor.

FRENCH DOOR
RADIUS WINDOW

Vaulted Living Room 15⁶ x 20²
13'-6" HIGH CEILING
FPL.

Bedroom 2 11² x 11⁰

LINEN
Bath

STAIRS

Foyer 13'-6" HIGH CEILING
COATS

Bedroom 3 11² x 11⁶

Dining Room 11³ x 12⁰
13'-6" HIGH CEILING

Covered Porch

STAIRS TO OPT. BSMT.

Garage 23⁰ x 19⁵

Bath
W.i.c.
STAIRS DN

Optional Bonus Room 11⁰ x 19²

Width 56'-0"
Depth 60'-0"

QUOTE ONE®
Cost to build? See page 434 to order complete cost estimate to build this house in your area!

■ The stucco exterior and combination roof lines give a stately appearance to this traditional home. Inside, the well-lit foyer leads to an elegant living room with a vaulted ceiling, a fireplace, a radius window and a French door leading to the rear yard. Two family bedrooms share a full bath on the right side of the home, while an impressive master suite is located on the left side for privacy. The master suite includes a tray ceiling and a vaulted master bath with dual sinks, a separate tub and shower and a walk-in closet. A formal dining room and an open kitchen area with plenty of counter space and a serving bar complete this plan. An optional bonus room with a full bath, perfect for a college student, could be added later. Please specify basement or crawlspace foundation when ordering.

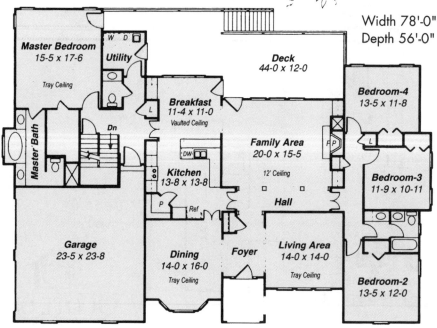

Master Bedroom
15-5 x 17-6

Tray Ceiling

W D

Utility

Master Bath

Dn

Breakfast
11-4 x 11-0
Vaulted Ceiling

Deck
44-0 x 12-0

Bedroom-4
13-5 x 11-8

Kitchen
13-8 x 13-8

DW

Family Area
20-0 x 15-5

12' Ceiling

Bedroom-3
11-9 x 10-11

P Ref

Hall

Garage
23-5 x 23-8

Dining
14-0 x 16-0

Tray Ceiling

Foyer

Living Area
14-0 x 14-0

Tray Ceiling

Bedroom-2
13-5 x 12-0

Width 78'-0"
Depth 56'-0"

Design X033

Square Footage: 2,720

■ Inside this stylish stucco home, elegant columns separate front-facing, formal living and dining areas from rear-facing, informal living areas. The family room features a twelve-foot ceiling, a fireplace and a door leading to an expansive deck. The kitchen, breakfast room and leisure room areas flow together for entertaining ease. Split from the master suite for privacy, three secondary bedrooms share a full bath. The secluded master suite features a tray ceiling, large walk-in closet and bumped-out tub with dual vanities.

Design by
© Jannis Vann &
Associates, Inc.

Design A131

Square Footage: 2,765
Bonus Room: 367 square feet

■ Moulded window facades and corner quoins join with triple gables to decorate the exterior of this three-bedroom plus attic bonus room plan. Entertain in the formal dining room, the grand room or the gracious gathering room with wraparound windows and fireplace. Breakfast in the bay window breakfast nook that faces the covered lanai. The master bedroom suite stretches along the left wing of the house and features His and Hers walk-in closets, toilet compartment and garden tub. Two additional bedrooms on the other side of the house share a full bath.

Design by
LIVING CONCEPTS

MASTER RETREAT 15'-0" x 22'-6"

COVERED LANAI

BREAKFAST 11'-0" X 10'-0"

GATHERING ROOM 16'-3" X 15'-1"

GRAND ROOM 14'-4" x 18'-2"

KITCHEN 13'-10" X 13'-10"

DECK

HERS

HIS

SUITE 2 12'-0" X 14'-6"

MASTER BATH

FOYER

DINING ROOM 11'-0" X 11'-6"

HALL

BATH

BATH

LOGGIA

PDR.

LIN.

UTILITY

SUITE NO.3 12'-10"x11'-6"

Width 66'-0"
Depth 82'-9"

ATTIC

BONUS ROOM 11'-8" X 27'-2"

GARAGE 22'-10"x22'-2"

299

Design P122

Square Footage: 1,884

■ Keystones above the windows and stately corner quoins are just a hint of the attention to detail this well-crafted plan offers. Arched openings, decorative columns and elegant ceiling detail throughout highlight the very livable floor plan. The large country kitchen has a spacious work area, prep island and breakfast nook. The dining room is set to the rear for gracious entertaining and opens to the great room. The master suite is beautifully appointed with a compartmented bath and walk-in closet. Two family bedrooms share a private compartmented bath. Please specify basement, crawlspace or slab foundation when ordering.

Design by

Frank Betz
Associates, Inc.

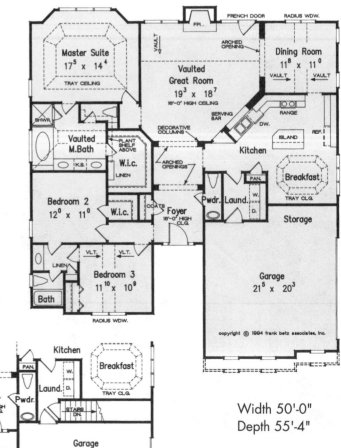

Width 50'-0"
Depth 55'-4"

copyright © 1994 frank betz associates, inc.

Optional Basement
Stair Location

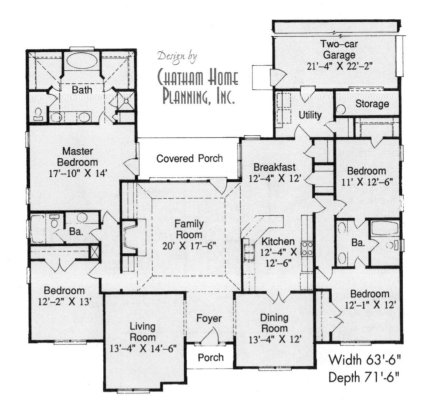

Design E138

Square Footage: 2,558

Two-car Garage 21'-4" X 22'-2"

Bath

Master Bedroom 17'-10" X 14'

Design by CHATHAM HOME PLANNING, INC.

Covered Porch

Utility

Storage

Breakfast 12'-4" X 12'

Bedroom 11' X 12'-6"

Ba.

Family Room 20' X 17'-6"

Kitchen 12'-4" X 12'-6"

Ba.

Bedroom 12'-2" X 13'

Living Room 13'-4" X 14'-6"

Foyer

Dining Room 13'-4" X 12'

Bedroom 12'-1" X 12'

Porch

Width 63'-6"
Depth 71'-6"

■ Heavy corner quoins make a rustic impression that is dressed up by a subtly asymmetrical design and arches on the windows. The floor plan is almost labyrinthine, sprawling over 2,500 square feet in a single story. The centerpiece of the home is a magnificent family room with tray ceiling, fireplace, built-in shelves and access to the rear covered porch. Adjacent are the breakfast room and the kitchen, which serves the formal dining room through elegant double doors. Two secondary bedrooms are secluded on the far right of the plan, each having private access to a full bath with twin vanities. To the far left are a third bedroom and the spacious master suite, which features His and Hers walk in closets, an oval tub, a separate shower, compartmented toilet and twin vanities.

Design M508

Square Footage: 2,618

Design by
© Andy McDonald
Design Group

■ This delightful French chateau features high rooflines and a stucco and brick exterior. The open floor plan begins with columns that define the formal living and dining rooms and separate them from the family room. A breakfast room connects to the island kitchen and also opens to a covered porch. Two family bedrooms share a full bath on the right side of the plan, while an additional bedroom with full bath is located behind the garage—a perfect hideaway for guests. The amenity-filled master suite features a salon with a tray ceiling.

br.4
11-10 X 12

porch

m bath

mbr
15-10 X 14

brkfst
11-5 X 17-7

br.2
12 X 12

kit
10-8 X 13-9

family
19 X 19

laundry

dining
11 X 14

foyer

living
11 X 13

br.3
12 X 11-5

garage
20 X 22

Width 71'-1"
Depth 74'-0"

302

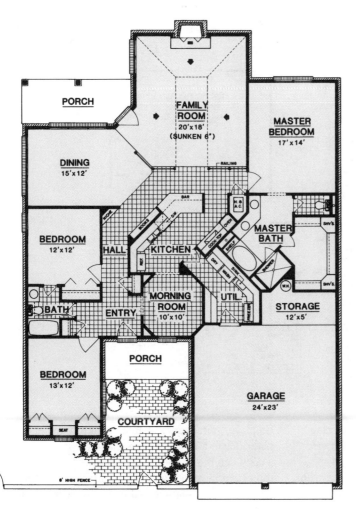

Design HPTM03059

Square Footage: 1,994

■ French accents inspire this European-influenced creation. A quaint courtyard introduces guests to this family compound. Inside, the central kitchen opens to the morning room. A sunken family room with sloped ceilings features a fireplace and access to the rear porch. The master bedroom, with a private bath and walk-in closet, is placed on the right side of the plan. Two additional family bedrooms reside on the left and share a full bath. Please specify crawlspace or slab foundation when ordering.

Design by
©BRELAND & FARMER DESIGNERS, INC.

Width 49'-0"
Depth 68'-0"

Design S130
Square Footage: 1,661

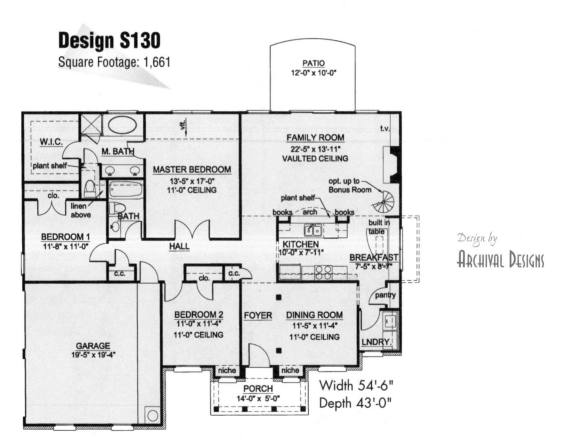

PATIO
12'-0" x 10'-0"

FAMILY ROOM
22'-5" x 13'-11"
VAULTED CEILING

t.v.

W.I.C.

plant shelf

M. BATH

MASTER BEDROOM
13'-5" x 17'-0"
11'-0" CEILING

opt. up to
Bonus Room

plant shelf

clo.

linen
above

BATH

books arch books

built in
table

KITCHEN
10'-0" x 7'-11"

BREAKFAST
7'-5" x 8'-7"

BEDROOM 1
11'-8" x 11'-0"

HALL

pantry

c.c.

clo.

c.c.

BEDROOM 2
11'-0" x 11'-4"
11'-0" CEILING

FOYER

DINING ROOM
11'-5" x 11'-4"
11'-0" CEILING

LNDRY.

GARAGE
19'-5" x 19'-4"

niche

niche

Width 54'-6"
Depth 43'-0"

PORCH
14'-0" x 5'-0"

Design by
Archival Designs

■ European accents grace the facade of this delightful plan and include an arched entry, circle detailing and a columned overhang. The floor plan is classically rendered as well, though with a nod to less formal living. The entry opens with a dining room on the right, defined by two columns at the foyer. The kitchen and breakfast room separate the dining room from the gigantic family room with its built-in shelves,

fireplace, spiral staircase to a small loft and access to the rear patio. There are three bedrooms in the plan—or make one into a cozy den if you choose. The master bedroom connects to a truly luxurious bath with spa tub, walk-in closet, separate shower and compartmented bath. The hall bath serves both family bedrooms.

Design P236

Square Footage: 1,978

■ A glass-paneled entry poses an inviting complement to stucco cornices and double-hung windows, and adds a generous dash of European spirit to this stunning country home. Inside, vaulted ceilings and radius windows inspire a broader sense of space and help bring in the outdoors. Arched openings decorate the interior, while an unrestrained floor plan provides a plentitude of well-lit bays and niches. Casual living space enjoys a wide serving bar, served by the gourmet kitchen and warmed by a centered hearth in the family room. A tray ceiling, a sunlit sitting area and a vaulted bath highlight the master suite, which enjoys a secluded wing to the rear of the plan. Two family bedrooms share a hall bath to the right of the breakfast/kitchen area. Please specify basement or crawlspace foundation when ordering.

Design by
FRANK BETZ
ASSOCIATES, INC.

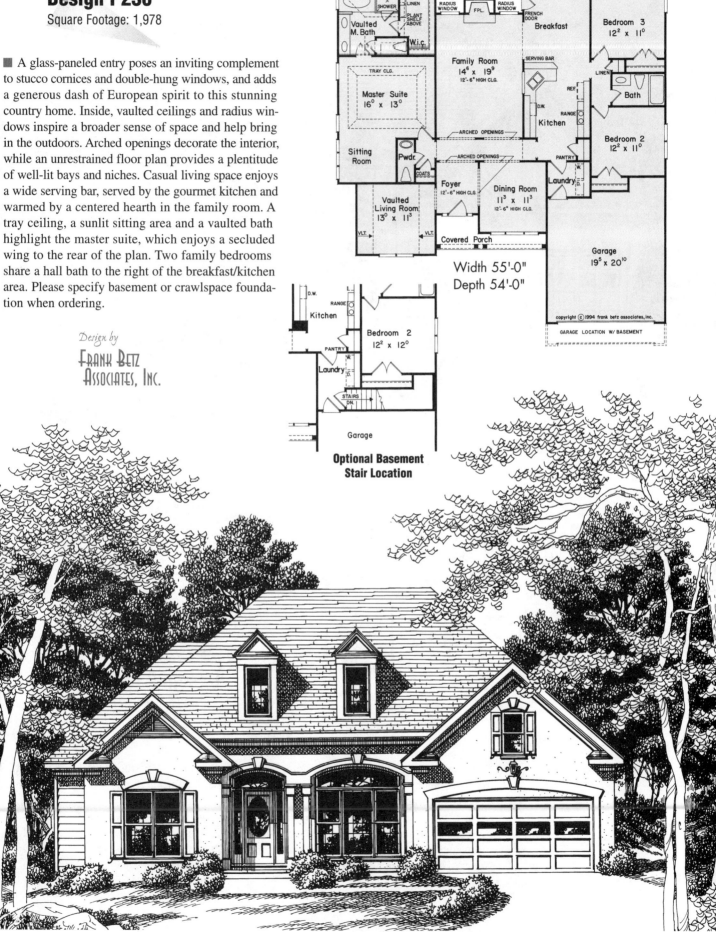

Width 55'-0"
Depth 54'-0"

**Optional Basement
Stair Location**

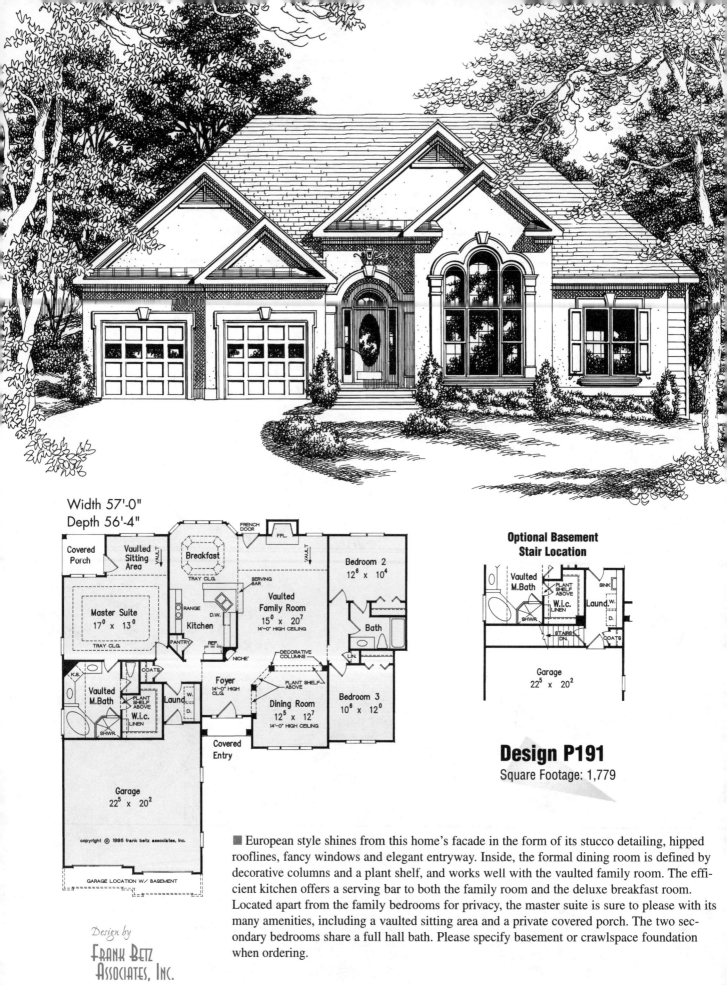

Width 57'-0"
Depth 56'-4"

Covered Porch

Vaulted Sitting Area

VAULT

Breakfast
TRAY CLG.

FRENCH DOOR

FPL.

VAULT

Bedroom 2
12⁶ x 10⁴

SERVING BAR

Master Suite
17⁰ x 13⁰
TRAY CLG.

RANGE

Kitchen

D.W.

PANTRY

REF.

Vaulted Family Room
15⁰ x 20⁷
14'-0" HIGH CEILING

Bath

NICHE'

DECORATIVE COLUMNS

LIN.

K.S.

Vaulted M.Bath

PLANT SHELF ABOVE

W.i.c.

COATS

Laund.
W. D.

Foyer
14'-0" HIGH CLG.

PLANT SHELF ABOVE

Dining Room
12⁵ x 12⁷
14'-0" HIGH CEILING

Bedroom 3
10⁶ x 12⁰

LINEN

SHWR.

Covered Entry

Garage
22⁵ x 20²

copyright © 1995 frank betz associates, inc.

GARAGE LOCATION W/ BASEMENT

Optional Basement Stair Location

Vaulted M.Bath

PLANT SHELF ABOVE

W.i.c.
LINEN

SINK

Laund.
W. D.

SHWR.

STAIRS DN.

COATS

Garage
22⁵ x 20²

Design P191
Square Footage: 1,779

■ European style shines from this home's facade in the form of its stucco detailing, hipped rooflines, fancy windows and elegant entryway. Inside, the formal dining room is defined by decorative columns and a plant shelf, and works well with the vaulted family room. The efficient kitchen offers a serving bar to both the family room and the deluxe breakfast room. Located apart from the family bedrooms for privacy, the master suite is sure to please with its many amenities, including a vaulted sitting area and a private covered porch. The two secondary bedrooms share a full hall bath. Please specify basement or crawlspace foundation when ordering.

Design by
FRANK BETZ
ASSOCIATES, INC.

Design S128

Square Footage: 2,588

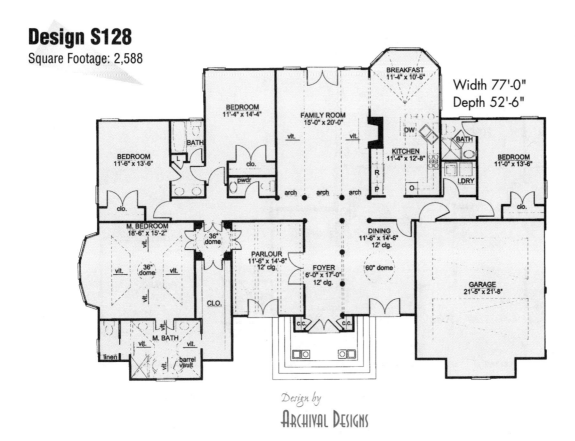

Width 77'-0"
Depth 52'-6"

BREAKFAST 11'-4" x 10'-6"

BEDROOM 11'-4" x 14'-4"

FAMILY ROOM 15'-0" x 20'-0"

BEDROOM 11'-6" x 13'-6"

BATH

vlt.

vlt.

clo.

pwdr

DW

BATH

KITCHEN 11'-4" x 12'-8"

R

P

LDRY

O

BEDROOM 11'-0" x 13'-6"

clo.

clo.

arch   arch   arch

M. BEDROOM 18'-6" x 15'-2"

vlt.

36" dome

36" dome

vlt.

vlt.

vlt.

vlt.

CLO.

PARLOUR 11'-6" x 14'-6" 12' clg.

DINING 11'-6" x 14'-6" 12' clg.

FOYER 6'-0" x 17'-0" 12' clg.

60" dome

GARAGE 21'-5" x 21'-8"

vlt.

M. BATH

vlt.

linen

vlt.

barrel vault

c.c.   c.c.

Design by
Archival Designs

■ A Mediterranean mansion or an Italian villa—these are the influences on the exterior of this grand one-story. The floor plan was designed for royalty, as well. Double doors open to an elegant entry foyer which opens on the left to the formal parlor and to the right to the formal dining room, accented with columns. The family room is also introduced by columns and is further enhanced by a fireplace and double doors to the rear yard. The kitchen area is large and magnified by a breakfast room full of light. A guest bedroom, or private suite, is down the hall behind the garage and has a private bath. Two family bedrooms are at the other end of the hall and share a bath. The master suite may be accessed through a private foyer, either at the hall or from the parlor. Its bath is superb with a gigantic walk-in closet, His and Hers sinks, a garden whirlpool and separate shower.

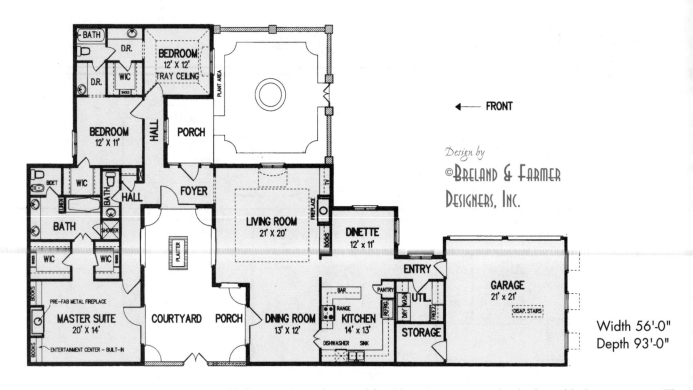

BATH
D.R.
WIC
D.R.

BEDROOM
12' X 12'
TRAY CEILING

PLANT AREA

← FRONT

Design by
©BRELAND & FARMER
DESIGNERS, INC.

BEDROOM
12' X 11'

HALL

PORCH

BIDET
WIC
BATH
HALL
FOYER

LINEN
SHOWER
BATH

WIC
WIC

BOOKS

PRE-FAB METAL FIREPLACE

MASTER SUITE
20' X 14'

PLAYER

COURTYARD

PORCH

FIREPLACE

LIVING ROOM
21' X 20'

BOOKS

tv

DINETTE
12' X 11'

ENTRY

UTL

DRY WASH
FREEZ

GARAGE
21' X 21'

DISAP. STAIRS

PANTRY

REFRIG

BAR

RANGE

DINING ROOM
13' X 12'

KITCHEN
14' X 13'

DISHWASHER   SINK

STORAGE

ENTERTAINMENT CENTER - BUILT-IN

Width 56'-0"
Depth 93'-0"

Design HPTM00041
Square Footage: 2,259

■ Courtyards set the mood for this country cottage, beginning with the entry court. The narrow design of this three-bedroom plan makes it perfect for high-density areas where the owner still wants privacy. A spacious high-ceilinged living room offers a fireplace and a built-in entertainment center; these special amenities are also found in the master suite, along with two walk-in closets and a full bath. Two secondary bedrooms—one with a tray ceiling—feature walk-in closets and share a full bath. Double doors in the kitchen open to the formal dining room, which offers access to the center courtyard. Please specify crawlspace or slab foundation when ordering.

Design 7634

Square Footage: 1,699
Bonus Room: 386 square feet

■ Keystone arches, asymmetrical gables and a stunning stucco exterior lend European sophistication to this great plan. The interior starts with an expansive great room, which features an extended-hearth fireplace and views to the outdoors. The U-shaped kitchen serves a spectacular dining room, with bay-window views that feast the soul. A private master suite nestles to the rear of the plan and offers a tray ceiling and a lavish bath with a garden tub, twin vanities and a corner whirlpool tub. Two additional bedrooms share a full bath nearby, while upstairs bonus space is available for future development.

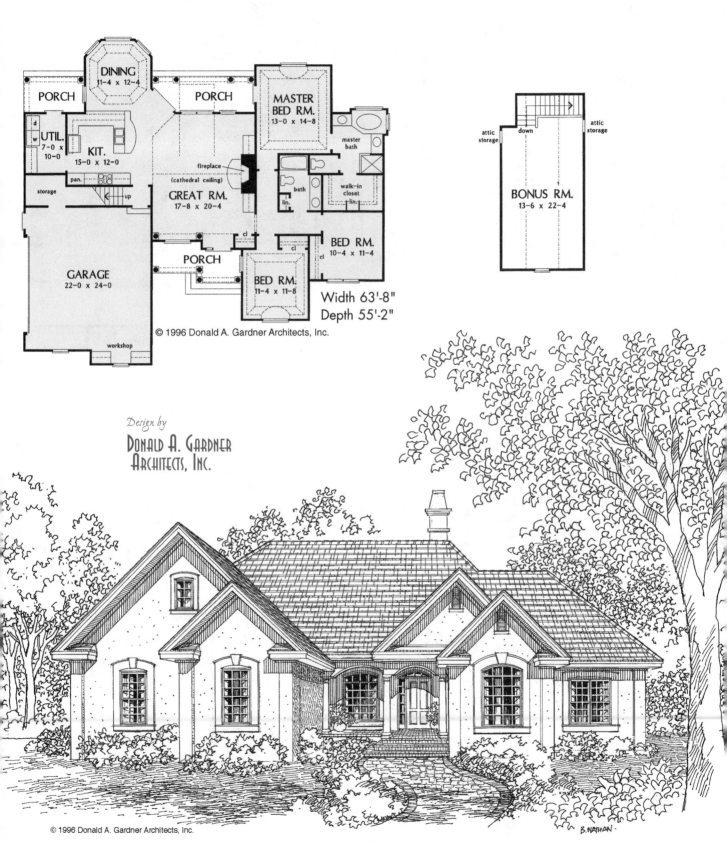

DINING
11-4 x 12-4

PORCH

PORCH

MASTER
BED RM.
13-0 x 14-8

UTIL.
7-0 x
10-0

KIT.
15-0 x 12-0

master bath

storage

pan.

fireplace
(cathedral ceiling)

GREAT RM.
17-8 x 20-4

bath

walk-in closet

lin.

lin.

up

BED RM.
10-4 x 11-4

cl

GARAGE
22-0 x 24-0

PORCH

cl

BED RM.
11-4 x 11-8

Width 63'-8"
Depth 55'-2"

workshop

© 1996 Donald A. Gardner Architects, Inc.

attic storage

down

attic storage

BONUS RM.
13-6 x 22-4

Design by
DONALD A. GARDNER
ARCHITECTS, INC.

B. NATHAN

© 1996 Donald A. Gardner Architects, Inc.

Design M526

Square Footage: 3,430

■ Wide-open windows grace this home and allow the rooms inside to enjoy natural light. Open living areas include a living room (or make it a study), a huge family room, a formal dining room and a breakfast room. The island kitchen sits between the two dining areas for convenience. A wonderful solarium provides light and warmth to the family room and breakfast room. Two bedrooms are split from the master suite and share a full bath that includes private vanities. An additional bedroom on the right side of the plan has a private bath. Note the extra storage in the two-car garage.

Design by
©Andy McDonald
Design Group

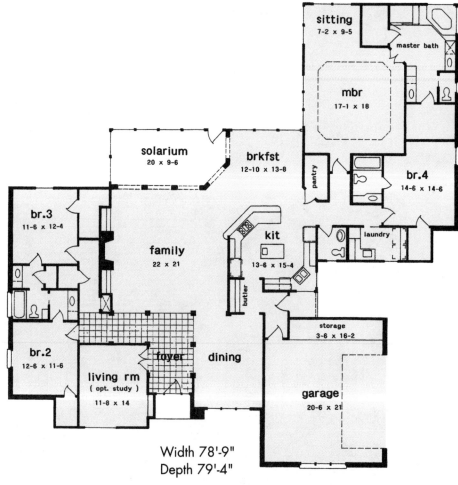

Width 78'-9"
Depth 79'-4"

© Design Traditions

Design T209
Square Footage: 2,140

Bedroom #3
11⁶ x 11⁰

Bedroom #2
11³ x 11⁰

Sun Room
12⁰ x 13⁹

Porch

Porch

Master Bedroom
13³ x 15⁶

Breakfast
10⁰ x 9⁰

Kitchen
12⁰ x 13³

Great Room
18⁰ x 14⁰

Dining Room
10⁷ x 10⁷

Den/ Guest Room
13⁴ x 14⁸

Two Car Garage
20⁸ x 21⁸

Width 62'-0"
Depth 60'-6"

■ Imagine the luxurious living you'll enjoy in this beautiful home! The natural beauty of stone combined with sophisticated window detailing represent the good taste you'll find carried throughout the design. Common living areas occupy the center of the plan and include a family room with fireplace, sun room and breakfast area, plus rear and side porches. A second fireplace is located in the front den. The master suite features private access to the rear porch and a wonderfully planned bath. This home is designed with a basement foundation.

Design by
DESIGN TRADITIONS

Design U217

Square Footage: 1,817

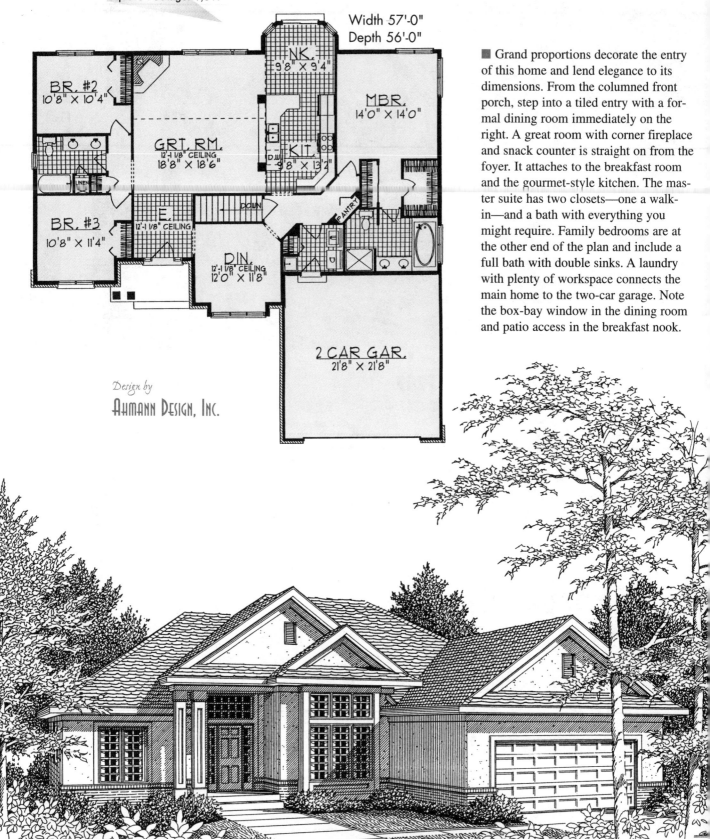

Width 57'-0"
Depth 56'-0"

NK.
9'8" × 9'4"

MBR.
14'0" × 14'0"

BR. #2
10'8" × 10'4"

GRT. RM.
12'-1 1/8" CEILING
18'8" × 18'6"

KIT.
9'8" × 13'2"

BR. #3
10'8" × 11'4"

E.
12'-1 1/8" CEILING

DOWN

PANTRY

DIN.
12'-1 1/8" CEILING
12'0" × 11'8"

2 CAR GAR.
21'8" × 21'8"

Design by
Ahmann Design, Inc.

■ Grand proportions decorate the entry of this home and lend elegance to its dimensions. From the columned front porch, step into a tiled entry with a formal dining room immediately on the right. A great room with corner fireplace and snack counter is straight on from the foyer. It attaches to the breakfast room and the gourmet-style kitchen. The master suite has two closets—one a walk-in—and a bath with everything you might require. Family bedrooms are at the other end of the plan and include a full bath with double sinks. A laundry with plenty of workspace connects the main home to the two-car garage. Note the box-bay window in the dining room and patio access in the breakfast nook.

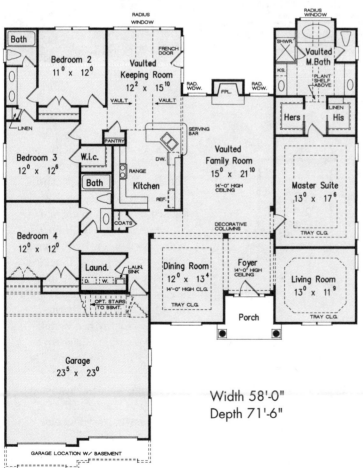

Bath

Bedroom 2
11⁰ x 12⁰

Vaulted Keeping Room
12² x 15¹⁰

RADIUS WINDOW

FRENCH DOOR

VAULT VAULT

RAD. WDW.

FPL.

RAD. WDW.

LINEN

Bedroom 3
12⁰ x 12⁶

PANTRY

W.i.c.

Bath

SERVING BAR

DW.

Kitchen

RANGE

REF.

Vaulted Family Room
15⁰ x 21¹⁰
14'-0" HIGH CEILING

RADIUS WINDOW

SHWR.

Vaulted M.Bath

KS.

PLANT SHELF ABOVE

Hers

LINEN

His

Master Suite
13⁰ x 17⁶

TRAY CLG.

Bedroom 4
12⁰ x 12⁰

COATS

Laund.

LAUN. SINK

D. W.

DECORATIVE COLUMNS

Dining Room
12⁰ x 13⁴
14'-0" HIGH CLG.

TRAY CLG.

Foyer
14'-0" HIGH CEILING

Living Room
13⁰ x 11⁹

TRAY CLG.

OPT. STAIRS TO BSMT.

Porch

Garage
23⁵ x 23⁰

GARAGE LOCATION W/ BASEMENT

Width 58'-0"
Depth 71'-6"

Design HPTM03060

Square Footage: 2,416

■ Arches and quoins lend a quaint appearance to this 21st-Century country home and harmonize with a thoroughly up-to-date interior. Decorative columns define formal rooms, which enjoy the soaring interior vistas of the vaulted family room, with wide views of the outdoors through radius windows. The lavish master suite boasts two walk-in closets, a windowed whirlpool tub and a knee-space vanity. Three family bedrooms share a full bath. Please specify basement or crawlspace foundation when ordering.

Design by
© Frank Betz Associates, Inc.

313

© Design Traditions

Design T234

Square Footage: 2,494

Porch

Master Bedroom 13³ x 19⁹

Breakfast 11⁶ x 9⁰

Great Room 15⁰ x 18⁰

Bedroom #2 12⁹ x 12³

Kitchen 11³ x 13⁵

Master Bath

Bedroom #3 12⁹ x 13⁰

Dining Room 12⁰ x 13⁵

Foyer

Living Room 15⁰ x 15⁰

Two Car Garage 24⁹ x 21⁹

Width 65'-4"
Depth 61'-8"

■ Stucco-and-stone, multi-pane windows, a covered porch—all elements to a fine European-flavored home. Inside, the foyer is flanked by formal living and dining rooms, and leads back to more casual areas. Here, a great room with a warming fireplace is framed by windows, with a nearby kitchen and breakfast room finishing off gathering areas. Two family bedrooms reside to the right and share a full bath with two vanities. The master suite is sure to please with a large walk-in closet and a sumptuous master bath. This home is designed with a basement foundation.

Design by
DESIGN TRADITIONS

314

keeping
14 x 15-10

brkfst
10 x 15-6

porch

kit
11-4 x 16

family
20 x 21

mbr
16 x 15

laundry

br.3
11-8 x 13-4

dining
12-4 x 14

foyer
12-4 x 7-6

br.2
(opt study)
12-8 x 13-3

master bath

Width 73'-8"
Depth 93'-3"

br.4
12 x 12

garage
21 x 22

Design M519
Square Footage: 3,039

Design by
©Andy McDonald
Design Group

■ A welcoming double-door glass entrance leads to this home reminiscent of a villa. The side-facing garage visually enlarges the home and provides extra storage at the back. Two fireplaces, in the keeping room and the family room, are a cozy touch. Stairs near the kitchen lead to the attic, which could be converted as living space or used for more storage. The smaller bedroom located near the luxurious master bedroom could be used for a home office. Two more bedrooms are found on the other side of the plan. An even blend of formal and informal spaces in this home makes it perfect for the lifestyle of today.

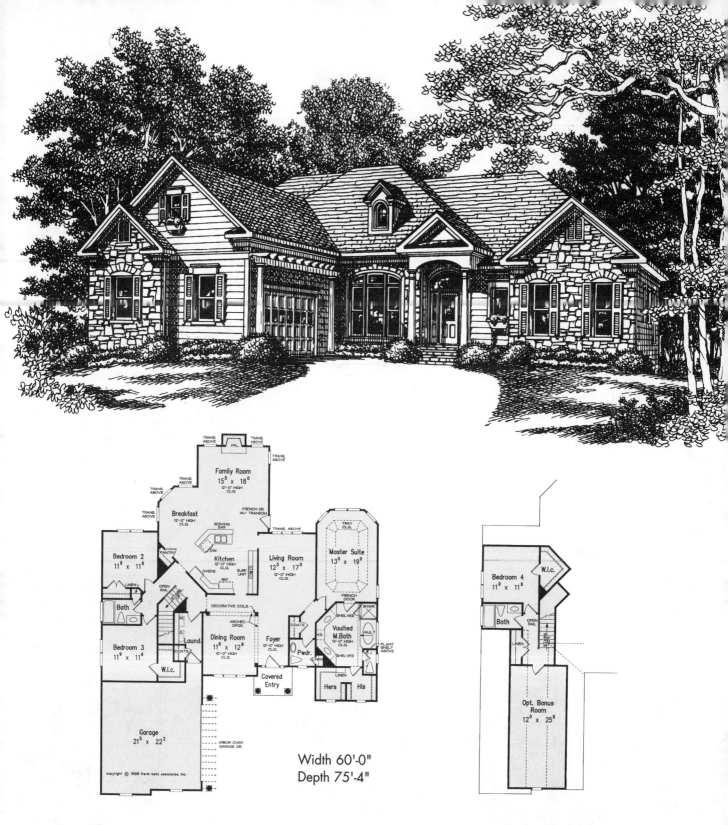

Width 60'-0"
Depth 75'-4"

Design HPTM03061

Square Footage: 2,282
Bonus Space: 629 square feet

Design by
©Frank Betz Associates, Inc.

■ Columns and keystone lintels lend a European aura to this stone-and-siding home. Arched openings and decorative columns define the formal dining room to the left of the foyer. A ribbon of windows with transoms above draws sunshine into the living room. The master suite opens from a short hallway and enjoys a tray ceiling and a vaulted bathroom with shelving, a compartmented toilet, separate shower and garden tub. Transoms abound in the open informal living areas of this home. A bay-windowed breakfast nook adjoins the kitchen with a central serving bar and the family room with a warming fireplace. Two additional bedrooms share a full bath to the left of the plan. Please specify basement or crawlspace foundation when ordering.

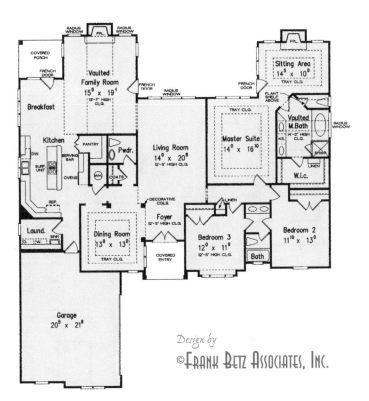

Design by
©Frank Betz Associates, Inc.

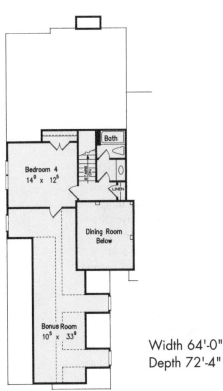

Width 64'-0"
Depth 72'-4"

■ Decorative columns adorn a pedimented porch on this charming brick home. Elegance marks the formal areas with high ceilings and columns. Radius windows enhance the family room, living room and master bath. The master suite and two additional bedrooms are located on the first floor, while an optional second floor contains space for another bedroom and bath. Please specify basement or crawlspace foundation when ordering.

Design HPTM03062

Square Footage: 2,499
Bonus Space: 733 square feet

Design M511

Square Footage: 2,678

■ In true French country style, this home begins with a fenced terrace that protects the double-door entry. The main foyer separates formal living and dining areas and leads back to a large family room with a fireplace and built-ins. The breakfast room overlooks a wrapping porch and opens to the island kitchen. Three bedrooms are found on the left side of the plan—two family bedrooms sharing a full bath and a master suite with a sitting area. A fourth bedroom is tucked behind the two-car garage and features a private bath.

Width 69'-4"
Depth 84'-8"

Design by
©Andy McDonald
Design Group

Design M131

Square Footage: 2,590

■ With a solid exterior of rough cedar and stone, this new country French design will stand the test of time. A wood-paneled study on the front features a large bay window. The heart of the house is found in a large, open great room with built-in entertainment center. The spacious master bedroom features a corner reading area and access to an adjacent covered patio. A three-car garage and three additional bedrooms complete this generous family home.

Design by
FILLMORE DESIGN GROUP

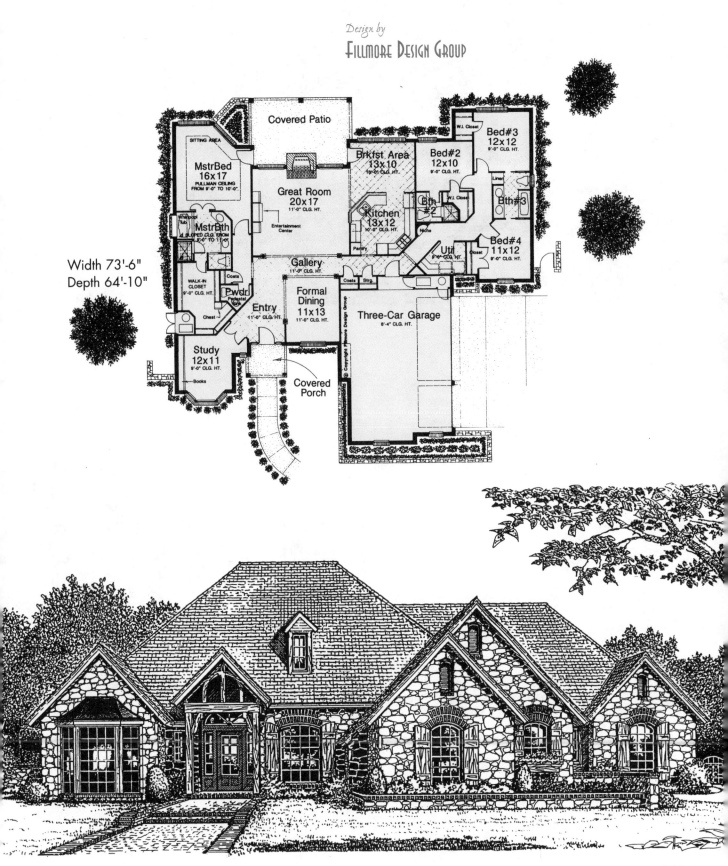

Width 73'-6"
Depth 64'-10"

© Design Traditions

Design T207

Square Footage: 1,751

Design by
DESIGN TRADITIONS

Deck

Bedroom #3
11⁶ x 11⁰

Great Room
14⁰ x 17⁶

Breakfast
11⁴ x 8⁶

Master
Bedroom
12⁴ x 15⁶

Kitchen
11⁴ x 10⁶

Bedroom
#2
11⁴ x 14⁸

Dining Room
11⁴ x 10⁶

Two Car
Garage
20⁴ x 19⁴

Width 55'-6"
Depth 59'-6"

■ A brick facade and central gable with an arched window introduce this English cottage design. The double-hung windows are crested by jack arches. The foyer opens to a large great room, emphasizing the open and airy floor plan, with French doors that lead to a back deck for a warm, inviting feeling. Convenient to both the great room and dining room, the kitchen opens to an attractive breakfast area with a bay window. To the left of the kitchen, two bedrooms—each with a walk-in closet—share a bath area. The luxurious master suite is located to the rear of the home, offering comfort and a peaceful retreat. The master bath contains a garden tub, a separate shower and double vanities. This home is designed with a basement foundation.

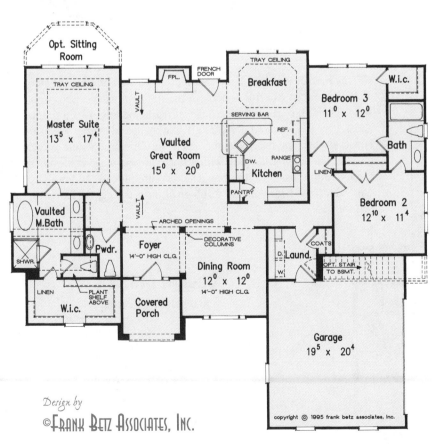

Opt. Sitting Room

TRAY CEILING

Master Suite
13⁵ x 17⁴

Vaulted M.Bath

SHWR.

Pwdr.

LINEN

W.i.c.

PLANT SHELF ABOVE

Foyer
14'-0" HIGH CLG.

Covered Porch

VAULT

VAULT

ARCHED OPENINGS

DECORATIVE COLUMNS

Dining Room
12⁰ x 12⁰
14'-0" HIGH CLG.

FPL.

FRENCH DOOR

TRAY CEILING

Breakfast

SERVING BAR

REF.

DW.

RANGE

PANTRY

Vaulted Great Room
15⁰ x 20⁰

Kitchen

Bedroom 3
11⁰ x 12⁰

W.i.c.

Bath

LINEN

Bedroom 2
12¹⁰ x 11⁴

COATS

Laund.

D.

W.

OPT. STAIR TO BSMT.

Garage
19⁵ x 20⁴

copyright © 1995 frank betz associates, inc.

Design by
© FRANK BETZ ASSOCIATES, INC.

Design HPTMO3063

Square Footage: 1,832
Bonus Space: 68 square feet

■ This compact one-story home has plenty of living in it. The master suite features an optional sun-washed sitting area with views to the rear of the home. A vaulted great room with a fireplace conveniently accesses the kitchen via a serving bar. Meals can also be taken in the cozy breakfast area. For formal occasions, the dining room creates opulence with its decorative columns. Two family bedrooms sit to the right of the home with a shared bath, linen storage and easy access to laundry facilities. Please specify basement or crawlspace foundation when ordering.

Width 59'-6"
Depth 52'-6"

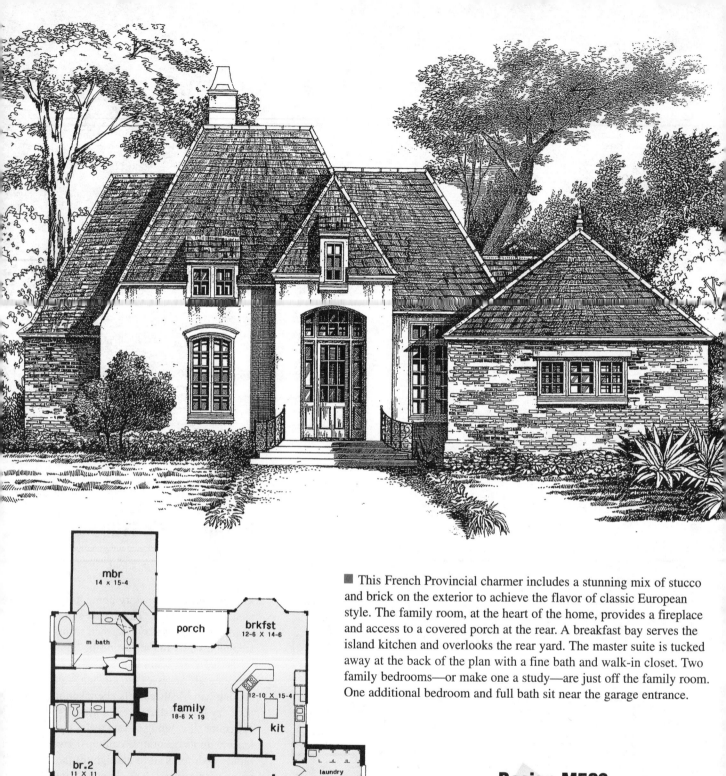

mbr
14 x 15-4

porch

brkfst
12-6 X 14-6

m bath

12-10 X 15-4

family
18-6 X 19

kit

br.2
11 X 11

br.3
(opt. study)
11-8 X 11

foyer

laundry

dining
11 X 14

Design M503

br.4
11 X 12-4

Width 58'-10"
Depth 83'-0"

garage
21 X 21

■ This French Provincial charmer includes a stunning mix of stucco and brick on the exterior to achieve the flavor of classic European style. The family room, at the heart of the home, provides a fireplace and access to a covered porch at the rear. A breakfast bay serves the island kitchen and overlooks the rear yard. The master suite is tucked away at the back of the plan with a fine bath and walk-in closet. Two family bedrooms—or make one a study—are just off the family room. One additional bedroom and full bath sit near the garage entrance.

Design M503
Square Footage: 2,300

Design by
© Andy McDonald
Design Group

Design T054

Square Footage: 2,935

■ This spacious one-story easily accommodates a large family, providing all the luxuries and necessities for gracious living. For formal occasions, there is a grand dining room just off the entry foyer. It features a vaulted ceiling and is just across the hall from the gourmet kitchen. The great room offers a beautiful ceiling treatment and access to the rear deck. For more casual times, the breakfast nook and adjoining keeping room with a fireplace fill the bill. The master suite is spacious and filled with amenities that include sitting room, a walk-in closet and access to the rear deck. Two family bedrooms share a full bath. Each of these bedrooms has its own lavatory. This home is designed with a basement foundation.

Width 71'-0"
Depth 66'-0"

Design by
DESIGN TRADITIONS

© Design Traditions

■ The favorite gathering place of this beautiful home is certain to be its sun-filled breakfast and keeping room complemented by the full kitchen. Thoughtful placement of the kitchen provides easy service to both formal and informal eating areas. A large living room enjoys two sets of double French doors that open to outdoor living areas. French doors open onto the spacious master suite and its elegant master bath. Here, a soothing whirlpool tub takes center-stage. Three other bedrooms, or two bedrooms and a study, are positioned at the opposite end of the house for privacy. Bedrooms 2 and 3 have their own walk-in closets. Please specify slab or crawl-space foundation when ordering.

Design 8076
Square Footage: 2,733

Width 88'-0"
Depth 54'-2"

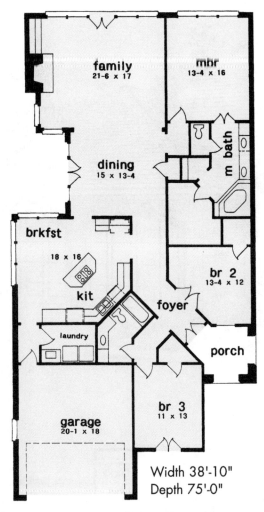

family
21-6 x 17

mbr
13-4 x 16

dining
15 x 13-4

m bath

brkfst

18 x 16

br 2
13-4 x 12

kit

foyer

laundry

porch

br 3
11 x 13

garage
20-1 x 18

Width 38'-10"
Depth 75'-0"

Design M533

Square Footage: 2,048

■ Presenting a narrow frontage, this plan provides
spacious rooms for a family. Enter through a front
corner porch or through a side courtyard that opens to
the dining room. A fireplace warms the family room,
which accesses the rear yard through French doors. A
bright corner breakfast nook highlights the kitchen,
which provides a cooktop island and laundry-room
access. The master suite features a walk-in closet and
separate vanities in the compartmented bath. Two
family bedrooms share a full bath.

Design by
©Andy McDonald
Design Group

Design HPTM03064

Square Footage: 1,891

■ The gated courtyard adds privacy and
personality to this charming two-bedroom home. The open interior includes
a sunken family room with a sloped
ceiling, a gracious fireplace, built-ins
and access to a rear porch. A brilliantly
sunny dining room sits opposite an open
and cleverly angled kitchen—allowing
for ease of service between the dining
room and the morning room. The living
room could be replaced as a third bedroom or a study. The master suite
includes a dual-bowl vanity, a separate
bath and shower, and a large walk-in
closet. Please specify crawlspace or slab
foundation when ordering.

Design by
©Breland & Farmer Designers, Inc.

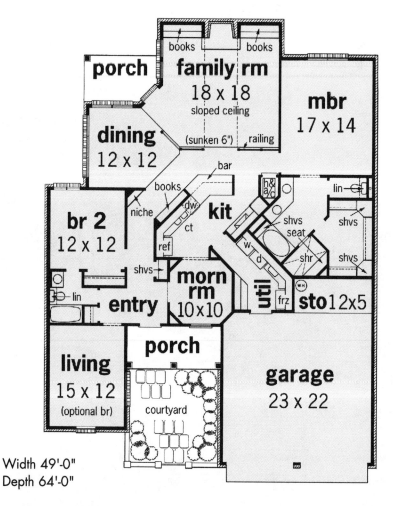

Width 49'-0"
Depth 64'-0"

326

Look to the Future:
One-story contemporary homes

Design by
Homes For Living, Inc.

TERR

Width 77'-2"
Depth 39'-5"

TWO CAR GAR
20' x 20'

STOR

LAUN

LAV

COUNTRY KIT
17'-6" x 11'-4"

GREAT RM
20'-6" x 16'-8"

sloping ceiling
skylights

high ceiling

columns

DR
12'-4" x 15-10"

sloping ceiling

skylight

f.p.

wall cabinet

fireplace
logs

MB high ceil.
whirlpool tub
shr.

MBR
13'-4" x 16-8"

WIC

WIC

HALL

BR
11'-2" x 10

BR
10' x 13-4"

Design N120
Square Footage: 1,926

■ A crisp, contemporary exterior combines with great interior elements to produce a home that accommodates today's active lifestyles. Inside, a skylit foyer opens onto a large great room that extends a hospitable welcome to all gatherings, whether cozy or lavish. The country kitchen, adjacent to the columned dining room, features an island counter, a multi-windowed eating area and its own fireplace with wood storage.

Bedrooms are contained in the right wing of the plan. Enjoying views of the backyard, the master bedroom features twin walk-in closets and a pampering bath with a whirlpool tub. Two family bedrooms—each with a bumped-out window—share a full bath. A laundry room and powder room complete this outstanding plan. Please specify basement or slab foundation when ordering.

Design N104

Square Footage: 1,530

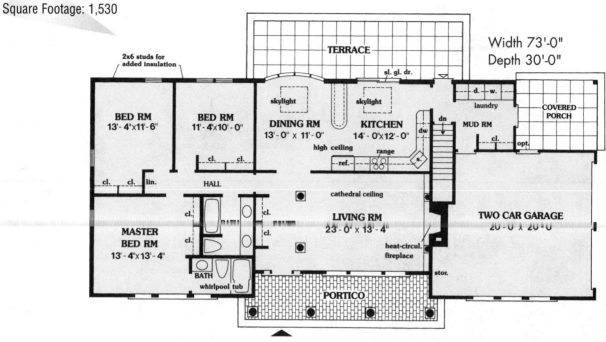

Width 73'-0"
Depth 30'-0"

- TERRACE
- 2x6 studs for added insulation
- BED RM 13'-4"x11'-6"
- BED RM 11'-4"x10'-0"
- sl. gl. dr.
- d. — w.
- laundry
- COVERED PORCH
- skylight
- DINING RM 13'-0" X 11'-0"
- skylight
- KITCHEN 14'-0"x12'-0"
- MUD RM
- cl.
- opt.
- cl. cl.
- high ceiling
- range
- ref.
- s.
- dw
- dn
- cl. cl. lin.
- HALL
- cathedral ceiling
- TWO CAR GARAGE 20'-0" x 20'-0"
- cl.
- MASTER BED RM 13'-4"x13'-4"
- BATH
- cl.
- cl.
- LIVING RM 23'-0" x 13'-4"
- heat-circul. fireplace
- stor.
- BATH
- whirlpool tub
- PORTICO

■ Doric columns add drama to the portico and are repeated in the interior of this three-bedroom design. The cathedral living room features a heat circulating fireplace. The open dining room and kitchen have skylights, a large bow window and a sliding glass door onto the terrace. A covered porch at the back of the two-car garage leads into the house through the separate mud room and laundry. Please specify basement or slab foundation when ordering.

Design by
Homes For Living, Inc.

Design F148

Square Footage: 1,732

DECK

MORNING ROOM
14'-0'' x 8'-0''
VAULTED CEILING

LIVING ROOM
20'-0'' x 16'-0''
VAULTED CEILING

FP

MASTER BATH

MASTER BEDROOM
12'-0'' x 16'-0''

KITCHEN
14'-0'' x 10'-0''

BATH

UP DN

W D

DINING ROOM
11'-0'' x 14'-0''

ENTRY FOYER

LINEN

WIC

TWO-CAR GARAGE
21'-0'' x 21'-0''

PORCH

BEDROOM
10'-0'' x 10'-0''

BEDROOM
10'-0'' x 10'-0''

Width 60'-0"
Depth 46'-4"

■ This cozy one-story plan features a volume roofline that allows vaulted ceilings in the living room, morning room and master bedroom. The dining room opens, through gracious columns, at the foyer and the living room. Special features in the living areas include a fireplace in the living room and doors leading to the rear yard from the living room and the morning room. The kitchen is designed with the gourmet cook in mind. It contains an island cooktop, over-the-sink window and loads of counter space. Family bedrooms share a hall bath and have box windows that would be perfect for window seats. The master suite is appointed with all the expected amenities including a garden whirlpool, separate shower and double sinks. A hall linen closet provides plenty of storage space, as does the two-car garage.

Design by
The Housing Associates

■ With clean, contemporary accents, the exterior of this home features circle and half-circle windows, sidelites at the entry and horizontal wood siding. The wide front porch is set up a few steps and leads to an entry with a small foyer opening to the great room. Here you'll enjoy a corner fireplace and access to a massive terrace with a built-in bench. The dinette also opens to this terrace and connects to the U-shaped kitchen. A more formal dining room is nearby and has its own private din-

ing terrace. The master suite is situated on the left side of the foyer. Look for a box bay window and walk-in closet in the bedroom and separate shower and whirlpool tub in the bath. Family bedrooms are to the right of the foyer and share a full bath with double sinks. The two-car garage is to the rear of the plan and connects to the home via a convenient mud room. Please specify basement or slab foundation when ordering.

Design N142
Square Footage: 1,658

Design by
Homes For Living, Inc.

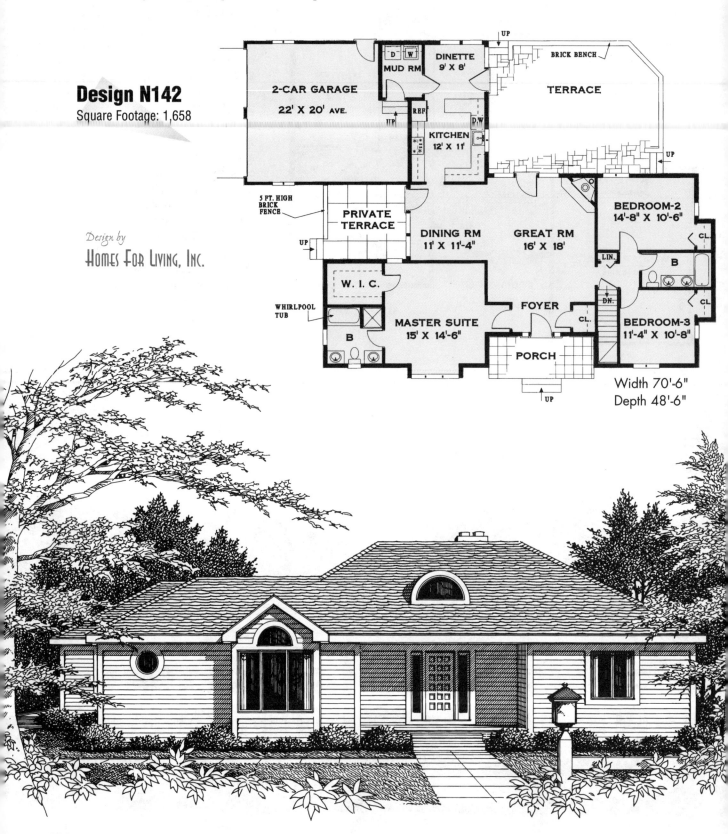

Width 70'-6"
Depth 48'-6"

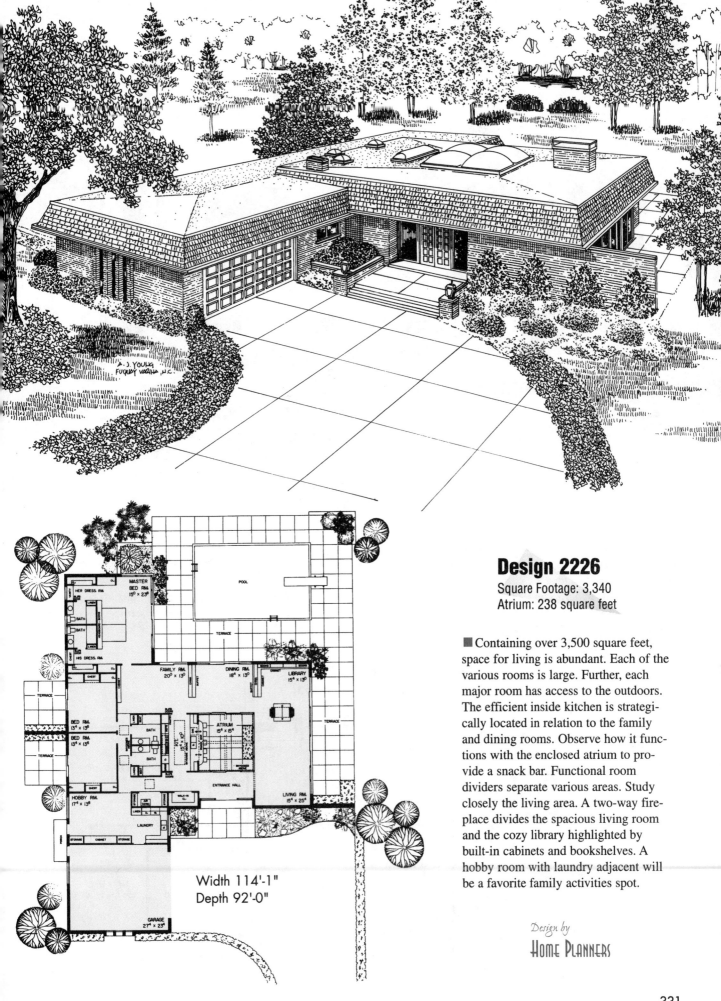

Design 2226

Square Footage: 3,340
Atrium: 238 square feet

■ Containing over 3,500 square feet, space for living is abundant. Each of the various rooms is large. Further, each major room has access to the outdoors. The efficient inside kitchen is strategically located in relation to the family and dining rooms. Observe how it functions with the enclosed atrium to provide a snack bar. Functional room dividers separate various areas. Study closely the living area. A two-way fireplace divides the spacious living room and the cozy library highlighted by built-in cabinets and bookshelves. A hobby room with laundry adjacent will be a favorite family activities spot.

Design by
Home Planners

Width 114'-1"
Depth 92'-0"

Design N108

Square Footage: 1,771

■ This ground-hugging ranch was designed for maximum use of space. The large family room with fireplace, and the kitchen and breakfast area are clustered around a covered porch with built-in barbecue. The formal living room and dining room are to the left of the large entry foyer and are separated by a partition. The fully equipped kitchen is easily accessible to the formal dining room and to the covered porch by sliding glass doors. The right wing holds a spacious master bedroom suite with plenty of closet space and separate bath. Two additional bedrooms share a hall bath with two sinks. Stairs to the full basement are located just off the combination mudroom/laundry area and rear service entrance. Please specify basement or slab foundation when ordering.

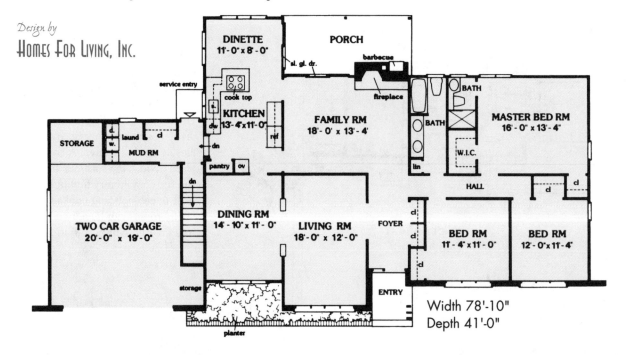

Design by
HOMES FOR LIVING, INC.

DINETTE
11'-0" x 8'-0"

PORCH

barbecue

sl. gl. dr.

fireplace

BATH

service entry

cook top

KITCHEN
13'-4" x 11'-0"

FAMILY RM
18'-0" x 13'-4"

BATH

MASTER BED RM
16'-0" x 13'-4"

W.I.C.

STORAGE

laund

w.

MUD RM

pantry   ov

ref

lin

HALL

d   d

TWO CAR GARAGE
20'-0" x 19'-0"

dn

DINING RM
14'-10" x 11'-0"

LIVING RM
18'-0" x 12'-0"

FOYER

BED RM
11'-4" x 11'-0"

BED RM
12'-0" x 11'-4"

storage

ENTRY

Width 78'-10"
Depth 41'-0"

planter

Room	Metric	Imperial
	2,90 X 3,60	9'-8" X 12'-0"
	3,90 X 3,60	13'-0" X 12'-0"
	3,90 X 2,70	13'-0" X 9'-0"
	2,80 X 3,50	9'-4" X 11'-8"
	3,70 X 3,90	12'-4" X 13'-0"

Width 32'-8"
Depth 36'-0"

Design HPTM03065

Square Footage: 1,067

■ This clearly contemporary home offers an exciting exterior with a non-traditional arched wing wall and a multi-level roof that mimics the interior's sunken living room. Inside, the living room rises to the central gallery and formal dining area—these spaces make entertaining a delight. To the right are the bedrooms, each with plenty of closet space. The master bedroom enjoys a private access to the share full bath. Off to the left is the angled kitchen where a snack bar offers a place for casual dining. This home is designed with a basement foundation.

■

Design by
©DRUMMOND DESIGNS, INC.

Design HPTM03066

Square Footage: 1,085

■ This charming one-story design offers a petite layout for the young or growing family. The foyer opens to a spacious great room that's warmed by a fireplace. Vaulted ceilings are found throughout the home—in the great room, kitchen, dining room and master bedroom. The master suite also features a private bath and walk-in closet. Bedrooms 2 and 3 share a hall bath. A two-car garage and a laundry room that's accessed from the kitchen complete the plan. Please specify basement or crawlspace foundation when ordering.

Design by
©Frank Betz Associates, Inc.

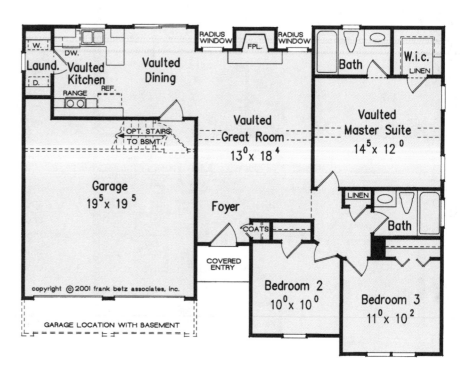

Width 48'-0"
Depth 36'-0"

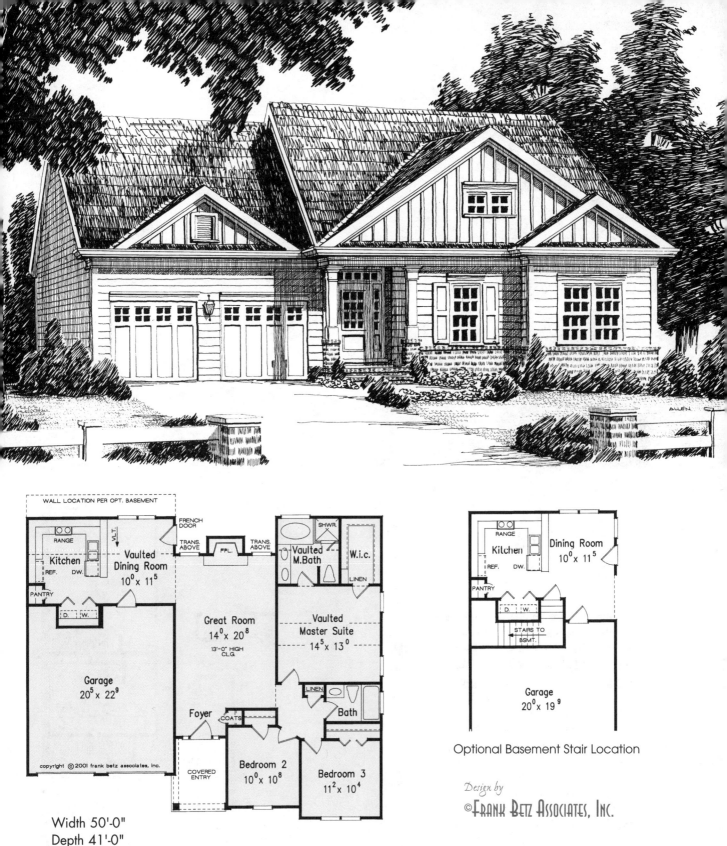

WALL LOCATION PER OPT. BASEMENT

FRENCH DOOR

RANGE

Kitchen
REF.   DW.

PANTRY

D.   W.

VLT.

Vaulted
Dining Room
10⁰ x 11⁵

TRANS. ABOVE   FPL.   TRANS. ABOVE

SHWR.

Vaulted
M.Bath

W.i.c.

LINEN

Great Room
14⁰ x 20⁸

13'-0" HIGH
CLG.

Vaulted
Master Suite
14⁵ x 13⁰

Garage
20⁵ x 22⁹

LINEN

Bath

copyright © 2001 frank betz associates, inc.

Foyer   COATS

COVERED
ENTRY

Bedroom 2
10⁰ x 10⁸

Bedroom 3
11² x 10⁴

Width 50'-0"
Depth 41'-0"

RANGE

Kitchen
REF.   DW.

PANTRY

Dining Room
10⁰ x 11⁵

D.   W.

STAIRS TO
BSMT.

Garage
20⁰ x 19⁹

Optional Basement Stair Location

Design by
© Frank Betz Associates, Inc.

Design HPTM03067
Square Footage: 1,304

■ Country simplicity is the dominant voice of this cottage plan. Horizontal and vertical siding highlight the exterior, while a family-friendly layout is found within. Inside, the foyer opens to the great room, which is warmed by a fireplace. The U-shaped kitchen serves the dining room and features a storage pantry. The vaulted master bedroom enjoys its own vaulted bath and walk-in closet. Two additional bedrooms nearby share a hall bath. A two-car garage completes the plan. Please specify basement or crawlspace foundation when ordering.

Design HPTM03068

Square Footage: 1,197

■ This contemporary design boasts a multitude of windows filling the interior with an abundance of sunlight. The living room enjoys one of two front-facing Palladian windows offering a breathtaking view. The formal dining room adjoins the well-equipped kitchen, which opens to the backyard with sliding glass doors—an ideal location for a future deck and barbecue. Wrapping around the centrally located utility room are the three family bedrooms and a lavish bath. The master bedroom finds privacy raised above ground level while the full bath and closets do double-duty as a sound barrier. This home is designed with a basement foundation.

Design by
©Drummond Designs, Inc.

Width 34'-0"
Depth 36'-8"

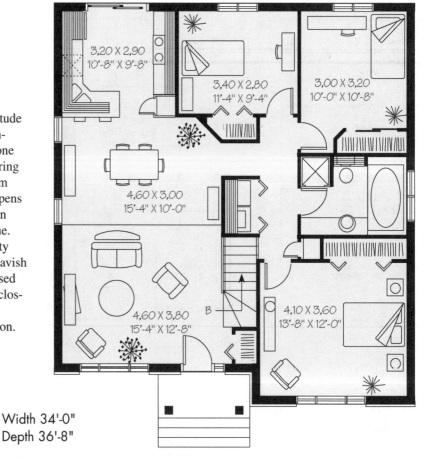

Design 8611

Square Footage: 1,413

■ An angled side entry to this home allows for a majestic, arched window that dominates its facade. The interior, though small in square footage, holds an interesting and efficient floor plan. Because the breakfast room is placed to the front of the plan, it benefits from two large, multi-pane windows. The dining and family rooms form a single space enhanced by a volume ceiling and an optional fireplace, which is flanked by sets of optional double doors. Both the family room and master bedroom boast access to the covered patio. A volume ceiling further enhances the master bedroom, which also has a dressing area, walk-in closet and full bath. The plans include options for a family room with corner fireplace with French doors or a sliding glass door instead of a fireplace. The package includes plans for three different elevations.

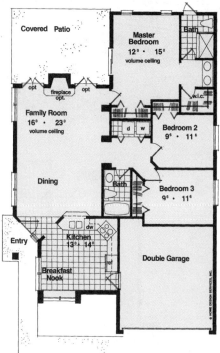

Width 38'-0"
Depth 58'-0"

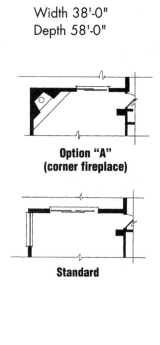

Option "A"
(corner fireplace)

Standard

Design by
Home Design Services

Alternate Elevation

337

Design U107

Square Footage: 1,830

■ This beautiful contemporary ranch-style home offers interesting windows and varied siding textures. The tiled entry opens to the great room with a tray ceiling, arched thresholds and a fireplace. The casual dining area opens to the kitchen with a bar and built-in desk. The master suite is accented by double doors, a walk-in closet and a bath with an oval tub and a separate shower. A secondary bedroom is on the opposite side of the house, and a study to the front might also be used as a den or third bedroom.

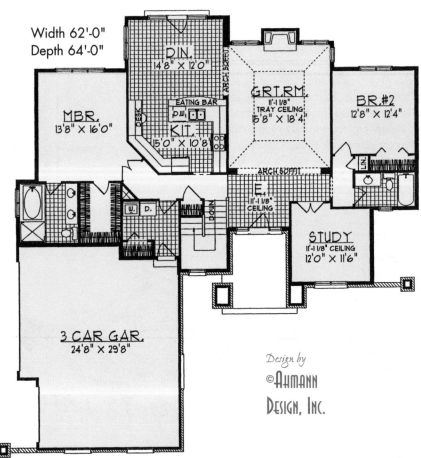

Width 62'-0"
Depth 64'-0"

DIN.
14'8" X 12'0"

GRT. RM.
11'-1 1/8"
TRAY CEILING
15'8" X 18'4"

BR. #2
12'8" X 12'4"

MBR.
13'8" X 16'0"

EATING BAR

KIT.
15'0" X 10'8"

E.
11'-1 1/8"
CEILING

ARCH SOFFIT

STUDY
11'-1 1/8" CEILING
12'0" X 11'6"

W. D.

3 CAR GAR.
24'8" X 29'8"

Design by
©Ahmann
Design, Inc.

338

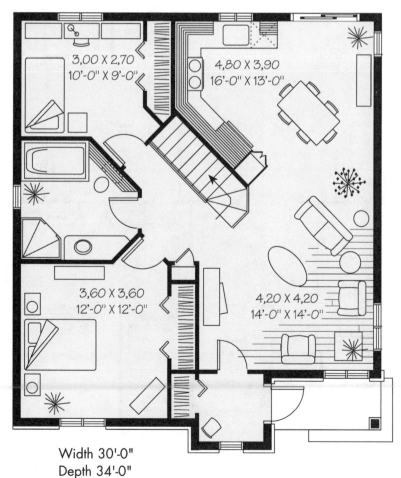

3,00 X 2,70
10'-0" X 9'-0"

4,80 X 3,90
16'-0" X 13'-0"

3,60 X 3,60
12'-0" X 12'-0"

4,20 X 4,20
14'-0" X 14'-0"

Width 30'-0"
Depth 34'-0"

Design HPTM03069

Square Footage: 936

■ The Mansard roof atop the bumped-out foyer adds panache to this charming two-bedroom home. The enclosed entry offers a coat closet and a full-length window. The angled floor plan offers open planning in the living areas with an easy flow from the family room to the dining room. Sliding glass doors lead to the outdoors where a deck or patio would be a welcome addition. The angled kitchen includes a pantry and a casement window over the sink. On the left, a short angled hall leads to the rear bedroom or to the master bedroom and shared full bath. This home is designed with a basement foundation.

Design by
©DRUMMOND DESIGNS, INC.

Design HPTM03070

Square Footage: 1,865

■ Arches and French doors characterize the exterior of this fascinating home. Inside the entry, a formal dining room has arched-door views of the living room. To the left and through French doors are two secondary bedrooms sharing a full bath. The focal point of the living room is the beautiful fireplace centered by two sets of sliding glass doors to the patio. Skylights bring in additional natural light from above. The modified galley kitchen includes a breakfast bar. Adorning the master suite is a tray ceiling; the breathtaking master bath has an enormous triangular bathtub under a skylight. Please specify crawlspace or slab foundation when ordering.

Design by
©BRELAND & FARMER DESIGNERS, INC.

Width 62'-0"
Depth 64'-0"

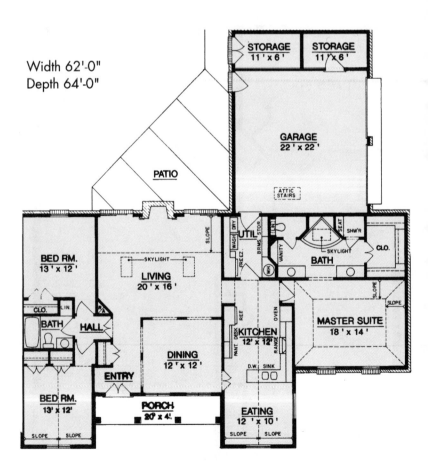

GARAGE
34' X 24'

STORAGE 2
12' X 10'

STORAGE 1
10' X 9'

PORCH 3

CLOSET
14' X 9'

SITTING AREA
11' X 11'

EATING
16' X 16'

DECK

PORCH 2
18' X 12'

BEDROOM 3
15' X 14'

CLOSET
7' X 6'

BATH 4
8' X 7'

BATH 3
15' X 6'

SUN ROOM
16' X 12'

BEDROOM 4
/ OFFICE
14' X 11'

CLOSET

VANITY

MASTER
BATH
20' X 12'

MASTER SUITE
18' X 16'

BAR

HALL

BATH 5

UTILITY

KITCHEN
15' X 14'

FAMILY ROOM
26' X 20'
12' CEILING

CLO.

BEDROOM 2
15' X 14'

BATH 2
12' X 6'

FREEZE

PANTRY
12' X 8'

DINING
16' X 16'
12' CEILING

FOYER
12' X 8'
12' CEILING

LIVING
16' X 16'
12' CEILING

CLOSET
12' X 6'

PORCH 1
40' X 8'

Width 98'-0"
Depth 90'-0"

Design HPTM03071

Square Footage: 4,038

■ Reminiscent of the old Newport mansions, this luxury house has volume ceilings, a glamorous master suite with a hearth-warmed sitting area, a glassed-in sun room, a home office, three porches with a deck, and a gourmet kitchen with a pantry. Graceful French doors are used for all the entrances and in the formal living and dining rooms. The kitchen is magnificent and boasts a large pantry. A centrally positioned family room is graced with a large fireplace and is accessed by the rear porch, living room and dining room. Please specify basement, crawlspace or slab foundation when ordering.

Design by
©Breland & Farmer Designers, Inc.

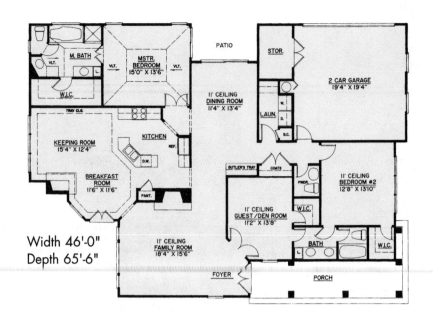

Design S124
Square Footage: 2,026

Design by
Archival Designs

Width 46'-0"
Depth 65'-6"

■ This home has elegant European styling and a most contemporary floor plan. Stuccoed walls and corner quoins accent the exterior, as does the narrow, columned porch leading to an offset entry. The entry opens directly into the huge family room, or go to the right through double doors to the guest room or den. The dining room is at the center of the plan and has sliding glass doors that open to a private patio. Casual dining takes place in the breakfast room—octagonal in shape and opening to the side yard. The keeping room is attached and both are joined by a lovely tray ceiling. The kitchen has an island sink that separates it from these two casual spaces. A private foyer introduces the master suite. The bedroom has a tray ceiling and patio access. The bath features a walk-in closet, double sinks and separate shower and tub. One additional bedroom is located on the opposite side of the plan and shares a bath with the guest room/den.

Design P146

Square Footage: 2,592

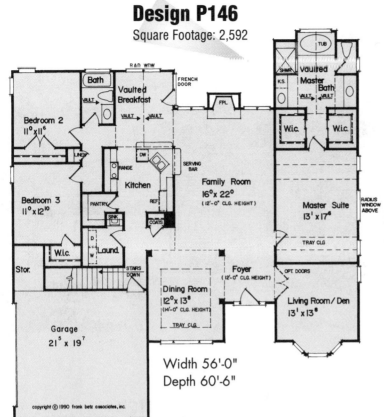

Width 56'-0"
Depth 60'-6"

copyright © 1990 frank betz associates, inc.

■ A blend of contemporary layout with traditional themes places a formal dining room and living room to either side of the foyer, while still allowing an open view to the family room. The efficient kitchen has a welcome walk-in pantry and a serving bar facing both the vaulted breakfast room and the family room. The master suite is located on the opposite side of the plan from the family bedrooms and features twin walk-in closets and a lush bath. Two family bedrooms, both with ample closet space, and a hall bath complete this plan. A two-car garage offers more storage space. Please specify basement, crawlspace or slab foundation when ordering.

Design by
Frank Betz
Associates, Inc.

Design U129

Square Footage: 1,947

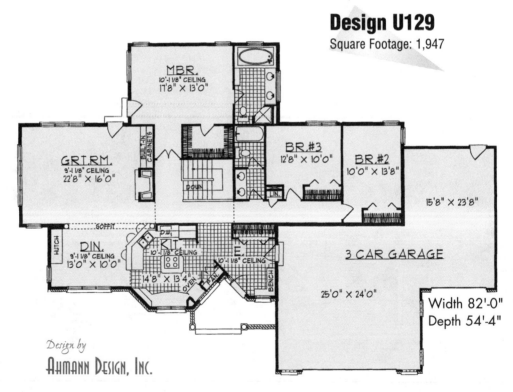

MBR.
10'-1 1/8" CEILING
17'8" X 13'0"

GRT. RM.
9'-1 1/8" CEILING
22'8" X 16'0"

BUILT-IN CABINETS

DOWN

BR. #3
12'8" X 10'0"

BR. #2
10'0" X 13'8"

LIN.

15'8" X 23'8"

3 CAR GARAGE

25'0" X 24'0"

SOFFIT

HUTCH

DIN.
9'-1 1/8" CEILING
13'0" X 10'0"

KIT.
10'-1 1/8" CEILING
14'8" X 13'4"

10'-1 1/8" CEILING

BENCH

OVEN

Width 82'-0"
Depth 54'-4"

Design by
Ahmann Design, Inc.

■ This contemporary home is not the standard one-story plan—it is filled with unusual features that make it a real standout. For instance, the columned entry is angled for interest and opens to a tiled foyer with built-in bench, coat closet and garage access. The kitchen is octagonal in shape and has an island cooktop and snack-bar counter to the dining room. Hutch space here makes this room convenient and attractive.

The great room also has built-ins and a warming hearth for chilly evenings. The master bedroom opens through double doors in the central hall. A walk-in closet and bath with corner shower, spa tub and double sinks grace this suite. Two family bedrooms are found at the other end of the hall and share a full bath. A three-car garage includes space for recreational vehicles.

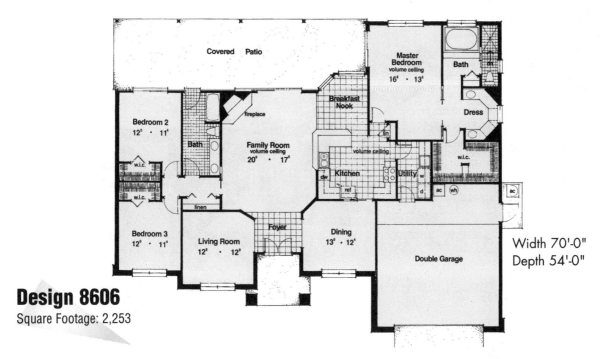

Covered Patio

Bedroom 2
12⁶ · 11⁴

Bath

Family Room
volume ceiling
20⁶ · 17⁰

fireplace

Breakfast Nook

Master Bedroom
volume ceiling
16⁶ · 13⁰

Bath

Dress

w.i.c.

Kitchen

volume ceiling

Utility

w.i.c.

Bedroom 3
12⁶ · 11⁴

linen

Living Room
12⁶ · 12⁶

Foyer

Dining
13⁰ · 12⁴

Double Garage

Width 70'-0"
Depth 54'-0"

Design 8606
Square Footage: 2,253

■ Brick detailing makes an elegant statement in this one-story contemporary; large multi-pane windows add a touch of distinction. Past the front-facing living room and tiled foyer, the large family room is provided extra dimension by its high volume ceiling and corner fireplace. A tiled breakfast nook and kitchen are separated by a convenient eating bar; nearby is the formal dining room. The master bedroom features a walk-in closet, a U-shaped dressing area with double vanity and a full bath. Two additional large bedrooms, each with a walk-in closet, share a full bath with double vanity.

Design by
HOME DESIGN SERVICES

© HOME DESIGN SERVICES, INC.

Design 8646

Square Footage: 2,352

■ An array of varied, arched windows sets off this striking Italianate home. Double doors reveal the foyer, which announces the living room accented by a wet bar, niche and patio access. The coffered dining room combines with the living room to create a perfect space for formal entertaining. An arched entry to the informal living area presents a bayed breakfast nook and adjoining family room warmed by a fireplace. A pass-through kitchen comes with a deep pantry and informal eating bar. Double doors open to the coffered master bedroom. Its sumptuous bath has two walk-in closets, a dual vanity and spa tub. Arched entries lead to three additional bedrooms: two share a full bath and the third boasts a private bath with yard access. Blueprints include an alternate elevation at no extra charge.

Width 61'-8"
Depth 64'-8"

Design by
HOME DESIGN SERVICES

Alternate Elevation

Width 82'-0"
Depth 75'-0"

Design 3667
Square Footage: 2,085

Design by
HOME PLANNERS

QUOTE ONE®
Cost to build? See page 434
to order complete cost estimate
to build this house in your area!

■ The luxurious exterior of this Mediterranean dream home conceals an interior that wears a simple theme of casual comfort. From the stylish tiled entry, the spacious great room extends an invitation to relax with a fireplace and wide views of the outdoors. The nearby gourmet kitchen serves all occasions, grand and cozy, and leads through an eating nook outdoors to the entertainment terrace. A rambling master suite enjoys its own wing, with a private covered porch and a courtyard patio. On the opposite side of the plan, two family bedrooms—or one could be a study—share a full bath with two vanities. Service access from the two-car garage is available through the utility room and the courtyard patio.

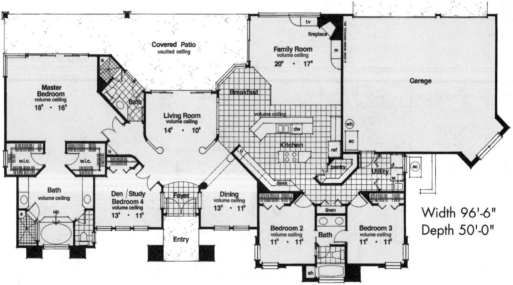

Design 8663
Square Footage: 2,597

Width 96'-6"
Depth 50'-0"

■ The angles in this home create unlimited views and spaces that appear larger. Majestic columns of brick add warmth to a striking elevation. Inside, the foyer commands special perspective on living areas including the living room, dining room and the den. The island kitchen services the breakfast nook and the family room. A large pantry provides ample space for food storage. In the master bedroom suite, mitered glass and a private bath set the tone for simple luxury. Two secondary bedrooms share privacy and quiet at the front of the house. The den may also convert to a fourth bedroom, if desired.

Design by
HOME DESIGN SERVICES

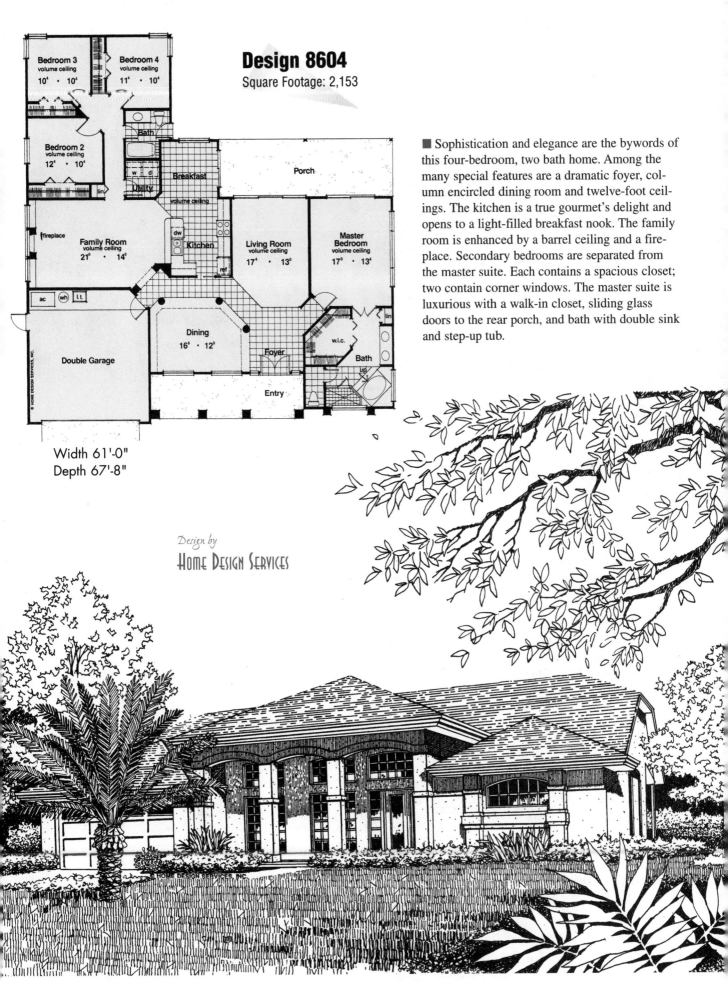

Design 8604

Square Footage: 2,153

Bedroom 3
volume ceiling
10⁴ · 10⁴

Bedroom 4
volume ceiling
11⁴ · 10⁴

Bedroom 2
volume ceiling
12⁴ · 10⁴

Bath

Breakfast
volume ceiling

Utility
w d

lin

Porch

fireplace

Family Room
volume ceiling
21⁰ · 14⁰

dw

Kitchen

ref

Living Room
volume ceiling
17⁴ · 13⁰

Master Bedroom
volume ceiling
17⁰ · 13⁴

lin

ac wh l.t.

Dining
16⁶ · 12⁰

Double Garage

Foyer

w.i.c.

Bath

up

Entry

Width 61'-0"
Depth 67'-8"

Design by
HOME DESIGN SERVICES

■ Sophistication and elegance are the bywords of this four-bedroom, two bath home. Among the many special features are a dramatic foyer, column encircled dining room and twelve-foot ceilings. The kitchen is a true gourmet's delight and opens to a light-filled breakfast nook. The family room is enhanced by a barrel ceiling and a fireplace. Secondary bedrooms are separated from the master suite. Each contains a spacious closet; two contain corner windows. The master suite is luxurious with a walk-in closet, sliding glass doors to the rear porch, and bath with double sink and step-up tub.

Design HPTM03072

Square Footage: 2,409
Bonus Space: 709 square feet

■ A pedimented entry marries Old World charm with New World tradition. The great room of this home provides a large masonry fireplace. Built-ins are included on one wall for entertainment equipment and books. The master suite is located to the rear of the house and has a luxury bath that includes large walk-in closets. The kitchen, equipped with a snack bar, walk-in pantry and desk, is well designed for the busy cook. From the kitchen area, the staircase rises to an expandable second floor. With a future bedroom, game room and bath upstairs, this home will fit the needs of a growing family. Please specify basement, crawlspace or slab foundation when ordering.

Design by
©Larry E. Belk Designs

QUOTE ONE®
Cost to build? See page 434 to order complete cost estimate to build this house in your area!

Width 85'-8"
Depth 68'-4"

Design 8664
Square Footage, 2,660

This charming one-story home will accommodate families of all sizes. The entry opens onto the living room and glass doors leading to the covered patio. The kitchen leads to a family room with a fireplace and shelves that create a relaxed setting. A massive master suite provides a sitting room and an expansive master bath featuring a walk-in closet and His and Hers vanities. Two secondary bedrooms share a full bath.

Covered Patio

Family Room
20⁰ · 16⁰
10⁰ Clg.

fireplace

shelves

Breakfast

Sitting Rm
23⁰ · 15⁰
10⁰ Clg.

Bath

Living Room
15⁰ · 13⁴
12⁸ Clg.

Kitchen

dw

desk

ref

pantry

Bedroom 2
12⁰ · 11⁰
10⁰ Clg.

Master Bedroom

Bath

lin

w.i.c.

Bath

Den   Study
Bedroom 4
11⁰ · 11⁰
10⁰ Clg.

Foyer

Dining
11⁰ · 11⁰
14⁸ Clg.

linen

Utility
d   w

Bedroom 3
12⁰ · 11⁰
10⁰ Clg.

ac

ac

wh

Entry

Width 66'-4"
Depth 74'-4"

Double Garage

Design by
Home Design Services

J.N. HANSEN P.T.L.

© HOME DESIGN SERVICES, INC.

Design HPTM03073

Square Footage: 1,104

■ A covered front porch welcomes friends and family to this fine three-bedroom cottage. From the Palladian window in front to the rear sliding glass doors, the living/dining area is open under a cathedral ceiling. A large bay provides natural light to the dining room and the kitchen. Three bedrooms share a roomy bath that includes a garden tub and a separate shower. This home is designed with a basement foundation.

Design by
© DRUMMOND DESIGNS, INC.

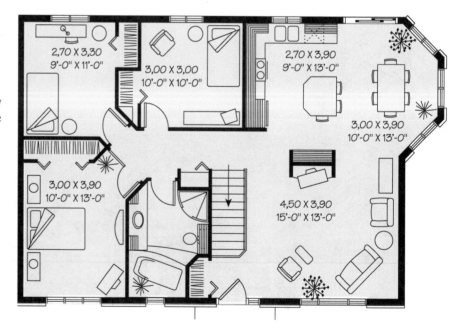

2,70 X 3,30
9'-0" X 11'-0"

3,00 X 3,00
10'-0" X 10'-0"

2,70 X 3,90
9'-0" X 13'-0"

3,00 X 3,90
10'-0" X 13'-0"

3,00 X 3,90
10'-0" X 13'-0"

4,50 X 3,90
15'-0" X 13'-0"

Width 42'-0"
Depth 28'-0"

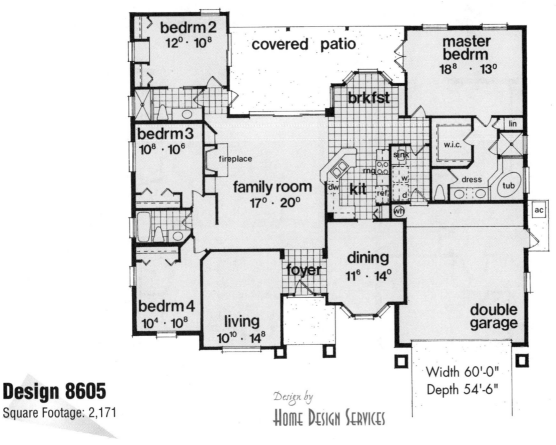

bedrm 2
12⁰ · 10⁸

covered patio

master bedrm
18⁸ · 13⁰

brkfst

bedrm 3
10⁸ · 10⁶

fireplace

w.i.c.

lin

family room
17⁰ · 20⁰

sink

mg

kit

w

dw

ref

d

dress

tub

wh

ac

bedrm 4
10⁴ · 10⁸

foyer

dining
11⁶ · 14⁰

living
10¹⁰ · 14⁸

double garage

Width 60'-0"
Depth 54'-6"

Design 8605

Square Footage: 2,171

Design by
HOME DESIGN SERVICES

■ This four-bedroom, three-bath home is designed to minimize wasted space, such as hallways. There are loads of living options, especially in the placement of the secondary bedrooms. Bedroom 2 can be a much needed mother-in-law room, with semi-private bath that doubles as a pool bath for outdoor living. The classic family room/nook area and kitchen work well together for convenient living. The secluded living room and bay windowed dining room are a special bonus for formal entertaining. The master suite provides the best of everything from twin vanities to handy linen storage. There's also a huge walk-in closet and private commode. The interior architecture of this home boasts soaring vaulted ceilings throughout.

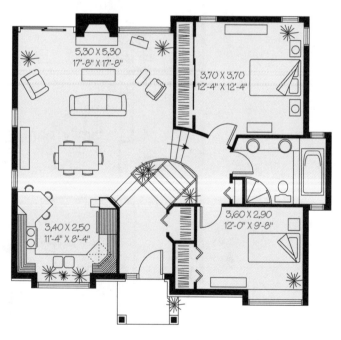

Design HPTM03074

Square Footage: 1,514
Finished Basement: 1,514 square feet

Design by
©DRUMMOND DESIGNS, INC.

Width 34'-8"
Depth 32'-0"

■ The dramatic elevation of this split-level home enjoys two Palladian windows of a non-traditional design as well as a covered porch with asymmetrical supports. The foyer leads up to the dining/living room where a bevy of windows offers dramatic views and a fireplace offers warmth and charm. The U-shaped kitchen enjoys a snack bar for casual dining. From the dining area, follow a curved wall up a brief flight of stairs to the sleeping quarters where a full bath creates privacy by its placement. The finished basement offers a third bedroom and a second bath as well as an exercise room and family/game room.

2,70 X 4,30
9'-0" X 14'-4"

2,90 X 3,40
9'-8" X 11'-4"

3,00 X 3,40
10'-0" X 11'-4"

3,60 X 4,50
12'-0" X 15'-0"

3,70 X 3,50
12'-4" X 11'-8"

Width 38'-0"
Depth 28'-0"

Design HPTM03075

Square Footage: 1,064

■ The stunning covered entry of this home enjoys storage space with glass-block illumination and brickwork that mimics the Palladian window of the living room. Up a short flight of steps from the angular entry sits the kitchen with its double-sided pantry. To the right is the adjoining dining room with access to the rear porch via sliding glass doors. The living room faces forward with a fireplace centered on the right wall. Two bedrooms are on the left sharing a full bath with a double-sink vanity. The unfinished basement allows for future development.

Design by
©Drummond Designs, Inc.

Design Z109

Square Footage: 1,277

Width 52'-0"
Depth 38'-0"

■ This one-story contemporary home, though smaller, holds a wealth of livability. An angled entry opens to the foyer, which features a large closet to store coats and hats. The living and dining rooms are open to one another and are conveniently located near the U-shaped kitchen. The two large bedrooms share an oversized bath that includes a separate shower and tub. The garage opens to the main house at a door near the entry. This home is designed with a basement foundation.

4,40 X 3,30
14'-8" X 11'-0"

5,30 X 4,50
17'-8" X 15'-0"

4,70 X 7,30
15'-8" X 24'-4"

4,80 X 3,30
16'-0" X 11'-0"

3,60 X 3,30
12'-0" X 11'-0"

3,40 X 3,90
11'-4" X 13'-0"

Design by
©Drummond
Designs, Inc.

Design 8636
Square Footage: 2,010

Bedroom 2
14⁰ · 10⁰

Covered Patio

Bath

Breakfast

Master Bedroom
15⁰ · 13⁴

w.i.c.

Bedroom 3
11⁰ · 10⁴

shelf

Family Room
16⁸ · 14¹⁰

fireplace

shelf

dw

Kitchen

Bath

ref

pan

Utility

w

d

ac

ac

wh

Bedroom 4
11⁰ · 10⁴

Living Room
11⁰ · 10²

Foyer

Dining
11⁰ · 10²

Double Garage

Entry

Width 62'-8"
Depth 56'-0"

■ Not only does this house look exciting from the outside with its contemporary use of glass, but upon entering this home, the excitement continues. The classic split living room and dining room sets this house apart from the rest. The family room, breakfast nook and kitchen all share the views to the rear yard. The efficient placement of the bedrooms creates privacy for family members. The master suite is ample, with a wonderful bath featuring a lounging tub, shower, private toilet room, double vanities and generous walk-in closet. Plans for this home include a choice of two exterior elevations.

Design by
HOME DESIGN SERVICES

Alternate Elevation

Design 4183

Square Footage: 1,885

L

■ Nothing is excluded in this delightful contemporary one-story design. Enter the home from a deck entry to the oversized great room. A fireplace and sliding glass doors are nice accents here. The dining room is separated from this area by a divider wall, and it is embellished with a greenhouse unit and sloped ceiling. The breakfast area and kitchen access the rear yard as well as a side deck. Four bedrooms include three family bedrooms (two with sliding glass doors) and a master suite with a private deck.

Design by
©HOME PLANNERS

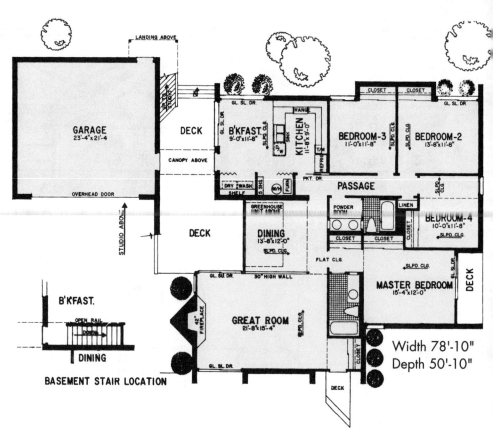

Width 78'-10"
Depth 50'-10"

BASEMENT STAIR LOCATION

Design 8613
Square Footage: 1,872

Alternate Elevation

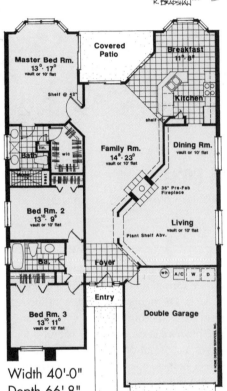

Master Bed Rm.
13⁰·17⁰
vault or 10' flat

Shelf @ 42"

Covered Patio

Breakfast
11⁴·8⁰

Kitchen

shelf

Bath

lin.

wic

Family Rm.
14⁴·23⁰
vault or 10' flat

Dining Rm.
vault or 10' flat

36" Pre-Fab Fireplace

Bed Rm. 2
13¹⁰·9⁶
vault or 10' flat

Living
vault or 10' flat

Plant Shelf Abv.

Ba.

Foyer

wh   A/C   W   D

Bed Rm. 3
13¹⁰·11⁰
vault or 10' flat

Entry

Double Garage

Width 40'-0"
Depth 66'-8"

■ Vaulted ceilings throughout this home suggest the innovative touches that add interest in a one-story plan. Sidelight and overhead windows brighten a foyer that opens to the family room and living room. A plant shelf spans the entry into the living room, which is united with the dining room under a high ceiling. A vaulted ceiling also augments the family room. Notice the two-way fireplace and access to a covered patio here. The kitchen is convenient to the dining room and to a bayed breakfast nook. The master bedroom also has a bay window plus a full bath with oversized shower. Two additional bedrooms share a full bath. Plans include two different elevation choices!

Design by
HOME DESIGN SERVICES

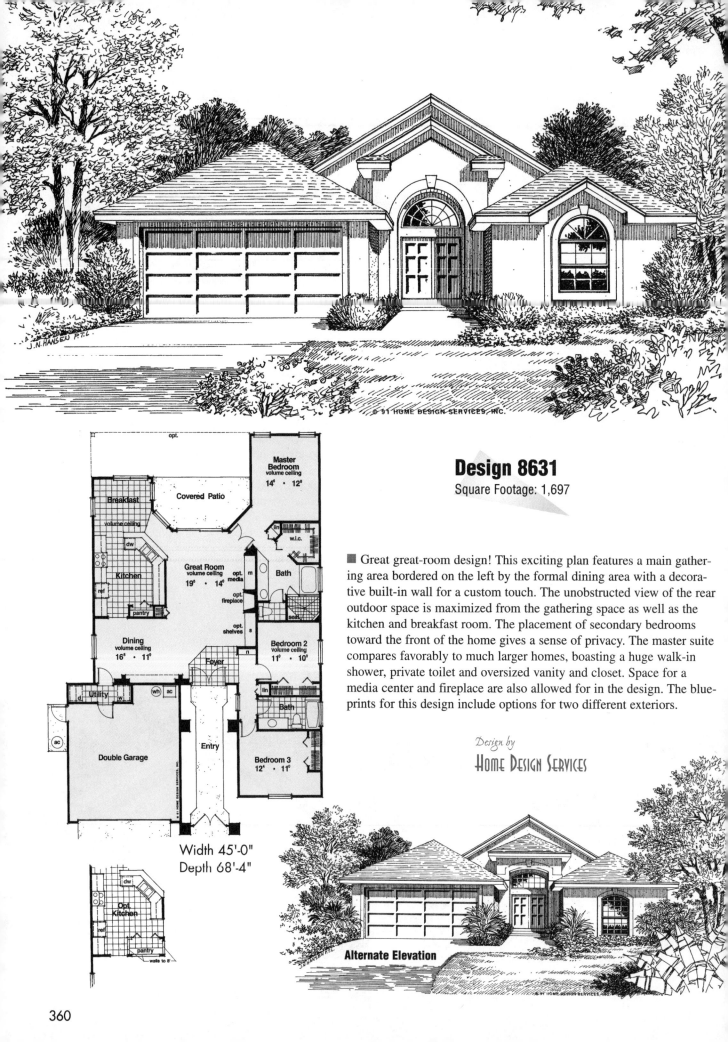

Design 8631
Square Footage: 1,697

■ Great great-room design! This exciting plan features a main gathering area bordered on the left by the formal dining area with a decorative built-in wall for a custom touch. The unobstructed view of the rear outdoor space is maximized from the gathering space as well as the kitchen and breakfast room. The placement of secondary bedrooms toward the front of the home gives a sense of privacy. The master suite compares favorably to much larger homes, boasting a huge walk-in shower, private toilet and oversized vanity and closet. Space for a media center and fireplace are also allowed for in the design. The blueprints for this design include options for two different exteriors.

Design by
HOME DESIGN SERVICES

Width 45'-0"
Depth 68'-4"

Alternate Elevation

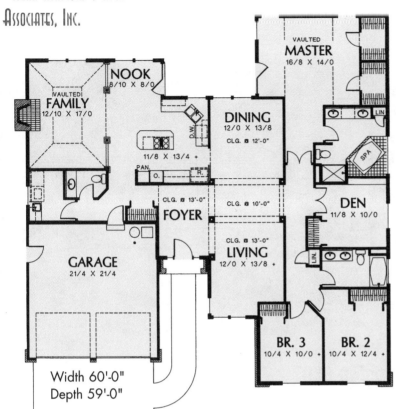

VAULTED MASTER 16/8 X 14/0

NOOK 8/10 X 8/0

VAULTED FAMILY 12/10 X 17/0

DINING 12/0 X 13/8 CLG. @ 12'-0"

11/8 X 13/4 +

PAN.

FOYER CLG. @ 13'-0" CLG. @ 10'-0"

DEN 11/8 X 10/0

GARAGE 21/4 X 21/4

LIVING 12/0 X 13/8 + CLG. @ 13'-0"

BR. 3 10/4 X 10/0 +

BR. 2 10/4 X 12/4 +

LIN

SPA

Width 60'-0"
Depth 59'-0"

Design 9450

Square Footage: 2,378

L

■ Spacious living all on one story—this traditional design has a place for everything. The foyer leads directly into the living room that enjoys elegant columns and a tall corner window. A large central kitchen with an island serves the dining room, living room, nook and family room with ease. Note the fireplace and vaulted ceiling in the family room. Four bedrooms—or three bedrooms and a den—occupy the right wing of the house. The master suite with a vaulted ceiling comes in two versions—the choice is up to you.

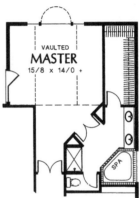

VAULTED MASTER 15/8 X 14/0 +

SPA

Alternate Layout

Design 8607

Square Footage: 2,271

■ The family room, with volume ceiling, serves as a hub in this spacious home. It blends with a large covered patio to form an expansive, informal space. Special amenities here include a fireplace and sliding glass doors. The high ceiling extends to the kitchen and beyond to the bayed breakfast nook. A pass-through counter permits easy access between the kitchen and family room. The master bedroom is highlighted by a volume ceiling and patio access. A tiled shower and step-up tub in the master bath overlook the solarium. Three additional bedrooms, two flanking a tiled bath, are found beyond the living room. A third bedroom is located off the family room and features its own private bath.

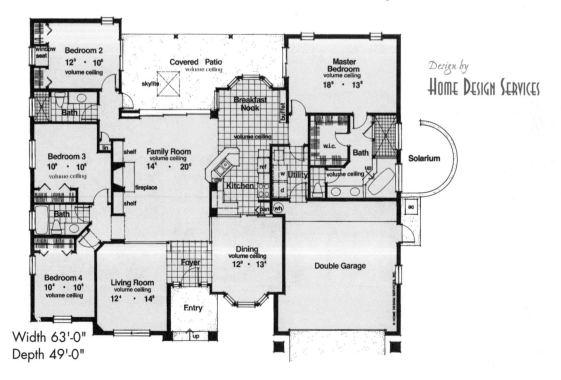

Width 63'-0"
Depth 49'-0"

Design 8253

Square Footage: 2,910

Multiple rooflines, shutters, a bayed tower and a covered porch combine to create a fine facade for this three-bedroom home. Inside, the foyer opens to the formal dining room off to the right, with the formal living room and its fireplace directly ahead. The island kitchen easily serves the sunny breakfast room and the spacious family room, while also offering a large pantry and plenty of counter and cabinet space. Located in the left wing for privacy, the master bedroom suite features His and Hers walk-in closets and a lavish bath with a separate tub and shower. Two family bedrooms share a full bath. Please specify basement, crawlspace or slab foundation when ordering.

Width 79'-8"
Depth 69'-6"

Design by
©Larry E. Belk
Designs

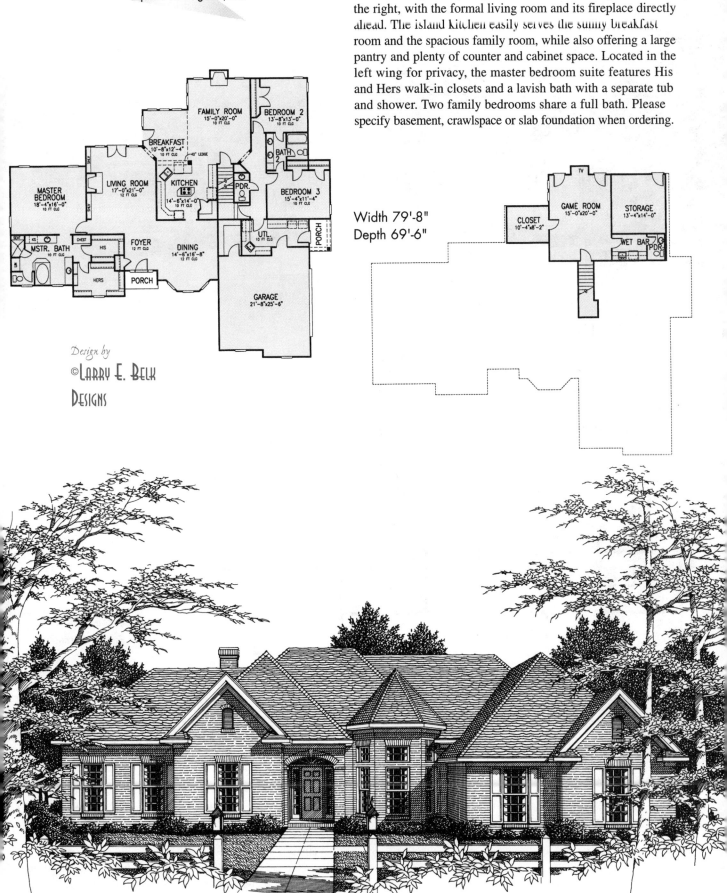

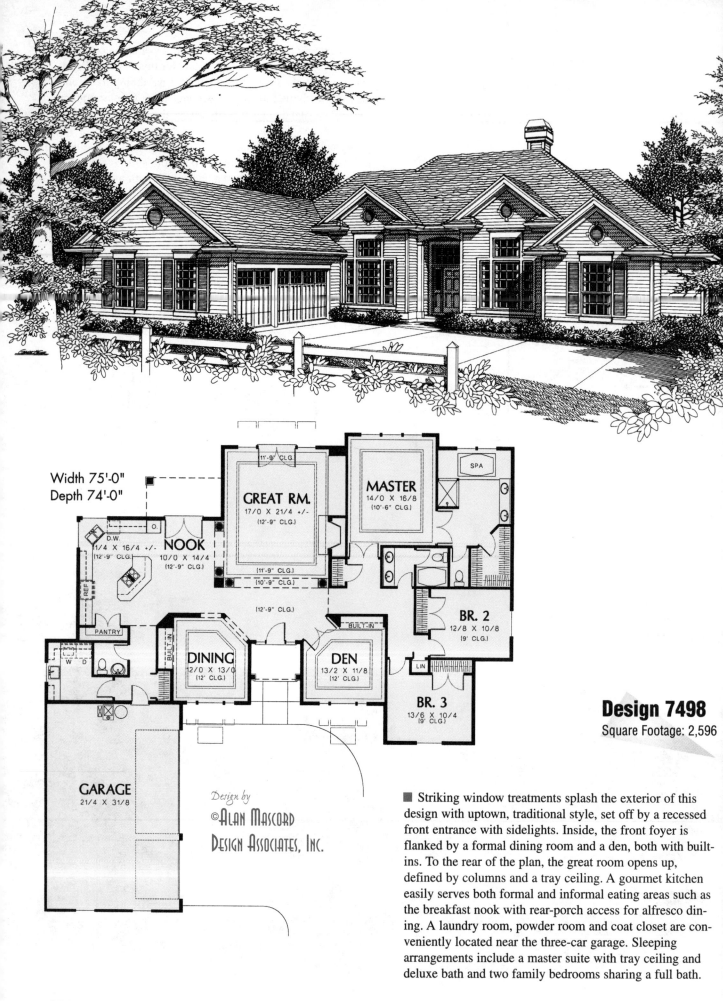

Width 75'-0"
Depth 74'-0"

GREAT RM.
17/0 X 21/4 +/-
(12'-9" CLG.)
11'-9" CLG.
(11'-9" CLG.)
(10'-9" CLG.)

MASTER
14/0 X 16/8
(10'-6" CLG.)

SPA

NOOK
10/0 X 14/4
(12'-9" CLG.)

D.W.
1/4 X 16/4 +/-
(12'-9" CLG.)

O.

REF

PANTRY

(12'-9" CLG.)

BUILT-IN

BR. 2
12/8 X 10/8
(9' CLG.)

BUILT-IN

DINING
12/0 X 13/0
(12' CLG.)

DEN
13/2 X 11/8
(12' CLG.)

LIN

BR. 3
13/6 X 10/4
(9' CLG.)

W   D

GARAGE
21/4 X 31/8

Design by
©Alan Mascord
Design Associates, Inc.

Design 7498
Square Footage: 2,596

■ Striking window treatments splash the exterior of this design with uptown, traditional style, set off by a recessed front entrance with sidelights. Inside, the front foyer is flanked by a formal dining room and a den, both with built-ins. To the rear of the plan, the great room opens up, defined by columns and a tray ceiling. A gourmet kitchen easily serves both formal and informal eating areas such as the breakfast nook with rear-porch access for alfresco dining. A laundry room, powder room and coat closet are conveniently located near the three-car garage. Sleeping arrangements include a master suite with tray ceiling and deluxe bath and two family bedrooms sharing a full bath.

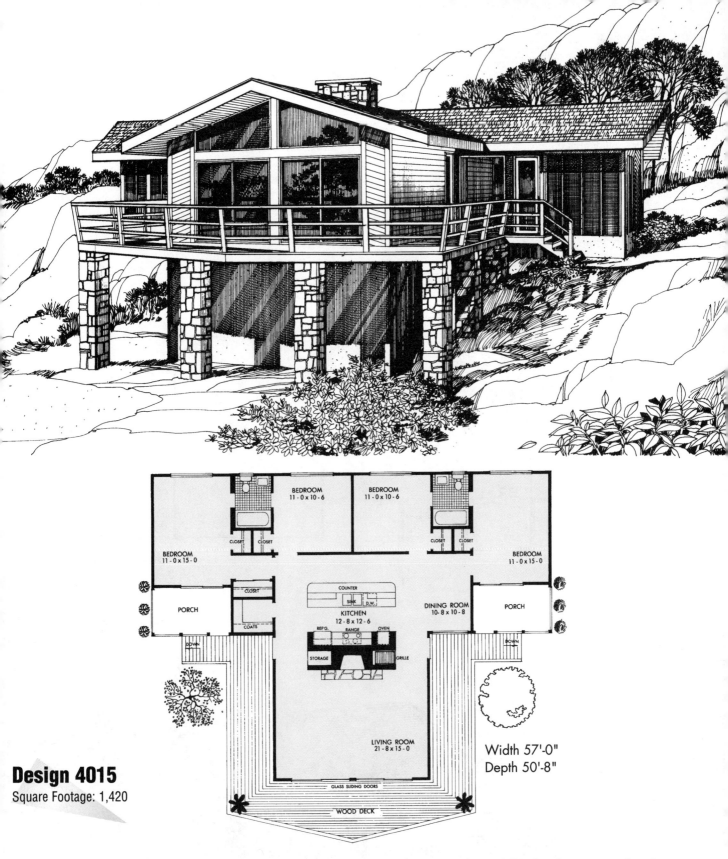

BEDROOM
11 - 0 x 10 - 6

BEDROOM
11 - 0 x 10 - 6

CLOSET CLOSET

CLOSET CLOSET

BEDROOM
11 - 0 x 15 - 0

BEDROOM
11 - 0 x 15 - 0

COUNTER

CLOSET

SINK D.W.

PORCH

KITCHEN
12 - 8 x 12 - 6

DINING ROOM
10 - 8 x 10 - 8

PORCH

COATS

REF'G. RANGE OVEN

DOWN

STORAGE GRILLE

DOWN

LIVING ROOM
21 - 8 x 15 - 0

Width 57'-0"
Depth 50'-8"

GLASS SLIDING DOORS

WOOD DECK

Design 4015

Square Footage: 1,420

■ The perfect vacation home, this symmetrical plan combines open, informal living spaces with lots of sleeping space. The spacious living room has a warming fireplace, sliding glass doors to the deck and is graced with ceiling-to-floor windows, allowing for beautiful views. Convenient to the dining room, the efficient kitchen is carefully placed so as not to interfere with the living room. Notice the four spacious bedrooms—plenty of room for accommodating guests. Two of the bedrooms boast private porches.

Design by

© HOME PLANNERS

Design U257

Square Footage: 1,868

■ A large living area dominates the center of this contemporary-flavored traditional one-story. It opens off of a vaulted foyer through a doorway with soffit. At one end is a warming hearth; at the other, another soffitted opening to the dining area and island kitchen. The dining area is enhanced by a bay window with sliding glass doors to the outdoors. There is a large laundry room with a closet and space for a washer and dryer and a freezer. It connects to the two-car garage with storage space. The bedrooms are at the opposite end of the plan and include two family bedrooms and a master suite. Accents in the master suite: a sliding glass door to the rear yard, corner shower, whirlpool tub, double sinks and a large walk-in closet.

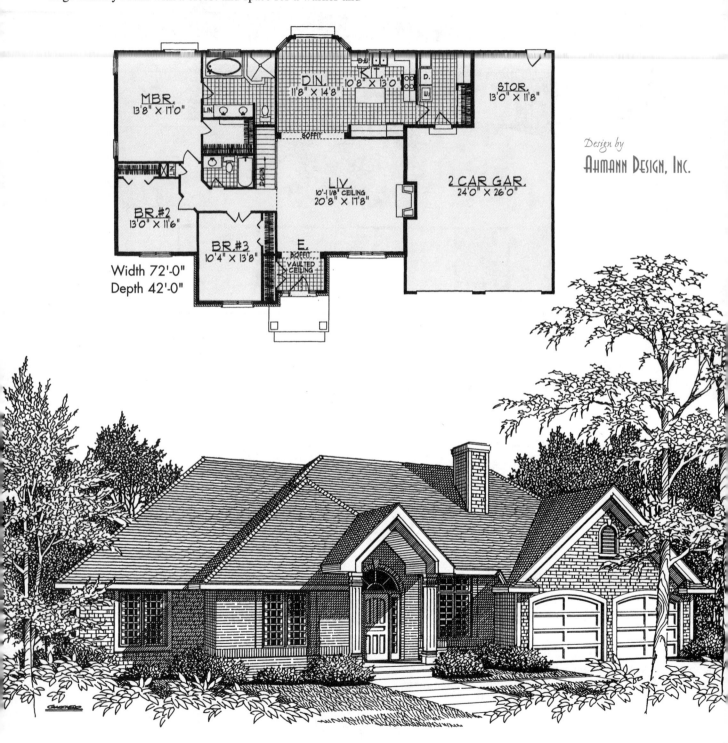

MBR.
13'8" X 17'0"

DIN.
11'8" X 14'8"

KIT.
10'8" X 13'0"

STOR.
13'0" X 11'8"

LIV.
10'-1 1/8" CEILING
20'8" X 17'8"

2 CAR GAR.
24'0" X 26'0"

BR.#2
13'0" X 11'6"

BR.#3
10'4" X 13'8"

E.

VAULTED CEILING

Width 72'-0"
Depth 42'-0"

Design by
AHMANN DESIGN, INC.

■ In this plan, a large tiled area extends from the entry foyer through to the breakfast nook and island kitchen. It unites the areas and helps to separate them from the massive great room. Look for a warming fireplace and abundant windows in this grand living area. The dining room is distinguished by soffits and columns, but is near to the kitchen for convenience. The master bedroom is exquisite with a tray-ceiling accent, walk-in closet and bath with double sinks, spa tub and separate shower. Two family bedrooms share the use of a full bath with double sinks. One of these bedrooms has a walk-in closet. A two-car garage sits to the front of the plan, but offers a side entry that does not detract from the beauty of the facade.

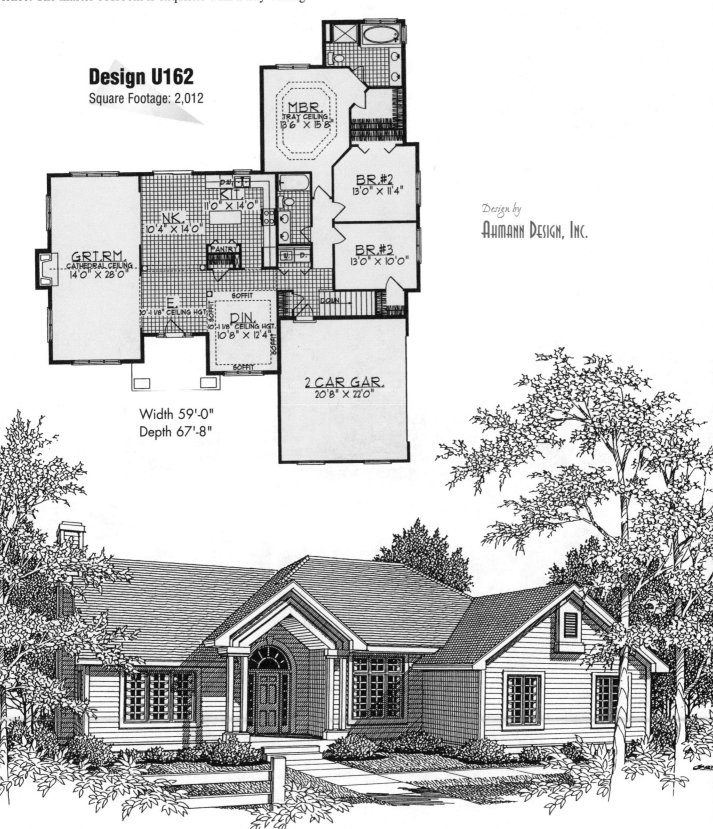

Design U162
Square Footage: 2,012

MBR.
TRAY CEILING
13'6" X 15'8"

BR. #2
13'0" X 11'4"

BR. #3
13'0" X 10'0"

KIT.
11'0" X 14'0"

NK.
10'4" X 14'0"

GRT. RM.
CATHEDRAL CEILING
14'0" X 28'0"

PANTRY

DIN.
10'8" X 12'4"

2 CAR GAR.
20'8" X 22'0"

Width 59'-0"
Depth 67'-8"

Design by
AHMANN DESIGN, INC.

Design 1404

Square Footage: 1,336

■ Here is an exciting design, unusual in character, yet fun to live in. This design, with its frame exterior and large glass areas, has as its dramatic focal point a hexagonal living area that gives way to interesting angles. The spacious living area features sliding glass doors through which traffic may pass to the terrace stretching across the entire length of the house. The wide overhanging roofs project over the terraces, thus providing partial protection from the weather. The sloping ceilings converge above the unique, open fireplace. The sleeping areas are located in each wing from the hexagonal center.

Design by

HOME PLANNERS

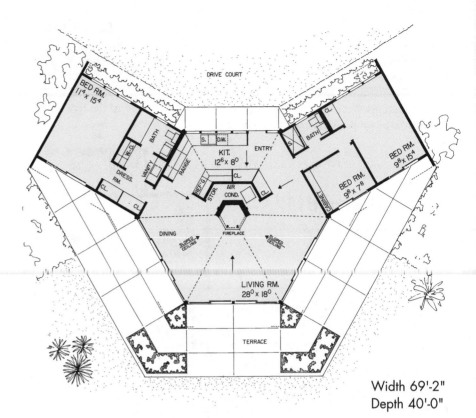

Width 69'-2"
Depth 40'-0"

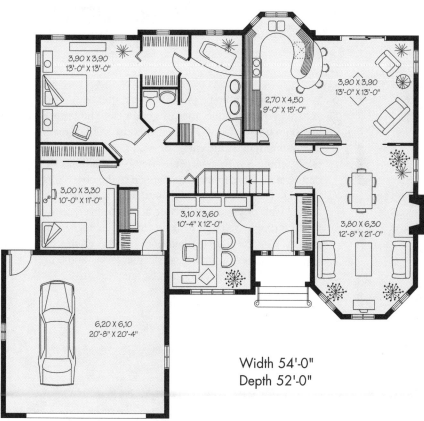

3,90 X 3,90
13'-0" X 13'-0"

2,70 X 4,50
9'-0" X 15'-0"

3,90 X 3,90
13'-0" X 13'-0"

3,00 X 3,30
10'-0" X 11'-0"

3,10 X 3,60
10'-4" X 12'-0"

3,80 X 6,30
12'-8" X 21'-0"

6,20 X 6,10
20'-8" X 20'-4"

Width 54'-0"
Depth 52'-0"

Design HPTM03076

Square Footage: 1,572

■ The rooflines, Palladian window and turreted bay window of this home blend together to create a delightful facade that brightens any neighborhood. The private office to the left of the foyer offers a wonderful view. The dining/living room to the right of the foyer boasts a warming fireplace. Privacy is offered with pocket doors to the family/kitchen area and double doors to the foyer. The kitchen delights with a second bay window and a dramatically curved snack bar. The master bedroom privately accesses the shared full bath which is complete with a compartmented toilet. This home is designed with a basement foundation.

Design by
©DRUMMOND DESIGNS, INC.

Design HPTM03077

Square Footage: 1,120

■ This charming home puts a modern spin on the European cottage. Following the rules of good Feng Shui, this two-bedroom home places the kitchen at the front of the house and to the right of the entry. Beyond the snack bar is the family room—with a gorgeous view—that adjoins the formal dining area. Here French doors open to the covered porch in the rear. The master bedroom is situated in the rear with an angled wall of windows. Private access to the shared bath is found through the large walk-in closet. The lavish bath, in tandem with the flanking bedroom closets, assures privacy and noise reduction for sound sleeping. This home is designed with a basement foundation.

Front View

3,90 X 4,20
13'-0" X 14'-0"

3,30 X 4,20
11'-0" X 14'-0"

3,90 X 4,20
13'-0" X 14'-0"

2,40 X 3,90
8'-0" X 13'-0"

3,10 X 3,30
10'-4" X 11'-0"

3,10 X 6,10
10'-4" X 20'-4"

Width 36'-0"
Depth 48'-0"

Design by
© DRUMMOND DESIGNS, INC.

Design 2439

Square Footage: 1,312

■ Here is a wonderfully organized plan with an exterior that will command the attention of each and every passerby. The rooflines and the pointed glass gable-end wall will be noticed immediately—the delightful deck will be quickly noticed, too. Inside, visitors will be thrilled by the spaciousness of the huge living room. The ceilings slope upward to the exposed ridge beam. A freestanding fireplace will make its contribution to a cheerful atmosphere. The sleeping zone has two bedrooms, two bunk rooms, two full baths, two built-in chests and fine closet space.

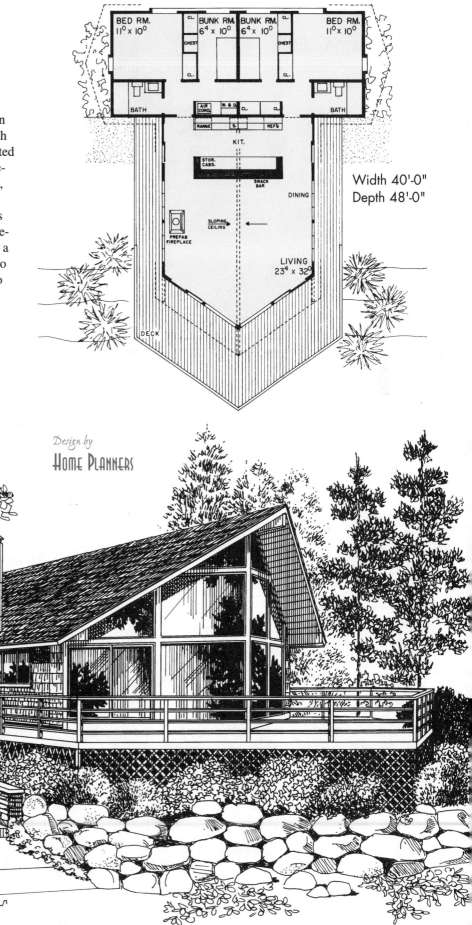

Width 40'-0"
Depth 48'-0"

Design by
HOME PLANNERS

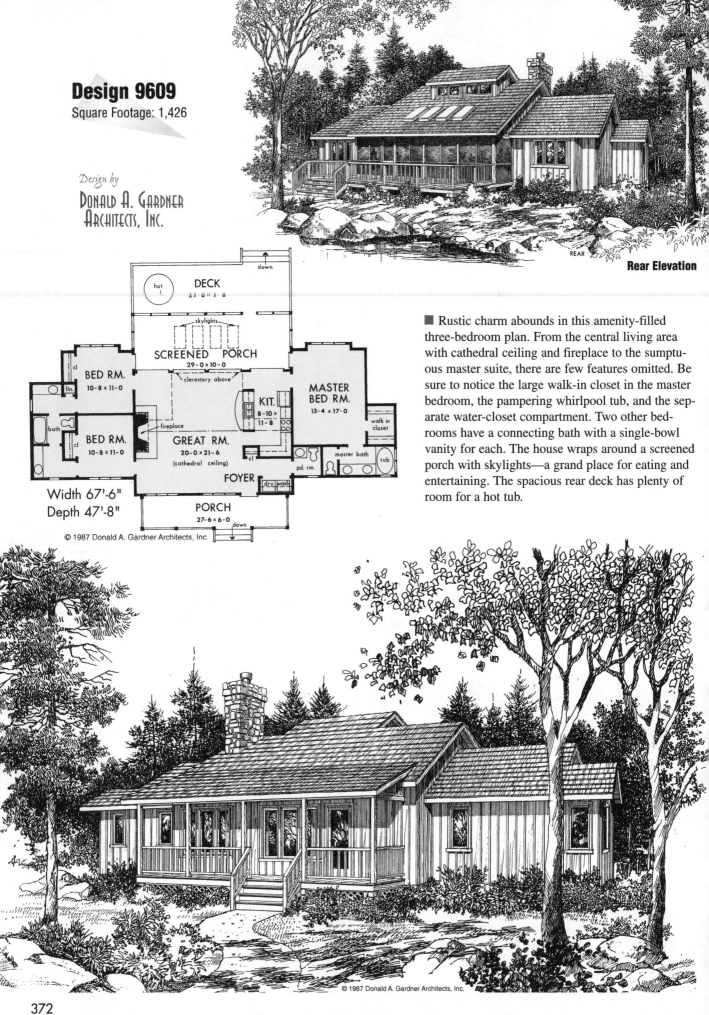

Design 9609

Square Footage: 1,426

Design by

**DONALD A. GARDNER
ARCHITECTS, INC.**

Rear Elevation

REAR

DECK

down

hot

skylights

SCREENED   PORCH
29-0 x 10-0

clerestory above

BED RM.
10-8 x 11-0

cl

lin.

KIT.
8-10 x
11-8

**MASTER
BED RM.**
13-4 x 17-0

walk in
closet

bath

BED RM.
10-8 x 11-0

cl

fireplace

GREAT RM.
20-0 x 21-6
(cathedral ceiling)

cl

pd. rm.

master bath

tub

FOYER

dry wash

Width 67'-6"
Depth 47'-8"

PORCH
27-6 x 6-0

down

© 1987 Donald A. Gardner Architects, Inc.

■ Rustic charm abounds in this amenity-filled three-bedroom plan. From the central living area with cathedral ceiling and fireplace to the sumptuous master suite, there are few features omitted. Be sure to notice the large walk-in closet in the master bedroom, the pampering whirlpool tub, and the separate water-closet compartment. Two other bedrooms have a connecting bath with a single-bowl vanity for each. The house wraps around a screened porch with skylights—a grand place for eating and entertaining. The spacious rear deck has plenty of room for a hot tub.

© 1987 Donald A. Gardner Architects, Inc.

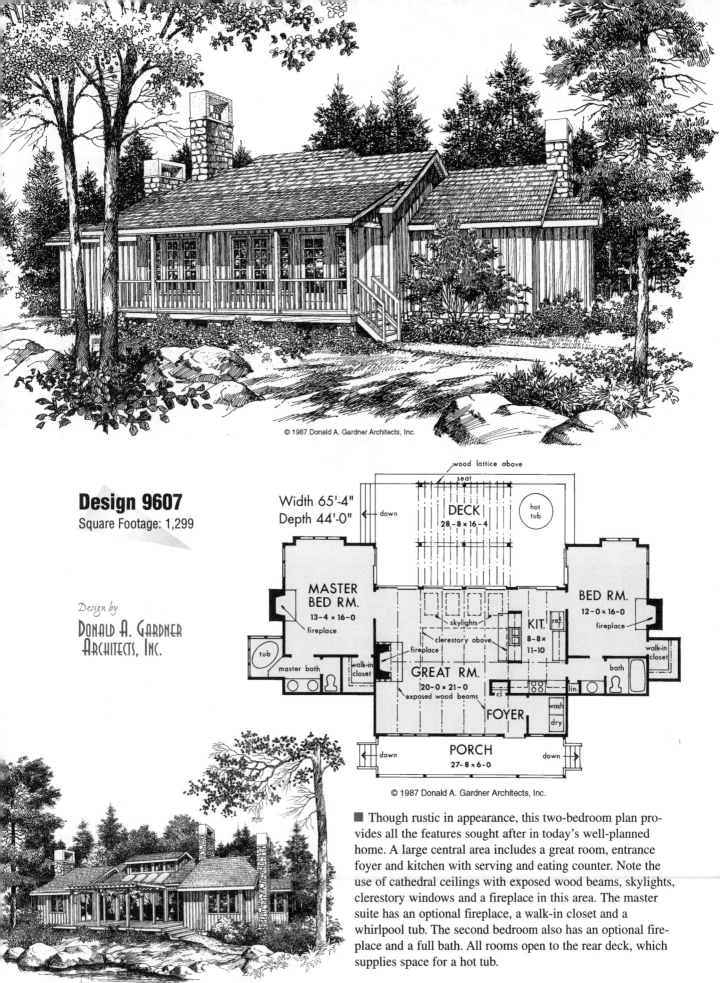

© 1987 Donald A. Gardner Architects, Inc.

Design 9607

Square Footage: 1,299

Design by

Donald A. Gardner Architects, Inc.

Width 65'-4"
Depth 44'-0"

wood lattice above

seat

down

DECK
28-8 × 16-4

hot tub

MASTER BED RM.
13-4 × 16-0

fireplace

skylights

clerestory above

KIT.
8-8 × 11-10

ref.

BED RM.
12-0 × 16-0

fireplace

tub

master bath

walk-in closet

fireplace

GREAT RM.
20-0 × 21-0

exposed wood beams

FOYER

bath

walk-in closet

cl

lin.

wash

dry

PORCH
27-8 × 6-0

down

down

© 1987 Donald A. Gardner Architects, Inc.

■ Though rustic in appearance, this two-bedroom plan provides all the features sought after in today's well-planned home. A large central area includes a great room, entrance foyer and kitchen with serving and eating counter. Note the use of cathedral ceilings with exposed wood beams, skylights, clerestory windows and a fireplace in this area. The master suite has an optional fireplace, a walk-in closet and a whirlpool tub. The second bedroom also has an optional fireplace and a full bath. All rooms open to the rear deck, which supplies space for a hot tub.

Rear Elevation

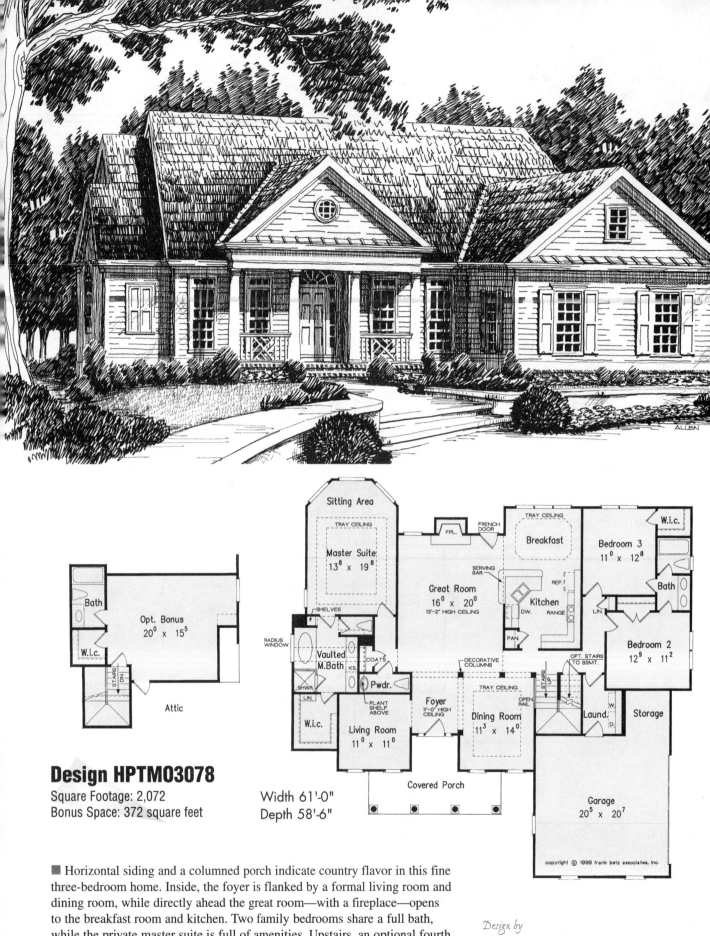

Design HPTM03078

Square Footage: 2,072
Bonus Space: 372 square feet

Width 61'-0"
Depth 58'-6"

■ Horizontal siding and a columned porch indicate country flavor in this fine three-bedroom home. Inside, the foyer is flanked by a formal living room and dining room, while directly ahead the great room—with a fireplace—opens to the breakfast room and kitchen. Two family bedrooms share a full bath, while the private master suite is full of amenities. Upstairs, an optional fourth bedroom provides plenty of future expansion opportunities. Please specify basement or crawlspace foundation when ordering.

Design by
©Frank Betz Associates, Inc.

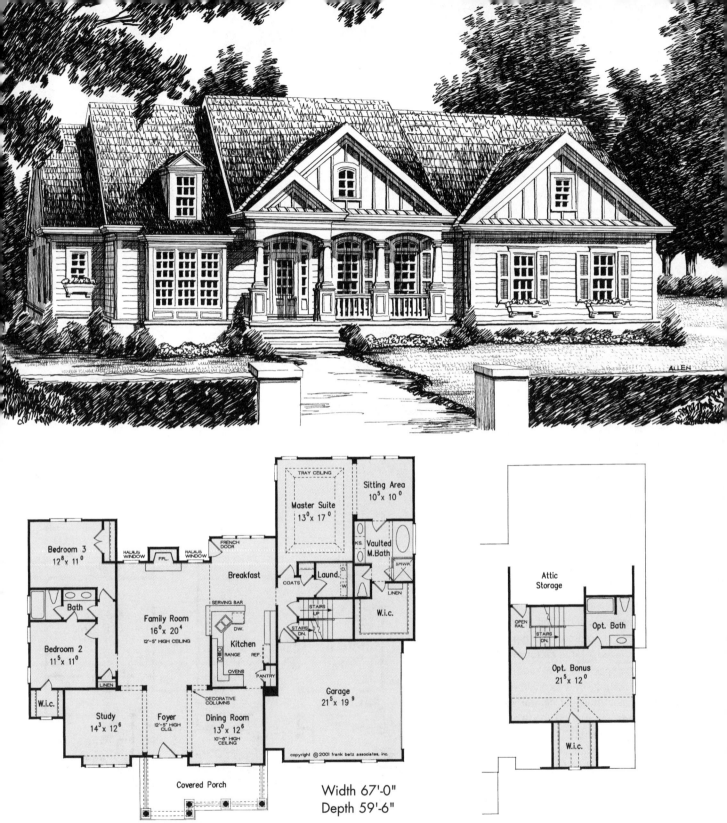

Design HPTM03079

Square Footage: 2,258
Bonus Space: 441 square feet

Design by
© FRANK BETZ ASSOCIATES, INC.

■ This charming cottage design offers rustic character and traditional simplicity. The quaint covered porch welcomes you inside to a foyer flanked by the formal dining room and study. The central family room features a cozy fireplace. The kitchen serves the breakfast room, which accesses the rear through a French door. Two family bedrooms that share a hall bath are located to the left side of the plan. The secluded master suite is on the opposite side of the home and is enhanced by a sitting room. Please specify basement or crawlspace foundation when ordering.

© 1989 Donald A. Gardner Architects, Inc.

Design 9611

Square Footage: 1,817

■ This inviting ranch offers many special features uncommon to a typical house this size. A large entrance foyer leads to the spacious great room with cathedral ceiling, fireplace and operable skylights that allow for natural ventilation. A bedroom just off the foyer doubles nicely as a study. The large master suite contains a walk-in closet and a pampering master bath with double-bowl vanity, shower and whirlpool tub. For outdoor living, look to the open deck with spa at the great room and kitchen, as well as the covered deck at the master suite.

Design by
DONALD A. GARDNER
ARCHITECTS, INC.

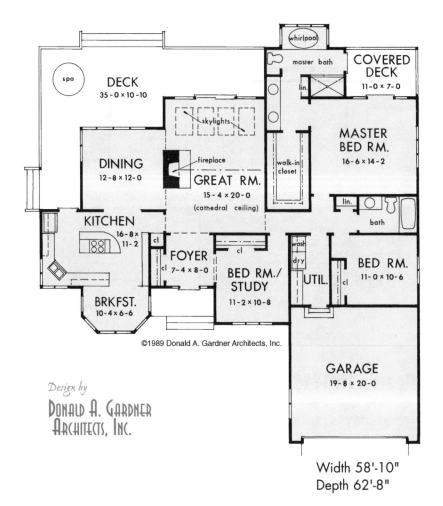

whirlpool

master bath

COVERED DECK
11-0 × 7-0

spa

DECK
35-0 × 10-10

skylights

MASTER BED RM.
16-6 × 14-2

DINING
12-8 × 12-0

fireplace

GREAT RM.
15-4 × 20-0
(cathedral ceiling)

walk-in closet

lin.

lin.

bath

KITCHEN
16-8 × 11-2

cl

cl

FOYER
7-4 × 8-0

cl

BED RM./STUDY
11-2 × 10-8

wash

dry

UTIL.

cl

BED RM.
11-0 × 10-6

BRKFST.
10-4 × 6-6

©1989 Donald A. Gardner Architects, Inc.

GARAGE
19-8 × 20-0

Width 58'-10"
Depth 62'-8"

376

Sun Country Vistas:

One-story homes designed for sunny climes

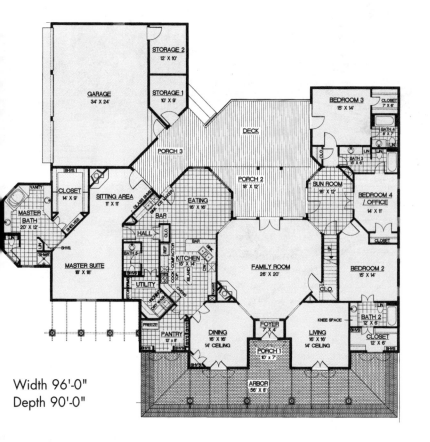

Width 96'-0"
Depth 90'-0"

Design HPTM03080
Square Footage: 3,960

■ A hipped roofline, with varying elevations, accents this stunning Mediterranean design and lends superb curb appeal. Double doors in the uniquely shaped family room open to the rear porch and deck. The large family room, complete with a corner fireplace, is accessible from all points of the house—kitchen area, deck, dining room, living room and the hallway leading to the sleeping quarters on the right side of the plan—creating a perfect hub of activity. The master suite features a private bath, a large walk-in closet and a sitting room with a fireplace. The three-car garage holds a convenient storage area. Please specify basement, crawlspace or slab foundation when ordering.

Design by
©Breland & Farmer Designers, Inc.

Design HPTM03081

Square Footage: 2,473

L

■ Luxurious living begins as soon as you step into the entryway of this home. Double doors open to the foyer, which features columns and a barrel-vaulted ceiling; combined living and dining rooms are straight ahead. The octagonal kitchen serves this area with a pass-through counter. Two master suites characterize this plan as the perfect vacation retreat. Two guest rooms enjoy quiet locales and direct access to the master baths. Outdoor living areas include a master lanai and another lanai that stretches around the back of the house. A pool bath is easily accessible from the lanai. A two-car garage and a utility room finish off the plan.

Design by
©THE SATER DESIGN COLLECTION

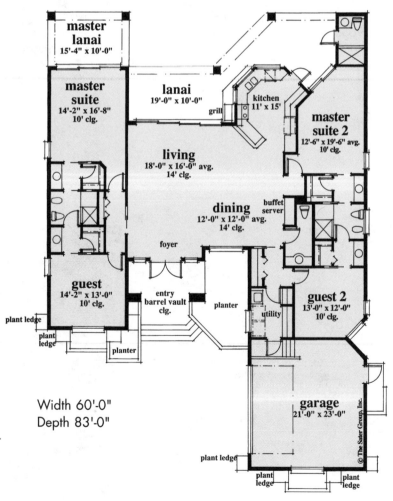

Width 60'-0"
Depth 83'-0"

Design HPTM03082

Square Footage: 2,387

■ This sunny design opens through double doors into the great room. A rounded dining area contributes a sense of the dramatic and is easily served by the roomy kitchen. A relaxing study provides outdoor access. Two secondary bedrooms enjoy ample closet space and share a bath that includes dual vanities. In the master suite, a tiered ceiling and lots of windows gain attention. A luxury bath with a compartmented toilet, a garden tub, dual vanities and a separate shower also offers a walk-in closet. A bath with a stall shower serves the outdoor living areas.

Design by
© The Sater Design Collection

Width 53'-6"
Depth 94'-6"

379

Design HPTM03083

Square Footage: 1,575

■ A lovely facade opens this one-story home, with gable ends and dormer windows as decorative features. The interior opens with vaulted family and dining rooms. The family room holds a fireplace; the dining room is defined by columns. The kitchen attaches to a bayed breakfast nook with a vaulted ceiling. Bedrooms are separated, with family bedrooms on the right side of the plan and the master suite on the left. The master bedroom has a tray ceiling; the bath is vaulted. A large walk-in closet graces the suite. Please specify basement or crawlspace foundation when ordering.

Design by
© FRANK BETZ ASSOCIATES, INC.

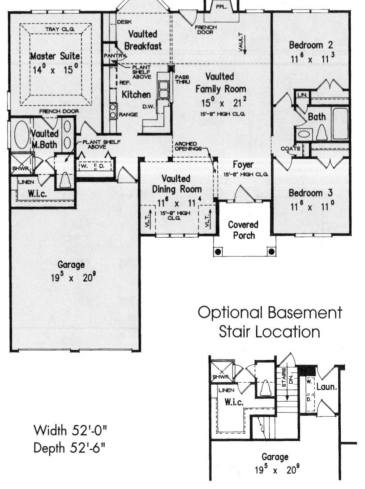

Width 52'-0"
Depth 52'-6"

Optional Basement Stair Location

380

Design HPTM03084

Square Footage: 1,271

Design by
© FRANK BETZ ASSOCIATES, INC.

■ Spaciousness is the key to this charming three-bedroom home. The decorative columns that define the formal dining room create an open living area at the center of this floor plan. Intimate dining is enjoyed in the breakfast nook which is nestled between the galley kitchen and the utility closet. The great room boasts an elegant fireplace flanked by radius windows. The sleeping quarters are found on the left where two family bedrooms share a full bath. The master suite pampers with a large walk-in closet and a lavish private bath—note the tray ceiling in the master bedroom. Please specify basement or crawlspace foundations when ordering.

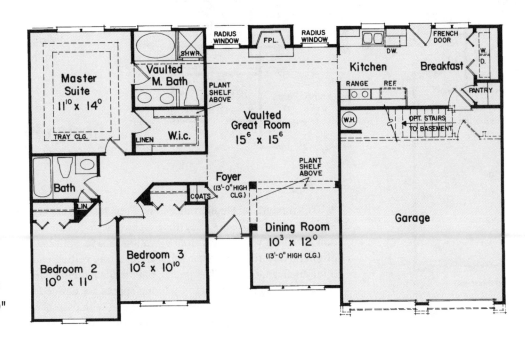

Width 56'-6"
Depth 33'-10"

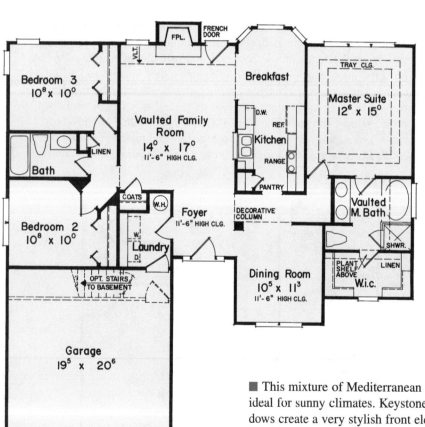

Width 49'-0"
Depth 49'-0"

Design HPTM03085
Square Footage: 1,392

■ This mixture of Mediterranean and French styles makes for a home that is ideal for sunny climates. Keystone arches, nested gables and shuttered windows create a very stylish front elevation. Inside, split-bedroom planning offers privacy for the master suite. Here, a tray ceiling and a magnificent view offer an elegant touch. The private bath holds a double-sink vanity and separate tub and shower. The family living spaces are defined with archways and a decorative column—perfect for entertaining with ease of movement. Please specify basement or crawlspace foundation when ordering.

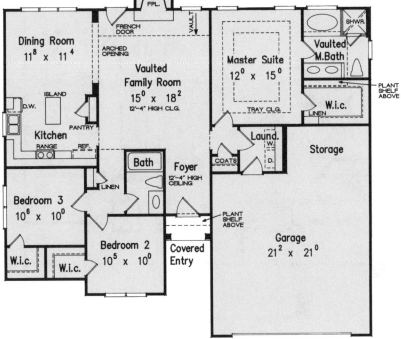

Dining Room
11⁸ x 11⁴

FRENCH DOOR

ARCHED OPENING

FPL.

VAULT

Vaulted Family Room
15⁰ x 18²
12'-4" HIGH CLG.

ISLAND

D.W.

Kitchen

RANGE   REF.

PANTRY

Bath

LINEN

Foyer
12'-4" CEILING

Bedroom 3
10⁶ x 10⁰

W.i.c.   W.i.c.

Bedroom 2
10⁵ x 10⁰

Covered Entry

PLANT SHELF ABOVE

COATS

Laund.
W.

D.

Master Suite
12⁰ x 15⁰

TRAY CLG.

SHWR.

Vaulted M.Bath

PLANT SHELF ABOVE

W.i.c.

LINEN

Storage

Garage
21² x 21⁰

PLANT SHELF ABOVE

Design by
© Frank Betz Associates, Inc.

Width 49'-6"
Depth 45'-4"

Design HPTM03086
Square Footage: 1,361

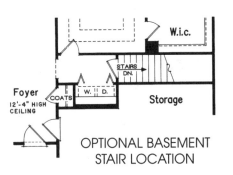

Foyer
12'-4" CEILING

COATS   W.   D.

STAIRS DN.

W.i.c.

Storage

OPTIONAL BASEMENT
STAIR LOCATION

■ An elegant addition to any neighborhood, this one-story stucco home offers Old World charm. The twelve-foot-plus ceiling of the foyer continues through to the spacious family room that holds an impressive fireplace flanked by views to the backyard. An arched opening leads to the formal dining room with its own expansive view. The island kitchen is sure to please the family cook. Two family bedrooms, each with a walk-in closet, are found at the end of a short angled hall where they share a full bath. The master suite, on the right, features a tray ceiling, walk-in closet and lavish bath complete with a garden tub. The utility room doubles as a mudroom leading to and from the garage. Please specify basement or crawlspace foundation when ordering.

© HOME DESIGN SERVICES, INC.

J.N. HANSEN PIL

Design 8634

Square Footage: 1,869

Design by
HOME DESIGN SERVICES

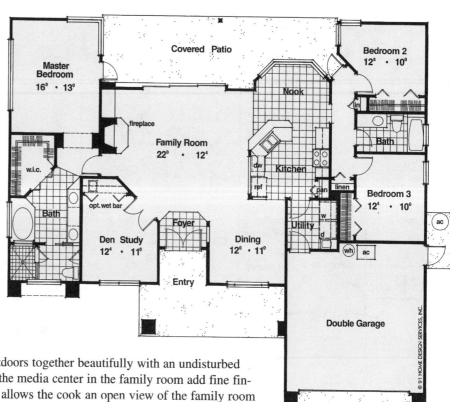

Master Bedroom
16⁰ · 13⁰

Covered Patio

Bedroom 2
12⁸ · 10⁰

fireplace

Nook

Bath

w.i.c.

Family Room
22⁰ · 12⁴

dw   Kitchen

ref

pan linen

Bath

opt. wet bar

Bedroom 3
12⁴ · 10⁰

Foyer

Utility

w

d

ac

Den Study
12⁴ · 11⁰

Dining
12⁰ · 11⁰

wh ac

Entry

Double Garage

© '91 HOME DESIGN SERVICES, INC.

■ This open plan brings indoors and outdoors together beautifully with an undisturbed view of the rear yard. The fireplace and the media center in the family room add fine finishing touches. The open kitchen design allows the cook an open view of the family room and easy service to the breakfast nook and dining room. The secondary bedrooms feature a "kids" door off the hall ideal for bathroom access from the patio area. The super master suite features mitered glass for a great view of the patio area as well as a bath with a walk-in closet, dual lavatories and spa tub. There is even a courtesy door off the toilet area accessing the den/study.

Width 61'-8"
Depth 55'-0"

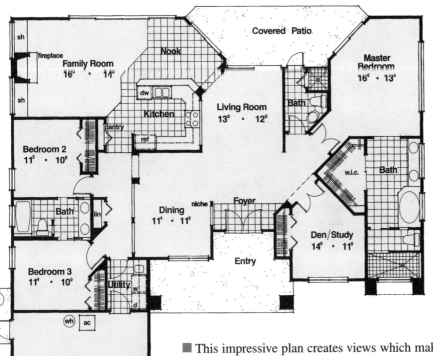

Family Room
16⁰ · 14⁰

sh
fireplace
sh

Nook

Covered Patio

Master
Bedroom
16⁶ · 13⁴

Bath

dw
Kitchen
ref
pantry

Living Room
13⁰ · 12⁰

Bedroom 2
11² · 10⁰

Bath
lin

Bath
w.i.c.

Dining
11⁴ · 11⁰

niche
Foyer

Entry

Den/Study
14⁰ · 11⁰

Bedroom 3
11⁴ · 10⁰

Utility
w
d

wh   ac
ac

Double Garage

© 91 HOME DESIGN SERVICES, INC.

Width 60'-8"
Depth 62'-8"

Design 8639

Square Footage: 2,149

Design by
Home Design Services

■ This impressive plan creates views which make this house look much larger than it really is. Upon entry into this four-bedroom, three-bath home, the formal living room overflows to outdoor living space. The formal dining room is designed with open wall areas for an air of spaciousness. A decorative arch leads to the family spaces of the home. The two bedrooms share a "pullman" bath, accessible only from the rooms themselves for total privacy. The kitchen/family room/nook area is large and inviting, all with beautiful views of the outdoor living spaces. The master wing of the home is off the den/study and the pool bath. Double doors welcome you into the master suite with a glass bedwall and angled sliding glass doors to the patio. The efficient use of space makes the bath as functional as it is beautiful.

J.N.HANSEN P.T.L.

Design HPTM03087

Square Footage: 2,456

■ Multi-paned windows, a hipped roof and a columned, vaulted entry lend a Mediterranean aura to this three-bedroom home. Elegance continues inside with columns defining the living room and dining area. Entertaining will be easy in this sizable living room with a fireplace and built-in entertainment center. The master suite enjoys a tray ceiling, walk-in closet and sumptuous bath including dual vanity sinks, a garden tub set off by a glass-block window, and separate shower. A guest suite with a private bath lies nearby. A bay-windowed breakfast nook features views of the rear covered patio and access to the convenient kitchen with a walk-in pantry.

Design by
© HOME DESIGN SERVICES, INC.

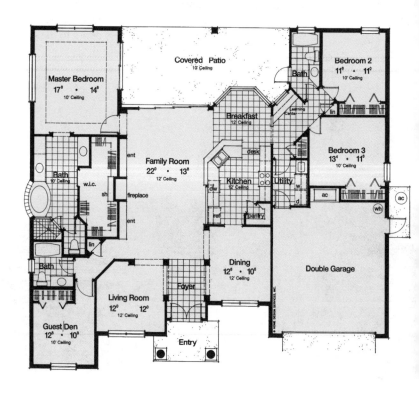

Width 63'-8"
Depth 58'-0"

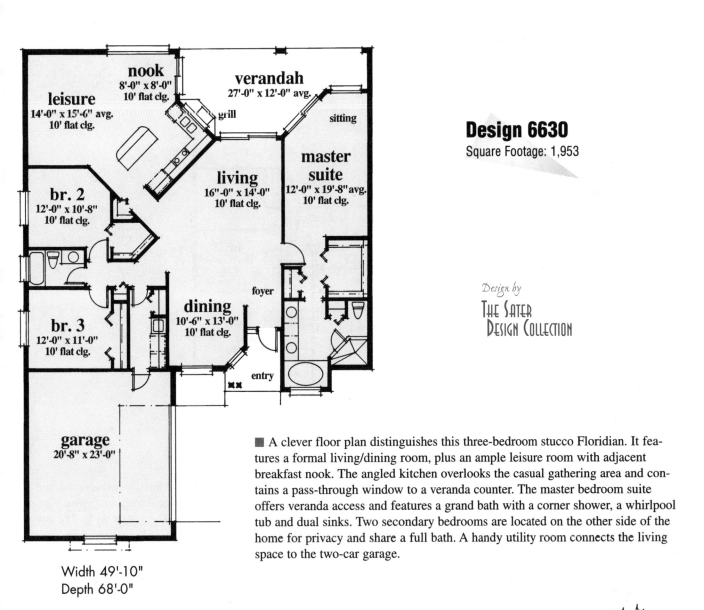

leisure
14'-0" x 15'-6" avg.
10' flat clg.

nook
8'-0" x 8'-0"
10' flat clg.

verandah
27'-0" x 12'-0" avg.

grill

sitting

Design 6630
Square Footage: 1,953

br. 2
12'-0" x 10'-8"
10' flat clg.

living
16"-0" x 14'-0"
10' flat clg.

master
suite
12'-0" x 19'-8" avg.
10' flat clg.

br. 3
12'-0" x 11'-0"
10' flat clg.

foyer

dining
10'-6" x 13'-0"
10' flat clg.

entry

Design by
The Sater
Design Collection

garage
20'-8" x 23'-0"

Width 49'-10"
Depth 68'-0"

■ A clever floor plan distinguishes this three-bedroom stucco Floridian. It features a formal living/dining room, plus an ample leisure room with adjacent breakfast nook. The angled kitchen overlooks the casual gathering area and contains a pass-through window to a veranda counter. The master bedroom suite offers veranda access and features a grand bath with a corner shower, a whirlpool tub and dual sinks. Two secondary bedrooms are located on the other side of the home for privacy and share a full bath. A handy utility room connects the living space to the two-car garage.

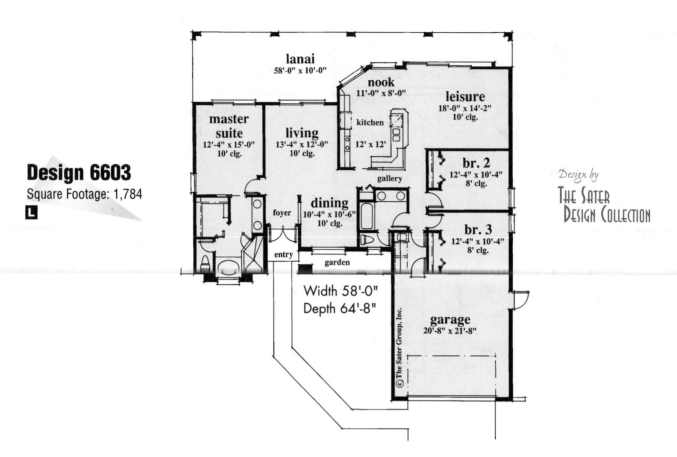

lanai
58'-0" x 10'-0"

nook
11'-0" x 8'-0"

leisure
18'-0" x 14'-2"
10' clg.

master
suite
12'-4" x 15'-0"
10' clg.

living
13'-4" x 12'-0"
10' clg.

kitchen
12' x 12'

br. 2
12'-4" x 10'-4"
8' clg.

gallery

Design 6603

Square Footage: 1,784

L

foyer

dining
10'-4" x 10'-6"
10' clg.

br. 3
12'-4" x 10'-4"
8' clg.

Design by
**THE SATER
DESIGN COLLECTION**

entry

garden

Width 58'-0"
Depth 64'-8"

© The Sater Group, Inc.

garage
20'-8" x 21'-8"

■ This one-story home is filled with amenities. A raised entry features double doors that lead to the grand foyer. From the formal living room, large sliding glass doors open to the lanai, providing natural light and outdoor views. The dining room is separated from the foyer and living area by a half-wall and a column. The large kitchen, breakfast nook and leisure room round out the informal gathering areas. The secondary bedrooms are split from the master wing. The cozy master suite sports a large walk-in closet, a walk-in shower, a whirlpool tub and a private water closet.

Design 6629

Square Footage: 2,214

■ Make yourself at home in this delightful one-story home. The dramatic entry—with an arched opening—leads to a comfortable interior. Volume ceilings highlight the main living areas which include a formal dining room and a great room with access to one of the lanais. In the turreted study, quiet time is assured with double doors closing off the rest of the house. Nearby, the master bedroom suite features a luxury bath with a double-bowl vanity, a bumped-out whirlpool tub and a separate shower. The secondary bedrooms reside on the other side of the house and utilize a full bath that also accommodates outdoor living areas.

Design by
The Sater
Design Collection

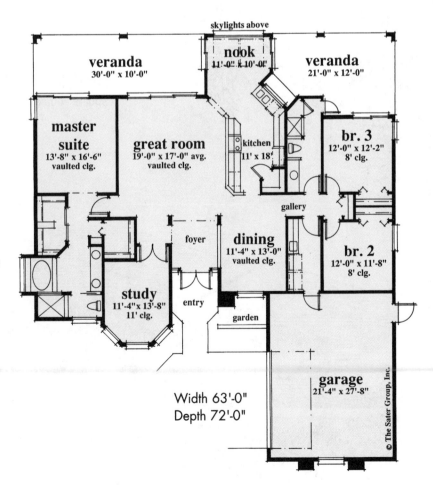

This Florida classic has been an award winner, as well as a family favorite. Just looking at the flow of this plan will tell you why it's a best seller. The formal living/dining area provides impact as you enter this home. Tiered ceiling treatments add crisp contemporary flair to the ceilings. The double-door entry to the master's retreat leads you to a portico-style space, which adds privacy when the doors are opened. The mitered glass treatment in the large sleeping area provides unobstructed views of the outdoor living areas. The master bath is second to none in terms of amenities and intelligent use of space, right down to His and Hers walk-in closets. The secondary bedroom wing has everything for the large family. Note the "kids' door" which accesses the rear patio area from the hallway to the bedrooms and bath. A summer kitchen for outdoor entertaining is icing on the cake!

Width 68'-8"
Depth 72'-8"

Design by
HOME DESIGN SERVICES

Design 8619
Square Footage: 2,385

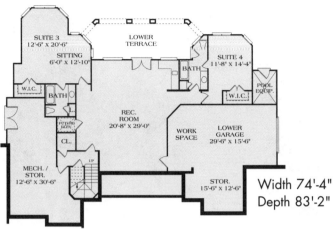

Design A379

Main Level: 2,747 square feet
Lower Level: 1,735 square feet
Total: 4,482 square feet

Width 74'-4"
Depth 83'-2"

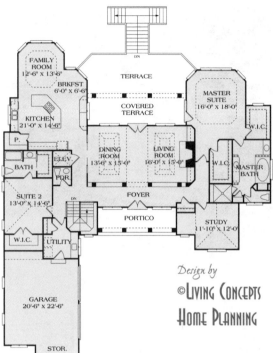

Design by
© LIVING CONCEPTS
HOME PLANNING

■ The towering entry of this stucco beauty makes for a gracious entrance to the floor plan inside. Double doors open off the covered front porch to a dining room and a living room defined by columns. A fireplace warms the living room. To the back are the casual areas: a family room, breakfast nook and gourmet kitchen. A bedroom with full bath and a utility area sit directly behind the two-car garage. The master suite features a study and private bath. The lower level can be developed into a recreation room or additional bedroom suites.

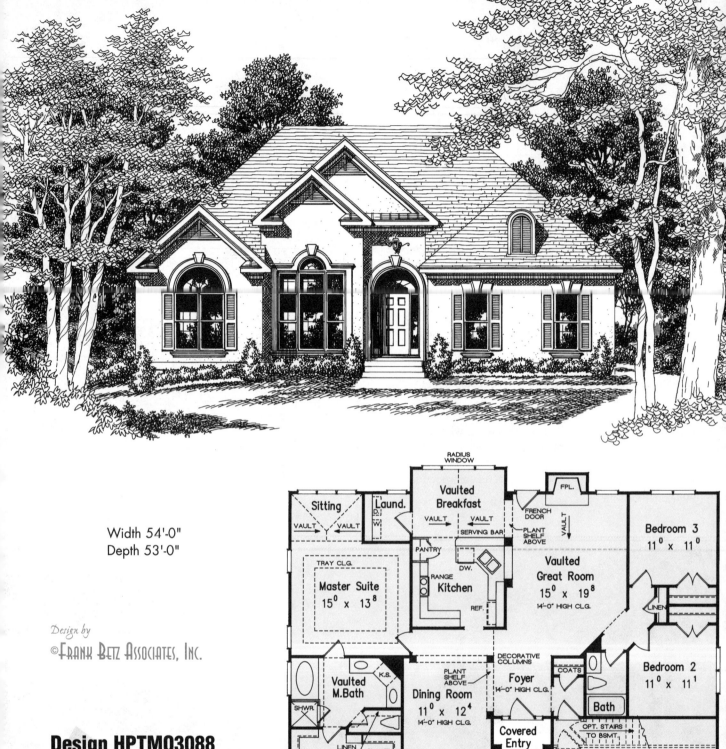

Width 54'-0"
Depth 53'-0"

Design by
©FRANK BETZ ASSOCIATES, INC.

Design HPTM03088

Square Footage: 1,694

■ Keystone arches and a stucco exterior create a sense of the Mediterranean on this one-story plan—perfect for a sunny climate. The recessed entry opens to the foyer leading to the vaulted great room. Breathtaking views and a magnificent fireplace create a memorable first impression. Decorative columns are used throughout to define areas and keep the living spaces open and airy. Both the formal dining room and the vaulted breakfast nook boast opulent views of the outdoors. To the left, the master suite delights with a vaulted sitting room that looks out to the back. Two family bedrooms reside on the right where they share a full bath. Please specify basement or crawlspace foundation when ordering.

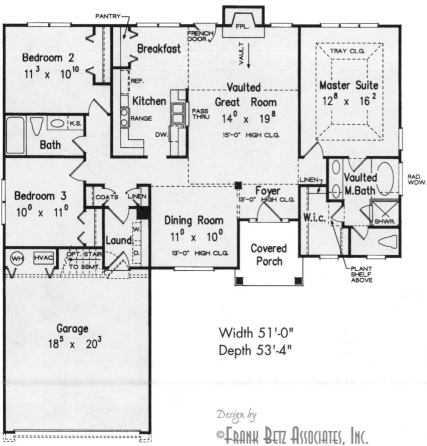

PANTRY

Breakfast

FRENCH DOOR

FPL.

Bedroom 2
11³ x 10¹⁰

REF.

Kitchen

RANGE

VAULT

Vaulted
Great Room
14⁰ x 19⁸

15'-0" HIGH CLG.

Master Suite
12⁸ x 16²

TRAY CLG.

K.S.

Bath

PASS THRU

DW.

Bedroom 3
10⁰ x 11⁰

COATS

LINEN

Foyer
13'-0" HIGH CLG.

LINEN

Vaulted
M.Bath

RAD. WDW.

Laund

W.i.c.

SHWR.

WH

HVAC

OPT. STAIR TO BSMT.

W.

D.

Dining Room
11⁰ x 10⁰
13'-0" HIGH CLG.

Covered
Porch

PLANT SHELF ABOVE

Garage
18⁵ x 20³

Width 51'-0"
Depth 53'-4"

Design by
© Frank Betz Associates, Inc.

Design HPTMO3089

Square Footage: 1,459

■ The floor plan of this stylish one-story home is both functional and attractive. The foyer, great room and dining room combine in one open area, with a single column acting as a partition. The master suite is found to the right of the great room, secluded from Bedrooms 2 and 3 and general traffic. The compartmented master bath boasts a vaulted ceiling, separate tub and shower, and walk-in closet. The kitchen, to the left of the great room, is flanked by the dining room and breakfast room, which features a large pantry. The laundry room also serves as a mudroom and is conveniently near the two family bedrooms. Please specify basement or crawlspace foundation when ordering.

Design 8602

Square Footage: 2,564

■ The living areas of this
Mediterranean home are enhanced
by interesting angles and are
designed to take advantage of sunlight. Double doors reveal a dramatic foyer that opens to the living and
dining rooms. In the sunken dining
room, columns add to the formality.
The kitchen is centered around the
breakfast nook and dining room for
casual eating or formal entertaining.
The master suite offers seclusion as
well as a fine view of the deck area.
A walk-in closet and a tiled master
bath with a double vanity and spa
tub complete the master suite.

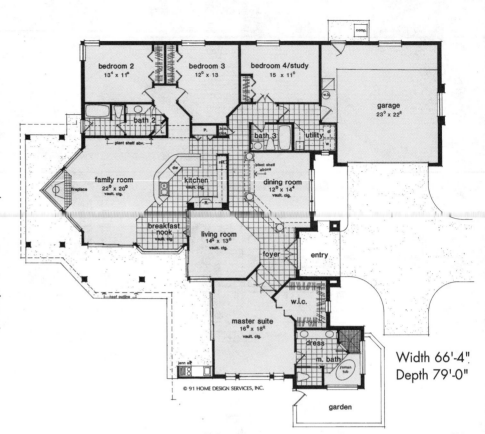

bedroom 2
13⁴ x 11⁸

bedroom 3
12⁰ x 13

bedroom 4/study
15 x 11⁰

garage
23⁰ x 22⁸

bath 2

bath 3

utility

plant shelf abv.

family room
22⁸ x 20⁰
vault. clg.

fireplace

kitchen
vault. clg.

plant shelf
above

dining room
12⁰ x 14⁴
vault. clg.

breakfast
nook
vault. clg.

living room
14⁰ x 13⁰
vault. clg.

foyer

entry

roof outline

w.i.c.

master suite
16⁰ x 18⁰
vault. clg.

dress

m. bath

roman
tub

jenn air

garden

© 91 HOME DESIGN SERVICES, INC.

Width 66'-4"
Depth 79'-0"

Design by
HOME DESIGN SERVICES

© HOME DESIGN SERVICES, INC.

R. BRADSHAW

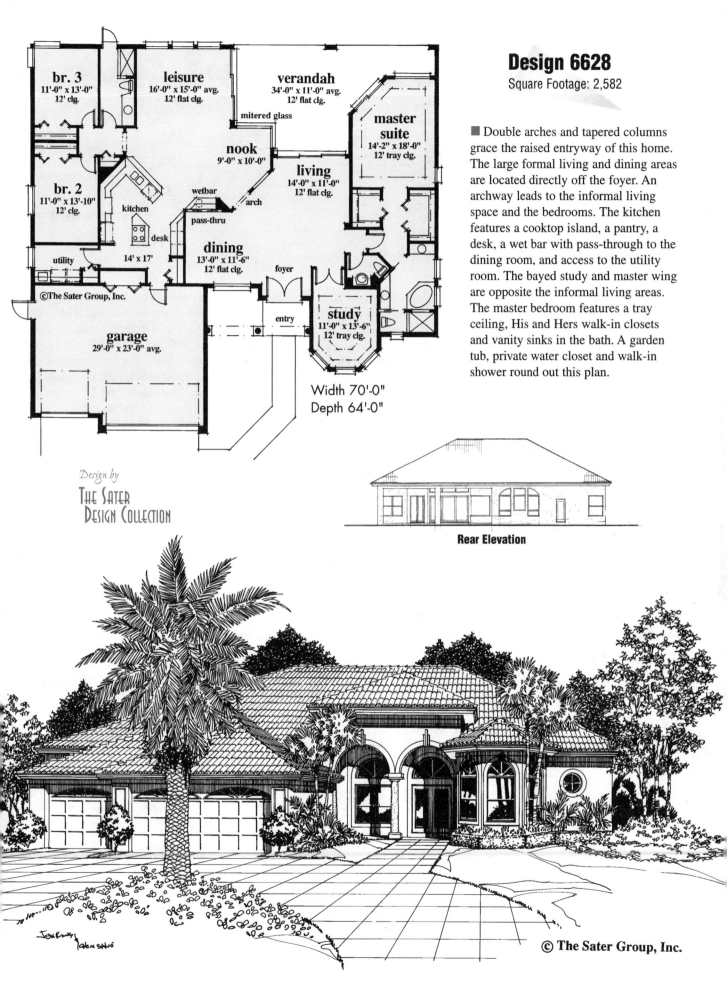

br. 3
11'-0" x 13'-0"
12' clg.

leisure
16'-0" x 15'-0" avg.
12' flat clg.

verandah
34'-0" x 11'-0" avg.
12' flat clg.

mitered glass

master suite
14'-2" x 18'-0"
12' tray clg.

nook
9'-0" x 10'-0"

living
14'-0" x 11'-0"
12' flat clg.

br. 2
11'-0" x 13'-10"
12' clg.

wetbar

arch

pass-thru

kitchen

desk

14' x 17'

dining
13'-0" x 11'-6"
12' flat clg.

foyer

utility

©The Sater Group, Inc.

garage
29'-0" x 23'-0" avg.

entry

study
11'-0" x 13'-6"
12' tray clg.

Width 70'-0"
Depth 64'-0"

Design by
THE SATER DESIGN COLLECTION

Design 6628

Square Footage: 2,582

■ Double arches and tapered columns grace the raised entryway of this home. The large formal living and dining areas are located directly off the foyer. An archway leads to the informal living space and the bedrooms. The kitchen features a cooktop island, a pantry, a desk, a wet bar with pass-through to the dining room, and access to the utility room. The bayed study and master wing are opposite the informal living areas. The master bedroom features a tray ceiling, His and Hers walk-in closets and vanity sinks in the bath. A garden tub, private water closet and walk-in shower round out this plan.

Rear Elevation

© The Sater Group, Inc.

395

© The Sater Group, Inc.

Alternate Elevation

Design 6658
Square Footage: 1,647

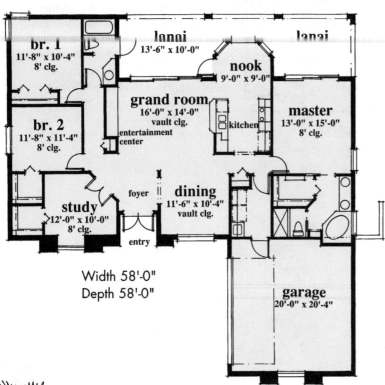

br. 1
11'-8" x 10'-4"
8' clg.

lanai
13'-6" x 10'-0"

lanai

nook
9'-0" x 9'-0"

grand room
16'-0" x 14'-0"
vault clg.

kitchen

master
13'-0" x 15'-0"
8' clg.

br. 2
11'-8" x 11'-4"
8' clg.

entertainment center

study
12'-0" x 10'-0"
8' clg.

foyer

dining
11'-6" x 10'-4"
vault clg.

entry

garage
20'-0" x 20'-4"

Width 58'-0"
Depth 58'-0"

■ This glorious sun-country cottage gives you the option of two elevations: choose from a hipped or gabled roof at the front entrance. Either way, this plan gives a new look to comfortable resort living. Designed for casual living, the foyer opens to the dining room and grand room while providing great views of the rear lanai and beyond. The grand room has a built-in entertainment center and a snack bar served from the kitchen. The galley kitchen has a gazebo dining nook with a door to the lanai. The master suite is split from the family sleeping wing and features a walk-in closet and a compartmented bath. Two secondary bedrooms, a study and full cabana bath complete this luxurious home.

Design by
The Sater
Design Collection

© The Sater Group, Inc.

Design by
©ALAN MASCORD
DESIGN ASSOCIATES, INC.

Design 7411
Square Footage: 2,755

PATIO

DEN
12/0 X 10/8
(9' CLG.)

NOOK
9/2 X 10/0

VAULTED
FAMILY
16/6 X 21/4 +

LIVING
16/0 X 16/4
(13'-4" CLG.)

MASTER
15/8 X 15/8
(9' CLG.)

BR. 2
11/6 X 12/0

DESK

PANTRY

LIN.

15/8 X 9/6

DINING
11/0 X 16/8

(13'-4" CLG.)

REF.

BR. 3
12/8 X 11/0

Width 84'-0"
Depth 73'-0"

GARAGE
20/6 X 19/8 +

25/2 X 11/0

■ Squared columns flank an appealing entrance to this three-bedroom home. Columns continue inside, helping to define the formal dining room and formal living room, and separating the family room/nook area from the kitchen. The gourmet cook of the family will be ecstatic when presented with this amenity-filled kitchen. The living room and the vaulted family room share a through-fireplace. A cozy den opens through double doors just off the nook area. To the left of the plan, two family bedrooms share a full bath between them. Located at the opposite end of the home, the master bedroom suite is sure to please with a double-door entry, walk-in closet, sumptuous bath and private access to the rear yard.

Design W014

Square Footage: 2,407

■ With clean lines, a tiled roof and a multi-windowed portico, this one-story contemporary home possesses plenty of curb appeal. Inside, the living/dining area is flooded with light from two walls of windows and French-door access to the spacious courtyard. Located in the left wing, the living area includes a U-shaped kitchen with a huge walk-in pantry, breakfast area and large great room with a fireplace. To the right of the foyer is the sleeping wing. Here, a deluxe master bedroom features two walk-in closets, a round tub and access to the courtyard. Two secondary bedrooms share a hall bath.

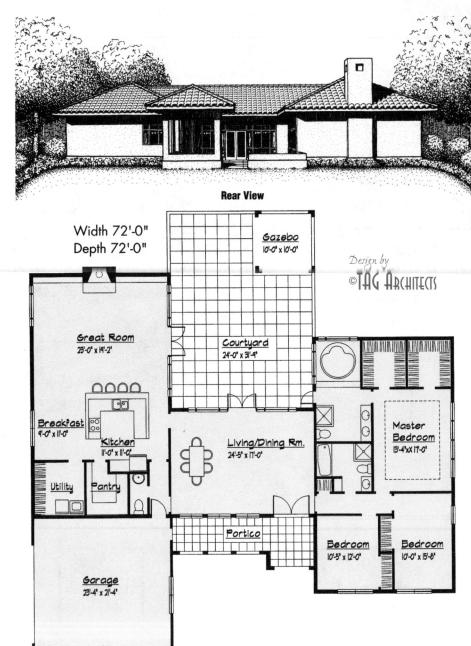

Rear View

Width 72'-0"
Depth 72'-0"

Design by
©TAG Architects

Gazebo
10'-0" x 10'-0"

Great Room
23'-0" x 19'-2"

Courtyard
24'-0" x 31'-4"

Master Bedroom
13'-4" X 17'-0"

Breakfast
9'-0" x 11'-0"

Kitchen
11'-0" x 11'-0"

Living/Dining Rm.
24'-5" x 17'-0"

Utility

Pantry

Portico

Bedroom
10'-5" x 12'-0"

Bedroom
10'-0" x 15'-8"

Garage
23'-4" x 21'-4"

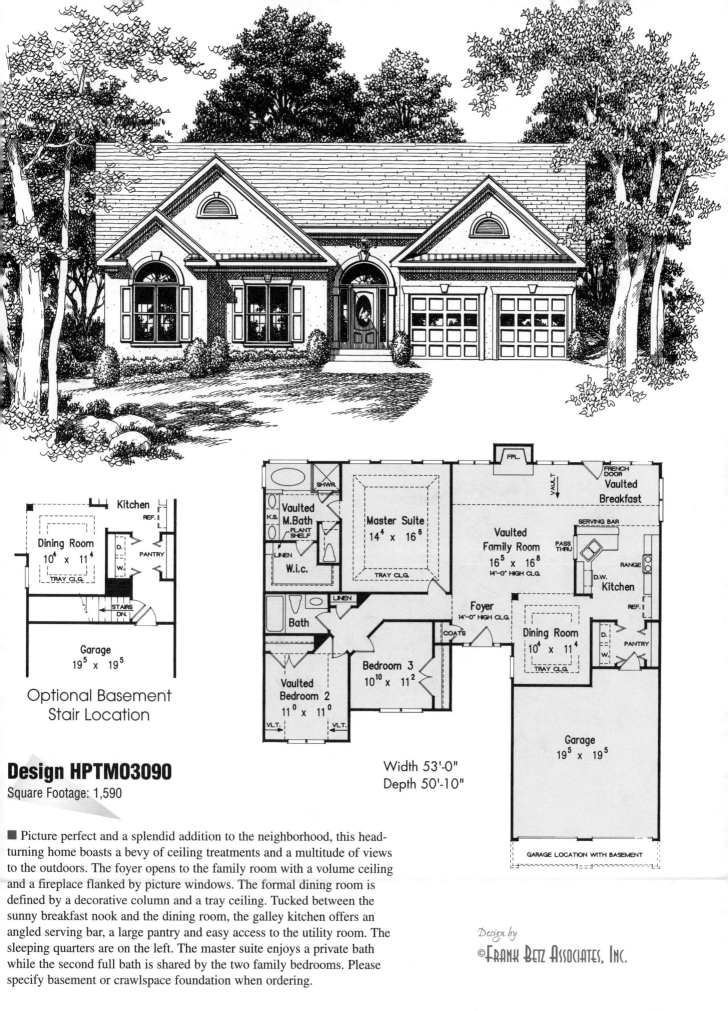

Kitchen

Dining Room
10⁴ x 11⁴
TRAY CLG.

REF.

PANTRY

D.
W.

STAIRS
DN.

Garage
19⁵ x 19⁵

Optional Basement Stair Location

Design HPTM03090

Square Footage: 1,590

SHWR.

K.S.

Vaulted M.Bath

PLANT SHELF

LINEN

W.i.c.

Bath

LINEN

Vaulted Bedroom 2
11⁰ x 11⁰

VLT.   VLT.

Master Suite
14⁴ x 16⁶
TRAY CLG.

Bedroom 3
10¹⁰ x 11²

FPL

VAULT

Vaulted Breakfast

Vaulted Family Room
16⁵ x 16⁸
14'-0" HIGH CLG.

SERVING BAR

PASS THRU

D.W.

RANGE

Kitchen

REF.

Dining Room
10⁴ x 11⁴
TRAY CLG.

Foyer
14'-0" HIGH CLG.

COATS

D.
W.

PANTRY

Garage
19⁵ x 19⁵

GARAGE LOCATION WITH BASEMENT

Width 53'-0"
Depth 50'-10"

■ Picture perfect and a splendid addition to the neighborhood, this head-turning home boasts a bevy of ceiling treatments and a multitude of views to the outdoors. The foyer opens to the family room with a volume ceiling and a fireplace flanked by picture windows. The formal dining room is defined by a decorative column and a tray ceiling. Tucked between the sunny breakfast nook and the dining room, the galley kitchen offers an angled serving bar, a large pantry and easy access to the utility room. The sleeping quarters are on the left. The master suite enjoys a private bath while the second full bath is shared by the two family bedrooms. Please specify basement or crawlspace foundation when ordering.

Design by
© FRANK BETZ ASSOCIATES, INC.

Width 151'-6"
Depth 54'-0"

Design by
©Home
Planners

Design 2258
Square Footage: 2,504

■ This Western ranch house is perfectly outfitted with all the amenities an active family desires. From the covered front porch, the angled foyer leads directly to the library and the grand living room. An expanse of windows and a rustic fire-place give the living room a casual elegance. The large, gal-ley-style kitchen is designed for efficient cooking and has an abundance of storage space along with a large snack bar. Two

family bedrooms feature walk-in closets and share a hall bath. The master suite boasts His and Her walk-in closets and a compartmented bath with dual vanities. The three-car garage joins the house with a service entrance complete with a full bath and large utility area. Don't miss the views from the nos-talgic look-out tower—the finishing touch for every home on the range!

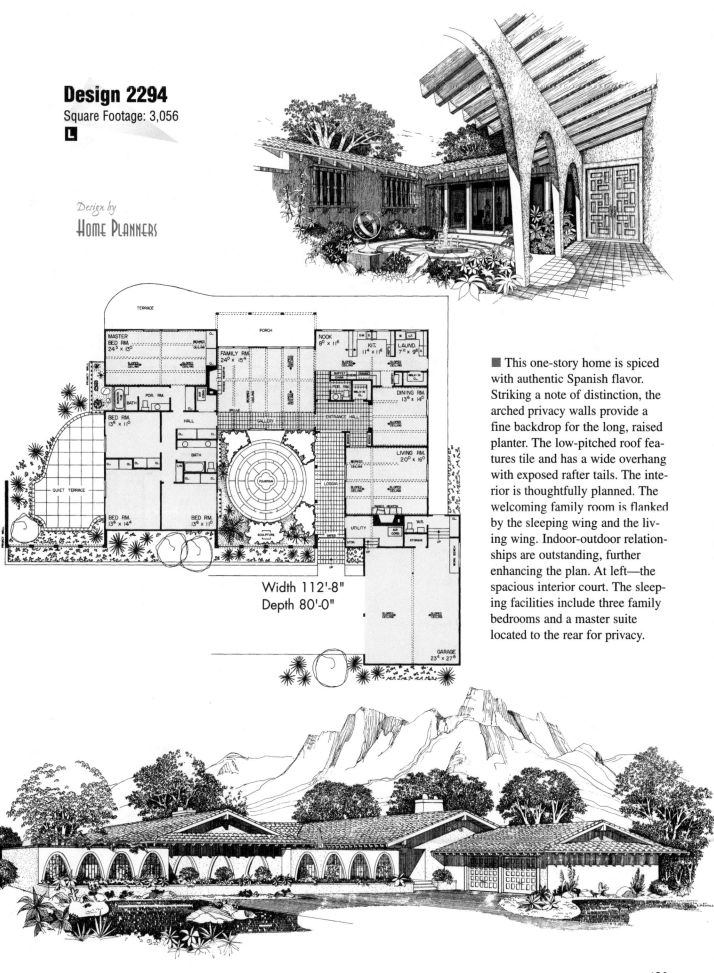

Design 2294

Square Footage: 3,056

L

Design by

HOME PLANNERS

■ This one-story home is spiced with authentic Spanish flavor. Striking a note of distinction, the arched privacy walls provide a fine backdrop for the long, raised planter. The low-pitched roof features tile and has a wide overhang with exposed rafter tails. The interior is thoughtfully planned. The welcoming family room is flanked by the sleeping wing and the living wing. Indoor-outdoor relationships are outstanding, further enhancing the plan. At left—the spacious interior court. The sleeping facilities include three family bedrooms and a master suite located to the rear for privacy.

Width 112'-8"
Depth 80'-0"

Design HPTM03091

Square Footage: 1,226

■ European detailing gives this house special appeal. Corner quoins, keystone lintels and multiple gables are just some of its exterior charms. Amenities abound inside with built-in plant shelves, niches and a tray ceiling in the master bedroom. The focal point of the vaulted great room is the fireplace, framed by a window and a French door. The galley kitchen leads to a well-lit breakfast area and convenient access to the garage. The split floor plan has two family bedrooms sharing a full bath to the left of the great room, and the master suite privately tucked at the right. Please specify basement or crawlspace foundation when ordering.

Design by
© FRANK BETZ ASSOCIATES, INC.

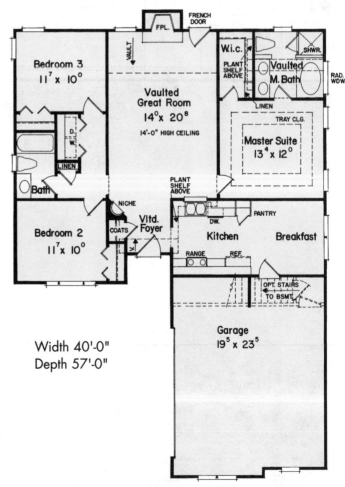

Width 40'-0"
Depth 57'-0"

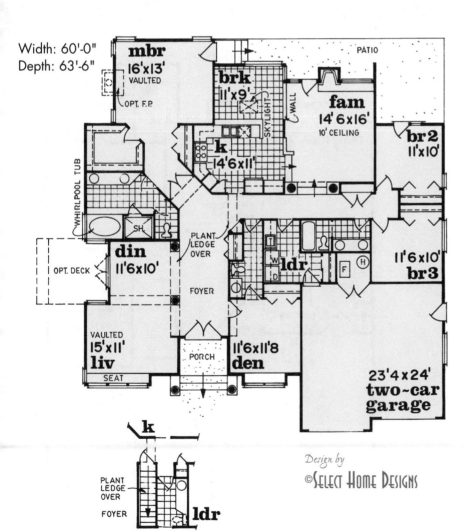

Width: 60'-0"
Depth: 63'-6"

mbr 16'x13' VAULTED
OPT. F.P.

brk 11'x9'

PATIO

fam 14'6x16'
10' CEILING

br2 11'x10'

k 14'6x11'

SKYLIGHT

WALL

WHIRLPOOL TUB

SH

PLANT LEDGE OVER

11'6x10'
br3

din 11'6x10'

OPT. DECK

W D

ldr

F

H

FOYER

VAULTED 15'x11' **liv**

SEAT

PORCH

11'6x11'8 **den**

23'4x24'
two~car garage

k

PLANT LEDGE OVER

FOYER

ldr

Optional Basement Stair Location

Design Q597
Square Footage: 2,471

■ Decorative columns with a plant ledge entablature define the living and dining room entrances. The den, tucked off the foyer, can double as a guest room or home office. The well-planned kitchen serves the eating bar and skylit breakfast room. Large walk-in and wall closets, a luxurious ensuite with double vanity, whirlpool tub and oversized shower, and patio access are just some of the master suite features. Two additional bedrooms share a main bath that includes a twin vanity. The large laundry area holds extra storage and a folding counter.

Design by
©Select Home Designs

403

Design HPTM03092

Square Footage: 1,346

■ Outdoor enthusiasts will adore the multitude of windows meticulously placed throughout this delightful three-bedroom home—and what better location than the Sun Belt? The foyer opens dramatically to the vaulted living room. The neighboring dining room sits in the bay window at the rear. The kitchen boasts a pantry and access to the laundry room while efficiently offering a serving bar to the dining and living rooms. The master suite is situated in the rear for privacy where luxury is defined with a tray ceiling, a walk-in closet and a lavish private bath. A vaulted bedroom sits to the immediate right of the foyer, perfect for weekend guests. Please specify basement or crawlspace foundation when ordering.

Design by
© Frank Betz Associates, Inc.

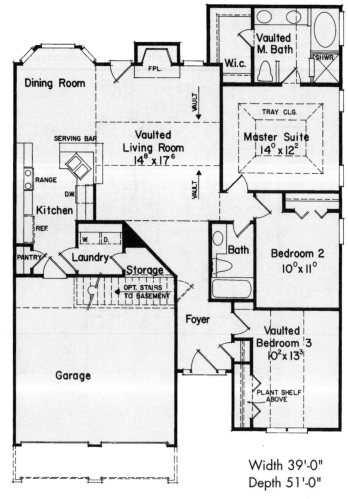

Width 39'-0"
Depth 51'-0"

404

Width 68'-10"
Depth 52'-0"

Design HPTM03093
Square Footage: 2,010

■ An arched entrance, a sunburst and sidelights around the four-panel door provide a touch of class to this European-style home. An angled bar opens the kitchen and breakfast room to the living room with bookcases and a fireplace. The master suite boasts a sloped ceiling and a private bath with a five-foot turning radius, dual vanities, and a separate tub and shower. Two family bedrooms provide ample closet space and share a full hall bath and linen closet. Don't miss the two-car garage located to the far right of the plan.

Design by
©Larry E. Belk Designs

Design HPTM03094

Square Footage: 1,259

■ Delighting with opulent windows, this one-story home is a perfect choice for the warmer climates of the Sun Belt region. The shaded front entry opens to the inviting vaulted great room. To the right, the efficient kitchen is flanked by the sun-dappled breakfast nook and the formal dining room—note the French door leading out to the covered porch where barbecues can be served rain or shine. The left side is reserved for the sleeping quarters. Here the master suite is steeped in elegance with a tray ceiling in the bedroom and a vaulted ceiling in the bath. Two family bedrooms share an additional full bath. Please specify basement or crawlspace foundation when ordering.

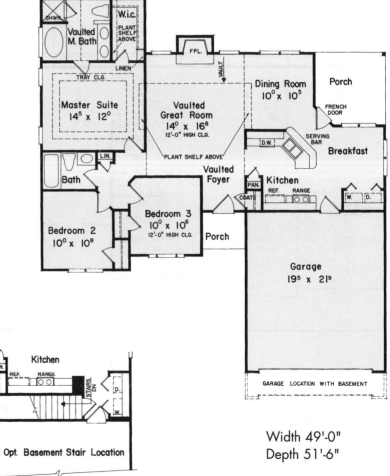

Width 49'-0"
Depth 51'-6"

Design by
©Frank Betz Associates, Inc.

406

Basic Plan

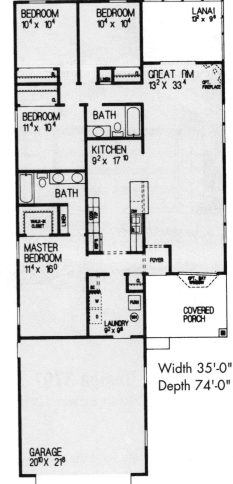

BEDROOM 10⁴ × 10⁴
BEDROOM 10⁴ × 10⁴
LANAI 13² × 9⁸
GREAT RM 13² × 33⁴ OPT. FIREPLACE
BEDROOM 11⁴ × 10⁴
BATH
KITCHEN 9² × 17¹⁰
BATH
WALK-IN CLOSET LINEN
MASTER BEDROOM 11⁴ × 16⁰
FOYER
OPT. BAY WINDOW
COVERED PORCH
LAUNDRY 9² × 9⁶
FURN
GARAGE 20¹⁰ × 21⁸

Width 35'-0"
Depth 74'-0"

Design 3719

Square Footage: 1,634

■ This modest but handsome ranch design provides an open living environment in an excellent home for narrow lots. The master bedroom features a large walk-in closet and a full-sized bath. Three additional bedrooms are served by another full bath. A galley kitchen, with an eat-in nook, opens up to a huge great room. Indoor/outdoor livability may be expanded with the addition of a rear lanai or deck with railing. A fireplace in the great room, front bay windows and a two-car garage are wonderful options. The blueprints for this home show how to build both the basic and the expanded version.

Design by
HOME PLANNERS

Enhanced Plan

Enhanced Plan

Design 3707
Square Footage: 1,345

■ Enhanced livability for warm climates is an appropriate theme for this well-laid-out ranch house. The split-bedroom plan separates the master bedroom from two family bedrooms. One of the bedrooms would make a perfect office, if needed. A large L-shaped kitchen has loads of counter space and includes an alcove for a washer and dryer. Two baths and a large great room complete the layout. Enhance livability by including the fireplace, rear deck or lanai and the two-car garage. The blueprints for this house show how to build both the basic and the enhanced version.

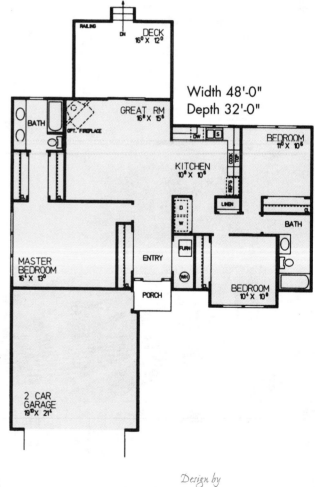

Width 48'-0"
Depth 32'-0"

DECK 16⁰ X 12⁰
RAILING
DN
BATH
GREAT RM 16⁰ X 15⁰
OPT. FIREPLACE
DW S
BEDROOM 11⁰ X 10⁵
KITCHEN 10⁰ X 10⁶
LINEN
BATH
D W
MASTER BEDROOM 16⁴ X 13⁰
ENTRY
FURN
WH
BEDROOM 10⁴ X 10⁰
PORCH
2 CAR GARAGE 19⁰ X 21⁴

Design by
Home Planners

Basic Plan

408

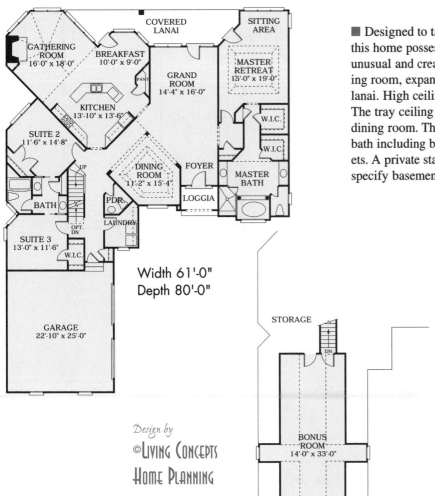

GATHERING ROOM
16'-0" x 18'-0"

COVERED LANAI

SITTING AREA

BREAKFAST
10'-0" x 9'-0"

MASTER RETREAT
15'-0" x 19'-0"

GRAND ROOM
14'-4" x 16'-0"

PANT.

KITCHEN
13'-10" x 13'-6"

W.I.C.

SUITE 2
11'-6" x 14'-8"

W.I.C.

UP

DINING ROOM
11'-2" x 15'-4"

FOYER

MASTER BATH

BATH

PDR.

LOGGIA

OPT. DN

LAUNDRY

SUITE 3
13'-0" x 11'-6"

W.I.C.

Width 61'-0"
Depth 80'-0"

GARAGE
22'-10" x 25'-0"

STORAGE

DN

BONUS ROOM
14'-0" x 33'-0"

Design by
© Living Concepts
Home Planning

■ Designed to take full advantage of panoramic rear vistas, this home possesses some great visual effects of its own. Its unusual and creative use of space includes an angled gathering room, expansive grand room and continuous covered lanai. High ceilings throughout create an air of spaciousness. The tray ceiling reflects the pentagonal shape of the open dining room. The master retreat features a sitting area and a bath including both His and Hers vanities and walk-in closets. A private staircase leads to a large bonus room. Please specify basement or crawlspace foundation when ordering.

Design A106

Square Footage: 2,585
Bonus Room: 519 square feet

Design HPTM00043

Square Footage: 2,046

■ Curb appeal abounds in this three-bedroom farmhouse with its columned porch, keystone lintel windows and stucco facade. A fireplace with adjacent built-ins in the great room can be viewed from the foyer and breakfast area. Light pours in from the rear porch with windows at every turn. Counter space is abundant in this interesting kitchen, which adjoins the breakfast area. The private master suite enjoys a luxurious bath with twin vanity sinks, a garden tub and separate shower. At the opposite end of the home, two secondary bedrooms share a bath. One features French-door access to the rear porch. Please specify basement, crawlspace or slab foundation when ordering.

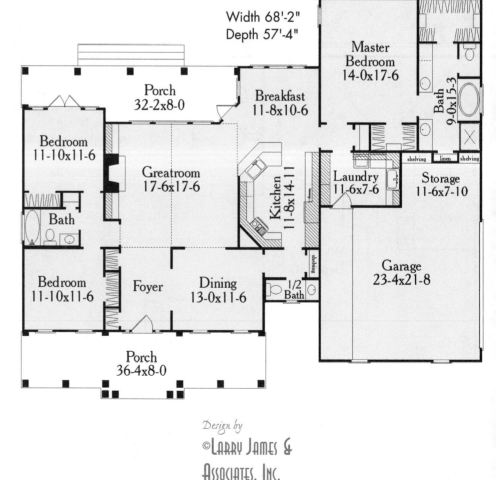

Width 68'-2"
Depth 57'-4"

Master Bedroom 14-0x17-6

Bath 9-0x15-3

Porch 32-2x8-0

Breakfast 11-8x10-6

Bedroom 11-10x11-6

Greatroom 17-6x17-6

Kitchen 11-8x14-11

Laundry 11-6x7-6

Storage 11-6x7-10

Bath

Bedroom 11-10x11-6

Foyer

Dining 13-0x11-6

1/2 Bath

Garage 23-4x21-8

Porch 36-4x8-0

Design by
©Larry James & Associates, Inc.

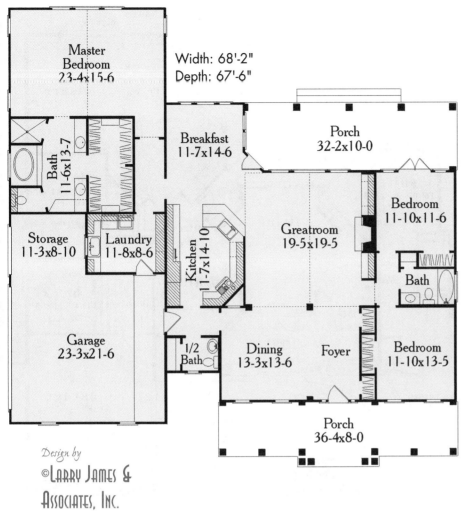

Master
Bedroom
23-4x15-6

Width: 68'-2"
Depth: 67'-6"

Bath
11-6x13-7

Breakfast
11-7x14-6

Porch
32-2x10-0

Storage
11-3x8-10

Laundry
11-8x8-6

Kitchen
11-7x14-10

Greatroom
19-5x19-5

Bedroom
11-10x11-6

Bath

Garage
23-3x21-6

1/2
Bath

Dining
13-3x13-6

Foyer

Bedroom
11-10x13-5

Porch
36-4x8-0

Design by
©Larry James &
Associates, Inc.

Design HPTM00044

Square Footage. 2,424

■ Beyond this home's beautiful
columned porch and keystone
arches is a successful plan. Enter
the foyer to find the formal
dining room and two closets.
Straight ahead lies the great
room, which includes a fireplace
and built-ins. Between the spacious kitchen and the breakfast
area, a hallway leads to the
master bedroom. The private
bath here provides convenience
with dual vanities, a separate
shower and an enormous walk-in
closet. Two additional bedrooms
to the far right of the plan share
a full bath that includes a linen
closet. The rear bedroom boasts
French doors that access a covered porch. Please specify crawlspace or slab foundation when
ordering.

Design 6605

Square Footage: 2,762

L

A different and exciting floor plan defines this three-bedroom home. Clear and simple rooflines and a large welcoming entryway make it unique. A large archway frames the dining room entry to the gallery hall. The hall leads past the kitchen toward the informal leisure and nook area. High glass above the built-in fireplace allows for natural light and rear views. Greenhouse-style garden windows light the nook. The large master suite has a morning kitchen and sitting area. The bath features a make-up space, a walk-in shower and a private garden tub.

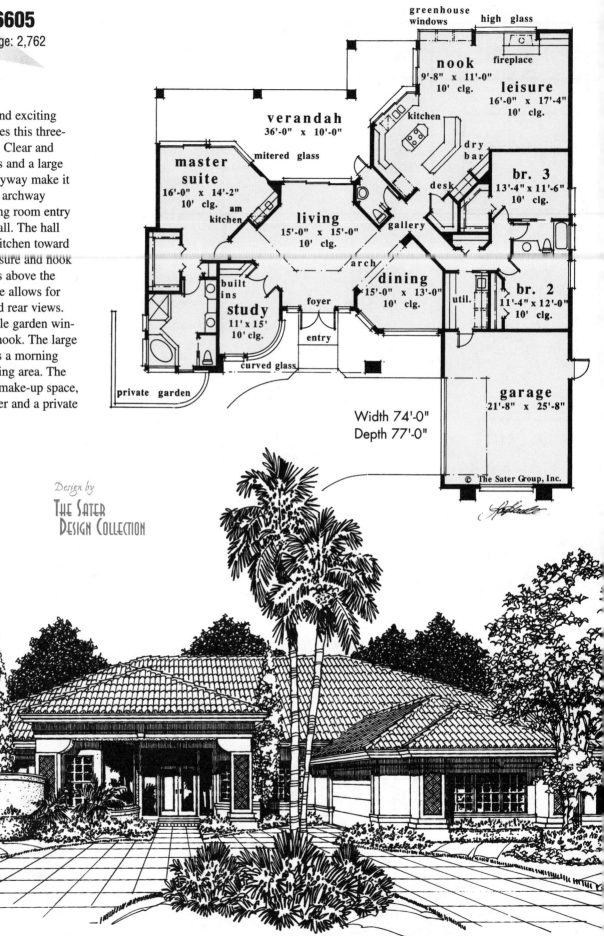

Design by
**The Sater
Design Collection**

greenhouse windows

high glass

fireplace

nook
9'-8" x 11'-0"
10' clg.

leisure
16'-0" x 17'-4"
10' clg.

kitchen

verandah
36'-0" x 10'-0"

mitered glass

dry bar

br. 3
13'-4" x 11'-6"
10' clg.

master suite
16'-0" x 14'-2"
10' clg.

am kitchen

desk

living
15'-0" x 15'-0"
10' clg.

gallery

built ins

study
11' x 15'
10' clg.

foyer

arch

dining
15'-0" x 13'-0"
10' clg.

util.

br. 2
11'-4" x 12'-0"
10' clg.

entry

curved glass

private garden

Width 74'-0"
Depth 77'-0"

garage
21'-8" x 25'-8"

© The Sater Group, Inc.

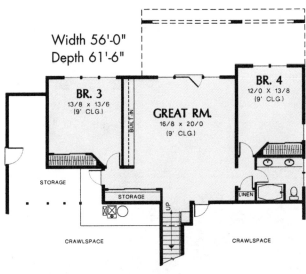

Width 56'-0"
Depth 61'-6"

BR. 3
13/8 x 13/6
(9' CLG.)

GREAT RM.
16/8 X 20/0
(9' CLG.)

BR. 4
12/0 X 13/8
(9' CLG.)

STORAGE

STORAGE

LINEN

UP

CRAWLSPACE

CRAWLSPACE

Design 7546

Main Level: 2,300 square feet
Lower Level: 1,114 square feet
Total: 3,414 square feet

Design by
©ALAN MASCORD DESIGN
ASSOCIATES, INC.

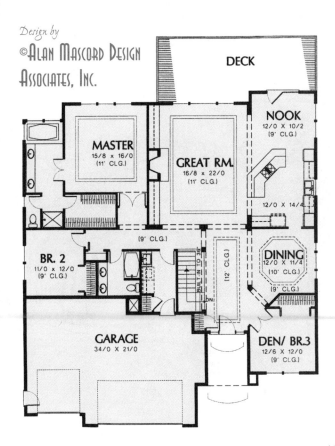

DECK

MASTER
15/8 x 16/0
(11' CLG.)

GREAT RM.
16/8 x 22/0
(11' CLG.)

NOOK
12/0 X 10/2
(9' CLG.)

12/0 X 14/4

BR. 2
11/0 x 12/0
(9' CLG.)

(9' CLG.)

DINING
12/0 X 11/4
(10' CLG.)

(9' CLG.)

GARAGE
34/0 X 21/0

DEN/ BR.3
12/6 X 12/0
(9' CLG.)

■ Looking for all the world like a one-story plan, this elegant hillside design has a surprise on the lower level. Reach the main level through an arched, recessed entry that opens to a twelve-foot ceiling. The formal dining room is on the right, next to a cozy den or Bedroom 3. Columns decorate the hall and separate it from the dining room and great room, which contains a tray ceiling and a fireplace flanked by built-ins. The breakfast nook and kitchen are just steps away on the left. Lower-level space includes another great room with built-ins and two family bedrooms sharing a full bath.

Design 6626

Square Footage: 2,589

■ This plan has an Old World Mediterranean look with a contemporary floor plan that's easy to live in. The formal living areas are just off the grand foyer. The large living and dining rooms are easily accessible to the wet bar. An archway leads to the family areas. An ample kitchen has a walk-in pantry and desk message center. The nook and leisure room face the rear. The owners wing features a bayed study with bookshelves, large sleeping quarters and a bayed sitting area. The bath has His and Hers walk-in closets, a glass shower and a garden tub.

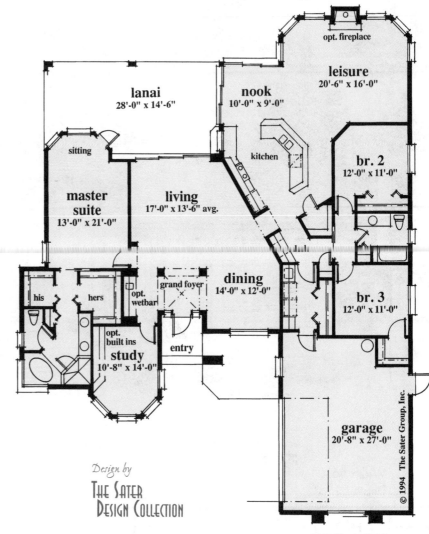

opt. fireplace

leisure
20'-6" x 16'-0"

lanai
28'-0" x 14'-6"

nook
10'-0" x 9'-0"

sitting

kitchen

br. 2
12'-0" x 11'-0"

master suite
13'-0" x 21'-0"

living
17'-0" x 13'-6" avg.

his   hers

opt. wetbar

grand foyer

dining
14'-0" x 12'-0"

br. 3
12'-0" x 11'-0"

opt. built ins

study
10'-8" x 14'-0"

entry

garage
20'-8" x 27'-0"

© 1994 The Sater Group, Inc.

Design by

THE SATER
DESIGN COLLECTION

Width 64'-0"
Depth 81'-0"

© The Sater Group, Inc.

Jenkins &
Johnston

414

Arched windows and a dramatic arched entry enhance this exciting Southwestern home. The expansive great room, highlighted by a cathedral ceiling and a fireplace, offers direct access to the rear patio and the formal dining room—a winning combination for both formal and informal get-togethers. An efficient U-shaped kitchen provides plenty of counter space and easily serves both the dining room and the great room. Sunlight fills the master bedroom through a wall of windows which affords views of the rear grounds. The master bath invites relaxation with its soothing corner tub and separate shower. Two secondary bedrooms (one serves as an optional study) share an adjacent bath.

Design 9740

Square Footage: 1,838

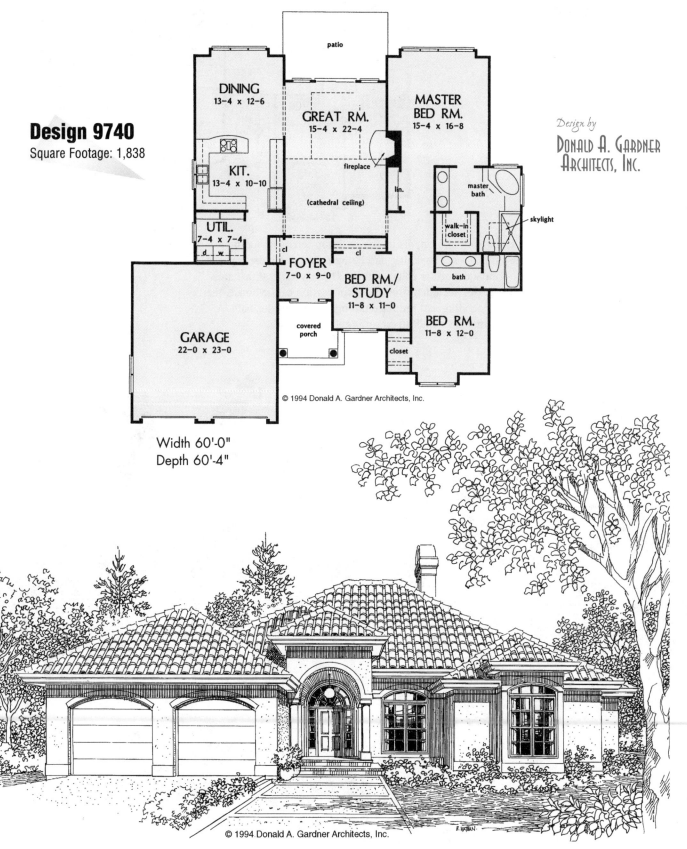

Width 60'-0"
Depth 60'-4"

415

Design 8620
Square Footage: 2,454

Design by
HOME DESIGN SERVICES

Floor plan labels:

Covered Patio

Bed Rm. #2
13⁰10⁸
10' flat ceiling

Master Bed Rm
17⁴13⁰
tray ceiling

Brkfst. Nook
11⁴8

Bath

fireplace

Family Rm.
17⁰19⁰
vaulted ceiling

Kitchen
11⁰13⁴
vaulted ceiling

M. Bath
vaulted ceiling

Bed Rm. #3
11⁴11⁸
10' flat ceiling

skylite

8' high wall

Lau.

W.I.C.

A/C

Bath

w.h.

arch

Foyer
8⁰10⁰
10' flat ceiling

Dining Rm.
10⁸13⁰
10' flat ceiling

Bed Rm. #4
11⁴13⁰
10' flat ceiling

Living Rm.
12⁴14⁸
tray ceiling

Entry

Double Garage

■ This one-story sports many well-chosen, distinctive exterior details including a cameo window and hipped rooflines. The dining and living rooms flank the foyer. A tray ceiling in the living room adds further enhancement. The bayed breakfast area admits light softened by the patio. Secluded from the main portion of the house, the master bedroom features a tray ceiling and fireplace through to the master bath. A raised tub, double vanity and immense walk-in closet highlight the bath.

Width 66'-8"
Depth 56'-8"

©1997 Donald A. Gardner Architects, Inc.

Design by

Donald A. Gardner Architects, Inc.

Width 64'-10"
Depth 58'-10"

SCREEN PORCH
24-11 x 8-7
(12' ceiling)

BRKFST.
11-8 9-0
(12' ceiling)

MASTER BED RM.
15-0 x 13-4

fireplace

GREAT RM.
19-0 x 15-0
(12' ceiling)

KIT.
11-8 x 11-8
(12' ceiling)

bath

BED RM.
11-0 x 12-0

(8' high wall)

master bath

pd. rm.

FOYER
6-0 x 7-4

DINING
11-0 x 12-0
(12' ceiling)

BED RM.
12-0 x 11-0

walk-in closet

STUDY/ BED RM.
11-4 x 12-0
(10' ceiling)

PORCH

GARAGE
21-8 x 22-10

© 1997 Donald A Gardner Architects, Inc.

Optional Full Bath

Design 7659
Square Footage: 1,954

■ Direct from the Mediterranean, this Spanish-style one-story is not only decorous, it also offers a very practical floor plan. The facade features arch-top, multi-pane windows, a columned front porch, tall chimney stack and a tiled roof. The interior has a wealth of livability. What you'll appreciate first is the juxtaposition of the great room and the formal dining room—both defined by columns. A more casual eating area is attached to the L-shaped kitchen and has access to a screen porch, as does the great room. Three bedrooms mean abundant sleeping space. The study could be a fourth bedroom—choose the full bath option in this case. A tray ceiling decorates the master bedroom, which is further enhanced by a bath with separate shower and tub, a walk-in closet and double sinks. You can also access the porch from the master bedroom.

Width 61'-0"
Depth 65'-4"

Design by
© Frank Betz Associates, Inc.

Design HPTM03095

Square Footage: 2,311
Bonus Space: 425 square feet

■ With elegant hipped rooflines, stucco-and-brick detailing, arched windows and gabled roofs, this home presents its European heritage with pride. The covered entryway leads to a formal dining room defined by graceful columns and arched openings. Columns and arched openings also lead into the vaulted family room, where a welcoming fireplace waits to warm cool evenings, while radius windows flood the room with light. The kitchen is sure to please with its angled counter and accessibility to the vaulted breakfast nook. Two family bedrooms are to the right of the design while the master suite is to the left. Please specify basement or crawl-space foundation when ordering.

Width 64'-5"
Depth 52'-11"

BED RM.
12-0 x 11-4

walk-in closet

walk-in closet

BED RM.
12-0 x 11-4

bath

DINING
11-0 x 14-0
(11' ceiling)

SCREEN PORCH
16-8 x 12-5
(11' ceiling)

storage

up

KIT.
11-0 x 15-0
(11' ceiling)

GREAT RM.
17-0 x 20-0
(11' ceiling)

fireplace

MASTER BED RM.
13-4 x 15-0

GARAGE
21-0 x 21-0

UTIL.
5-6 x 6-0

d   w

cl

lin.

walk-in closet

PORCH

master bath

storage

© 1997   Donald A Gardner Architects, Inc.

Design 7655

Square Footage: 1,782
Bonus Room: 229 square feet

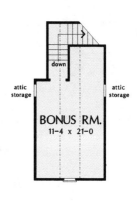

down

attic storage

attic storage

BONUS RM.
11-4 x 21-0

■ Though tending toward Spanish-style, this home carries a more classic, formal look than the traditional Mediterranean of its genre. More symmetrical than most, it offers a raised porch with columns and multi-pane windows with jack-arch detailing. The interior is pure modern floor planning. The living areas are open, with eleven-foot ceilings and an easy flow from great room to dining room to kitchen. The rear screen porch supplies outdoor enchantment. The bedrooms are designed in the split style that is popular with new homes. The master suite features a tray ceiling, walk-in closet and grandly appointed master bath. Two family bedrooms have walk-in closets and share a full bath. Top it all off with a two-car garage with extra storage space and you've got one great design.

Design by
DONALD A. GARDNER
ARCHITECTS, INC.

©1997 Donald A. Gardner Architects, Inc.

■ Discreet placement of bedrooms provides for the utmost in privacy in this one story home. The dining and living rooms flank the foyer—note the columns that add drama to the living room. A volume-ceilinged family room includes a fireplace which is flanked by sliding doors leading to a covered rear patio. The master suite includes a walk-in closet and bath with a dual vanity and step-up corner spa tub set between columns. Two bedrooms and a full bath occupy the opposite wing, which is reached via a pocket door off the family wing. Blueprints for this design include three different elevations.

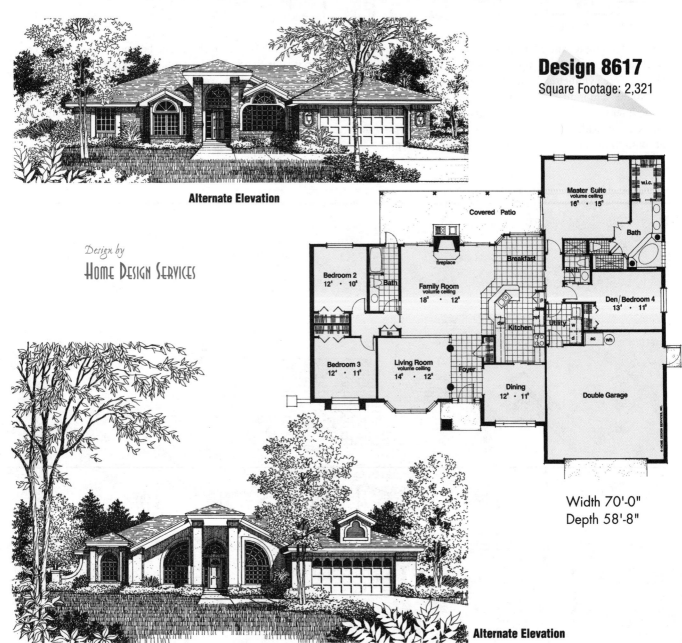

Alternate Elevation

Design by
HOME DESIGN SERVICES

Design 8617
Square Footage: 2,321

Width 70'-0"
Depth 58'-8"

Alternate Elevation

Make the most of warmer climes in this striking three-bedroom home. A grand entry gives way to a great room with skylights and a fireplace. A cathedral ceiling furthers the open feeling in this room. A large dining room surveys views on two sides. Adjacent, the kitchen will delight with its large island work space and abundance of counter and cabinet space.

Facing the front, the breakfast room offers ample space along with elegant ceiling detail. Three bedrooms—or two with a study—make up the sleeping quarters of this plan. In the master bedroom, large proportions include a private bath with a walk-in closet and a bumped-out garden tub. A secluded covered porch provides the opportunity for outdoor enjoyment.

Design 9737
Square Footage: 1,929

Design by
Donald A. Gardner Architects, Inc.

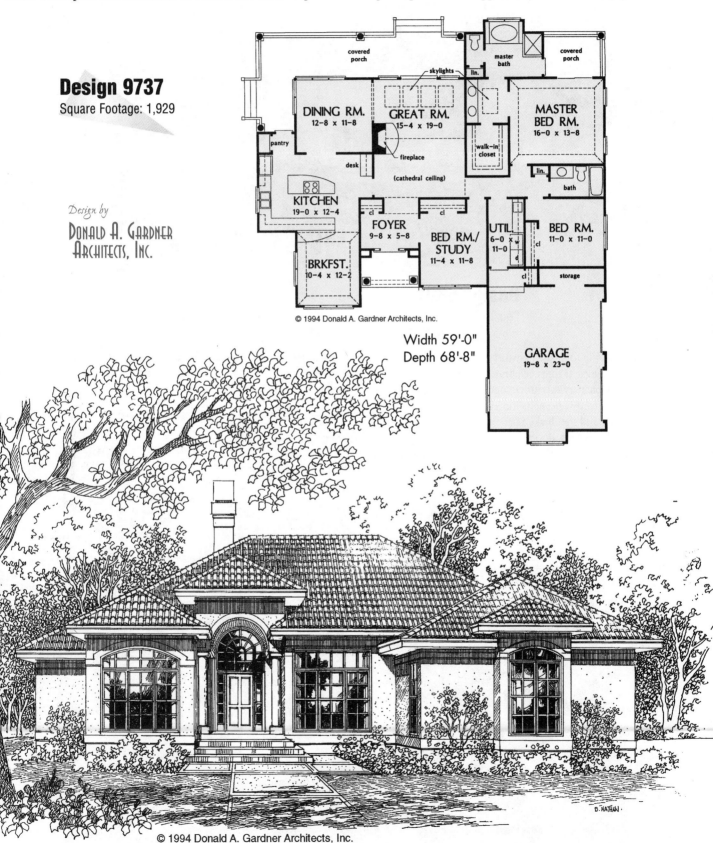

Width 59'-0"
Depth 68'-8"

© 1994 Donald A. Gardner Architects, Inc.

© 1994 Donald A. Gardner Architects, Inc.

Design 6691
Square Footage: 1,288

■ Welcome home to casual, unstuffy living with this comfortable tidewater design. Asymmetrical lines celebrate the turn of the new century, and blend a current Gulf Coast style with vintage panache brought forward from its regional past. The heart of this home is the great room, where a put-your-feet-up atmosphere prevails, and the dusky hues of sunset can mingle with the sounds of ocean breakers. French doors open the master suite to a private area of the covered porch, where sunlight and sea breezes mingle with a spirit of bon vivant.

Design by

The Sater Design Collection

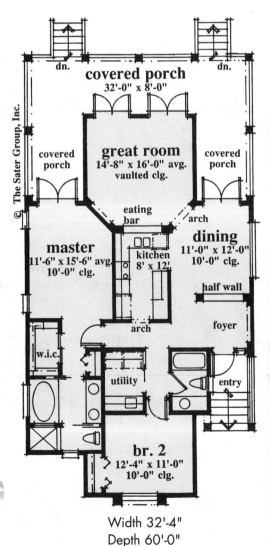

Rear Elevation

© The Sater Group, Inc.

dn.   **covered porch**   dn.
32'-0" x 8'-0"

covered porch

great room
14'-8" x 16'-0" avg.
vaulted clg.

covered porch

eating bar   arch

master
11'-6" x 15'-6" avg.
10'-0" clg.

kitchen
8' x 12'

dining
11'-0" x 12'-0"
10'-0" clg.

half wall

foyer

arch

w.i.c.

utility

entry

br. 2
12'-4" x 11'-0"
10'-0" clg.

Width 32'-4"
Depth 60'-0"

Garages-Plus:

More than just a convenient parking space

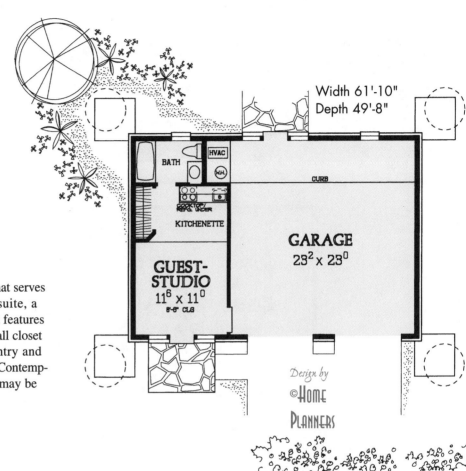

Width 61'-10"
Depth 49'-8"

BATH

HVAC

W.H.

CURB

COOKTOP
REF.& UNDER
KITCHENETTE

GARAGE
23² x 23⁰

GUEST-
STUDIO
11⁶ x 11⁰
8'-6" CLG

Design by
©Home
Planners

Design G201A

Square Footage: 610

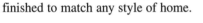

■ This two-car garage has an addition that serves multiple purposes—it can be a guest suite, a mother-in-law suite or a handy studio. It features a kitchenette and full bath, plus a large hall closet for storage. A stone patio graces the entry and provides a bit of outdoor space to enjoy. Contemporary in design, this garage/guest house may be finished to match any style of home.

Design G256

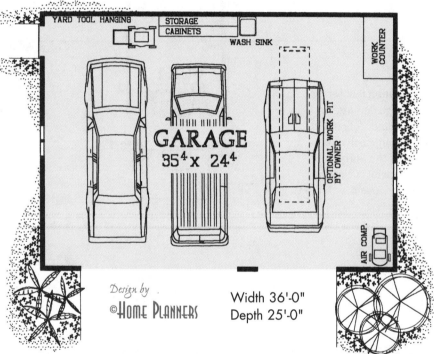

YARD TOOL HANGING

STORAGE
CABINETS

WASH SINK

WORK COUNTER

GARAGE
35⁴ x 24⁴

OPTIONAL WORK PIT BY OWNER

AIR COMP.

Design by
©Home Planners

Width 36'-0"
Depth 25'-0"

Design G257

Design G255
Square Footage: 900

■ Is it a garage? Is it a workshop? The answer is both. You can put this 900-square-foot area to work however it suits you best—and modify the exterior to match your house. Providing space enough for three cars is only the first benefit. Convert the third parking bay to an optional work pit—perfect for the devoted mechanic's do-it-yourself car maintenance. A gener-ous work area adjacent to the parking bay allows space for a counter, air compressor, welders and other tool-time essen-tials. The back wall storage area includes optional cabinets and a wash sink, with handy side-door access for bringing the mower and other yard equipment in out of the weather. Four different exterior elevations are available.

Design G254

425

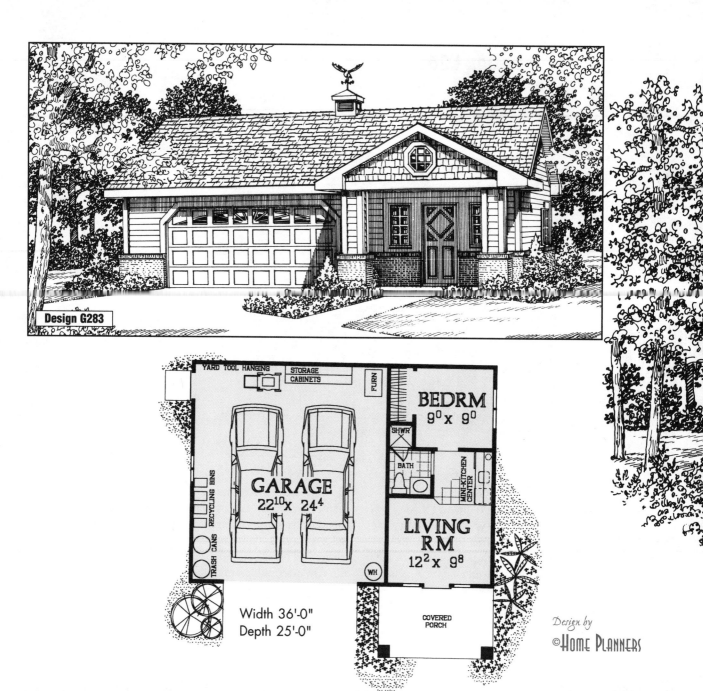

Design G283

YARD TOOL HANGING

STORAGE CABINETS

FURN

BEDRM
9⁰ x 9⁰

SHWR

BATH

MINI-KITCHEN CENTER

RECYCLING BINS

TRASH CANS

GARAGE
22¹⁰ x 24⁴

WH

LIVING RM
12² x 9⁸

Width 36'-0"
Depth 25'-0"

COVERED PORCH

Design by
©Home Planners

Design G284

Design G285

Square Footage: 321

■ This well-thought-out floor plan is the perfect solution for a home office addition. A single 16'x7' garage door provides shelter for two cars, plus storage areas for yard and garden equipment, garbage cans and recycling bins. A four-column porch provides entry to the compact apartment or office area.

A mini-kitchen (or make this extra work area) and a bath with a shower provide added convenience. The bedroom at the back could also be used for additional storage. Four different exterior elevations are available.

Design G282

Design by
©HOME PLANNERS

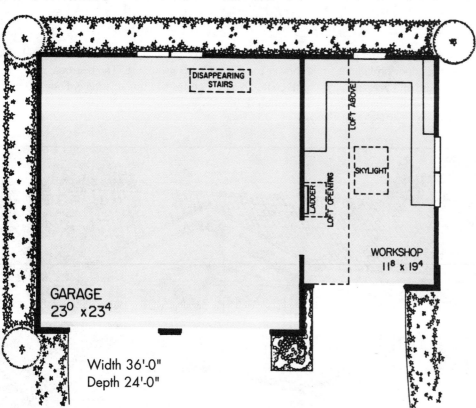

DISAPPEARING
STAIRS

LOFT ABOVE

SKYLIGHT

LADDER
LOFT OPENING

WORKSHOP
11⁸ x 19⁴

GARAGE
23⁰ x 23⁴

Width 36'-0"
Depth 24'-0"

Design G111

Square Footage: 225

■ This Tudor-style garage is
more than just a handy place
to park two cars—it also features a large workshop area
with a skylight and wrapping
countertops. Disappearing
stairs in both the garage section and the workshop section gain access to attic
space, which may be finished
into a studio or used for storage as needed. The outside
could be modified to suit any
style of home, using different
materials for a different look.

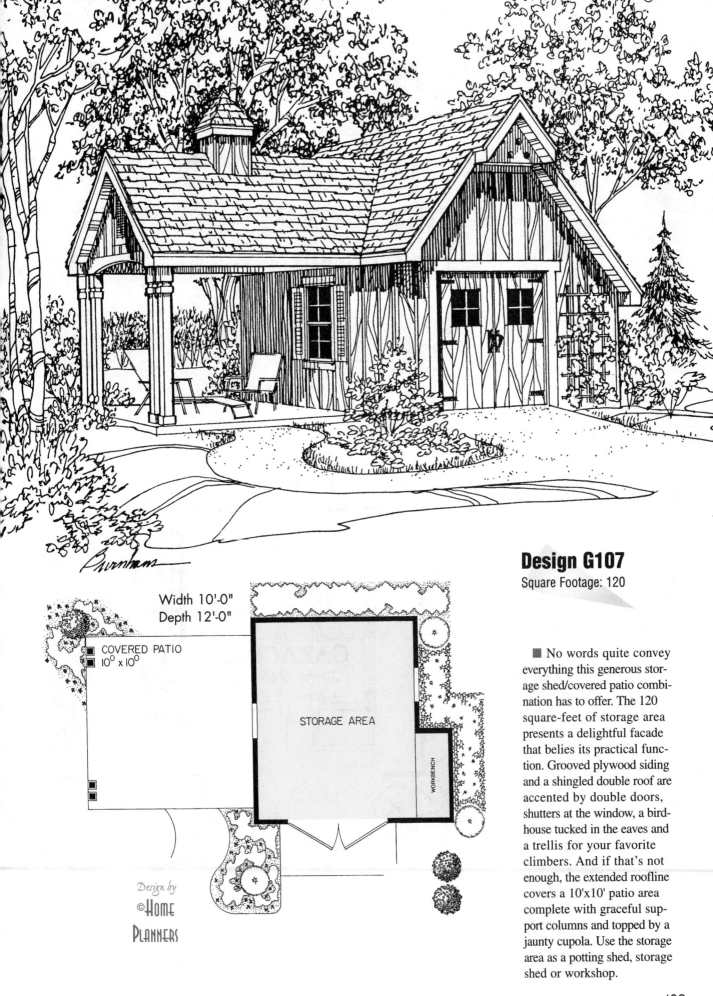

Design G107
Square Footage: 120

Width 10'-0"
Depth 12'-0"

COVERED PATIO
10⁰ x 10⁰

STORAGE AREA

WORKBENCH

Design by
©Home
Planners

■ No words quite convey everything this generous storage shed/covered patio combination has to offer. The 120 square-feet of storage area presents a delightful facade that belies its practical function. Grooved plywood siding and a shingled double roof are accented by double doors, shutters at the window, a birdhouse tucked in the eaves and a trellis for your favorite climbers. And if that's not enough, the extended roofline covers a 10'x10' patio area complete with graceful support columns and topped by a jaunty cupola. Use the storage area as a potting shed, storage shed or workshop.

Design HPTM03096

Square Footage: 306

Greet your clients in the business side of this multi-use structure. There's room enough for a reception/waiting room area in front with an impressive entryway through a columned porch. Decorative recessed windows flanking the door and two more in the side wall allow for plenty of natural light. In the back is ample space for an office with a storage closet and file space. Add a half-bath for maximum convenience. Choose from four different elevations to fit your particular style.

Quote One®

Cost to build? See page 434
to order complete cost estimate
to build this house in your area!

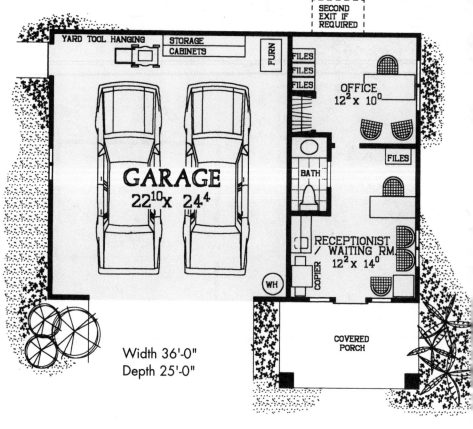

SECOND EXIT IF REQUIRED

YARD TOOL HANGING

STORAGE CABINETS

FURN

FILES
FILES
FILES

OFFICE
12² x 10⁰

FILES

BATH

GARAGE
22¹⁰ x 24⁴

RECEPTIONIST / WAITING RM.
12² x 14⁰

COPIER

WH

Width 36'-0"
Depth 25'-0"

COVERED PORCH

Design by
© Home Planners

Design HPTM03097

Design HPTM03098

Design HPTM03099

Design HPTM02006

Square Footage: 320

Design by
©HOME PLANNERS

Width 20'-0"
Depth 16'-0"

■ The ultimate luxury for any craft enthusiast—a separate, free-standing building dedicated to your craft of choice! Functional as well as a beautiful addition to your landscape, this cottage provides ample counter space and shelving to spread out or store all your materials and tools. And at break time, relax from your hobby in the attached sun room with a vaulted ceiling, French doors and lots of elegant windows. Orient the structure on your property to face south for the sun room and the north-facing work area receives soft, even light. A built-in and well-thought-out work table is flanked by additional countertop work space. Outside, an open 10' x 12' deck off the sun room makes this little cottage just about perfect.

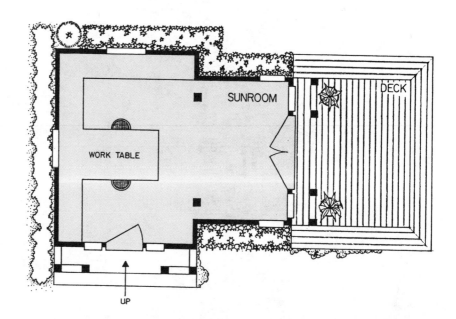

SUNROOM

DECK

WORK TABLE

UP

LET US SHOW YOU OUR HOME BLUEPRINT PACKAGE.

BUILDING A HOME? PLANNING A HOME?

OUR BLUEPRINT PACKAGE HAS NEARLY EVERYTHING YOU NEED TO GET THE JOB DONE RIGHT,

whether you're working on your own or with help from an architect, designer, builder or subcontractors. Each Blueprint Package is the result of many hours of work by licensed architects or professional designers.

QUALITY

Hundreds of hours of painstaking effort have gone into the development of your blueprint plan. Each home has been quality-checked by professionals to insure accuracy and buildability.

VALUE

Because we sell in volume, you can buy professional quality blueprints at a fraction of their development cost. With our plans, your dream home design costs substantially less than the fees charged by architects.

SERVICE

Once you've chosen your favorite home plan, you'll receive fast, efficient service whether you choose to mail or fax your order to us or call us toll free at 1-800-521-6797. After you have received your order, call for customer service toll free 1-888-690-1116.

SATISFACTION

Over 50 years of service to satisfied home plan buyers provide us unparalleled experience and knowledge in producing quality blueprints.

ORDER TOLL FREE 1-800-521-6797

After you've looked over our Blueprint Package and Important Extras, call toll free on our Blueprint Hotline: 1-800-521-6797, for current pricing and availability prior to mailing the order form on page 445. We're ready and eager to serve you. After you have received your order, call for customer service toll free 1-888-690-1116.

Each set of blueprints is an interrelated collection of detail sheets which includes components such as floor plans, interior and exterior elevations, dimensions, cross-sections, diagrams and notations. These sheets show exactly how your house is to be built.

SETS MAY INCLUDE:

FRONTAL SHEET

This artist's sketch of the exterior of the house gives you an idea of how the house will look when built and landscaped. Large floor plans show all levels of the house and provide an overview of your new home's livability, as well as a handy reference for deciding on furniture placement.

FOUNDATION PLANS

This sheet shows the foundation layout including support walls, excavated and unexcavated areas, if any, and foundation notes. If slab construction rather than basement, the plan shows footings and details for a monolithic slab. This page, or another in the set, may include a sample plot plan for locating your house on a building site.

DETAILED FLOOR PLANS

These plans show the layout of each floor of the house. Rooms and interior spaces are carefully dimensioned and keys are given for cross-section details provided later in the plans. The positions of electrical outlets and switches are shown.

HOUSE CROSS-SECTIONS

Large-scale views show sections or cut-aways of the foundation, interior walls, exterior walls, floors, stairways and roof details. Additional cross-sections may show important changes in floor, ceiling or roof heights or the relationship of one level to another. Extremely valuable for construction, these sections show exactly how the various parts of the house fit together.

INTERIOR ELEVATIONS

Many of our drawings show the design and placement of kitchen and bathroom cabinets, laundry areas, fireplaces, bookcases and other built-ins. Little "extras," such as mantelpiece and wainscoting drawings, plus molding sections, provide details that give your home that custom touch.

EXTERIOR ELEVATIONS

These drawings show the front, rear and sides of your house and give necessary notes on exterior materials and finishes. Particular attention is given to cornice detail, brick and stone accents or other finish items that make your home unique.

IMPORTANT EXTRAS TO DO THE JOB RIGHT!

*INTRODUCING IMPORTANT PLANNING AND CONSTRUCTION
AIDS DEVELOPED BY OUR PROFESSIONALS TO HELP YOU
SUCCEED IN YOUR HOME-BUILDING PROJECT*

MATERIALS LIST

*(Note: Because of the diversity
of local building codes, our
Materials List does not include
mechanical materials.)*

For many of the designs in our portfolio, we offer a customized materials take-off that is invaluable in planning and estimating the cost of your new home. This Materials List outlines the quantity, type and size of materials needed to build your house (with the exception of mechanical system items). Included are framing lumber, windows and doors, kitchen and bath cabinetry, rough and finish hardware, and much more. This handy list helps you or your builder cost out materials and serves as a reference sheet when you're compiling bids. Some Materials Lists may be ordered before blueprints are ordered, call for information.

SPECIFICATION OUTLINE

This valuable 16-page document is critical to building your house correctly. Designed to be filled in by you or your builder, this book lists 166 stages or items crucial to the building process. It provides a comprehensive review of the construction process and helps in choosing materials. When combined with the blueprints, a signed contract, and a schedule, it becomes a legal document and record for the building of your home.

QUOTE ONE®

SUMMARY COST REPORT   **MATERIAL COST REPORT**

A product for estimating the cost of building select designs, the Quote One® system is available in two separate stages: The Summary Cost Report and the Material Cost Report.

The **Summary Cost Report** is the first stage in the package and shows the total cost per square foot for your chosen home in your zip-code area and then breaks that cost down into various categories showing the costs for building materials, labor and installation. The report includes three grades: Budget, Standard and Custom. These reports allow you to evaluate your building budget and compare the costs of building a variety of homes in your area.

Make even more informed decisions about your home-building project with the second phase of our package, our **Material Cost Report.** This tool is invaluable in planning and estimating the cost of your new home. The material and installation (labor and equipment) cost is shown for each of over 1,000 line items provided in the Materials List (Standard grade), which is included when you purchase this estimating tool. It allows you to determine building costs for your specific zip-code area and for your chosen home design. Space is allowed for additional estimates from contractors and subcontractors, such as for mechanical materials, which are not included in our packages. This invaluable tool includes a Materials List. A Material Cost Report cannot be ordered before blueprints are ordered. Call for details. In addition, ask about our Home Planners Estimating Package.

If you are interested in a plan that is not indicated as Quote One®, please call and ask our sales reps. They will be happy to verify the status for you. To order these invaluable reports, use the order form.

CONSTRUCTION INFORMATION

IF YOU WANT TO KNOW MORE ABOUT TECHNIQUES—
and deal more confidently with subcontractors —
we offer these useful sheets. Each set is an excellent
tool that will add to your understanding of these
technical subjects. These helpful details provide
general construction information and
are not specific to any single plan.

PLUMBING

The Blueprint Package includes locations for all the plumbing fixtures, including sinks, lavatories, tubs, showers, toilets, laundry trays and water heaters. However, if you want to know more about the complete plumbing system, these Plumbing Details will prove very useful. Prepared to meet requirements of the National Plumbing Code, these fact-filled sheets give general information on pipe schedules, fittings, sump-pump details, water-softener hookups, septic system details and much more. Sheets also include a glossary of terms.

ELECTRICAL

The locations for every electrical switch, plug and outlet are shown in your Blueprint Package. However, these Electrical Details go further to take the mystery out of household electrical systems. Prepared to meet requirements of the National Electrical Code, these comprehensive drawings come packed with helpful information, including wire sizing, switch-installation schematics, cable-routing details, appliance wattage, doorbell hook-ups, typical service panel circuitry and much more. A glossary of terms is also included.

CONSTRUCTION

The Blueprint Package contains information an experienced builder needs to construct a particular house. However, it doesn't show all the ways that houses can be built, nor does it explain alternate construction methods. To help you understand how your house will be built—and offer additional techniques—this set of Construction Details depicts the materials and methods used to build foundations, fireplaces, walls, floors and roofs. Where appropriate, the drawings show acceptable alternatives.

MECHANICAL

These Mechanical Details contain fundamental principles and useful data that will help you make informed decisions and communicate with subcontractors about heating and cooling systems. Drawings contain instructions and samples that allow you to make simple load calculations, and preliminary sizing and costing analysis. Covered are the most commonly used systems from heat pumps to solar fuel systems. The package is filled with illustrations and diagrams to help you visualize components and how they relate to one another.

THE HANDS-ON HOME FURNITURE PLANNER

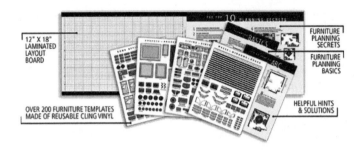

Effectively plan the space in your home using The **Hands-On Home Furniture Planner**. It's fun and easy—no more moving heavy pieces of furniture to see how the room will go together. And you can try different layouts, moving furniture at a whim.

The kit includes reusable peel and stick furniture templates that fit onto a 12" x 18" laminated layout board—space enough to layout every room in your home.

Also included in the package are a number of helpful planning tools. You'll receive:

- ✓ Helpful hints and solutions for difficult situations.
- ✓ Furniture planning basics to get you started.
- ✓ Furniture planning secrets that let you in on some of the tricks of professional designers.

The **Hands-On Home Furniture Planner** is the one tool that no new homeowner or home remodeler should be without. It's also a perfect housewarming gift!

To Order, Call Toll Free
1-800-521-6797

After you've looked over our Blueprint Package and Important Extras on these pages, call for current pricing and availability prior to mailing the order form. We're ready and eager to serve you. After you have received your order, call for customer service toll free 1-888-690-1116.

THE FINISHING TOUCHES...

THE DECK BLUEPRINT PACKAGE

Many of the homes in this book can be enhanced with a professionally designed Home Planners Deck Plan. Those homes marked with a **D** have a complementary Deck Plan, sold separately, which includes a Deck Plan Frontal Sheet, Deck Framing and Floor Plans, Deck Elevations and a Deck Materials List. A Standard Deck Details Package, also available, provides all the how-to information necessary for building *any* deck. Our Complete Deck Building Package contains one set of Custom Deck Plans of your choice, plus one set of Standard Deck Building Details, all for one low price. Our plans and details are carefully prepared in an easy-to-understand format that will guide you through every stage of your deck-building project. This page shows a sample Deck layout to match your favorite house. See Blueprint Price Schedule for ordering information.

THE LANDSCAPE BLUEPRINT PACKAGE

For the homes marked with an **L** in this book, Home Planners has created a front-yard Landscape Plan that is complementary in design to the house plan. These comprehensive blueprint packages include a Frontal Sheet, Plan View, Regionalized Plant & Materials List, a sheet on Planting and Maintaining Your Landscape, Zone Maps and Plant Size and Description Guide. These plans will help you achieve professional results, adding value and enjoyment to your property for years to come. Each set of blueprints is a full 18" x 24" in size with clear, complete instructions and easy-to-read type. A sample Landscape Plan is shown below. See Blueprint Price Schedule for ordering information.

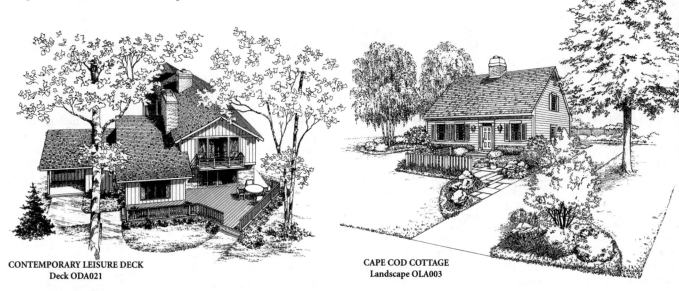

CONTEMPORARY LEISURE DECK
Deck ODA021

CAPE COD COTTAGE
Landscape OLA003

REGIONAL ORDER MAP

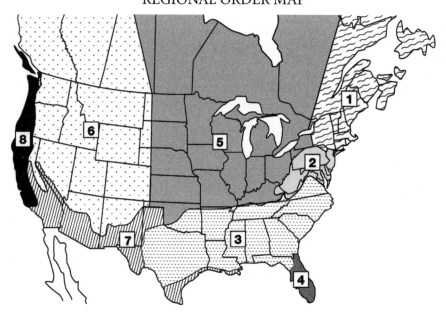

Most Landscape Plans are available with a Plant & Materials List adapted by horticultural experts to 8 different regions of the country. Please specify the Geographic Region when ordering your plan. See Blueprint Price Schedule for ordering information and regional availability.

Region	1	Northeast
Region	2	Mid-Atlantic
Region	3	Deep South
Region	4	Florida & Gulf Coast
Region	5	Midwest
Region	6	Rocky Mountains
Region	7	Southern California & Desert Southwest
Region	8	Northern California & Pacific Northwest

BLUEPRINT PRICE SCHEDULE

TIERS	1 SET STUDY PACKAGE	4-SET BUILDING PACKAGE	8-SET BUILDING PACKAGE	1-SET REPRODUCIBLE*
P1	$20	$50	$90	$140
P2	$40	$70	$110	$160
P3	$70	$100	$140	$190
P4	$100	$130	$170	$220
P5	$140	$170	$210	$270
P6	$180	$210	$250	$310
A1	$440	$490	$540	$660
A2	$480	$530	$580	$720
A3	$530	$590	$650	$800
A4	$575	$645	$705	$870
C1	$625	$695	$755	$935
C2	$670	$740	$800	$1000
C3	$715	$790	$855	$1075
C4	$765	$840	$905	$1150
L1	$870	$965	$1050	$1300
L2	$945	$1040	$1125	$1420
L3	$1050	$1150	$1240	$1575
L4	$1155	$1260	$1355	$1735
SQ1				.35/SqFt

* Requires a fax number

OPTIONS FOR PLANS IN TIERS A1–L4

Additional Identical Blueprints
in same order for "A1–L4" price plans ....$50 per set
Reverse Blueprints (mirror image)
with 4- or 8-set order for "A1–L4" plans..$50 fee per order
Specification Outlines..$10 each
Materials Lists for "A1–C3" plans ....$70 each
Materials Lists for "C4–L4" plans..$70 each

OPTIONS FOR PLANS IN TIERS P1–P6

Additional Identical Blueprints
in same order for "P1–P6" price plans..$10 per set
Reverse Blueprints (mirror image) for "P1–P6" price plans ....$10 fee per order
1 Set of Deck Construction Details ....$14.95 each
Deck Construction Package ....**add $10 to Building Package price**
(Includes 1 set of "P1–P6" plans, plus 1 set Standard Deck Construction Details)

IMPORTANT NOTES

SQ one-set building package includes one set of reproducible vellum construction drawings plus, one set of study blueprints.
The 1-set study package is marked "not for construction."
Prices for 4- or 8-set Building Packages honored only at time of original order.
Some foundations carry a $225 surcharge.
Right-reading reverse blueprints, if available, will incur a $165 surcharge.
Additional identical blueprints may be purchased within 60 days of original order.

TO USE THE INDEX, refer to the design number listed in numerical order (a helpful page reference is also given). Note the price tier and refer to the Blueprint Price Schedule above for the cost of one, four or eight sets of blueprints or the cost of a reproducible drawing. Additional prices are shown for identical and reverse blueprint sets, as well as a very useful Materials List for some of the plans. Also note in the Plan Index those plans that have Deck Plans or Landscape Plans. Refer to the schedules above for prices of these plans. The letter "Y" identifies plans that are part of our Quote One® estimating service and those that offer Materials Lists.

TO ORDER, Call toll free 1-800-521-6797 for current pricing and availability prior to mailing the order form. FAX: 1-800-224-6699 or 520-544-3086.

PLAN INDEX

DESIGN	PRICE	PAGE	MATERIALS LIST	QUOTE ONE*	DECK	DECK PRICE	LANDSCAPE	LANDSCAPE PRICE	REGIONS
1404	A3	368	Y						
2226	C3	331	Y						
2258	C1	400	Y						
2294	C2	401	Y				OLA037	P4	347
2439	A3	371	Y						
3345	A3	242	Y	Y			OLA021	P3	123568
3487	A4	245	Y	Y			OLA010	P3	1234568
3489	A4	246	Y	Y	ODA013	P2	OLA021	P3	123568
3667	C1	347	Y	Y					
3699	A4	16	Y	Y	ODA016	P2	OLA093	P3	12345678
3707	A4	408	Y						
3719	A3	407	Y						
3804	A4	151	Y	Y			OLA010	P3	1234568
4015	A3	365	Y						
4183	A4	358	Y				OLA032	P4	12345678
6602	C2	5					OLA004	P3	123568
6603	A3	388					OLA014	P4	12345678
6604	C2	92					OLA001	P3	123568
6605	C1	412					OLA012	P3	12345678
6606	C1	99					OLA008	P4	1234568
6609	C2	98					OLA012	P3	12345678
6624	C1	101					OLA001	P3	123568
6626	C1	414					OLA012	P3	12345678
6628	C2	395					OLA001	P3	123568
6629	C1	389					OLA012	P3	12345678
6630	A3	387					OLA014	P4	12345678
6636	C4	9	Y				OLA008	P4	1234568
6639	C3	8					OLA012	P3	12345678
6641	C4	96					OLA017	P3	123568
6643	C4	100	Y				OLA004	P3	123568
6657	C2	95							
6658	A3	396							
6691	A2	422							
6712	C2	84							

BEFORE FILLING OUT THE ORDER FORM, PLEASE CALL US ON OUR TOLL-FREE BLUEPRINT HOTLINE 1-800-521-6797. YOU MAY WANT TO LEARN MORE ABOUT OUR SERVICES AND PRODUCTS. HERE'S SOME INFORMATION YOU WILL FIND HELPFUL.

OUR EXCHANGE POLICY

With the exception of reproducible plan orders, we will exchange your entire first order for an equal or greater number of blueprints within our plan collection within 90 days of the original order. The entire content of your original order must be returned before an exchange will be processed. Please call our customer service department for your return authorization number and shipping instructions. If the returned blueprints look used, redlined or copied, we will not honor your exchange. Fees for exchanging your blueprints are as follows: 20% of the amount of the original order...plus the difference in cost if exchanging for a design in a higher price bracket or less the difference in cost if exchanging for a design in a lower price bracket. **(Reproducible blueprints are not exchangeable or refundable.)** Please call for current postage and handling prices. Shipping and handling charges are not refundable.

ABOUT REPRODUCIBLES

When purchasing a reproducible you may be required to furnish a fax number. The designer will fax documents that you must sign and return to them before shipping will take place.

ABOUT REVERSE BLUEPRINTS

Although lettering and dimensions will appear backward, reverses will be a useful aid if you decide to flop the plan. See Price Schedule and Plans Index for pricing.

REVISING, MODIFYING AND CUSTOMIZING PLANS

Like many homeowners who buy these plans, you and your builder, architect or engineer may want to make changes to them. We recommend purchase of a reproducible plan for any changes made by your builder, licensed architect or engineer. As set forth below, we cannot assume any responsibility for blueprints which have been changed, whether by you, your builder or by professionals selected by you or referred to you by us, because such individuals are outside our supervision and control.

ARCHITECTURAL AND ENGINEERING SEALS

Some cities and states are now requiring that a licensed architect or engineer review and "seal" a blueprint, or officially approve it, prior to construction due to concerns over energy costs, safety and other factors. Prior to application for a building permit or the start of actual construction, we strongly advise that you consult your local building official who can tell you if such a review is required.

ABOUT THE DESIGNS

The architects and designers whose work appears in this publication are among America's leading residential designers. Each plan was designed to meet the requirements of a nationally recognized model building code in effect at the time and place the plan was drawn. Because national building codes change from time to time, plans may not comply with any such code at the time they are sold to a customer. In addition, building officials may not accept these plans as final construction documents of record as the plans may need to be modified and additional drawings and details added to suit local conditions and requirements. We strongly advise that purchasers consult a licensed architect or engineer, and their local building official, before starting any construction related to these plans.

LOCAL BUILDING CODES AND ZONING REQUIREMENTS

At the time of creation, our plans are drawn to specifications published by the Building Officials and Code Administrators (BOCA) International, Inc.; the Southern Building Code Congress (SBCCI) International, Inc.; the International Conference of Building Officials (ICBO); or the Council of American Building Officials (CABO). Our plans are designed to meet or exceed national building standards. Because of the great differences in geography and climate throughout the United States and Canada, each state, county and municipality has its own building codes, zone requirements, ordinances and building regulations. Your plan may need to be modified to comply with local requirements regarding snow loads, energy codes, soil and seismic conditions and a wide range of other matters. In addition, you may need to obtain permits or inspections from local governments before and in the course of construction. Prior to using blueprints ordered from us, we strongly advise that you consult a licensed architect or engineer—and speak with your local building official—before applying for any permit or beginning construction. We authorize the use of our blueprints on the express condition that you strictly comply with all local building codes, zoning requirements and other applicable laws, regulations, ordinances and requirements. Notice: Plans for homes to be built in Nevada must be re-drawn by a Nevada-registered professional. Consult your building official for more information on this subject.

TOLL FREE
1-800-521-6797

REGULAR OFFICE HOURS:
24 hours, 7 days a week

If we receive your order by 3:00 p.m. EST, Monday-Friday, we'll process it and ship within **two business days**. When ordering by phone, please have your credit card or check information ready. We'll also ask you for the Order Form Key Number at the bottom of the order form.

By FAX: Copy the Order Form on the next page and send it on our FAX line: 1-800-224-6699 or 520-544-3086.

Canadian Customers
Order Toll Free 1-877-223-6389

DISCLAIMER

The designers we work with have put substantial care and effort into the creation of their blueprints. However, because they cannot provide on-site consultation, supervision and control over actual construction, and because of the great variance in local building requirements, building practices and soil, seismic, weather and other conditions, WE CANNOT MAKE ANY WARRANTY, EXPRESS OR IMPLIED, WITH RESPECT TO THE CONTENT OR USE OF THE BLUEPRINTS, INCLUDING BUT NOT LIMITED TO ANY WARRANTY OF MERCHANTABILITY OR OF FITNESS FOR A PARTICULAR PURPOSE. **ITEMS, PRICES, TERMS AND CONDITIONS ARE SUBJECT TO CHANGE WITHOUT NOTICE. REPRODUCIBLE PLAN ORDERS MAY REQUIRE A CUSTOMER'S SIGNED RELEASE BEFORE SHIPPING.**

TERMS AND CONDITIONS

These designs are protected under the terms of United States Copyright Law and may not be copied or reproduced in any way, by any means, unless you have purchased Reproducibles which clearly indicate your right to copy or reproduce. We authorize the use of your chosen design as an aid in the construction of one single family home only. You may not use this design to build a second or multiple dwellings without purchasing another blueprint or blueprints or paying additional design fees.

HOW MANY BLUEPRINTS DO YOU NEED?

Although a standard building package may satisfy many states, cities and counties, some plans may require certain changes. For your convenience, we have developed a Reproducible plan which allows a local professional to modify and make up to 10 copies of your revised plan. As our plans are all copyright protected, with your purchase of the Reproducible, we will supply you with a Copyright release letter. The number of copies you may need: 1 for owner; 3 for builder; 2 for local building department and 1-3 sets for your mortgage lender.

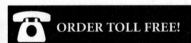

ORDER TOLL FREE!

For information about any of our services or to order call 1-800-521-6797

Browse our website: www.eplans.com

BLUEPRINTS ARE NOT REFUNDABLE EXCHANGES ONLY

For Customer Service, call toll free 1-888-690-1116.

HOME PLANNERS, LLC wholly owned by Hanley-Wood, LLC
3275 WEST INA ROAD, SUITE 220 • TUCSON, ARIZONA • 85741

THE BASIC BLUEPRINT PACKAGE

Rush me the following (please refer to the Plans Index and Price Schedule in this section):

___Set(s) of reproducibles*, plan number(s) _____ $_____
   indicate foundation type _____ surcharge (if applicable): $_____
___Set(s) of blueprints, plan number(s) _____ $_____
   indicate foundation type _____ surcharge (if applicable): $_____
___Additional identical blueprints (standard or reverse) in same order @ $50 per set $_____
___Reverse blueprints @ $50 fee per order. Right-reading reverse @ $165 surcharge $_____

IMPORTANT EXTRAS

Rush me the following:

___Materials List: $60 (Must be purchased with Blueprint set.) Add $10 for Schedule C4–L4 plans $_____
___**Quote One®** Summary Cost Report @ $29.95 for one, $14.95 for each additional,
   for plans _____ $_____
   Building location: City _____ Zip Code _____
___**Quote One®** Material Cost Report @ $120 Schedules P1–C3; $130 Schedules C4–L4,
   for plan _____ (Must be purchased with Blueprints set.) $_____
   Building location: City _____ Zip Code _____
___Specification Outlines @ $10 each $_____
___Detail Sets @ $14.95 each; any two $22.95; any three $29.95; all four for $39.95 (save $19.85) $_____
   ❑ Plumbing ❑ Electrical ❑ Construction ❑ Mechanical
___Home Furniture Planner @ $15.95 each $_____

DECK BLUEPRINTS

(Please refer to the Plans Index and Price Schedule in this section)

___Set(s) of Deck Plan _____ $_____
___Additional identical blueprints in same order @ $10 per set. $_____
___Reverse blueprints @ $10 fee per order. $_____
___Set of Standard Deck Details @ $14.95 per set. $_____
___Set of Complete Deck Construction Package (Best Buy!) Add $10 to Building Package.
   Includes Custom Deck Plan _____ Plus Standard Deck Details

LANDSCAPE BLUEPRINTS

(Please refer to the Plans Index and Price Schedule in this section.)

___Set(s) of Landscape Plan _____ $_____
___Additional identical blueprints in same order @ $10 per set $_____
___Reverse blueprints @ $10 fee per order $_____

Please indicate appropriate region of the country for Plant & Material List. Region _____

POSTAGE AND HANDLING *SIGNATURE IS REQUIRED FOR ALL DELIVERIES.*	1–3 sets	4+ sets
DELIVERY No CODs (Requires street address—No P.O. Boxes)		
•Regular Service (Allow 7–10 business days delivery)	❑ $20.00	❑ $25.00
•Priority (Allow 4–5 business days delivery)	❑ $25.00	❑ $35.00
•Express (Allow 3 business days delivery)	❑ $35.00	❑ $45.00
OVERSEAS DELIVERY	fax, phone or mail for quote	

Note: All delivery times are from date Blueprint Package is shipped.

POSTAGE (From box above) $_____
SUBTOTAL $_____
SALES TAX (AZ & MI residents, please add appropriate state and local sales tax.) $_____
TOTAL (Subtotal and tax) $_____

YOUR ADDRESS (please print legibly)

Name _____

Street _____

City _____ State _____ Zip _____

Daytime telephone number (required) (_____) _____

* Fax number (required for reproducible orders) _____
TeleCheck® Checks By Phone℠ available

FOR CREDIT CARD ORDERS ONLY

Credit card number _____ Exp. Date: (M/Y) _____

Check one ❑ Visa ❑ MasterCard ❑ American Express

Order Form Key

HPTMO4

Signature (required) _____

Please check appropriate box: ❑ Licensed Builder-Contractor ❑ Homeowner

☎ **ORDER TOLL FREE!**
1-800-521-6797

BY FAX: Copy the order form above and send it on our FAXLINE: 1-800-224-6699 OR 520-544-3086

1 BIGGEST & BEST

1001 of our best-selling plans in one volume. 1,074 to 7,275 square feet. 704 pgs $12.95 1K1

2 ONE-STORY

450 designs for all lifestyles. 800 to 4,900 square feet. 384 pgs $9.95 OS

3 MORE ONE-STORY

475 superb one-level plans from 800 to 5,000 square feet. 448 pgs $9.95 MO2

4 TWO-STORY

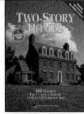

443 designs for one-and-a-half and two stories. 1,500 to 6,000 square feet. 448 pgs $9.95 TS

5 VACATION

430 designs for recreation, retirement and leisure. 448 pgs $9.95 VS3

6 HILLSIDE

208 designs for split-levels, bi-levels, multi-levels and walkouts. 224 pgs $9.95 HH

7 FARMHOUSE

300 Fresh Designs from Classic to Modern. 320 pgs. $10.95 FCP

8 COUNTRY HOUSES

208 unique home plans that combine traditional style and modern livability. 224 pgs $9.95 CN

9 BUDGET-SMART

200 efficient plans from 7 top designers, that you can really afford to build! 224 pgs $8.95 BS

10 BARRIER-FREE

Over 1,700 products and 51 plans for accessible living. 128 pgs $15.95 UH

11 ENCYCLOPEDIA

500 exceptional plans for all styles and budgets—the best book of its kind! 528 pgs $9.95 ENC

12 ENCYCLOPEDIA II

500 completely new plans. Spacious and stylish designs for every budget and taste. 352 pgs $9.95 E2

13 AFFORDABLE

300 Modest plans for savvy homebuyers.256 pgs. $9.95 AH2

14 VICTORIAN

210 striking Victorian and Farmhouse designs from today's top designers. 224 pgs $15.95 VDH2

15 ESTATE

Dream big! Eighteen designers showcase their biggest and best plans. 224 pgs $16.95 EDH3

16 LUXURY

170 lavish designs, over 50% brand-new plans added to a most elegant collection. 192 pgs $12.95 LD3

17 EUROPEAN STYLES

200 homes with a unique flair of the Old World. 224 pgs $15.95 EURO

18 COUNTRY CLASSICS

Donald Gardner's 101 best Country and Traditional home plans. 192 pgs $17.95 DAG

19 COUNTRY

85 Charming Designs from American Home Gallery. 160 pgs. $17.95 CTY

20 TRADITIONAL

85 timeless designs from the Design Traditions Library. 160 pgs. $17.95 TRA

21 COTTAGES

245 Delightful retreats from 825 to 3,500 square feet. 256 pgs. $10.95 COOL

22 CABINS TO VILLAS

Enchanting Homes for Mountain Sea or Sun, from the Sater collection. 144 pgs $19.95 CCV

23 CONTEMPORARY

The most complete and imaginative collection of contemporary designs available anywhere. 256 pgs $10.95 CM2

24 FRENCH COUNTRY

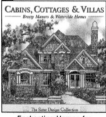

Live every day in the French countryside using these plans, landscapes and interiors. 192 pgs. $14.95 PN

25 SOUTHERN

207 homes rich in Southern styling and comfort. 240 pgs $8.95 SH

26 SOUTHWESTERN

138 designs that capture the spirit of the Southwest. 144 pgs $10.95 SW

27 SHINGLE-STYLE

155 Home plans from Classic Colonials to Breezy Bungalows. 192 pgs. $12.95 SNG

28 NEIGHBORHOOD

170 designs with the feel of main street America. 192 pgs $12.95 TND

29 CRAFTSMAN

170 Home plans in the Craftsman and Bungalow style. 192 pgs $12.95 CC

30 GRAND VISTAS

200 Homes with a View. 224 pgs. $10.95 GV

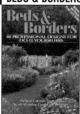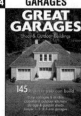
447

FOR FASTER SERVICE ORDER ONLINE AT
www.hwspecials.com